Method and Theory in
Historical Archeology

STUDIES IN ARCHEOLOGY

Consulting Editor: Stuart Struever

Department of Anthropology
Northwestern University
Evanston, Illinois

Charles R. McGimsey III. **Public Archeology**

Lewis R. Binford. **An Archaeological Perspective**

Muriel Porter Weaver. **The Aztecs, Maya, and Their Predecessors: Archaeology of Mesoamerica**

Joseph W. Michels. **Dating Methods in Archaeology**

C. Garth Sampson. **The Stone Age Archaeology of Southern Africa**

Fred T. Plog. **The Study of Prehistoric Change**

Patty Jo Watson (Ed.). **Archeology of the Mammoth Cave Area**

George C. Frison (Ed.). **The Casper Site: A Hell Gap Bison Kill on the High Plains**

W. Raymond Wood and R. Bruce McMillan (Eds.). **Prehistoric Man and His Environments: A Case Study in the Ozark Highland**

Kent V. Flannery (Ed.). **The Early Mesoamerican Village**

Charles E. Cleland (Ed.). **Cultural Change and Continuity: Essays in Honor of James Bennett Griffin**

Michael B. Schiffer. **Behavioral Archeology**

Fred Wendorf and Romuald Schild. **Prehistory of the Nile Valley**

Michael A. Jochim. **Hunter-Gatherer Subsistence and Settlement: A Predictive Model**

Stanley South. **Method and Theory in Historical Archeology**

in preparation

Timothy K. Earle and Jonathon E. Ericson (Eds.). **Exchange Systems in Prehistory**

Lewis R. Binford. **For Theory Building in Archaeology: Essays on Faunal Remains, Aquatic Resources, Spatial Analysis, Systemic Modeling**

Stanley South (Ed.). **Research Strategies in Historical Archeology**

John E. Yellen. **Archeological Approaches to the Present: Models for Reconstructing the Past**

Method and Theory in Historical Archeology

STANLEY SOUTH

Institute of Archeology and Anthropology
University of South Carolina
Columbia, South Carolina

ACADEMIC PRESS NEW YORK SAN FRANCISCO LONDON
A Subsidiary of Harcourt Brace Jovanovich, Publishers

ACADEMIC PRESS, INC.
111 Fifth Avenue, New York, New York 10003

United Kingdom Edition published by
ACADEMIC PRESS, INC. (LONDON) LTD.
24/28 Oval Road, London NW1

Library of Congress Cataloging in Publication Data

South, Stanley A
      Method and theory in historical archeology.

      (Studies in archeology)
      Includes bibliographies and index.
        1.   United States–Antiquities.   2.   Indians of North
America–Antiquities.   3.   Archaeology–Methodology.
I.   Title。
E159.5.S65   970   75-40616
ISBN 0–12–655750–0

PRINTED IN THE UNITED STATES OF AMERICA

For Joffre L. Coe

A critically rigorous mentor, who questions,
stresses faults, and raises objections. His
stringent and often frustrating manner
serves well those who pass his way.

Contents

Foreword

Rarely is a book published that is more than of passing interest. This is one of the rare ones in that it is the first systematic comparative study of archaeological data relative to the historic period in North America. Additionally it is a book with vision; it looks beyond the data and comparative material presented to the advancement of archaeological science. It is much more, however, than a polemic-laden thesis. It is solidly based in the use of empirical material, and it is modest in that while looking beyond the materials and specific arguments presented it does not attempt to go beyond the current state of the field; instead it is concerned with building a sound research foundation for envisioned progress in science.

Stanley South is doing in this book what Francois Bordes did for European paleolithic studies, namely arguing the necessity for quantitative studies as the very basis for pattern recognition. In the absence of demonstrated patterning—spatial, structural, or temporal—there is in fact nothing to which the investigator may direct a *why* question, for as long as there are only particular facts there are only particular questions. Once there are demonstrated general facts, then one may ask general questions. Only with the latter is scientific progress possible. Once such general facts are demonstrated and the focus of study moves to comparative pattern recognition and evaluation of variability, particularistic approaches are thereafter trivial, uninteresting, and boring—even to their advocates. I anticipate a major change in the character of historic sites literature after the publication of this book.

While I anticipate that this book is an important "turning point" in the field of historic sites archaeology, it will be of great interest to anthropologists concerned with other time periods. For instance, I am curious as to *why* South's ceramic formula works so well on historic period materials. He has already demonstrated that there is a great deal of functional variability among sites of the historic period, for example, contrasts between his Carolina Pattern and the Frontier Pattern. Were there not functional differences among sites in the types and kinds of containers used? Is stylistic or production variability independent of vessel function in the Historic Period? If so, is this always the case, and if not, why are there differences in the relationships between design characteristics related to functional differences in containers versus design characteristics reflecting stylistic, symbolic, or simple informational aspects of production? Were replacement rates similar in all settings? If not, variability in the accuracy of the "ceramic dates" may be anticipated. Investigation of such questions may lead to greater understanding of the archaeological record, as well as to what it tells us about the dynamics of cultural systems and the causal conditions which bring about their modification.

Welcome historic sites archaeology to the science of archaeology.

Lewis R. Binford

Preface

This book is based on the premise that the archeologist is concerned with understanding past lifeways, culture history, and culture process by examining the material remains of culture reflecting these processes. The conceptual framework for this understanding is that of evolutionary theory. The method whereby these phenomena of the past are examined pivots on the recognition of pattern in the archeological record. Once pattern is abstracted and synthesized with other patterns, these demonstrated regularities are often expressed as empirical laws. The explanation of why these lawlike regularities exist is the goal of archeology. The explanation is addressed to the causal processes in the past cultural system in the form of hypotheses to be tested with new data through research designs specifically constructed to fit the questions being asked. The understanding of culture process and how it works comes through this basic procedure of archeological science. This understanding provides a conceptual environment within which new theory is invented to explain the phenomena the archeologist has observed.

With this procedure as basic to archeological science, it follows that the use of ethnographic data and historical documentation by the archeologist does not result in a different kind of archeology merely because a wider data base is available. This fact has been obvious to me throughout two decades of full-time archeological research during which I have excavated a range of sites from Early Archaic, to Mississippian, to eighteenth-century historic, to the twentieth century. This viewpoint is not generally shared by archeologists, however. Many colleagues assume historical archeology is a particularistic involvement with details of history, cataloging, and classification. This book is designed to demonstrate that this is not enough, that the archeologist has a responsibility to go further than this and to address the culture process by scientific procedures.

There is historical reason for the more limited approach in that historical archeology has so frequently been done by archeologists with a particularistic point of view. This historical development, accompanied by the publication of a number of books emphasizing the particularistic approach, has resulted in historical archeology having a particularistic image. I hope that this book can contribute to a realization by archeologists that we can, and in fact must, do more than this in an area of archeological research that offers great promise for the development of archeological science.

Unless there is an effort made to go beyond the particularistic approach to historical archeology there can be no concern for pattern recognition. Pattern recognition, however, is a basic step in any analysis. Judging from many recently published reports by historical archeologists as well as a number of doctoral dissertations, none of which contains any attempt at pattern recognition, it is apparent to me that the training these people received did not prepare them to carry out scientific archeology. Pattern recognition is a basic methodological approach demonstrated throughout this book. Without quantification, however, there can be no explicit pattern recognition. Without pattern recognition, there can be no archeological science. Without archeological science, our ideas about man's past cannot be predictably tested, which is the basic goal of archeology. Without predictability, man's ideas about the past amount to antiquarianism. Therefore, pattern recognition and quantification are basic to the archeological process. These are, however, merely the first steps in that process, but archeologists must take them before they can ever hope to contribute through their work to a science of archeology.

The figures and tables in this book illustrate points made in the text. Some figures are referred to by number; other photographs and drawings are not numbered. They are used to illustrate the archeological process of excavation, data recording, conservation, stabilization, and historic site development. Some photographs illustrate the technique of combining archeological artifacts into settings for suggesting past lifeways in a manner not possible through words alone. Artists' renderings of past environmental settings, costumes, and events are tools used in interpreting past lifeways, and some of these are included here.

A reconstructive step beyond such interpretive tools is the development of explanatory exhibits on archeological sites. These take the form of palisades placed in archeologically revealed ditches, parapets placed beside excavated moats, kivas stabilized and restored, ceremonial structures rebuilt on top of temple mounds, and masonry ruins stabilized—all under the guidance of the archeologist. Photographs illustrating these aspects of archeology are included.

These visual reminders of the wide range of archeological activities are intended as constant reminders throughout the book of the variety of activity underlying the process of pattern recognition.

Stanley South

Acknowledgments

In preparing this book, I received excellent conceptual, organizational, and editorial suggestions, for which I am most grateful, from my colleagues, Lewis Binford, Richard Carrillo, Leland Ferguson, Roseline Hunter-Anderson, John Idol, and Robert L. Stephenson. Other colleagues read and commented on various chapters or parts, and offered valuable suggestions. These are John Combes, Albert C. Goodyear, Michael Hartley, John House, Kenneth Lewis, Audrey Noël Hume, Ivor Noël Hume, Richard Polhemus, David South, and George Teague. I am also indebted to Lewis Binford for writing the foreword.

Assistance with statistical and computer handling of data was gratefully received from Joan Combes, Leland Ferguson, Albert C. Goodyear, and David South. A valuable contribution was received from colleagues who made data available for use in this book, for which I am most grateful. These are Richard Carrillo, William Faulk, Leland Ferguson, Stephen Gluckman, John Combes, and Robert L. Stephenson.

I would like to thank Gordon Brown for photographic assistance with reproducing line drawings and photographs. Permission to use photographs previously published elsewhere was provided as follows:

Frontispiece; Pp. 54, 59, 70, 155, 190: From State of North Carolina Department of Cultural Resources, Division of Archives and History.

Pp. 46, 200: From the Brunswick County Historical Society, Winnabow, North Carolina.

Pp. 54, 59, 98, 99, 205, 296, 298, 299, 300, 307: From South, Stanley, Photography in historical archaeology, *Historical Archaeology 1968* 1969, 2:73–113. Reproduced by courtesy of the Society for Historical Archaeology.

Pp. 78, 79, 215, 237, 240, 250, 279–281, 310, 329: From the Conference on Historic Site Archaeology.

Pp. 91, 101, 140, 142, 144, 283, 284, 286, 287, 290, 293, 301, 304, 325, 327:

From the Institute of Archeology and Anthropology, University of South Carolina, Columbia.

P. 100: From the Florida Anthropological Society.

Pp. 100, 206, 208, 209, 213, 252–253: From the Southeastern Archaeological Conference.

Pp. 152, 181, 186, 276, 319, 320, 322–324: From Bethabara Historic Park, Winston-Salem, North Carolina, the Moravian Archives.

P. 185: From South, Stanley, The lowly flax hackle, *Antiques Magazine* 1968, August:224–227, Fig. 9. From the collection of the Mercer Museum of the Bucks County Historical Society. Reproduced by courtesy of the magazine *Antiques*.

P. 329: From the Society for American Archaeology.

I wish to thank the following individuals for their cooperation in the use of these previously published photographs: John Combes, editor of *Historical Archaeology*; R. V. Asbury Jr., Historic Wilmington Foundation, Inc.; Dr. E. L. Stockton for the Southern Province of the Moravian Church, and Historic Bethabara Park, Inc.; Larry E. Tise for the North Carolina Department of Cultural Resources; Robert L. Stephenson for the Institute of Archeology and Anthropology, University of South Carolina; Charles McGimsey for the Society for American Archeology; and Lynne Poirier for the Mercer Museum of the Bucks County Historical Society.

I wish to thank the following publishers for permission to quote from their publications:

P. 7: From Agee, James and Evans, Walker, *Let us now praise famous men,* Boston, Houghton-Mifflin, 1969.

P. 7: From Ascher, Robert and Fairbanks, Charles, Excavation of a slave cabin: Georgia, U.S.A., *Historical Archaeology* 1971, **v**:3–17.

Pp. 8, 10, 11: From Noël Hume, Ivor, *Historical archaeology,* New York, Knopf, 1969, pp. 15, 12, 13.

P. 9: From Dollar, Clyde D., Some thoughts on theory and method in historical archaeology, in *The Conference on Historic Site Archeology Papers, 1967,* 1968, **2** (Part 2): 3–30. Reproduced by permission of the Conference on Historic Site Archaeology.

Pp. 9, 14–15: From Binford, Lewis R., Evolution and horizon as revealed in ceramic analysis in historical archaeology—A step toward the development of archaeological science, in *The Conference on Historic Site Archaeology Papers, 1971,* 1972, **6**:117–125. Reproduced by permission of the Conference on Historical Site Archaeology.

P. 9: From Walker, Iain C., *Historical Archaeology* 1967, **26**.

P. 11: From Noël Hume, Ivor, *Historical Archaeology in America, Post Medieval Archaeology 1967* 1968, **I**:104; 13.

P. 13: From Ayala, Francisco J., Biological evolution: Natural selection or random walk:? *American Scientist* 1974, **62**(6):700. Reprinted by permission of *American Scientist* (journal of Sigma Xi), The Scientific Research Society of North America.

P. 13: From Binford, Lewis R., Archaeology as anthropology, *American Antiquity* 1962, **28**:224. Reproduced by permission of the Society for American Archaeology.

P. 13: From Parker, Arthur C., Getting down to facts, *American Antiquity* 1935, **1**:2–3. Reproduced by permission of the Society for American Archaeology.

P. 13: From South, Stanley, Evolutionary theory in archaeology, *Southern Indian Studies* 1955, **7**:9, 22. Reproduced by permission of the Archaeological Society of North Carolina.

P. 14: From Adams, Robert, Discussion, in *Research and theory in current archeology*, edited by Charles L. Redman, New York, Wiley, 1973, p. 322.

P. 14: From Fogel, R. W., The new economic history: Its findings and methods, *Economic History Review* (2nd series) 1966, xix.

P. 16: From Watson, Patty Jo, The future of archeology in anthropology: Culture history and social science, in *Research and theory in current archeology*, edited by Charles L. Redman, New York, Wiley, 1973, p. 114.

Pp. 31–32, 201–235: From South, Stanley, Evolution and horizon as revealed in ceramic analysis in historical archeology, in *The Conference on Historic Site Archaeology Papers 1971*, 1972 **6**:71–116. Reproduced by permission of the Conference on Historic Site Archaeology.

P. 33: From Kroeber, A. L., *The nature of culture*, Chicago, The University of Chicago Press, 1952, p. 336 (c)

P. 203: From Dunnell, Robert C., Seriation method and its evaluation, *American Antiquity* 1970, **35**:309. Reproduced by permission of the Society for American Archaeology.

P. 203: From Willey, Gordon R. and Phillips, Philip, *Method and theory in American archaeology*, Chicago, The University of Chicago Press, 1958, pp. 31–34 (c) The University of Chicago Press.

P. 209: From Washburn, S. L., The strategy of physical anthropology, in *Anthropology today*, edited by A. L. Kroeber, Chicago, The University of Chicago Press, 1953, pp. 714–715. (c)

P. 235: From Hempel, Carl G., *Philosophy of natural science*, Englewood Cliffs, N.J., Prentice-Hall, 1966, p. 15.

Pp. 238–274: From South, Stanley, The horizon concept revealed in the application of the mean ceramic date formula to Spanish majolica in the new world, in *The Conference on Historic Site Archaeology Papers 1972*, 1974 **7**:96–122. Reproduced by permission of the Conference on Historic Site Archaeology.

Pp. 277–296: From South, Stanley, The function of observation in the archeological process, in *The Conference on Historic Site Archaeology Papers 1972*, 1974, **7**:123–137.

Pp. 299–308: From South, Stanley, Methodological phases in the archeological process, in *The Conference on Historic Site Archaeology Papers 1972,* 1974, **7:**138–145. Reproduced by permission of the Conference on Historic Site Archaeology.

Pp. 305–306: From South, Stanley, Exploratory archeology at Holmes' Fort, the blockhouse, and jail redoubt at Ninety Six; in *The Conference on Historic Site Archaeology Papers, 1970,* 1971, **5** (Part 1):48. Reproduced by permission of the Conference on Historic Site Archaeology.

Pp. 308–314: From South, Stanley, Evaluation of analysis situations relative to the archeological data bank, in *The Conference on Historic Site Archaeology Papers 1972,* 1974, **7:**146–150. Reproduced by permission of the Conference on Historic Site Archaeology.

Pp. 317–330: From South, Stanley, Historical archeology reports: a plea for a new direction, in *The Conference on Historic Site Archeology Papers 1972,* 1974, **7:**151–158. Reproduced by permission of the Conference on Historic Site Archaeology.

P. 321: From South, Stanley, What archaeology can do to expand historical research, in *The Conference on Historic Site Archaeology Papers, 1968,* 1968. Reproduced by permission of the Conference on Historic Site Archaeology.

P. 324: From Harrington, Jean C., Archeology as auxiliary to American history, *American Anthropologist* 1955, **6** (Part 1):1127. Reproduced by permission of the American Anthropological Association.

Pp. 324–325: From Noël Hume, Ivor, Historical archaeology: Who needs it? *Historical Archaeology* 1973, **vii:**7.

The author wishes to thank the following for permission to quote from data they have published:

P. 4: Data from Steward, Julian, *Theory of culture change,* Urbana, Ill., University of Illinois Press, 1955.

Pp. 117, 148: Data from Jelks, Edward B., Archaeological explorations at Signal Hill, Newfoundland, 1965–1966, *Occasional Papers in Archaeology and History* 1973, No. 7, Tables 4–10.

Pp. 144, 145: Data from Grimm, Jacob L., Archaeological investigation of Fort Ligonier 1960–1965, *Annals of Carnegie Museum* 1970, **42.**

Pp. 210–212: From Noel Hume, Ivor, *A guide to artifacts of Colonial America,* New York, Knopf, 1970.

Pp. 239, 241, 245, 246: Data from Goggin, John M., Spanish Majolica in the new world, *Yale University Publications in Anthropology* 1968, No. 72.

I wish to thank the following individuals for their cooperation in the use of previously published work: Lewis R. Binford, Joffre L. Coe, John

D. Combes, Clyde D. Dollar, Margaret Knox Goggin, Jacob L. Grimm, J. C. Harrington, Ivor Noël Hume, Edward Jelks, Iain C. Walker, and Patty Jo Watson.

I received assistance for some illustrations from Darby Erd, Jim Frierson, Don Mayhew, and Michael Hartley, for which I am most grateful. Analysis help was provided by Michael Hartley and my wife, Jewell, whose reliable work provided a basis for some of the chapters in the book. I am also grateful for Jewell's help with preparation of the index, and for proofreading assistance. Thanks are also due to Susan Jackson for her help in proofing the galleys.

I am indebted to my 8-year-old son, Robert, for suggesting the conceptual framework for the "Relativity" chart seen in Figure 4. I am grateful to my wife, Jewell, and children Robert and Lara, for their patience throughout the many months during which I was obsessed with this book and out of touch with their world.

Particular thanks to Stuart Struever, who suggested that I write it.

The fabric of this book is woven on a warp of theory provided by a man I never met but to whom I owe a particular debt of gratitude, Leslie A. White.

List of Cited Figures and Tables

FIGURES

TABLES

Theoretical
Foundation

The archeological scientist digs to find
Within apparent chaos from the past,
Hidden order in the refuse man has left behind.
Explanation of the pattern lies
In answer to the question "why?"
Creatively invented in the scientific mind.

The emphasis of this book is on the exploration of archeological methods being used to abstract answers relevant to questions about processes governing past human behavior. Each archeological decision is dictated by theoretical assumptions. The decision ranges from whether to use a grid to record data in the field, to count artifact pieces or estimate whole artifacts represented by fragments, to undertake quantification studies designed to abstract culture process, or to concentrate on the particular historical story an artifact has to reveal. Therefore, any presentation of method implies presentation of relevant theory and the assumptions that stand behind the method. This chapter is designed to examine the foundations upon which the methodology used in this book is built. The importance of an evolutionary perspective in archeology is examined, as well as the role played by archeology in the humanities, in particularistic archeology, and scientific archeology. Trends in historical archeology are evaluated through a study of papers published during the past 15 years, and a personal view of the slow emergence of archeological science is presented.

The data used here have been generated through the application of some archeological strategies to sites occupied during the period of recorded history. Those studies using both archeological and historical data have come to be called "historical archeology." This term refers to the data base, not a different kind of archeology from any other. This book is concerned with archeologically relevant methods for exploring the data recovered from sites of the historic period, methods having relevance to archeology regardless of the temporal or cultural origins of the data. This chapter is concerned with examining the concepts that guided the way in which archeology on historic sites has been traditionally executed, and the contrasting approach used in the studies presented here.

TOWARD A SCIENCE OF CULTURAL EVOLUTION

A long range diachronic perspective is basic to archeology in its concern with culture change as revealed through the archeological record (Flannery 1972a: 404; 1972b: 102). This traditional involvement does not alter when surviving material remains of culture in the form of archival documents, in addition to those remains of human behavior recovered from archeological sites, are utilized by the archeologist. The basic nature of diachronic studies in archeology has been pointed out by the Binfords (1968), Plog (1974), and Spaulding (1973: 354). Each emphasized the leading role to be played by the anthropological archeologist in the development of a science of cultural evolution.

The archeologist uses a range of data that may be archeological, historical, archival, and ethnographic in order to evaluate ideas regarding the dynamics of past human behavior and the processes of cultural evolution. This format is anthropological in its concern with cultural systems and behavioral processes as revealed through archeology. Archeologists trained in history tend to see the archeological record as an elaboration on the historical record, while archeologists trained as ethnographers tend to use ethnographic models in the interpretation of the archeological data. This book emphasizes an approach to archeological data designed to abstract information relating to cultural process.

The first half of the twentieth century was characterized by a reaction against the nineteenth-century evolutionism and scientific functionalism to the point that a particularistic approach dominated much of anthropological thought as late as the middle of the century. Because patterned regularity and variability exist as ever present mirrors of past cultural behavior, and because change is basically what evolutionary theory seeks to understand, archeology in the 1950s, with its concern for pattern recognition and interest in documenting change, appeared strangely oblivious to evolution. There was a strong antievolutionary attitude taken by many archeologists, and a lack of recognition on the part of others (Phillips and Willey 1953, 1955) of the potential a viable evolutionary theory had to offer (South 1955).

Some archeologists of the 1950s, particularly those in the eastern United States, were fortunate enough to have been fed a diet of evolutionary theory (White 1938, 1945a, 1945b, 1946, 1947b, 1948; Morgan 1877; Tylor 1891; Steward 1948, 1955, 1956) by former students of Leslie White. As a result, a response appeared as a counterpoint in the antievolutionary climate. The argument was made that archeologists dealing with temporal processes are of necessity concerned with evolutionary theory, a requisite theoretical foundation for a science of archeology (South 1955: 22; Haag 1959). In a recent discussion of the "re-emergence of cultural evolution," Willey and Sabloff (1974: 178–179) acknowledge that the reluctance of Phillips and Willey to separate evolution from history—and their refusal to recognize the evolutionary hand that fed archeologists their theoretical food—"was a hesitancy in keeping with the anti-evolutionary attitude of the times."

Fortunately other archeologists had long since realized the potential importance of evolutionary theory to archeology, and by the 1960s a "new" archeological banner incorporating evolutionary theory and archeological science was being carried by Lewis Binford (1962, 1964, 1965, 1967; Binford and Binford 1968). The new look had roots in the past, however, in the work of those concerned with demonstrating regularities in ethnographic and archeological data and providing empirical generalizations. One such fundamental inspiration was seen in the work of Julian H. Steward. In the face of an intellectual climate that virtually denied that regularities exist, Steward insisted on the need to "establish a genuine interest in the scientific objective and a clear conceptualization of what is meant by regularities" (Steward 1955: 179–180). Steward's strategy was primarily inductive, attempting to recognize regularities to be stated as empirical generalizations. His strategy is best summarized in the following abstract of attitude expressed in 1949 (Table 1) taken from his work published in 1955 (179–180, 208–209).

Statements similar to these can be seen in many contemporary works, and these attitudes are presented here as a reminder that such views, popular now, were expressed a quarter century ago in a far different intellectual climate. The ferment of the 1960s was generated from the fruitful work of men such as Steward, who insisted on the need for an empirical base for inductively arriving at empirical laws useful to archeological science. The emphasis on the hypothetico-deductive half of the scientific cycle was yet to come, but Steward took a basic step toward generating the new wine beginning to mature in the 1970s, explicitly scientific archeology. Parts of Steward's work are still having considerable influence on studies in American archeology, an excellent example being David Hurst Thomas' (1973) empirical validation for Steward's model of Great Basin settlement patterns.

With recent emphasis in archeology on general systems models studies

TABLE 1

Abstract of Steward's Attitude and Conceptual Stance

Steward's attitude	Conceptual stance
1. Cultural particulars provide the data necessary for any generalizations.	(Induction)
2. The discovery of cultural laws is an ultimate goal of anthropology.	(Nomothetic)
3. Comparative cultural studies should interest themselves in the unique as well as recurrent phenomena.	(Particularistic-nomothetic)
4. Anthropology explicitly recognizes the need to see through the differences of cultures to the similarities, to ascertain processes that are duplicated independently in cultural sequences, and to recognize cause and effect in both temporal and functional relationships.	(Nomothetic-processual studies)
5. Trial formulations of regularities on varying levels are sought, unencumbered by a requirement that they be absolutes and universals, or that they provide ultimate explanations.	(Nomothetic, law-like, regularities. Statistically based trial laws)
6. Valid formulations of cultural data are based on empirical procedures, hypotheses arising from interpretations of fact and being revised as new facts become available.	(Inductively derived hypotheses and theory)
7. In densely settled areas, internal needs will produce an orderly interrelationship of environment, subsistence patterns, social groupings, occupational factors. These interrelated institutions do not have unlimited variability, for they must be adapted to the requirements of subsistence patterns established in particular environments; they involve a cultural ecology.	(Ecosystem studies)
8. Unless anthropology is to interest itself mainly in the unique, exotic, and nonrecurrent particulars, it is necessary that formulations be attempted no matter how tentative they may be. It is formulations that will enable us to state new kinds of problems and to direct attention to new kinds of data which have been slighted in the past. Fact-collecting of itself is insufficient scientific procedure; facts exist only as they are related to theories, and theories are not destroyed by facts—they are replaced by new theories which better explain the facts.	(Nomothetic, problem-oriented research and trial laws. Inductively derived theory)

designed to test laws of culture process, there has been some slackening of interest in evolutionary theory. For those waving its banner in the polemic battles of the 1950s, the view that evolutionary theory is somehow less than basic to contempoary archeology has the familiar ring of a call to arms. Willey and Sabloff have noted this trend (1974:

193), however, a look beyond immediate contemporary problem solving reveals a systemic relationship between evolutionary theory, the ecosystem concept, and the general systems model in archeology (Steward 1955: 208; Spaulding 1973: 352–354; Willey and Sabloff 1974: 189). When we look deep within the hub of systems for causes of change, we are addressing ourselves to the concept of cultural evolution, a paradigm for the processual theorist (Flannery 1972b: 102).

In 1959, William Haag correctly predicted the rise of a new theoretical position within the field of archeology, but it is unlikely that he realized that the "new archeology" he was forecasting would arrive so soon (Haag 1959: 104–105). He was entirely correct, however, in suggesting that the new processual perspective would emerge "from the active body of evolutionism."

THE POLEARM OF ARCHEOLOGY—A BILL OF PARTICULARS FOR THEORETICAL THRUSTS

As we have suggested, archeological theory must be evolutionary in nature, and this applies equally to the classical, anthropological, and historical branches of the discipline. These branches of archeology can be visualized as forming a polearm[1] (Figure 1). This heuristic device illustrates that the branches of archeology are subject in their temporal dimensions to evolutionary theory. They also derive specific conceptual tools from the humanities, mathematics, social science, and science. As a result three paradigms under which archeological excavation is conducted can be defined. These are archeology in the humanities, particularistic archeology, and scientific archeology. We will look at these approaches through the attitudes characteristic of each, as revealed by those conducting archeology on historic sites.

Archeology in the Humanities

Archeology in the humanities is concerned with human sensuality, sociability, wisdom, ideational internalization, cultivation of the intellect, and education toward the enjoyment of life. These are admirable goals against which hardly anyone would argue. The methods used to achieve these goals are often nonscientific and subjective, though there is no reason why they have to be (Ford 1973: 83). Iain Walker clearly reflects

[1] This was a weapon used by foot soldiers against the possibility of a cavalry charge while the musketeers were loading their muskets. A particular form of this weapon was the bill, used as a general bush-cutting tool as well as for making fascines, palisades, and other fortification features in the seventeenth century (Noël Hume 1963: 59–60).

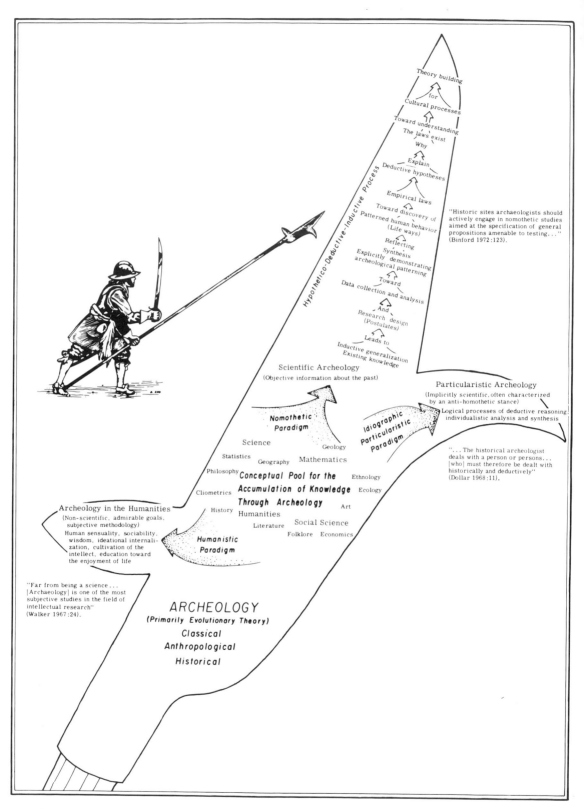

Theory building

for

Cultural processes

Toward understanding

The laws exist

Why

Explain

Deductive hypotheses

Empirical laws

Toward discovery of

Patterned human behavior
(Life ways)

Reflecting

Synthesis

Explicitly demonstrating
archeological patterning

Toward

Data collection and analysis

And

Research design
(Postulates)

Leads to

Inductive generalization
Existing knowledge

Hypothetico-Deductive-Inductive Process

"Historic sites archaeologists should actively engage in nomothetic studies aimed at the specification of general propositions amenable to testing..." (Binford 1972:123).

Scientific Archeology

(Objective information about the past)

Nomothetic
Paradigm

Particularistic Archeology

(Implicitly scientific, often characterized by an anti-homothetic stance)

Logical processes of deductive reasoning, individualistic analysis and synthesis

Idiographic
Particularistic
Paradigm

Science

Statistics

Geography

Geology

Mathematics

Philosophy

Cliometrics

Conceptual Pool for the Accumulation of Knowledge Through Archeology

Ethnology

Ecology

History

Art

Humanities

Literature

Folklore

Social Science

Economics

"... The historical archeologist deals with a person or persons... |who| must therefore be dealt with historically and deductively" (Dollar 1968:11).

Archeology in the Humanities

(Non-scientific, admirable goals, subjective methodology)

Human sensuality, sociability, wisdom, ideational internalization, cultivation of the intellect, education toward the enjoyment of life

Humanistic
Paradigm

"Far from being a science... |Archaeology| is one of the most subjective studies in the field of intellectual research" (Walker 1967:24).

ARCHEOLOGY

(Primarily Evolutionary Theory)

Classical

Anthropological

Historical

the humanistic attitude when he says that archeology is one of the most subjective studies "in the field of intellectual research" (Walker 1967: 24).

The humanistic attitude is manifested in archeological site reports in statements such as "Artifacts are three dimensional: they are visual and tactile and sometimes they smell and make noise. Word pictures and flat representations in photographs and drawings offer only limited help [Ascher and Fairbanks 1971: 3]."

This same source uses a quote from Agee and Evans (1969) which is an expression of the humanistic viewpoint used in interpreting arche-ological data and illustrates a basic philosophy behind many house museums, restoration efforts, and some museum exhibits: "If I could do it, I'd do no writing at all here. It would be photographs: the rest would be fragments of cloth, bits of cotton, lumps of earth, records of speech, pieces of wood and iron, phials of odors, plates of food and excrement [Agee and Evans 1969: 12, in Ascher and Fairbanks 1971: 3]."

This appeal to the senses through a subjective, personalized approach is used by Noël Hume when speaking of "period rooms" and their frequent failure in "re-creating the past," when he makes the point that by cleaning up the human disorder in a room the personal presence in scattered books, papers and ashes in ashtrays is removed (Noël Hume 1970: 30–31). A personal confrontation with the past, Noël Hume sug-gests, is what visitors to historic houses and archeological sites are seek-ing. Archeology in the humanities emphasizes this personalized, human-istic, subjective viewpoint.

For historical reasons which we will not go into here, humanities departments, departments of anthropology, history, and American studies, as well as high schools, are using potentially scientific data sealed in archeological sites primarily as a means for achieving the goals of the humanities. Granting agencies are often involved, providing funds for conducting archeology where the primary result expected is education of the grantee. These same data are of great potential value to a science—sadly, under exclusive humanistic management they are generally lost to science.

The future of such projects may be in jeopardy, however, with the passage of a resolution by the American Anthropological Association and the Society for American Archaeology. It states that it is an unethical practice to collect from or excavate an archeological site "solely or pri-marily for 'teaching purposes,' since no site deserves less than

---

Figure 1. The polearm of archeology—a bill of particulars. To face the charge of arche-ology as antiquarianism the polearm of archeology must be forged from the nomothetic metal of explicitly scientific archeology. The bill was a seventeenth-century polearm used by foot soldiers against charging cavalry (Hume 1963:59–60).

professional excavation, analysis and publication" (Whitney 1975). Such projects, with humanistic goals, may well be forced into resorting to the scientific paradigm for their research designs. Certainly if *reliable, predictive* results are sought, this is the *only* avenue toward such ends, since any reliable understanding of the past must be achieved through scientific methods.

Particularistic Archeology

Particularistic archeology (pertaining to one person, thing, group, class, event, etc.—special, not general) emphasizes individualistic analysis and synthesis. The paradigm (idea set) is idiographic (intensive study of an individual case) and particularistic (often characterized by an antinomothetic stance against the search for general laws). Archeologists operating under a particularistic approach are often implicitly scientific, using principles of rigor in collecting field data, analyzing, and forming generalized conclusions from empirical data, while at the same time disdaining the use of the hypothetico-deductive method (reasoning from the general to the particular through hypothesis testing) and the scientific search for general laws (nomothetics). The methods of intensive inquiry into the specific case is sometimes mistaken for science by the particularistic archeologist, and the greater the intensity of the detail involved, the more "scientific" the research may be thought to be. Rigorous work often results from such inquiry, but, without the required theoretical and methodological base of science, such work is only implicitly scientific. It appears particularistic, but must be based on implied assumptions having lawlike characteristics (Schiffer 1973).

The particularistic approach has been accompanied by an antiscientific, antianthropology phenomenon. This viewpoint is seen in the following statement by Noël Hume (1969) who says that archeology should not be elevated to the ranks of the sciences:

> In truth it has no business there; its place is with the arts. The only skill that is peculiar to the archaeologist is his ability to study the artifacts in their relationship to the ground. That is what excavation is all about. But excavating is only a technique, and the excavator is, in theory, simply a technician who has mastered the art of taking the ground apart in such a way that it will give up its secrets. He is a detective, trained to expose the fingerprints of the past. He does not have to be a scientist (though his training as an anthropologist may make him one) to do a good job, but he must understand the contributions that such sciences as physics, microbiology, chemistry, botany, and computer mathematics can make to archaeological detection, dating, conservation, and interpretation. He must know when to call for the assistance of scientists [p. 15].

This attitude does not consider science as a way of organizing and examining data for more efficient problem solving, but rather as something that can be called on upon occasion as "experts" are needed. Such technical advice and expertise on a broad multidisciplinary front is certainly needed in archeology, but is not in itself scientific archeology.

Iain Walker (1967) also insists that archeology is not a science:

> Time and again the so-called scientific basis of New World archaeology is vaunated because New World archaeologists (anthropologists) wish to emphasize that their approach has evolved a Linnaean classification and terminology, and does follow pure, objective, immutable laws, and is thus superior to the historical approach [p. 26].

Walker appears to equate science with classification and terminology, not as a way of approaching data for the purpose of abstracting answers to questions. He seems to confuse the method with the goal. He apparently recognizes the nomothetic aspect of archeological science, but the words, "pure, objective, immutable laws" are Walker's, not those of a scientific archeologist.

The particularistic attitude is typified by Clyde Dollar (1968) when he says:

> The anthropologist deals with "people" and the historical archeologist deals with a person or persons. "People" have cultural expressions on a cultural center and peripheral area level; a "person" is basically a cultural variant, and must therefore be dealt with historically and deductively [p. 11].

In 1968, a paper by Clyde Dollar was used as a focal point for a forum of papers by a number of archeologists, some of who debated his particularistic stance. Lewis Binford (1972) has summarized Dollar's view:

> The debate largely boils down to an attempt on the part of Dollar to set forth the "uniqueness thesis" as the justification for adopting a set of goals commensurate with traditional historical perspectives. His concern is with specific events, dates, and actions of individuals summarized in the pursuit of reconstruction. Dollar offers further justification through a criticism of the accomplishments of "generalizing anthropology," which are set forth as a contrastive set of "failures," which he sees as further support for "uniqueness" claims and for the dismissal of generalizing propositions in historic sites archaeology [p. 121].

Dollar's paper and the accompanying forum papers (ed. South 1968) stimulated some interest in why archeologists dig, but the primary image maker in particularistic historical archeology has been Ivor Noël Hume (1963, 1966, 1969, 1970, 1974). His document-oriented archeology within the particularistic paradigm is the approach many view as primary to those working on historic sites. Through Noël Hume's work the layman or student receives the impression that the archeologist excavating an historic site is concerned with the unique, the historical, the idiographic. He concentrates upon the specifics of events, dates, individuals, and things. In the following passage Noël Hume provides us with his definition of archeology, the particularistic paradigm under which he operates, and the method relating to it:

> I would suggest that archaeology be described as the study of the material remains of both the remote and recent past in relationship to documentary history and the stratigraphy of the ground in which they are found.
> This relationship between the layers of the soil and the objects they contain enables the archaeologist to extract from his site the all-important information of what happened, when, and (it is hoped) to whom. Thus, to extract this information the archaeologist must be competent to do two things: he must be able to take the ground apart in such a way that its secrets can be wrested from it, and he must be sufficiently versed in the history and objects of the appropriate period or culture to properly interpret the site he is destroying [1969: 12].

This viewpoint is coupled with a disciplinary bias toward history where such a philosophy is at home. Noël Hume suggests it is imperative that archeologists excavating historic sites be trained in departments of history (1969: 19). Sympathetically, Dollar identifies the excavation of historic sites as basically historical research (1969: 188). Provided all the archeologist is looking for is facts to assimilate into what he already believes he knows, a particularistic training and methodology is certainly warranted (Ford 1973: 86). But scientists seek new understandings and means for evaluating what we think we know.

Noël Hume's particularism is consistently revealed in his attitude toward "relics," which he insists can be identified from the documents as to type, date of manufacture, factory, shipping date, value, and owner, since all these data are written down somewhere. In discovering the answers to these questions the archeologist is seen as fulfilling his responsibility (Noël Hume 1969: 13). He does indicate that a higher goal exists for the archeologist, learning something new about the past through looking "beyond the fragments to the whole and thence to the life of which that whole was a part" (Noël Hume 1970: 5). His emphasis on specific "relics," as identified by means of the written documents surviving from the past, contrasts markedly with attempts to use archeological data for evaluating ideas about cultural processes and with a goal of the specification of "laws" of such processes and the explanation for why such patterned regularity exists.

The fact that Noël Hume uses the particularistic approach does not mean that the descriptive classifications and data emerging from his work cannot be used for other purposes. However, his philosophy and bias condition what he considers "data." His work reveals that for him quantitative data are largely irrelevant, and therefore the products of his research are seen here as of limited utility, and extremely selfish in their limitations. Nevertheless, Noël Hume's dedication and intensive concern with identification, chronology, and the time of arrival of artifact types in this country have resulted in a series of formal-temporal artifact types of considerable classificatory value.

Anyone who has read Noël Hume's *A guide to artifacts of colonial America* (1970), knows of the historical and archeological research synthesis represented by each class of artifacts discussed, and of Noël Hume's concern with fixing these objects in time and place of manufacture. Noël Hume would be the first to insist that his temporal brackets as assigned in that book are merely the best estimate at the time the book was written, and these are continually being refined through the accumulation of more empirical material. An example of one of these formal-temporal types can be read as follows:

Artifact Type X: Described as having attributes 1 through 5, was manufactured in Bristol, England, from ca. 1750 to ca. 1765, and exported to the American colonies during most of that period.

For some objects, therefore, Noël Hume's identifications (shape and style through time) provide a basic set of information useful to others with far broader and more scientific interests than those questions ever to be asked by Noël Hume himself under the particularistic paradigm. These are isolated formal-functional regularities of considerable value to archeologists working under either a particularistic or a nomothetic paradigm. As stressed earlier, however, archeological data collected particularistically have a very limited value when used by another archeologist operating under a different framework (Flannery 1972b: 106–107). Noël Hume's limited data, therefore, serve well as a first step toward quantified analysis of archeological data directed at questions asked under a far different paradigm than that used by Noël Hume.

The tendency of anthropologically trained archeologists to depend on their own classifications of historic site artifacts rather than using the historical approach of going to the documents first has brought criticism of this approach from Noël Hume:

> Such categories often have neither value nor meaning, for it is generally possible to find a book containing the necessary information, often including the potter's original name for his product [1969: 13].
> The absence of knowledge on the part of the student prompts him to seek it in the only way he knows how—through the methods of anthropology and prehistory. Thus, he wastes time and funds laboriously compiling useless pottery typologies in the quest for dating and nomenclatures that should be sought amid the vast corpus of material already published on the subject [1968: 104].

Although the archeologist should certainly be aware of the historical documents relating to the artifacts he unearths, as Noël Hume is saying here, it is also true that Noël Hume appears to misunderstand the role of classification in scientific archeology. When the Moravian kiln waster dump of Gottfried Aust was excavated in Bethabara, N.C., it was not the documents that revealed how to classify the ware but rather the archeological record and my training as an anthropologist (South 1967: 33–52). Classifications should be designed as instruments for measuring something specifiable (a variable). There is no reason to believe that a taxonomy employed in England two hundred years ago would necessarily serve scientific needs today. For instance, an important classification of buttons used by the manufacturer and found impressed on the buttons was "BEST," "GILT," "DOUBLE GILT," "TREBLE GILT," and "**** GILT," but a scientific taxonomy would not necessarily utilize such a classification. The same is true of Indian pottery taxonomy. How the Indian who made the pot classified it is certainly not relevant to the criteria used by the archeological scientist classifying the same pot for asking questions relating to ceramic variability. The scientific archeologist does not depend on classifications written by merchants, priests, or craftsmen for measuring variability, but classifies his data in accordance with the variables he is measuring as determined by the questions he is asking.

The antianthropological view is expressed by Iain Walker when he admonishes his colleagues that it is still not too late to make historical archeology a field of distinction, "independent of the confining bounds of anthropology-oriented theory (1967: 32)." The ironic fact remains, however, that the literature reporting research on historic sites is a virtual desert when it comes to containing more than a sprig or two of anthropologically oriented research, and it is a difficult task to find demonstrated anthropological research that could be said to be "confining" historical archeology. Many anthropologically trained archeologists are involved in excavating historic sites, but reports reveal little more than a poor review of the historical documentation, and an inadequate classification of artifacts to show for such a background. Therefore, the criticism by particularists that the results of excavation on historic sites by anthropologically trained archeologists are inadequate is certainly often true. However, it is true not because they have used anthropological theory, methods, analyses, and interpretations, and have failed, but rather because they have not used such an approach, thus violating their anthropological heritage.

Incompetence is to be regretted wherever it is found, but anthropology is not responsible. It is hoped that this discussion will stimulate archeologists to take their anthropological responsibilities far more seriously. If they will reveal their anthropological training through their work, future criticism can be directed only at true failures in properly executing the anthropological goals rather than at results of archeological research that were never anthropologically guided to begin with.

Scientific Archeology

> The empirical sciences use the hypothetico-deductive method, consisting of two interdependent exercises or episodes—one imaginative, the other critical. To advance a hypothesis is an imaginative or creative exercise, but hypotheses must be subject to critical examination and test. Hypotheses and other imaginative exploits are the basis of scientific inquiry [Ayala 1974: 700].

In the face of a nonscientific bias in past archeological practice in this century, there have been those who have continued to insist that archeology can indeed be a science. The first president of the Society for American Archaeology, Arthur C. Parker, in the initial volume of *American Antiquity* expressed the hope that archeology could become a deductive science: "The older emphasis of gathering great quantities of archaeological material for its own sake has given way to that of selecting archaeological sites as specific problems. . . . Only by pursuing the latter method may archaeology be built up as a deductive science . . . [1935: 2–3]."

Twenty years later hope was expressed that the transition period of the 1950s would result in the emergence of a science of archeology: "American archaeology is now in a period of transition. It is breaking out of its Boasian shell of fact gathering, and is beginning to emerge as a science based upon a theoretical foundation [of evolution] for the interpretation of the cultural process [South 1955: 9, 22]."

In 1962, Lewis Binford, in the first of a series of influential articles to appear in the 1960s, emphasized the hypothetico-deductive approach in relation to the process of evolutionary change: "Archaeologists should be among the best qualified to study and directly test hypotheses concerning the process of evolutionary change, particularly processes of change that are relatively slow, or hypotheses that postulate temporal-processual priorities as regards total cultural systems [1962: 224]."

In 1968, Cleland and Fitting emphasized the need for problem-oriented, imaginative research based on the quantification of empirical data from the eighteenth and nineteenth centuries in order to enhance our knowledge in the areas of "trade, transportation, social stratification, political spheres, craft specialization, and acculturation of native peoples [pp. 134–136]."

Forty years have passed since Parker made his plea for a problem-oriented, deductive science of archeology. Throughout that period like a "great pulsation" surfacing from time to time in the words of a few individuals, was a conviction that a scientific archeology would eventually emerge.

The conceptual thrust of the 1960s toward scientific archeology has been paralleled by a similar phenomenon in other disciplines. A polemic battle is now raging in the field of history between the particularists and the cliometricians, or "new economic historians," who

> Attempt to cast all explanations of past economic development in the form of valid hypothetico-deductive models. This is another way of saying that the new generation seeks to continue an effort that was underway long before it appeared on the scene: namely, the construction of economic history on the basis of scientific methods [Fogel 1966, in Adams 1973: 322].

It is apparent that archeologists, historians, economic historians, and linguists are responding to a similar "wave length" toward a more scientific approach. This trend will not result in a dramatic replacement of the old entirely, since the continued reappearance of "young fogeys" will prevent a too-rash dash into the arms of science (Flannery 1973: 47). However, the revolution in thought is well under way, and dramatic changes will be seen in the decades to come in the results of archeological research.

In the polearm chart in Figure 1, the major paradigm is seen to be a nomothetic one, as urged by Steward, and more recently by Lewis Binford, Patty Jo Watson, Steven LeBlanc, Charles Redman, Fred Plog, Michael Schiffer, Jeff Reid, and others. The argument of these archeologists is that in order to face the charge of archeology as antiquarianism, the polearm of archeology must be forged from the nomothetic metal of explicitly scientific archeology. Fred Plog (1974) has said that archeology is a science examining data from the past to test hypotheses about past cultural processes, whereas antiquarianism merely collects data and attempts to do something with it (p. 4).

The scientific archeologist is compelled to ask himself, regardless of his background or training, whether the conceptual paradigm under which he is operating is consistent with the questions he is trying to answer, and which paradigm will give him the most reliable, predictive results, capable of being replicated by any trained investigator. Lewis Binford (1972) expresses the scientific point of view in his admonition to those excavating historic sites.

> Anthropology must become a science before it can adequately serve to enhance our historical understanding of man and his past. I suggest to historians, anthropologists, and interested bystanders alike, that insofar as we agree that our goals in historical sites archaeology are historical understanding of the events and the people which are responsible for the production of the archaeological record, such understanding will not be forthcoming until a science of archaeology is developed. Rejection of the pursuit of scientific or nomothetic understanding because of failures in this direction within the field of anthropology, or a commitment to particularistic approaches in the absence of such understanding is counterproductive. Historic sites archaeologists should actively

engage in nomothetic studies aimed at the specification of general propositions amenable to testing regarding (a) the processes responsible for the formation of the archaeological record and (b) the processes responsible for change and diversification in human lifeways [p. 123].

The procedure of scientific archeology outlined earlier, uses the inductively (reasoning from the particular to the general) derived generalizations from observed facts to specify problem areas. Trial solutions or theories are advanced and then evaluated through deduced consequences of such ideas. Such consequences are phrased as hypotheses, predictions, and deductions (reasoning from the general to the particular) and tested against further observation and collection of data. This is the hypothetico-deductive-inductive cycle of science clearly outlined by Kemeny (1959). The understanding of this scientific cycle is vital in distinguishing between traditional archeology and the new approach. The former holds that the problems and their solutions come directly from the data. The latter acknowledges that the solutions come from us—facts don't speak for themselves. The heuristic device in Figure 2 is designed to clarify the scientific cycle.

Traditional archeology emphasized the inductive reasoning from data as a means of developing general statements of theory. The new emphasis has been on the reasoning from data for purposes of problem recognition. The emphasis is on advancing trial idea solutions, potential

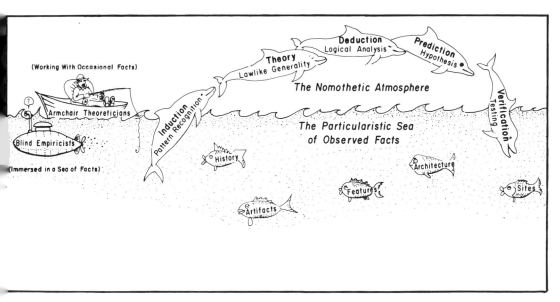

Figure 2.   Flowchart of the hypothetico-deductive-inductive scientific cycle (the Dolphin chart; after Kemeny 1959:86). The scientific archeologist completes the cycle of the dolphin.

explanations, and then, importantly, evaluating them by means other than simply how plausably such ideas accommodate the data, but going further to predict in hypothesis form toward verification through testing with new data (facts), thus completing the scientific cycle. An overemphasis on empirical data results in blind empiricists' being immersed in a sea of facts, whereas an overemphasis on construction of hypothetical models with only occasional reference to a factual data base is an imbalance in the opposite direction, resulting in armchair speculation.

Since the scientific cycle uses both inductive and deductive strategies in addressing the data, it is appropriate to look at the ways in which the empirical data of archeology can be used.

1. To furnish collectors' items and museum objects.
2. To furnish documentation for the study of art history or the history of architecture.
3. To attain knowledge of sequences of events and chronologies in the absence [or presence] of written documents (this is history *sensu stricto,* which Walter Taylor called "chronicle").
4. To help furnish data for much fuller historical studies (historiography, structural, or constructive history) with particularistic (idiographic) goals.
5. To furnish independent data that can be used to test hypotheses in order to confirm or disconfirm them as general laws about cultural processes (i.e., about the internal and external dynamics of human groups at one point in time or through time); this has to do with large-scale generalizing (nomothetic) goals; the general laws so confirmed provide us with an understanding of history (i.e., they are foundational in treating history as a science) [Watson 1973: 114].

The first four of these approaches to data handling have had extensive use in traditional archeology. The fifth addresses itself to the formulation of laws about cultural processes, a basic goal of scientific archeology. However, the confirmed general laws do not "provide us with an understanding of history" as stated here by Patty Jo Watson. Understanding comes only when we ask why the facts are the way they are. This is theory building. The expression of laws and lawlike statements are propositions directed at the empirical data base as generalizations from demonstrated patterning. Understanding does not come until we ask why the law is seen to be applicable to the data to which it is addressed. This allows for the presentation of alternative explanations for examination and testing relative to the dynamics of the cultural system. From this process understanding may then emerge.

As archeologists are swept into the intellectual ferment and professional challenge presented by the scientific approach to archeological data, their production will be revealed through the explanations of culture process emerging from their demonstrated patterning and laws derived from archeological data. At such a time, Flannery's goal of being able to spell archeology with a capital S (for science) will be nearer to being realized (Flannery 1973: 47). At that time, perhaps not too many decades in the future, those antiscientific particularists still among us will have as targets for their arrows a body of scientific reports on excavation and analysis of historic site data. Such a target will be far less vulnerable, I believe, than that presented by the reports on excavation of historic sites characterizing the decades just past.

A STUDY OF TRENDS IN HISTORICAL ARCHEOLOGY— EVALUATING THE STATE OF THE FIELD

The epistomological biases examined in the previous section provide a background against which an examination can be made of trends represented by the work of archeologists researching historic site data. An examination of papers presented by these archeologists during the past 15 years should reveal trends during that time that might provide some insight as to what we might expect for the decades to come.

Theoretical Assumptions

The assumptions for this study have been spelled out in the previous section of this chapter. They involve a commitment to the development of a theory of evolution of culture, the search for empirical laws or regularities and discovery of whether our theory is adequate to their explanation and, finally, the epistomological strategy of the hypothetico-deductive method whereby we evaluate our ideas, our theories.

To examine the intellectual trends among those excavating historic sites during the past decade, a quantitative analysis of attitudes reflected in published papers was undertaken. The data base for this study was the papers presented at the Conference on Historic Site Archaeology, and published in *The Conference on Historic Site Archaeology Papers,* and the Society for Historical Archaeology journal, *Historical Archaeology,* during the past 15 years. With this primary strategy in mind, several expectations were written down as to what the data might reveal based on my familiarity with the articles. These expectations are as follows:

1. Because of the rare occurrence of hypothetico-deductive papers in historical archeology until recent years it is thought that this type of paper will be seen to emerge only in recent years.
2. It is expected that reports concerning synthesizing classification and method will be seen to change little throughout this period since such papers are a necessary base for any archeological activity.

3. It is expected that the theory forum of 1967 in *The Conference on Historic Site Archaeology Papers* will have an effect on stimulating the occurrence of theory papers in the years following.
4. It is expected that because of the 1967 theory forum stimulus that there will be a heavier emphasis on theory in *The Conference on Historic Site Archaeology Papers,* where this forum appeared, than in the journal *Historical Archaeology.*
5. It is expected that site-specific reports of a narrative nature will decrease through time as emphasis is placed on method and theory.
6. It is expected that articles on underwater archeology should be seen in the early part of this period, but not so much after the founding of the International Conference on Underwater Archaeology in 1971.[2]
7. It is expected that articles on industrial archeology should be seen in the early part of this period, but not so much so after the founding of the Society for Industrial Archaeology in 1971 (see Footnote 2).

Method

With these guesses stated, each volume of the papers involved was examined in turn, as well as the program for the Conference on Historic Site Archaeology, and each paper was classified by type as the content was reviewed. The first meeting of the Conference on Historic Site Archaeology was held in 1960. The Society for Historical Archaeology followed 7 years later, in 1967, with a journal begun the same year. In the study of papers from these sources, a total of 285 papers are represented. Thirteen types of papers were defined and tabulated by year, not as a percentage but directly, each paper being represented by a symbol. These symbols were combined into bars reflecting the exact number of papers represented for each type for each year. The results were expected to take the form of bars centered on a line, perhaps in a microscopic manner revealing parts of "battleship curves" if normal curve trends were indeed to be revealed during this short time span. If not this type of trend, it was anticipated that the beginning dates at least, for various emphases reflected by the papers, might reveal a trend line through time. The results of this study are illustrated in Figure 3.

Observation and Classification of the Data

The 13 types of papers were assigned an attitude that in my judgment, reflected the primary content of the paper. These are (Table 2):

[2] The significant variable here proved not to be the founding of the conference, but whether or not a journal was begun.

TABLE 2

Type of Archeology Paper and Attitude Reflected

Type of paper	Attitude reflected
1. Narrative site report	*This is the site where I dug.*
2. Site descriptive report	*This is what I found on it.*
3. Synthesizing classification	*This is how I classified it.*
4. Conservation	*This is how I conserved the artifacts.*
5. Methodology	*This is how I did it.*
6. Site preservation and stabilization ⎫ 7. Restoration and reconstruction ⎭	*This is why my sponsor wanted me to dig.*
8. Theory	*This is why I dig.*
9. Hypothetico-deductive application	*I hypothesize, deduce, test, and predict.*
10. Ethnographic	
11. Underwater	
12. Industrial	
13. Humanistic	

Only eight of these were used to attempt to indicate trend within the basic historical archeology field; ethnographic, underwater, industrial, conservation, and humanistic papers were considered as adjunct disciplines. It becomes apparent from this list of types of papers that Type 1, narrative site report, is merely of the "show and tell" variety without even the redeeming feature of a description of the artifacts found on the site. That feature is left to the paper of Type 2, site descriptive, in that it includes some description of data related to the particular site. Type 3, synthesizing classification, includes those papers whose classificatory format is synthesized to the point that it has implications directly applicable to other sites. Type 4, conservation, is an adjunct discipline. Type 5, methodology, includes papers dealing primarily with various methodological considerations; a paper on photography in historical archeology, for instance, would fall in this type. Types 6 and 7, dealing with site preservation and stabilization, and with restoration and reconstruction, are primarily sponsor-oriented papers. Type 8 papers are concerned with theory, with the longest bars being the result of a section in *The Conference on Historic Site Archeology Papers* known as "The Historical Archaeology Forum," to which various papers on a single topic were solicited by the editor for publication. These papers resulted in a number of broad "blips" that tend to disturb the normal evolutionary development of trends that would be seen without them. Type 9, hypothetico-deductive application of this method to the paper content, was revealed in these papers.

Analysis

From the analyzing-synthesizing chart in Figure 3, we can note that the only "battleship" type curve that might be seen to be indicated is that

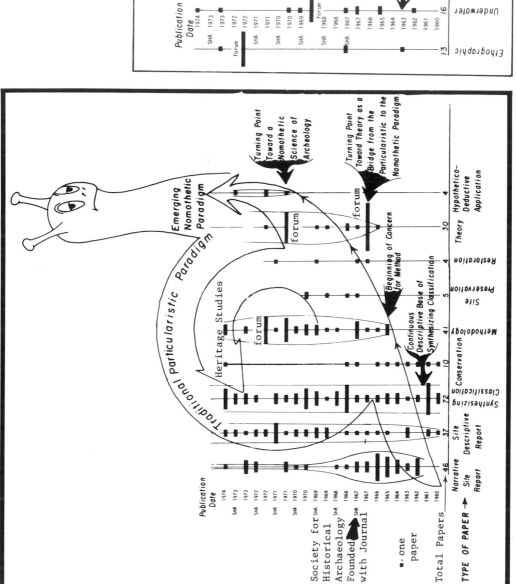

Figure 3. The slowly emerging trend in historical archeology toward archeological science revealed through 15 years of papers in *The Conference on Historic Site Archaeology Papers* and *Historical Archaeology* (S.H.A. journal).

for Type 1, the narrative site report. This decrease in the presentation of papers of this type was predicted by Expectation 5, and the continued infrequency of this type report is predicted as more emphasis is placed on method, theory, and definitive synthesizing classification in the years to come.

The site descriptive reports, and the synthesizing classification can be seen to maintain a straight line profile, definitely non-"battleship" in shape. This is in keeping with the prediction made by Expectation 2 regarding the uniformity expected of this group of papers, since such classification forms a basic foundation for historical archeology throughout time. The conservation profile stops abruptly in 1968, a fact that may well relate to the founding of the Association for Preservation Technology in that year, and the newsletter begun in 1969. An examination of papers in the newsletter compared with those published prior to 1969 might be warranted before a causal connection could be suggested.

Regarding the relationship between founding dates of societies and the frequency of papers presented after that date in these journals, we should look at the underwater profile. Expectation 6 suggests that with the founding of the International Conference on Underwater Archaeology in 1963 that there should be a decrease in the papers presented on this topic. Clearly this was not the case, so this expectation is negated. This may relate to the fact that no journal for underwater archeology papers has yet been established. This implies that when such a journal is established there should be a decrease in such papers in the journals of this study.

Also relating to this same question is the Industrial Archeology profile, where the last paper was presented in 1969, and the Society for Industrial Archaeology, founded in 1971 with a newsletter begun the following year. A causal relationship is suggested here, but a more definitive study would be needed in order to clearly establish the variables involved. Perhaps the establishment of a publication source for industrial archeology papers in England or Canada may be involved in the phenomenon we are seeing here.

The profile of papers on theory certainly is in conformity with the predictive Expectation 3, which suggested more papers after the 1967 forum. This theory profile also supports the prediction in expectation no. 4, which indicated that far more papers would appear in *The Conference on Historic Site Archaeology Papers* after 1967 than in *Historical Archaeology* as a result of the 1967 forum on theory. The majority of such papers indeed were published in *The Conference on Historic Site Archaeology Papers* as suggested.

The profile on method is virtually straight, with no dramatic trend indicated otherwise, which is as anticipated by part of Expectation 2, method being a basic, continually evolving consideration in the archeological process.

The hypothetico-deductive application profile reveals only four papers, beginning in 1971, that are of this type, a result in keeping with the prediction of Expectation 1, indicating that this type of paper would appear late in the time period involved.

Explanatory Synthesis

From this analysis, we can see that we can draw a line from the beginning of the temporal period at the left side of the chart in Figure 3, to the point in 1965 when the first papers on method were presented. From this point we can draw a slightly curving line to the point in 1971 when the first hypothetico-deductive paper was presented. This gradually ascending line is seen to reflect the slowly emerging emphasis on method and theory toward archeological science through hypothetico-deductive procedures.

This slowly emerging nomothetic paradigm in historical archeology as seen in this study represents only the beginning tail of a "battleship" curve that will be seen to expand in the decades to come as a scientific archeology is slowly developed. The hypothetico-deductive–inductive method depends on a firm foundation in archeological theory with corresponding methodological procedures, as indicated by the broad arrow on the chart in Figure 3. This arrow has its broad base in reliable synthesizing—classification with broad applicability. Archeological science builds on the entire spectrum of data represented by the various papers in this study.

THE SLOWLY EMERGING TREND IN HISTORICAL ARCHEOLOGY TOWARD ARCHEOLOGICAL SCIENCE: A PERSONAL VIEW

In contrast to this slowly developing trend, and continuing to form the major emphasis in historical archeology for many decades to come, is the traditional particularistic paradigm. This approach is not heavily dependent upon a theoretical base; in fact, it has been characterized by an overt antitheoretical position. The major body of literature in the field of historical archeology (86% in this study, not counting adjunct papers) is concerned with this traditional particularistic viewpoint, characterized by a cyclical phenomenon of archeological practice described as follows.

The sponsor who is concerned with the development and/or interpretation of an historic site for reasons of national heritage undertakes to finance an archeological excavation. The site is excavated; the features, particularly architectural features, are described. The artifacts are described, but only in rare instances are they afforded a synthesizing treatment. The documents relating to the site are examined in particular reference to the site, but seldom are documents synthesized in a systematic manner. A summary is written—a clotheshorse of history is draped with bits and pieces of archeological data—followed by recommendations to the sponsor as to the need for further research and historic site development. This has become a standard format in the examination of historic sites by archeologists, and it is circular in that the archeological data are merely used to reinforce written records by providing a few missing details of artifacts or architecture.

Since heritage goals have a primary focus in the history of a site, there is no need for a sponsor to look beyond this through archeological theory toward nomothetic goals and explanation. Indeed, why should he? He is not concerned with furthering the goals of archeology, or contributing to its evolution as a science. He is interested in contributing to classificatory, descriptive, documentary research oriented around a priori beliefs about the past (Figure 3). Historical archeology's problem lies in the willingness of most of its practitioners to accept the above procedure as their archeological goals, thus becoming sucked into the vortex of a circular particularistic historical whirlwind, at the center of which is a sponsor, with a heritage goal, regarding a site, on which is a ruin, from which a group of artifacts is recovered for exhibit in a museum.

In the decades to come there will continue to be a strong emphasis on site development research within agencies devoted to national heritage goals. Young archeologists should ask themselves, as they begin their professional careers, whether they will be conducting archeological science in their research. If so, they will have to face the fact that agencies employing archeologists will be emphasizing site-oriented research with limited goals (Swannack 1975). In some cases this viewpoint has imposed serious professional restraints on scholars through strictures on free and open inquiry. This is accomplished by agencies having a primary focus on site-development research, combined with strictures on time, funding, and planning. This focus restricts the archeologist who wishes to translate the scientific aspects of such site-oriented research into competent articles and analyses for publication in professional journals and books. As a result of this emphasis, such agencies cannot attract research archeologists whose primary responsibility, allegiance, and obligation lie with the research data rather than with site-specific, sponsor-dictated goals. To attract the best research minds agencies involved in site-specific research for historic site development must begin to accept their responsibility toward conducting both mission-oriented research and that directed toward archeological science. There is traditional pressure within such agencies toward achieving primarily the mission-oriented goals, and this trend continues (Swannack 1975). Rather than continuing to emphasize the use (and destruction through excavation) of precious cultural resource data in the management of sites for the visiting public, such agencies must begin to recognize higher research goals. Instead of restricting inquiry to specific, particularistic goals, they should urge their archeologists to make broader inquiry in order to realize the greatest potential of cultural resource management studies. In so doing, they will begin to foster an attitude compatible with a free and open inquiry of the human mind, a traditional value nurtured in a university climate. Only then will such agencies attract to their ranks the best research minds archeology has to offer.

Attracting such minds is important to archeology because mission-oriented agencies are responsible for excavating the vast majority of the archeological sites being examined today. It behooves us all that the best human resources be employed to conduct the destructive archeological process on the remaining cultural resources at our disposal.

Archeologists, therefore, should develop their own firm theoretical base for the archeology they are doing, to undertake excavation with the thought of carrying out their own research designs as well as those of the sponsor, and to demand of themselves that additional effort necessary to execute primary scientific archeological goals while at the same time fulfilling the goals of the sponsor. Historical archeologists must begin to do this on a far broader scale than is now the case if they are to move faster than a snail's pace toward conducting archeological science. In working toward this end, however, the sponsor's and archeologist's goals should not, indeed must not, be opposed.

Professional standards are now being established in the field of archeology in the form of guidelines for cultural resource management studies, and criteria for the registration of professional archeologists in a National Registry of Professional Archaeologists (Thompson 1974). These moves toward increased professional standards in archeology have a direct bearing on the points we have been making in this chapter in that the professional guidelines emphasize that archeological work should not be undertaken for the purpose of answering sponsor's goals only. They also emphasize that resource management studies must be subjected to the scientific archeological process in order to meet the standards of the guidelines. The final chapter in this book will examine in more detail the archeologist's responsibility in cultural resource management studies.

The chapters to follow will illustrate, through application, some of the theoretical, paradigmatic, methodological, and archeological considerations we have discussed here, drawing on data derived from archeology on historic sites. The literature in archeology is filled with models, hypotheses, and other "mouthtalk" (Service 1969), not relating directly to empirical archeological data, and there will no doubt be enough of that in this book also. However, our goal is to keep such business to a minimum in order to demonstrate the patterned regularity of the archeological record as well as the variability, under the belief that we can have no science without pattern recognition, and pattern cannot be refined without quantification. From pattern recognition, general empirical laws can be stated, and the explanation of why laws are operative through the hypothetico-deductive process leads to theory building through testing hypotheses with new data.

The concepts we have been concerned with in this chapter can be envisioned in terms of *archeology and the art of weaving*. The basic warp of the fabric is the process of evolution, interwoven with the weft of unique events trailed from the shuttle of history. The variable strands of the weft produce a pattern interlocked with the regularity of the warp. The resulting design, called "Carolina Pride," has determined the relationship each strand of yarn has to every other in the woof and warp of the fabric. This design can be equated with culture process. The fabric is that creation of man known as culture.

The particularist is involved primarily with the description of the weft strands as they cross the warp, tracing each step of the way, over and under, with every row of yarn representing a single archeological site. At the end of the row he writes his report and he is done.

The archeological scientist searches for pattern not only within each row of weft yarn as it repeats over two, under three, but he also notices that adjoining rows of weft (sites) have somewhat similar, yet varying patterns. Having recognized that pattern for a number of sites (weft rows), he makes a prediction as to what pattern the next row (site) will have. If his postulates are empirically verified, he then hypothesizes as to the design (culture process) that was the explanatory determinant for the pattern he has delineated from the empirical data. As his hypotheses are tested and found to be valid, he eventually is able to say, "The explanatory phenomenon is a design I will call 'Carolina Pride.'" Having thus addressed himself to culture process, he is well on the way to understanding something about the fabric of culture.

It is hoped that the discussion here has made clear that historical archeology is archeology carried out on sites of the historic period. This fact does not make it a different kind of archeology from any other. David Clarke (1968: 13) has emphasized that "archaeology is archaeology is archaeology," and Leslie White (1938) has stressed that "Science is Sciencing." In the decades to come, as more archeologists come under the continuing influence of the "great pulsation" toward archeological science, there may come a time when it can be said that archeology is sciencing, and no one will seriously challenge the proposition. At that time archeology can indeed be spelled with a capital S for science, as Flannery has suggested (1973: 47).

REFERENCES

Adams, Robert McC.
  1973 Discussion. In *Research and theory in current archeology,* edited by Charles L. Redman. New York: John Wiley.
Agee, J., and W. Evans
  1969 *Let us now praise famous men.* New York: Ballantine.
Ascher, Robert, and Charles H. Fairbanks
  1971 Excavation of a Slave Cabin: Georgia, U.S.A. *Historical Archaeology* **5:**3–17.
Ayala, Francisco J.
  1974 Biological Evolution: Natural Selection or Random Walk? *American Scientist* **62** (No. 6):692–700.
Binford, Lewis R.
  1962 Archaeology as Anthropology. *American Antiquity* **28** (No. 2):217–225.
  1964 A Consideration of Archaeological Research Design. *American Antiquity* **29** (No. 4):425–441.
  1965 Archaeological Systematics and the Study of Culture Process. *American Antiquity* **31** (No. 2):203–210.
  1967 Smudge Pits and Hide Smoking: The Role of Analogy in Archaeological Reasoning. *American Antiquity* **32** (No. 1):1–12.
  1972 'Evolution and Horizon as Revealed in Ceramic Analysis in Historical Archeology'—A Step Toward the Development of Archaeological Science. *The Conference on Historic Site Archaeology Papers 1971* **6:**117–125.
Binford, Sally R., and Lewis R. Binford (Eds.)
  1968 *New perspectives in archeology.* Chicago: Aldine.
Bronowski, J.
  1956 *Science and human values.* New York: Harper & Row.
Clarke, David
  1968 *Analytical archaeology.* London: Methuen.
Cleland, Charles E., and James E. Fitting
  1968 The Crisis of Identity: Theory in Historic Sites Archaeology. *The Conference on Historic Site Archaeology Papers 1967* **2** (No. 2):124–138.
Dollar, Clyde D.
  1968 Some Thoughts on Theory and Method in Historical Archaeology. *The Conference on Historic Site Archaeology Papers 1967* **2** (Part 2):3–30.
Ferguson, Leland G.
  1974 Historical Archeology and the Importance of Material Things (manuscript).
Flannery, Kent V.
  1972a The Cultural Evolution of Civilizations. *Annual Review of Ecology and Systematics* Richard F. Johnston, ed. **3:**399–426. Palo Alto, California: Annual Reviews, Inc.
  1972b Culture history versus cultural process: A debate in American archaeology. In *Contemporary Archaeology,* edited by Leone, Mark P. Carbondale and Edwardsville: Southern Illinois University Press.
  1973 Archeology with a capital "S." In *Research and theory in current archeology,* edited by Redman, Charles L. New York: John Wiley.
Fogel, R. W.
  1966 The New Economic History: Its Findings and Methods. *Economic History Review.* Second Series: 19. Also in McAdams, Robert, Discussion, in *Research and theory in current archeology,* edited by Redman, Charles L. New York: John Wiley, 1973.
Ford, Richard I.
  1973 Archeology serving humanity. In *Research and theory in current archeology,* edited by Redman, Charles L. New York: John Wiley.

Greer, Georgeanna H.
   1971   Preliminary Information on the Use of the Alkaline Glaze for Stoneware in the
          South 1800–1970. *The Conference on Historic Site Archaeology Papers* **5**:155–197.
Haag, William G.
   1959   The status of evolutionary theory in American archeology. In *Evolution and
          anthropology: A centennial appraisal,* edited by Meggers, Betty J. Washington,
          D.C.: The Anthropological Society of Washington.
Harrington, J. C.
   1952   Historic site archeology in the United States (1947). In *Archeology of eastern
          United States,* edited by Griffin, James B. Chicago: University of Chicago Press.
   1955   Archeology as Auxiliary to American History. *American Anthropologist* **55** (No.
          6):1121–1130.
Hill, J. N.
   1972   The methodological debate in contemporary archaeology: A model. In *Models in
          archaeology,* edited by Clarke, David L. London: Methuen.
Kemeny, John G.
   1959   *A philosopher looks at science.* New York: D. Van Nostrand.
LeBlanc, Steven A.
   1973   Two points of logic concerning data, hypotheses, general laws, and systems. In
          Research and theory in current archeology, edited by Redman, Charles L. New
          York: John Wiley.
Longacre, William A.
   1970   Current Thinking in American Archeology. *Current Directions in Anthropology.*
          Bulletins of the American Anthropological Association **3** (No. 3, Part 2):126–138.
Morgan, Lewis H.
   1877   *Ancient society.* Chicago: Kerr.
Noël Hume, Ivor
   1963   *Here lies Virginia.* New York: Knopf.
   1966   *1775: Another part of the field.* New York: Knopf.
   1968   Historical Archaeology in America. *Post-Medieval Archaeology* **1**:104–105.
   1969   *Historical archaeology.* New York: Knopf.
   1970   *A guide to artifacts of Colonial America.* New York: Knopf.
   1974   *All the best rubbish.* New York: Harper & Row.
Parker, Arthur C.
   1935   Getting Down to Facts. *American Antiquity* **1**:2–3.
Phillips, Phillip, and Gordon R. Willey
   1953   Method and Theory in American Archaeology: An Operational Basis for Culture-
          Historical Integration. *American Anthropologist* **55** (No. 5):615–633.
   1955   Method and Theory in American Archaeology II: Historical-Developmental
          Interpretation. *American Anthropologist* **57** (No. 4):723–819.
Pirsig, Robert M.
   1975   *Zen and the art of motorcycle maintenance.* New York: Bantam.
Plog, Fred T.
   1974   *The study of prehistoric change.* New York: Academic.
Reid, J. Jefferson, and Michael B. Schiffer
   1973   Prospects for a Behavioral Archaeology. Paper presented at the 1973 meeting of
          the American Anthropological Association, New Orleans.
Reid, J. Jefferson, Michael B. Schiffer, and Jeffrey M. Neff
   n.d.   Archaeological Considerations of Intrasite Sampling (manuscript).
Reid, J. Jefferson, Michael B. Schiffer, and William L. Rathje
   1974   Behavioral Archaeology: Four Strategies (manuscript).
Roth, Rodris

1961 Tea Drinking in 18th-Century America: Its Etiquette and Equipage. *Contributions from the Museum of History and Technology,* Paper 14. Washington, D.C.: Smithsonian Institution.

Schiffer, Michael B.
  1973 Several Archaeological Laws (manuscript), Fayetteville: Arkansas Archeological Survey.
  1975 Arrangement versus seriation of sites: A new approach to relative temporal relationships. In *The Cache River Archeological Project: An Experiment in Contract Archeology;* assembled by Michael B. Schiffer and John H. House (Arkansas Archeological Survey), *Research Series* (No. 8):257–264.

Schuyler, Robert L.
  1970 Historical and Historic Sites Archaeology as Anthropology: Basic Definitions and Relationships. *Historical Archaeology* 4:83–89.

Service, Elman R.
  1969 Models for the Methodology of Mouthtalk. *Southwestern Journal of Anthropology* 25:68–80.

South, Stanley
  1955 Evolutionary Theory in Archaeology. *Southern Indian Studies* 7:2–24.
  1967 The Ceramic Forms of the Potter Gottfried Aust at Bethabara, North Carolina, 1755 to 1771. *The Conference on Historic Site Archaeology Papers* 1:33–52.

(Editor)
  1968 Historical Archaeology Forum on Theory and Method in Historical Archaeology. *The Conference on Historic Site Archaeology Papers* 2 (No. 2):1–188.

Spaulding, Albert C.
  1973 Archeology in the active voice: The new anthropology. In *Research and theory in current archeology,* edited by Redman, Charles L. New York: John Wiley.

Steward, Julian H. (Editor)
  1948 A Functional-Developmental Classification of American High Cultures. *Memoir No. 4,* Society for American Archaeology.
  1955 *Theory of culture change.* Urbana: University of Illinois Press.
  1956 Cultural Evolution. *Scientific American* 194 (No. 5):69–80.

Stone, Lyle M.
  1974 Fort Michilimackinac 1715–1781. *Publications of the Museum.* East Lansing; Michigan: Michigan State University.

Struever, Stuart
  1968 Problems, methods and organization: A disparity in the growth of archeology. In *Anthropological archeology in the Americas,* edited by Meggers, Betty J. Washington, D.C.: Anthropological Society of Washington.
  1971 Comments on Archaeological Data Requirements and Research Strategy. *American Antiquity* 36:9–19.

Swannack, Jervis D.
  1975 Mission-oriented Agencies: Means and Ends of Historic Sites Archaeology. *Historical Archaeology* 9:80–81.

Taylor, Walter W.
  1948 A Study of Archaeology. *Memoir No. 69, American Anthropologist* 50 (No. 3), Part 2:1–256.

Thomas, David Hurst
  1973 An Empirical Test for Steward's Model of Great Basic Settlement Patterns. *American Antiquity* 38 (No. 2):115–176.

Thompson, Raymond H.
  1974 Society for American Archaeology Report of the Committee on Certification.

Tylor, E. B.
  1891 *Primitive culture.* London: John Murray.
Walker, Iain C.
  1967 Historic Archaeology—Methods and Principles. *Historical Archaeology 1967* **1**:23–
         33.
Watson, Patty Jo
  1973 The future of archeology in anthropology: Culture history and social science. In
         Research and theory in current archeology, edited by Redman, Charles L. New
         York: John Wiley.
Watson, Patty Jo, Steven A. LeBlanc, and Charles L. Redman
  1971 *Explanation in archeology: An explicitly scientific approach.* New York: Columbia
         University Press.
White, Leslie A.
  1938 Science is Sciencing. *Philosophy of Science* **5**:369–389.
  1945a Diffusion versus Evolution: An Anti-Evolutionist Fallacy. *American Anthropologist*
         47 (No. 3):339–356.
  1945b History, Evolutionism, and Functionalism: Three Types of Interpretation of Cul-
         ture. *Southwestern Journal of Anthropology* **1** (No. 2):221–248.
  1946 Kroeber's 'Configurations of Culture Growth.' *American Anthropologist* **48** (No.
         1):78–93.
  1947a Energy and the Development of Civilization. Serving Through Science (radio talk
         in New York sponsored by United States Rubber Co.).
  1947b Evolutionism in Cultural Anthropology: A Rejoinder. *American Anthropologist*
         49 (No. 3):400–413.
  1948 The individual and the culture process. In *Centennial.* Washington, D.C.:
         American Association for the Advancement of Science.
Whitney, Daniel D., ed.
  1975 Two Resolutions Passed by Council at Annual Meeting: Archeological Excavation
         for Teaching Purposes. *Anthropology Newsletter* **16**:10–11.
Willey, Gordon R., and Jeremy A. Sabloff
  1974 *A history of American archaeology.* San Francisco: W. H. Freeman.

Quantitative Analysis and Pattern Recognition

THE IMPORTANCE OF QUANTITATIVE ANALYSIS TO PATTERN RECOGNITION

The slowly emerging trend in historical archeology toward archeological science follows a similar general trend in American archeology. The impact of the ferment of the 1960s focused in the work of Lewis Binford, and the innovative work of Dethlefsen and Deetz (1965, 1966, 1971) with colonial tombstones from New England graveyards, has had little more than a shade of influence in conjuring up a scientific spirit within the body of historical archeology. Historical archeologists have concentrated on the reconstruction of culture history, and the reconstruction of lifeways, and have virtually ignored delineation of culture process (Binford 1968: 8). The key to understanding culture process lies in pattern recognition. Once pattern is recognized, the archeologist can then ask why the pattern exists, why it is often so predictive it can be expressed as laws. In so doing, he can begin to build a theory for explaining the demonstrated pattern. This chapter emphasizes the importance of quantitative analysis and pattern recognition for the development of theory explaining the dynamics of past cultural systems.

The vast majority of anthropologically trained archeologists now working on historic sites are operating under the same particularistic paradigm being used by those not trained in anthropology. The literature is filled with particularistic descriptions of architecture and artifacts revealing:

> No interpretation of any kind, historical, anthropological, cultural or archaeological to justify a catalog type publication of objects. . . . His-

torical archaeology has now reached the point where we should begin to explore [cultural concepts] rather than continuing to crowd our bookshelves with descriptive catalogs of our systematized relic collecting devoid of any redeeming analytical or interpretive value [South 1972:86,102].

The avenues for funding and the fact that we excavate only one site at a time need not prevent us from making some effort at addressing ourselves to the higher levels of classification in a synthesizing format (South 1974b), using quantification analyses to answer questions beyond the site-specific level.

Those of us who were taught that the ultimate goal of archeology is to explain laws of culture process through theory building accept quantitative analysis as a necessary means of demonstrating pattern in the material remains of culture. Therefore, it came as quite a shock in 1958, when I first encountered a strong antiquantification attitude in a colleague. When I told him I was involved in a ceramic frequency variation study of historic site ceramics from the eithteenth-century ruins at Brunswick Town, N.C. (South 1962a), his reply was that this approach was "sheer anthropological idiocy." Unfortunately this antinomothetic attitude is still reflected by some archeologists, who consider counting of artifacts a waste of time. These same critics often have the notion that historical data are somehow a more valid material remains of culture than are those from archeological contexts. This attitude is typified by the assumption that revealing another seventeenth-century set of house postholes and a collection of nonquantified objects associated with them somehow will automatically add to our accumulation of knowledge, when such an approach primarily adds only to our accumulation.

The quantification of data in itself will add no more to our knowledge than the collection of seventeenth-century postholes and relics, unless we are operating under a research design specifying why we are quantifying.

One of the studies that was influential in impressing nomothetic values on many of us trained in the 1950s was A. L. Kroeber's 1919 study of "Order in Changes of Fashion," which was later expanded in a quantification analysis of three centuries of women's dress fashions (Kroeber 1919; with Jane Richardson 1940; 1952:332, 358). This study, based on measurements of women's full evening dress, is an excellent model demonstrating the value of the nomothetic approach that many of us viewed as directly applicable to archeological data. Since it uses historical data it is particularly relevant to those archeologists excavating sites of the historic period, though its methodology is basic to all archeology as well as to anthropology.

It was in 1899 that Kroeber's creative imagination formulated the hypothesis that measurement of variables in women's dress should reveal the order in changes of fashion. He says that at that time "the project of inquiring into the principles that guide fashion arose in my mind . . . [1952:332]." It was not until 1919, however, that he began to gather data to test his hypothesis. He chose women's full evening dress as his data field, under an assumption that "If any principle could be determined, it would apply also to the more changeable kinds of clothing [1952:332]." In this first study he was able to demonstrate "great pulsations" in the various measurements representing "periods often exceeding the duration of human life . . . [1952:336]."

This approach necessarily involved an assumption of a normal curve phenomenon, but Kroeber (1952) carefully addressed himself to this point: "It is not to be expected that the development and decline of every trait of dress or civilization should follow a normal curve, that is, a symmetrical course. . . . A certain proportion of features should therefore follow irregular courses, or asymmetrical curves . . . [p. 336]." The "great pulsations" of normal curves revealing that "the major proportions of dress change rather with a slow majesty" were accompanied by the "glittering maze" of details, trimmings, pleats, and ruffles that left an "overwhelming impression of incalculably chaotic fluctuations."

Having proceeded this far, Kroeber allowed his study to remain dormant for 20 years more until in 1940 when with Jane Richardson he again addressed himself to this problem. This time the main question centered on variability and stability, and the problem of their causes. They concluded that a one-to-one, stimulus-reaction, reflex arc was not involved so much as basic multivariant patterns within different segments of the cultural system (Kroeber 1952:358).

Having established a basic pattern as something that must be recognized, with a "full wave length of periodicity" of about a century, this information was then used in an hypothesis projecting this data into the unknown of the seventeenth century (Kroeber 1952: 368–369). From this study Kroeber and Richardson were able to determine that the role of the individual in determining dress style was slight, the style's affecting the individuals far more than they are able to determine style (Kroeber 1952: 370).

The broader implications of this study were recognized by Kroeber and Richardson, as they were by many who read this study as a model in the 1950s.

> It is conceivable that the method pursued in this study may be of utility as a generic measure of sociocultural unsettlement. Also, it provides an objective description of one of the basic patterns characteristic of a given civilization for several centuries, and may serve as a precedent for the more exact definition of other stylistic patterns in the same or other civilizations [Kroeber 1952:372].

The importance of the method used here to the field of historical archeology is considerable if we are to move out of the particularistic into the
nomothetic paradigm in our studies.

Models having relevance to historic site archeological materials can
well be constructed by using Sears Roebuck catalogs from 1897 (Israel
1968) to the present in order to examine patterns in a manner similar to
that used by Kroeber. The pattern so revealed could be used as a base
from which to formulate postulates as to the relationships obtaining
among archeological patterns using similar artifact classes. Comparisons
of patterning from excavations could be made with the model, and
explanatory hypotheses formulated for further testing on other sites of
the twentieth century. Questions regarding such specifics as social class,
economic level, or function could be hypothesized and tested from such
an approach.

On a broader perspective, the motifs on stamps illustrated in a
comprehensive world stamp album could be used to determine variability in motifs used at various times and places, the contrast between
portraits of individuals, public buildings, nature scenes, and nationalistic
symbolism providing pattern-revealing trends through time. Such a study
would likely reveal both the "great pulsations" moving with "slow
majesty," and those smaller fluctuations described by Kroeber (see
Salwen 1973:155, for a "soup can" study along these lines).

I am not suggesting that detail is not important—certainly it is—but it
is only relevant to questions we ask. Making the first measurement of an
artifact is a useless exercise unless that measurement is relevant to our
inquiry. In historical archeology we can continue particularistic studies
aimed at describing each object from the Sears Roebuck Catalog, or
each stamp in a stamp collection, or each sherd and marble from an historic site; or we can begin treating the remains of material culture from
historic sites in a quantitative, pattern-recognizing manner similar to that
model suggested by Kroeber, and move toward nomothetic research.

Examples of frequency variability studies are relatively rare in historical
archeology, in spite of the fact that historic site data lend themselves
admirably to testing propositions in a controlled manner not possible
with prehistoric data. Some frequency variation studies using data from
historic sites, and making assumptions under a nomothetic paradigm,
include such diverse items as British colonial ceramics, Spanish olive jars,
buttons, tombstone motifs, tobacco pipestems, Spanish majolica, Victorian artifacts, and wine bottles (South 1962a, 1962b, 1964, 1972, 1974a;
Goggin 1960, 1968; Dethlefsen and Deetz 1966; Harrington 1954; Binford
1962, 1972; Brose 1967; Heighton and Deagan 1972; Carrillo 1974).

The fact that these studies deal with frequency variation in order to
arrive at statements of behavioral variability reflecting culture process
places them within a nomothetic paradigm far more than studies not so

oriented. The authors may not have stated this assumption explicitly, but such studies are a step up the ladder toward synthesizing data for question asking and hypothesis testing. Frequency variability studies are not in themselves nomothetic, but they are within the nomothetic paradigm.

Frequency variability studies of artifacts from historic sites should continue to be carried out, but to be most meaningful they must be anchored in relevant formal-temporal syntheses, such as the artifact types (primarily ceramics) defined by Noël Hume. Using one of these types as an example, I will illustrate how these kinds of data can be seen to have a definite utility in pattern recognition studies.

The hypothetical example used here is based on the actual application of these principles using Noël Hume's descriptions of ceramic types and temporal range of manufacture in combination with my own frequency-variation study of excavated ceramics from many ruins to establish a statistical model offered as a predictive tool in the form of a formula, which is presented in a later chapter (South 1972: 71). When tested, this formula has proved useful as a research tool for obtaining an interpreted median date for the time during which the sample was accumulated. This type of approach can lead to explicit hypothesis testing on historic sites in a manner never before achieved under the idiographic-particularistic paradigm. It is hoped that this, and other examples in this book, will encourage others to broaden their perspective from this viewpoint. The examples used here applies to eighteenth-century British colonial sites.

A Hypothetical Example of the Process of Pattern Recognition

Noël Hume's particularistic paradigm research (inductive) results in a formal-temporal definition of Artifact Type X, which can be considered as a postulate in the following pattern recognition process.

Artifact Type X (described by Noël Hume as having attributes 1
Inductive   through 5, was manufactured in Bristol, England, from
               ca. 1750 to ca. 1765, and exported to the American
               colonies during most of this period).

Site-specific historical research:
(particularistic paradigm)

Inductive   The Jones Manor was built in America in 1752, and
               destroyed by fire in 1762; no subsequent occupation
               revealed.

Deduced test implication (postulate):
(nomothetic paradigm)

Deductive   Assuming that a relatively uniform distribution of

Prediction 1.   Artifact Type X would occur in the American colonies, Artifact Type X should be found in the midden deposits and other features associated with the architecture representing the Jones Manor occupation from 1752 to 1762, when the ruin is excavated.

(Other postulates supporting assumptions of this type would need to be stated.)

Result of the test implication (testing; nomothetic)

Inductive
Testing   Archeology revealed a midden deposit at the rear door of the Jones Manor ruin, 15% of which was composed of Type X artifacts.

Results of the hypothetico-deductive–inductive process (particularistic)

Inductive   The prediction was verified by the discovery of Type X artifacts at the Jones Manor ruin as predicted. This tends to support the formal-temporal definition of Artifact Type X, and suggests that a uniform distribution of Artifact Type X may have occurred as predicted.

New postulate formulation (nomothetic paradigm)

Deductive   Since the above prediction was verified, we can deduce that perhaps the ruins of the period ca. 1750 to ca. 1765 will likely contain Type X artifacts.

Prediction 2.   nomothetic paradigm
Ruins of the period ca. 1752 to ca. 1762 will contain about 15% of Type X artifacts, and ruins of other decades will not (based on the 15% found at the Jones Manor ruin).

Prediction 3.   nomothetic paradigm
If Prediction 2 is verified through excavation and testing on a number of archeological sites, frequency variability among other artifact classes will be seen to be predictable for the decade ca. 1752 to ca. 1762.

Prediction 4.   nomothetic paradigm
If Prediction 3 is verified and tested on data from a number of sites, we can deduce that similar frequency variability will likely apply to other decades of the eighteenth century.

Prediction 5.   nomothetic paradigm
If Prediction 4 is verified, the frequency variability of artifacts can be used to predict the occupation period represented by artifacts from any particular decade.

Prediction 6.   nomothetic paradigm
If Prediction 5 is verified, a formula could be used to express the variability relationship between artifact classes as a single date for use in interpretation of the median date represented by the artifacts.

Prediction 7.   nomothetic paradigm
If Prediction 6 is verified, the median date for the artifact group could be compared with known historic median occupation date for the sites in question, and tested for goodness of fit between the two sets of dates. When goodness of fit is established, the formula dates could then be used to predict the median occupation date represented by the artifact relationships on the site.

Prediction 8.   nomothetic paradigm
If Prediction 7 is tested and verified, the formula dates would be seen to have predictive value for median occupation date estimates over a broad spatial area, since spatial continuity has been assumed.

Prediction 9.   nomothetic paradigm
If Prediction 8 is independently tested and verified, the broad and rapid spread of the artifacts involved will be demonstrated. This broad and rapid spread (horizon) demonstrated from the archeological record can then be compared with documented data to determine whether this information provides new insight on the interpretation of distribution of goods, trade routes, artifact function in the social context, etc.

Discussion: It matters not whether the horizon so demonstrated "matches" what is known from historical documentation, since the demonstration of variability and similarities in the archeological record and the explanation of these is the job of the archeologist. Such demonstrated consistency and variability could never have been known to exist by the carriers of the cultural artifacts, so historical documentation is virtually irrelevant to the archeologically demonstrated pattern except as adjunct information of interest. It can be analyzed in a quantification format to reveal pattern relevant to archeological pattern, however, and offers great promise in this direction.

Prediction 10   nomothetic paradigm
If the horizon phenomenon has been demonstrated

through the above procedure for one class of artifacts, the same situation would be seen to prevail among other classes of associated artifacts.

Prediction 11.   nomothetic paradigm
If Prediction 10 is negated for an associated class of artifacts, postulates regarding the effect of other variables should be formulated and tested.

Prediction 12.   nomothetic paradigm
If Prediction 10 is verified and firm associations established between artifact classes, then the associated artifact classes not well dated could be assigned approximate date ranges through the association established in Prediction 10.

Discussion: Through Prediction 12 the date range of artifacts for which the manufacture date range may never be known from historical documentation can be determined through the pattern recognition method used here with artifact variability and stability.

Here we have an illustration of how well-defined particularistic studies can have applicability to a quantitative, pattern recognition approach to arrive at far more controlled and reliable information of a predictive nature than would emerge from use of the particularistic data alone. In this case a statement regarding a broad and rapid spread of material culture as a horizon at any one moment in time throughout the eighteenth century on British colonial sites was demonstrated by the hypothetical example of the process of pattern recognition.

We still have not asked the question "why" of this data, which we must do in order to examine the explanation for the horizon phenomenon involved. The horizon phenomenon presented here as an hypothetical example will be explored more fully in a later chapter. Our primary concern here is to emphasize the importance of quantification to pattern recognition, and of pattern recognition to archeological science. Although pattern recognition is basic to a science of archeology, such procedures are just beginning to emerge from the excavation of historic sites. This has resulted from the past emphasis on particularistic archeology, and its primary concern with meaningless cataloging at the expense of broader goals. Unfortunately this procedure continues to constitute the basic approach for some archeologists (Adams, Gaw, and Leonhardy 1975).

Fortunately, broader questions relating to explanation of cultural dynamics are being asked. Examples of these broad questions can be seen in the well-known study of culture change using tombstone data which was carried out by Dethlefsen and Deetz (1965, 1966, 1967); Robert Schuyler's study of recent culture change through a multidisciplinary approach (1974: 13); Joel Klein's study on models and hypothesis testing (1973: 68); Mark Leone's study of Mormon town plans and fences (1973: 125); Kathleen Deagan's study of *Mestizaje* in colonial St. Augustine (1973: 55); John Solomon Otto's study of status differences between planters, overseers, and slaves (1975); and Kenneth Lewis' study of the frontier model in relation to archeology (1973: 84; 1975). These studies address themselves to questions of culture process in a manner badly needed in historical archeology. In asking these questions there will follow attempts to provide the answers through research designs using methods of quantification and pattern recognition. Such studies are few as yet, all those listed above having been published in the 1970s with the exception of Dethlefsen and Deetz's work. By the mid-1980s, it is hoped, many such studies will have been published, studies defining the patterned regularity of the empirical record with the goal of explaining the lawlike regularities and variability in terms of the cultural processes responsible.

The Relativity of Cultural Systems to the Orbit of Archeological Science

The illustration in Figure 4 represents the relativity of cultural systems to the orbit of archeological science. This heuristic device illustrates the role of causal processes in relation to the systemic context of British colonial culture. This in turn is shown in relation to the "Systemic Orbit with Historical Satellite," and "The Orbit of Archeological Science with Nomothetic Satellite," and the "Law of Behavioral By-Product Regularity." This law relates to an assumption of regularity in the archeological record upon which the studies in this book are based.

The methods of archeological science are involved with testing laws of cultural dynamics and stability using the material remains of culture. This requires pattern recognition to help define the parameters of regularity and variability in cultural systems, thus providing an inductive basis for formulating general laws. Hypotheses are deduced and tested through observation of new data. Methods of answering questions of culture process involve:

1. Defining empirical distinctions in the by-products from differing cultural systems to test laws of systemic variability.
2. Defining the by-products of a cultural system through time to reconstruct culture history, and test laws of culture change.
3. Defining the by-products of cultural systems in contact to test laws of culture contact, acculturation, and diffusion.

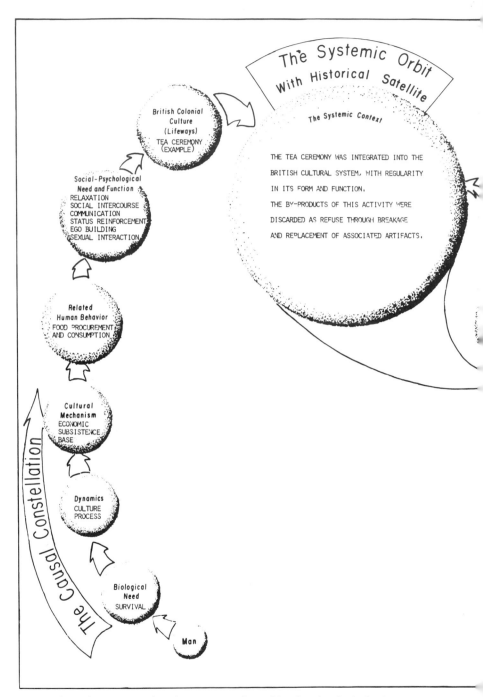

The systemic context labels within figure:

The Systemic Orbit With Historical Satellite

The Systemic Context

THE TEA CEREMONY WAS INTEGRATED INTO THE
BRITISH CULTURAL SYSTEM, WITH REGULARITY
IN ITS FORM AND FUNCTION.
THE BY-PRODUCTS OF THIS ACTIVITY WERE
DISCARDED AS REFUSE THROUGH BREAKAGE
AND REPLACEMENT OF ASSOCIATED ARTIFACTS.

British Colonial
Culture
(Lifeways)
TEA CEREMONY
(EXAMPLE)

Social-Psychological
Need and Function
RELAXATION
SOCIAL INTERCOURSE
COMMUNICATION
STATUS REINFORCEMENT
EGO BUILDING
SEXUAL INTERACTION

Related
Human Behavior
FOOD PROCUREMENT
AND CONSUMPTION

Cultural
Mechanism
ECONOMIC
SUBSISTENCE
BASE

Dynamics
CULTURE
PROCESS

Biological
Need
SURVIVAL

Man

The Causal Constellation

Figure 4. The relativity of cultural systems to the orbit of archeological science, exem-

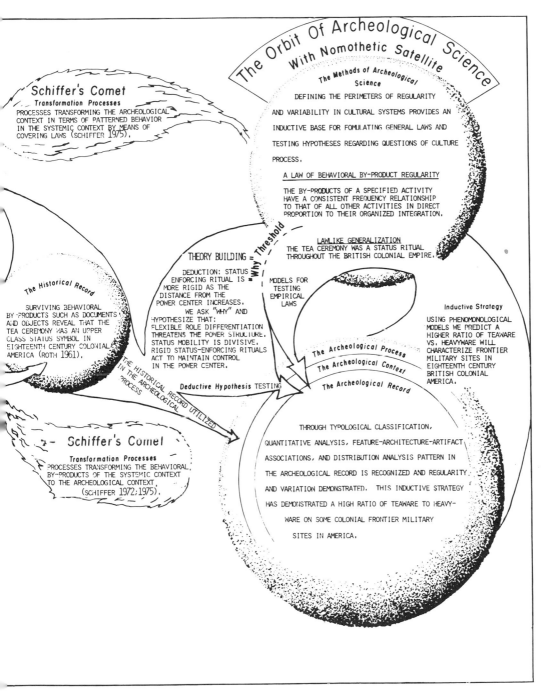

The Orbit Of Archeological Science
With Nomothetic Satellite

The Methods of Archeological Science

DEFINING THE PERIMETERS OF REGULARITY AND VARIABILITY IN CULTURAL SYSTEMS PROVIDES AN INDUCTIVE BASE FOR FORMULATING GENERAL LAWS AND TESTING HYPOTHESES REGARDING QUESTIONS OF CULTURE PROCESS.

A LAW OF BEHAVIORAL BY-PRODUCT REGULARITY

THE BY-PRODUCTS OF A SPECIFIED ACTIVITY HAVE A CONSISTENT FREQUENCY RELATIONSHIP TO THAT OF ALL OTHER ACTIVITIES IN DIRECT PROPORTION TO THEIR ORGANIZED INTEGRATION.

LAWLIKE GENERALIZATION
THE TEA CEREMONY WAS A STATUS RITUAL THROUGHOUT THE BRITISH COLONIAL EMPIRE.

Schiffer's Comet
Transformation Processes
PROCESSES TRANSFORMING THE ARCHEOLOGICAL CONTEXT IN TERMS OF PATTERNED BEHAVIOR IN THE SYSTEMIC CONTEXT BY MEANS OF COVERING LAWS (SCHIFFER 1975).

The Historical Record

SURVIVING BEHAVIORAL BY-PRODUCTS SUCH AS DOCUMENTS AND OBJECTS REVEAL THAT THE TEA CEREMONY WAS AN UPPER CLASS STATUS SYMBOL IN EIGHTEENTH CENTURY COLONIAL AMERICA (ROTH 1961).

THEORY BUILDING
Why Threshold

DEDUCTION: STATUS ENFORCING RITUAL IS MORE RIGID AS THE DISTANCE FROM THE POWER CENTER INCREASES.
WE ASK "WHY" AND HYPOTHESIZE THAT:
FLEXIBLE ROLE DIFFERENTIATION THREATENS THE POWER STRUCTURE, STATUS MOBILITY IS DIVISIVE, RIGID STATUS-ENFORCING RITUALS ACT TO MAINTAIN CONTROL IN THE POWER CENTER.

MODELS FOR TESTING EMPIRICAL LAWS

Deductive Hypothesis TESTING

THE HISTORICAL RECORD UTILIZED IN THE ARCHEOLOGICAL PROCESS

Inductive Strategy
USING PHENOMONOLOGICAL MODELS WE PREDICT A HIGHER RATIO OF TEAWARE VS. HEAVYWARE WILL CHARACTERIZE FRONTIER MILITARY SITES IN EIGHTEENTH CENTURY BRITISH COLONIAL AMERICA.

The Archeological Process
The Archeological Context
The Archeological Record

THROUGH TYPOLOGICAL CLASSIFICATION, QUANTITATIVE ANALYSIS, FEATURE-ARCHITECTURE-ARTIFACT ASSOCIATIONS, AND DISTRIBUTION ANALYSIS PATTERN IN THE ARCHEOLOGICAL RECORD IS RECOGNIZED AND REGULARITY AND VARIATION DEMONSTRATED. THIS INDUCTIVE STRATEGY HAS DEMONSTRATED A HIGH RATIO OF TEAWARE TO HEAVY-WARE ON SOME COLONIAL FRONTIER MILITARY SITES IN AMERICA.

Schiffer's Comet
Transformation Processes
PROCESSES TRANSFORMING THE BEHAVIORAL BY-PRODUCTS OF THE SYSTEMIC CONTEXT TO THE ARCHEOLOGICAL CONTEXT.
(SCHIFFER 1972;1975).

plified by the tea ceremony in eighteenth-century British colonial life.

4. Defining behavioral by-product rigidity and flexibility to explicate laws of cultural tradition and change.
5. Exploring behavioral by-product variability and regularity to discover functional relationships for reconstructing past lifeways.

The archeological process draws on the archeological record as well as other data, such as historical and ethnographic sources. An important consideration in bridging the gap between the systemic context and the archeological context are the cultural and noncultural formation processes transforming the behavioral by-products of the systemic context to the archeological context (Schiffer 1972; 1975). The return orbit involves the process of transforming the archeological context in terms of human behavior in the systemic context by means of covering laws and lawlike statements (Schiffer 1973). These processes are shown in Figure 4 as "Schiffer's Comet." Schiffer, Reid, Rathje, Binford and others have emphasized the use of archeological laws, and the need to explicitly define the transformation processes with which archeologists deal (Schiffer 1970, 1971, 1972, 1973, 1975; Schiffer and Rathje 1973; Reid, Rathje, and Schiffer 1974; Binford n.d.). The expression of recognized empirical patterning in the form of archeological laws is an area of primary concern to the archeologist. This is illustrated in Figure 4 by an arrow indicating the use of variability-examining models for testing empirical laws. However, to become involved in theory building the "why" threshold must be crossed, where the explanation of why the empirical laws prevail is examined through deductive hypotheses directed at the statics and dynamics of past cultural systems. If our concern is primarily with empirical laws, then the direction we are taking is by way of the "laws" arrow; if theory is to be built, the "theory" arrow must be used, after crossing the "why" threshold.

The tea ceremony in eighteenth-century British colonial life is used in Figure 4 to illustrate the steps involved in the archeological process in relation to the systemic and archeological contexts. This example sees the empirical pattern expressed as a lawlike inductive generalization as follows:

> *The tea ceremony was an important ritual in eighteenth-century British colonial life, relating to status even in the remote corners of the British Empire.*

When we apply this to the question of status-enforcing rituals generally, we can suggest that status-enforcing rituals will be more rigid as the distance from the power center increases. When we ask why this should be the case, three hypotheses can be seen as possible explanations: (1) Flexible role differentiation threatens the power structure; (2) status mobility is divisive; (3) rigid status-enforcing rituals act toward maintaining control in the power center. These hypotheses can then be tested through recovery of new data under research designs focused on these questions for addressing ourselves to the statics and dynamics of culture process.

As archeologists our first responsibility is pattern recognition. We must then ask why the patterns are distinct, why there is this regularity, why there is this variability. In 1960 I urged historical archeologists to use quantification of historic site pottery for pattern recognition and illustrated the validity of statistically dealing with ceramics from colonial American sites (South 1962 a: 1). The point made at that time was that quantification of European ceramics from eighteenth-century British-American sites would allow the archeologist to date the occupation period of a ruin. An assumption was that a comparison of the patterning from enough historically dated ruins would allow a prediction to be made as to the occupation period of ruins of unknown dates based on the frequency distribution of ceramic types.

As can be seen from the historic site literature since that admonition, there has been no general rush toward quantitative analysis and pattern recognition on the part of those excavating historic sites. As pointed out in the previous chapter, there has evolved an antiquantification climate having a detrimental effect on the field of historical archeology. In this chapter I have reiterated the importance of quantification to pattern recognition, and in the chapters to follow I will demonstrate the utility of this approach with empirical data on the level of the square and the ruin, and in intraruin, intrasite, intersite, and temporal contexts.

REFERENCES

Adams, William H., Linda P. Gaw, and Frank C. Leonhardy
   1975   Archaeological excavations at Silcott, Washington: The data inventory. In *Reports of investigations* (**No. 53**). Pullman: Laboratory of Anthropology, Washington State University.
Binford, Lewis R.
   1962   A New Method of Calculating Dates from Kaolin Pipe Stem Samples. *Southeastern Archaeological Conference Newsletter* **9** (No. 1):19–21.
   1972   The "Binford" Pipe Stem Formula: A Return from the Grave. *The Conference on Historic Site Archaeology Papers 1971* **6:**230–253.
   n.d.   47 Trips: A Case Study in the Character of Some Archaeological Formation Processes (in press).
Binford, Sally R., and Lewis R. Binford, eds.
   1968   *New perspectives in archeology.* Chicago: Aldine.
Brose, David S.
   1967   The Custer Road Dump Site: An Exercise in Victorian Archaeology. *The Michigan Archaeologist* **13** No. 2:37–128.

Carrillo, Richard
 1974 English Wine Bottles As Revealed By a Statistical Study: A Further Approach to
      Evolution and Horizon in Historical Archeology. *The Conference on Historic Site
      Archaeology Papers 1973.* **7**:290–317.
Deagan, Kathleen A.
 1973 *Mestizaje* in Colonial St. Augustine. *Ethnohistory* **20** (No. 1):55–65.
Deetz, James
 1968 Late man in North America: Archeology of European Americans. In *Anthropo-
      logical archeology in the Americas,* edited by Meggers, Betty J. Washington, D.C.:
      The Anthropological Society of Washington.
Deetz, James, and Edwin Dethlefsen
 1965 The Doppler Effect and Archaeology: A Consideration of the Spatial Aspects of
      Seriation. *Southwestern Journal of Anthropology* **21** (No. 3):196–206.
 1971 Some social aspects of New England Colonial mortuary art. In Approaches to the
      Social Demensions of Mortuary Practices, edited by Brown, J. A. *Society for
      American Archaeology, Memoir* **25**:30–38.
Dethlefsen, Edwin, and James Deetz
 1966 Death's Heads, Cherubs, and Willow Trees: Experimental Archaeology in Colonial
      Cemeteries. *American Antiquity* **31**: (No. 4):502–510.
 1967 Eighteenth Century Cemeteries: Demographic View. *Historical Archaeology 1967*
      1:66–68.
Goggin, John M.
 1960 The Spanish Olive Jar: An Introductory Study. Yale University Publications in
      Anthropology (No. 62).
 1968 Spanish Majolica in the New World. *Yale University Publications in Anthropology*
      (No. 72).
Harrington, J. C.
 1954 Dating Stem Fragments of Seventeenth and Eighteenth Century Clay Tobacco
      Pipes. *Quarterly Bulletin of the Archaeological Society of Virginia* **9** (No. 1):10–14.
Heighton, Robert F., and Kathleen A. Deagan
 1972 A New Formula for Dating Kaolin Clay Pipestems. *The Conference on Historic Site
      Archaeology Papers 1971* **6**:220–229.
Israel, Fred L., ed.
 1968 *1897 Sears Roebuck catalogue.* New York: Chelsea House.
Klein, Joel
 1973 Models and Hypothesis Testing in Historical Archaeology. *Historical Archaeology*
      7:68–77.
Kroeber, A. L.
 1919 Order in changes of fashion. In *The nature of culture.* Chicago: University of
      Chicago Press (1952).
 1952 *The nature of culture.* Chicago: University of Chicago Press.
Kroeber, A. L., and Jane Richardson
 1940 Three centuries of women's dress fashions: A quantitative analysis. In *The nature
      of culture.* Chicago: University of Chicago Press (1952).
Leone, Mark
 1973 Archeology as the Science of Technology: Mormon Town Plans and Fences. In
      Research and theory in current archeology, edited by Redman, Charles L. New
      York: John Wiley.
Lewis, Kenneth E.
 1973 An Archaeological Consideration of the Frontier. *Papers in Anthropology* **14**: (No.
      1): 84–103.
 1975 The Jamestown frontier: An archaeological view of colonization. Ph.D. disserta-
      tion, University of Oklahoma. (University Microfilms, Ann Arbor).

Otto, John Solomon
1975   Status Difference In the Archaeological Record of Planter, Overseer, and Slave Sites, Cannon's Point Plantation, St. Simon's Island, Georgia (1794–1861), Ph.D. dissertation, Department of Anthropology, University of Florida, Gainesville.

Reid, J. Jefferson, William L. Rathje, and Michael B. Schiffer
1974   Expanding Archaeology. *American Antiquity* **39:** (No. 1):125–26.

Richardson, Jane, and A. L. Kroeber
1940   Three centuries of women's dress fashions: A quantitative analysis. In *The nature of culture.* Chicago: University of Chicago Press (1952).

Roth, Rodris
1961   Tea Drinking in 18th-Century America: Its Etiquette and Equipage. *Contributions from the Museum of History and Technology,* Paper 14. Washington, D.C.: Smithsonian Institution.

Salwen, Bert
1973   Archeology in Megalopolis. In *Research and theory in current archeology,* edited by Redman, Charles L. New York: John Wiley.

Schiffer, Michael B.
1970   Cultural Laws and the Reconstruction of Past Lifeways. Paper presented at the 35th annual meeting of the Society for American Archaeology, Mexico City, May 1970. Manuscript on file with Arizona State Museum Library, University of Arizona, Tucson.
1971   Archaeology as Behavioral Science. Paper presented at the 36th Annual Meeting of the Society for American Archaeology in Norman, Oklahoma. Manuscript on file with Institute of Archeology and Anthropology, University of South Carolina, Columbia.
1972   Archaeological Context and Systemic Context. *American Antiquity* **37:**156–165.
1973   Several Archaeological Laws (manuscript); Arkansas Archeological Survey, Fayetteville.
1975   Cultural Formation Processes of the Archaeological Record: A General Formulation. Paper presented at the 8th Annual Meeting of the Society for Historical Archaeology, Charleston, South Carolina. Manuscript on file with The Institute of Archeology and Anthropology, University of South Carolina, Columbia.

Schiffer, Michael B., and William L. Rathje
1973   Efficient exploitation of the archeological record: Penetrating problems. In *Research and theory in current archeology,* edited by Redman, Charles L. New York: John Wiley.

Schuyler, Robert L.
1974   Sandy Ground: Archaeological Sampling in a Black Community in Metropolitan New York. *The Conference on Historic Site Archaeology Papers 1972* **7:**13–51.

South, Stanley
1962a   The Ceramic Types at Brunswick Town, North Carolina (1960). *Southeastern Archaeological Conference Newsletter* **9** (No. 1):1–5.
1962b   Kaolin Pipe Stem Dates from the Brunswick Town Ruins. *Southeastern Archaeological Conference Newsletter* **9** (No. 1):22–25.
1964   Analysis of the Buttons from Brunswick Town and Fort Fisher. *The Florida Anthropologist* **17** (No. 2):113–133.
1972   Evolution and Horizon as Revealed in Ceramic Analysis in Historical Archeology. *The Conference on Historic Site Archaeology Papers 1971* **6:**71–116.
1974a   The Horizon Concept Revealed in the Application of the Mean Ceramic Date Formula to Spanish Majolica in the New World. *The Conference on Historic Site Archaeology Papers 1972* **7:**96–122.
1974b   Palmetto Parapets. *Anthropological Studies No. 1.* Institute of Archeology and Anthropology, University of South Carolina, Columbia.

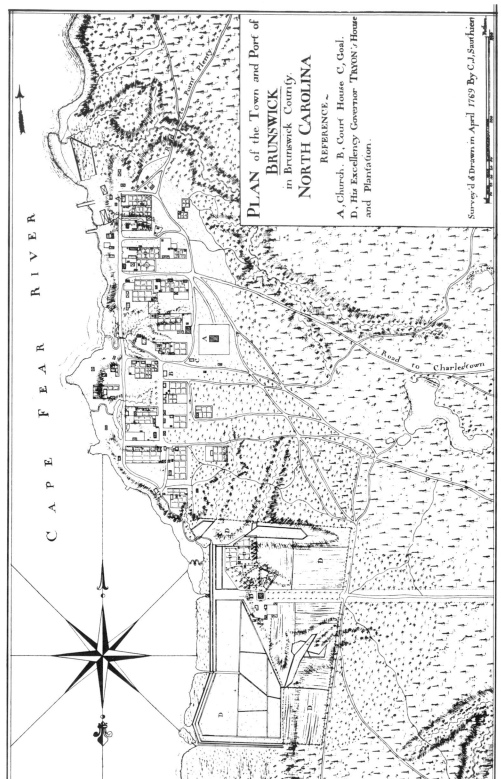

The 1769 map of Brunswick Town, N.C.

The Brunswick
Pattern of Refuse
Disposal

The study undertaken in this chapter will demonstrate the pattern of refuse disposal carried out at Brunswick Town, N.C., in the eighteenth century. This pattern reflects a British-American refuse disposal practice, and can well be compared with such demonstrated patterns on sites representing other cultural traditions. The importance is emphasized of distribution studies such as this for use in interpretation of the relationship between site structure, content, context, and function.

For more than a decade the pattern of refuse discard at the ruins of the town of Brunswick, N.C., has been used as a guide for predicting the location of refuse deposits reflecting eighteenth-century behavior on British-American sites. Excavations at Brunswick Town were carried out from 1958 to 1968, and revealed that the occupants of these structures from ca. 1725 to ca. 1776 discarded their refuse adjacent to their homes, primarily at the back door, but also adjacent to the front doorway. Nearby depressions were also used, as well as the public street. So firmly established was this pattern of refuse disposal that entrance areas to structures could be identified by the increased quantity of midden at the doorways, even if no architectural data had been present. This practice of discarding secondary refuse adjacent to the dwellings is the basis for what we call the Brunswick Pattern.

Two types of secondary refuse are defined elsewhere in this book on the basis of the ratio of bone to the total artifact count. A low bone–artifact ratio is seen in refuse deposits adjacent to occupied structures, whereas a high bone–artifact ratio is seen in those secondary midden deposits peripheral to occupied structures, allowing us to recognize adjacent secondary refuse and peripheral secondary refuse. The adjacent secondary refuse is the basis for the Brunswick pattern, peripheral secondary refuse not being found in large quantities at Brunswick Town.

The adjacent secondary refuse thrown into the yard cannot be assumed to remain forever untouched. On the contrary, even though it would accumulate in concentration is some areas through time, dispersal factors would work toward periodically scattering the refuse. Immediate dispersal would begin with humans displacing the accumulating refuse in landscaping efforts, chickens scratching in search of food, dogs scavenging for bones, pigs rooting for edible fragments, and raccoons going through the garbage. Despite these and other dispersal factors sufficient concentration of refuse accumulated at the entrances to the Brunswick Town structures to prompt recognition of the Brunswick Pattern of adjacent secondary refuse disposal.

It is this Brunswick Pattern that has served to allow prediction of the location of refuse areas on many other sites beyond the limits of the town of Brunswick. At the Paca House, in Annapolis, Md., predictions were made on the basis of the Brunswick Pattern and excavation proved these to be correct. At the 1670 fortifications at Charles Towne in South Carolina, the concentration of midden in one angle of the defensive ditch allowed an interpretation of the position of the original gateway across the ditch to be made, and the positioning of the roadway into the fort. This interpretation has not been independently verified but is based on the Brunswick Pattern (South 1967; 1971).

At Fort Moultrie, S.C., the exploratory excavations revealed the moat to the original fort, with a heavy concentration of both American and British midden limited to one concentrated area. This discovery allowed for the suggestion that the gateway to the original fort must have been in this area. When the map of the fort was positioned on the site using the architectural data provided by the angle in the moat, it was found that the original gateway was indeed opposite the midden concentration associated with the moat, again conforming to the Brunswick Pattern (South 1974). The Brunswick Pattern can be expressed as a lawlike generalization:

> On British-American sites of the eighteenth century a concentrated refuse deposit will be found at the points of entrance and exit in dwellings, shops, and military fortifications.

The demonstration of this pattern is seen in the distribution of several artifact classes from three Brunswick ruins, The Hepburn-Reonalds House (S7), Nath Moore's Front (S10), and the Public House–Tailor Shop (S25). The artifact classes chosen for this comparison are ceramics through creamware, ceramics-pearlware plus (pearlware and later types), wine bottle fragments, tobacco pipe fragments, nails, bone fragments,

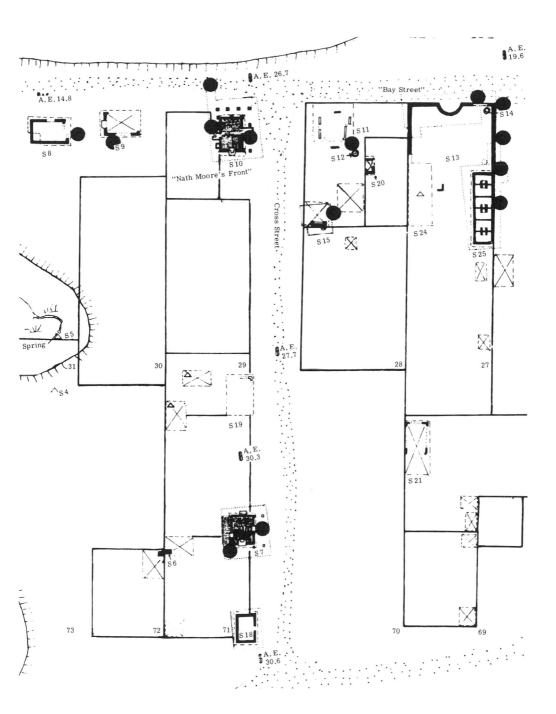

A. E.
19.6

A. E. 26.7

"Bay Street"

A.E.14.8

S 14

S 8

S 9

S 10

"Nath Moore's Front"

S 11

S 12

S 13

Cross Street

S 20

S 24

S 15

S 25

Spring

S 5

31

30

29

A. E.
27.7

28

27

S 4

S 19

A. E.
30.3

S 21

S 7

S 6

73

72

71

S 18

70

69

A. E.
30.6

Figure 5. A part of the Brunswick Town, archeological base map showing some of the excavated ruins, with dots indicating the concentration of adjacent secondary refuse representing how the Brunswick Pattern was constructed.

49

and tailoring objects, which includes scissors, hooks and eyes, baling seals, thimbles, buttons, buckles, pins, and beads.

The adjacent secondary refuse disposal pattern can be seen in Figure 5. The S7 and S10 ruins are representative of domestic dwellings having a shop in a downstairs room, with the Public House–Tailor Shop (S25) containing six rooms. Our goal here is to examine not only the specific areas where refuse was thrown from the doors of the structures, but to contrast these areas with the other areas around the ruins.

METHOD AND CONTEXT

Nath Moore's Front (S10) was excavated in 1958, The Hepburn-Reonalds House (S7) in 1959, and the Public House–Tailor Shop (S25) in 1960. Under the assumption that variability in artifact frequencies in various parts of an historic ruin will reflect behavioral activity, the Brunswick Town ruins were excavated using a grid system of 5- and 10-foot squares.

A one-quarter inch screen was used, with periodic testing of each square and level by a window screen mesh for recovering seed beads and pins, etc. Whenever testing indicated these were present, total screening through window screen was carried out, using water to assist in the screening process.

For the purpose of this study, artifact totals for all levels in the area around the ruins were combined by square, with separation inside the ruins based on the floor level, and the postdestruction levels. In the Public House–Tailor Shop no floor level was found, but the layer beneath the floor joists was used instead, revealing a large quantity of sewing objects.

In situ objects lying on the floor in the S7 and S10 ruins were sought by carefully isolating this layer of ash lying on the burned floor boards from the layers of rubble above. However, virtually no artifacts were found to indicate that there were furnishings in the structures at the time they were destroyed by fire. This finding is in agreement with the historical documents indicating that Brunswick had been virtually abandoned prior to its being burned by the British in 1776, an early casualty of the Revolution (South 1958; 1959; 1960). The absence of *in situ* refuse in these burned structures resulted in the artifact analysis being composed almost entirely of adjacent secondary refuse.

The Public House–Tailor Shop (S25) ruin revealed no burned floor, but burned floor joists were found beneath the rubble layer. The sand around these joists revealed objects that had fallen through the floorboards, or onto the floor after the floorboards had become rotten. This primary de facto refuse resulting from accidental loss at the area of use will be used in a comparison of such refuse with the adjacent secondary refuse surrounding the structure. (For a discussion of primary, secondary, and de facto refuse, see Chap. 8, and Schiffer 1972:161.)

THE HEPBURN–REONALDS HOUSE (S7)

The Hepburn–Reonalds House (S7) ruin is seen in Figure 6, with the brick patio on the private side to the north, a burned wooden floor in the west room, a cobblestone floor in the east room (interpreted as a public shop room), and stone footings for second floor porch supports.

By plotting the ceramics through creamware (no pearlware or later types were recovered) at the S7 ruin, using a symbol representing from 1 through 25 fragments, the distribution of ceramics around the ruin can be seen (Figure 7). A concentration of ceramics can be seen around the northwest corner of the house, at the end of the brick patio. A second concentration can be seen in the sunken, public entranceway on the street, at the south side of the structure. As we will see, this pattern prevails throughout Brunswick Town, and is referred to as the Brunswick Refuse Disposal Pattern.

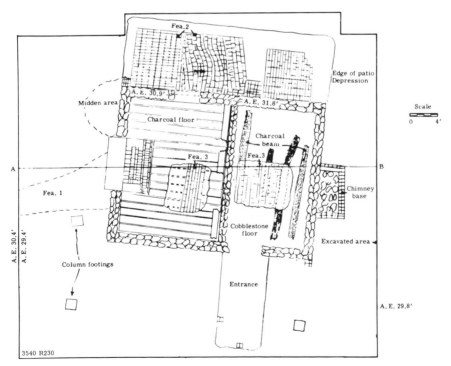

Figure 6. Foundation plan for the Hepburn–Reonalds House—field drawing (Unit S7, Lot 71).

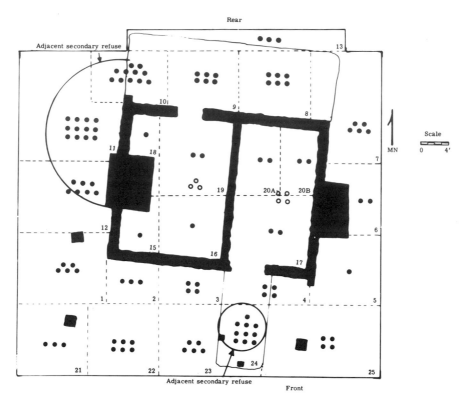

Figure 7. Foundation plan for the Hepburn–Reonalds House—Ceramics (Unit S7, Lot 71). Ceramics through Creamware: Solid symbol = total from yard and burned ash layer to floor; open symbol = above burned layer; symbol = I–25 frequency.

The nail distribution (Figure 8) follows the concentration seen for ceramics in the refuse deposit at the northwest corner of the structure, but reveals no increase in the sunken entranceway on the south side of the house. A high concentration is also seen for the east room compared with the west room. An important point to note in any of these distributions is the contrast between the area to the front of the house, the rear, inside, and in the adjacent refuse deposit. At this ruin there appear to have been a number of nails discarded in the adjacent refuse suggesting discard of old nails, boards, etc., probably from repairs inside. Such activity may result in a higher ratio of architecture-related artifacts in relation to kitchen-related artifacts in such cases. As was seen to be the case with the bone ratio, sampling of historic sites such as this will reveal differing ratios of artifacts depending on the area in relation to the structure, so that prediction should be able to be made from artifact ratios as to whether the artifacts are from the front, rear, inside or in adjacent refuse, even in the absence of architectural data.

The distribution of wine bottle and tobacco pipe fragments (Figure 9) reveals a surprising uniformity at this ruin, not reflecting the adjacent refuse concentration at the rear and front entrances seen for ceramics. A significant variable seen here is the fact that a high concentration of wine bottle fragments were recovered in the rubble above the burned layer of the house. This phenomenon reflects the disposal of wine bottles inside the house after it was in ruins, probably by people walking past the ruin in the street adjacent to the structure. This did not continue for long, however, since no objects later than creamware were recovered from the ruin.

The uniform distribution of tailoring objects in the S7 ruin is seen in Figure 10. This is in marked contrast to the high frequency found in the Tailor Shop Ruin (S25). Bone is also illustrated in Figure 10, and the low occurrence in the midden deposit areas suggests that careful control of peripheral refuse was in effect at this house, such refuse obviously being discarded elsewhere. The highest concentration of bone is seen in the

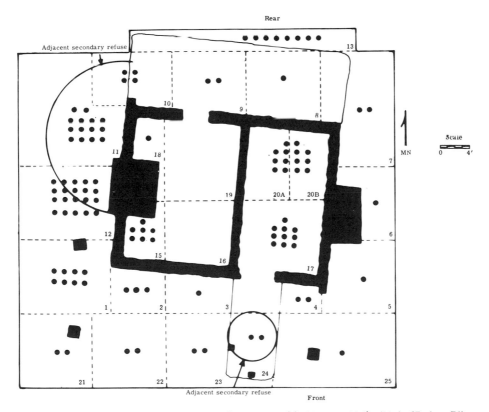

Figure 8. Foundation plan for the Hepburn-Reonalds House—Nails (Unit S7, Lot 71). Symbol = 1–25 frequency.

The burned remains of the Hepburn-Reonalds House beneath the fallen chimney in the east room on the cobblestone floor.

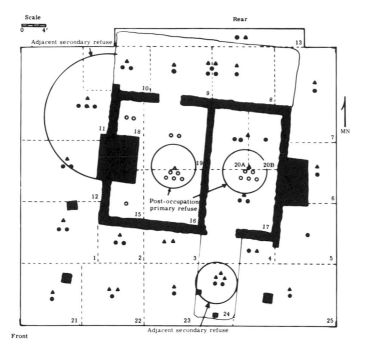

Figure 9. Foundation plan for the Hepburn-Reonalds House—Wine Bottle and Tobacco Pipe fragments (Unit S7, Lot 71): Solid symbol = total from yard and burned ash layer to floor; open symbol = above burned ash layer; symbol = 1–25 frequency; O = Wine bottle; Δ = Tobacco Pipe.

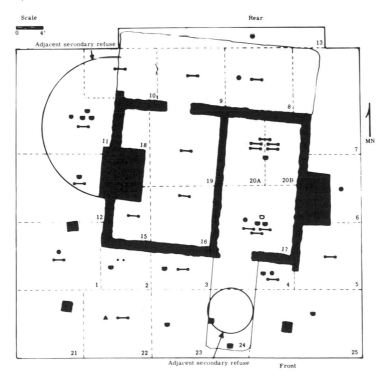

Figure 10. Foundation plan for the Hepburn-Reonalds House—Tailoring object distribution (Unit S7, Lot 71). ▽ = Buckle; • = Beads; ▲ = Scissors; ● = Buttons; □—□ = Bone; symbol = one object.

east room, where fragments were found in the yellow sand layer which was lying over the cobblestone floor at the time the house burned.

NATH MOORE'S FRONT (S10)

The field drawing of the features at the S10 ruin is seen in Figure 11, showing the rear, private entrance to the house, and the public street entranceway on the south. The typical Brunswick Town porch footings are shown for two sides of the house, with the public street passing close to the structure on the south and the east of this corner lot.

The ceramic distribution (Figure 12) for all types prior to pearlware reveals a concentration toward the east of the rear doorway, with very little to the left. This might be interpreted as caused by a person flinging refuse toward the right or, more likely, suggests that an architectural obstruction to the left prevented disposal of refuse in that direction. The refuse distribution has provided a suggestion relating to architectural data, an important factor when reconstruction of such structures is planned. Another major concentration of adjacent refuse is seen at the south, public entrance, also thrown toward the right facing away from the house. Again a similar architectural obstruction may have been located beside the sunken entranceway, which prevented discarding of refuse toward the east.

The distribution of refuse in this area between the porch footings and the sunken foundation wall indicates that there was no wooden floor covering this area at ground floor level, another important implication for interpreting the architectural details of the structure.

Notice the high concentration of ceramics above the burned ash layer of the house, in the rubble, postdating the burning of the building. This results from the use of the interior of this ruin as a refuse disposal area by occupants of the town after the Revolution. This is revealed dramatically in the distribution of the pearlware plus (postpearlware) ceramics seen in Figure 13.

A third concentration of ceramics to creamware is seen in the trench extending toward the east in the area of the public street. This concentration reveals refuse was being thrown into the street as well as around the house. A high drop off at the edge of the marsh is located another 30 feet or so toward the east, and it is over this embankment where quantities of peripheral refuse was likely discarded by the occupants of Nath Moore's Front.

The distribution of pearlware plus other associated, later types (post-1770s) emphasizes the concentration of refuse discarded inside this ruin (Figure 13), as well as scattered throughout the yard. The absence of

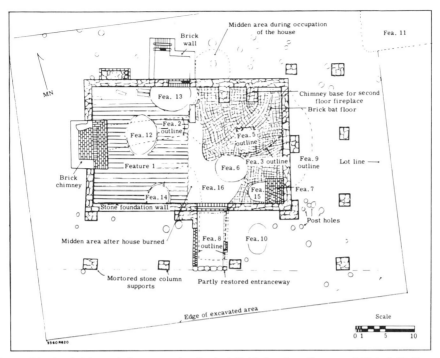

Figure 11. Nath Moore's Front—archeological field drawing (Structural Unit 5 10, Brunswick Town, Lot 29).

Archaeological features: (1) charcoal floor boards; (2) fallen brick chimney in west room; (3) fallen brick chimney in east room; (4) layer of clean sand above floor in east room; (5) fallen brick chimney section intact; (6) hole dug before house burned; (7) brick hearth platform built above rubble of burned house; (8) mortared brick doorway seal fallen intact; (9) pile of brick bats thrown from inside ruins; (10) pit dug during building of the house; (11) deeper midden in area of "Bay Street"; (12) Pit dug after house burned; before chimney fell; (13) shallow depression present before house burned; (14) pit dug after house burned; (15) pit dug after house burned, before Feature 7 was built; (16) pit dug after house burned.

Historical notes: Nath Moore's House (6/27/1728); Nath Moore to Edward Scott (Mariner) £700 (5/5/1733); Roger Moore (to Ed. Scott) to Hugh Blening £1300 (8/27/1744); Hugh Blening to Roger Moore £1300 (12/27/1744).

Interpretive notes: (1) The house was built before 1728; (2) The south entrance was sealed with bricks; (3) Outside footing added to west room; (4) Wooden floor in east room replaced by brick; (5) walls plastered over wooden lathing strips; (6) weatherboarded construction above first floor; (7) ballast stone foundation from below surface to several feet above ground; (8) porch or second floor overhang supported by columns on the east and south side; (9) posts on north side may have supported a porch and roof; (10) the windows were shuttered; (11) the house was abandoned in 1776; (12) a hole was dug in the floor of the east room; (13) burned by the British in 1776; (14) holes dug in the ruins in both rooms; (15) brick platform built above ashes of the ruins for use as a hearth to warm Confederate soldiers; (16) all whole bricks were salvaged for use in other houses; (17) the ruins were used as a garbage dump until 1830; (18) the ruins were hit during the shelling of Fort Anderson in 1865; (19) the ruins were discovered in 1958; (20) excavation was completed in 1959.

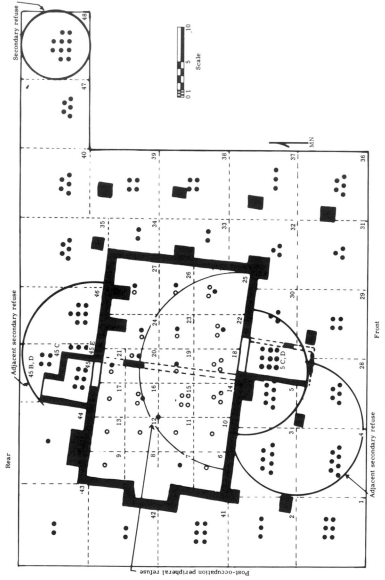

Figure 12. Nath Moore's Front—Ceramics through Creamware distribution (Structural Unit S 10, Brunswick Town, Lot 29). Solid symbol = total from yard and burned ash layer to floor; open symbol = above burned ash layer; symbol = 1-25 frequency.

58

The ruin of Nath Moore's Front at Brunswick Town, N.C., showing the burned wooden floor.

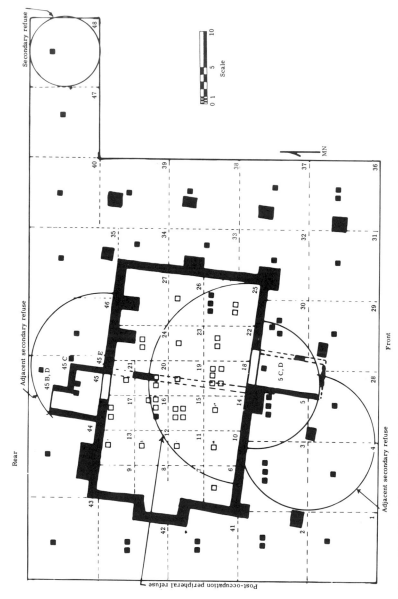

Figure 13. Nath Moore's Front—Ceramics—Pearlware plus distribution (Structural Unit S 10, Brunswick Town, Lot 29). Solid symbol = total from yard and burned ash layer to floor; open symbol = above burned ash layer; symbol = 1–25 frequency.

60

concentrations at the front and rear entrances and in the area of the street clearly reveals different behavioral practices regarding this class of artifacts. What we are seeing in contrasting the ceramics through creamware with those dating from pearlware to the early nineteenth century is the contrast in utilization of this area by occupants of the structure and occupants of another structure using this ruin as a refuse disposal area. Figure 13, therefore, reveals what might be seen as a "bomb burst" effect inside the ruin and a general scatter over the entire area, characteristic of peripheral middens.

An important point to be made here is that if we did not know the date of introduction of pearlware and associated types of ceramics and we nevertheless separated them on a typological attribute basis and conducted a comparative distributional analysis as we are doing here, we would be able to separate the occupation refuse from the postoccupation refuse on the basis of distribution and would be able to suggest a chronological relationship for the ceramic types involved.

The postoccupation refuse deposit phenomenon can be seen well in Figure 14, where the distribution of tailoring objects is illustrated. The concentration inside the ruin, above the burned ash layer of the house, suggests the discard activity of an individual standing in the doorway of the ruin and flinging refuse toward the left. This distribution is *not* that predicted by the Brunswick Refuse Disposal pattern of refuse disposal around an occupied structure. The high ratio of tailoring objects in this ruin above the burned floor level suggests considerable tailoring activity at a location other than this structure, at a time period revealed by ceramics to be ca. 1780 to ca. 1830. The distribution of artifacts at this ruin in relation to the architecture and the stratigraphy, therefore, is an important consideration to the proper interpretation of these objects in relation to this ruin. In the absence of such control, interpretation of artifacts from historic sites is often seen to be carried out on the assumption that all artifacts recovered from a ruin relate to the *occupation of than ruin,* clearly a faulty assumption to make in view of the findings revealed in this comparison of artifact distribution and relationships at Nath Moore's Front.

The wine bottle and bone fragment distribution is seen in Figure 15, where a relatively even distribution is indicated, with some increase at the rear doorway being observed. A similar uniform distribution is indicated for the tobacco pipe fragments (Figure 16), with a slight concentration present in the adjacent refuse entrance areas, and near the public street.

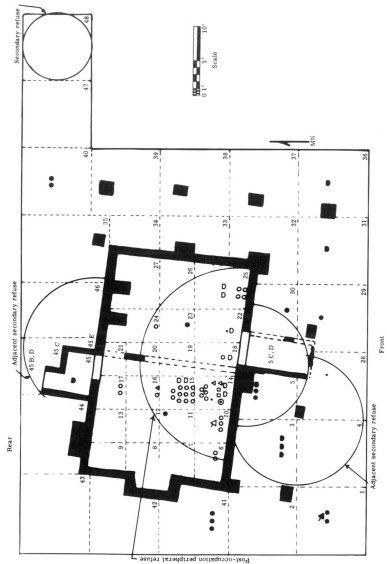

Figure 14. Nath Moore's Front—Tailoring objects distribution (Structural Unit S 10, Bruns-wick Town, Lot 29). Solid symbol = total from yard and burned ash layer to floor; open symbol = above burned ash layer; symbol = one object; ◉ = Thimble, ⋈ = Scissors; • = Pin, □ = Hook & Eye; ○ = Bale Seal; △ = Bead; ▷ = Buckle; ○ = Button.

62

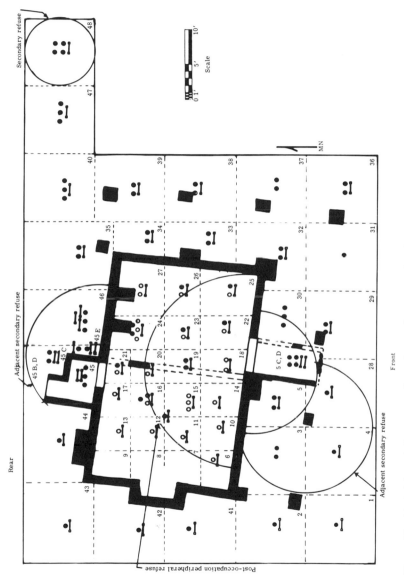

Figure 15. Nath Moore's Front—Bottle and Bone fragments distribution (Structural Unit S 10, Brunswick Town, Lot 29). Solid symbol = total from yard and burned ash layer to floor: open symbol = above burned ash layer; symbol = 1–25 frequency; O = Bottle; ▢—▢ = Bone.

63

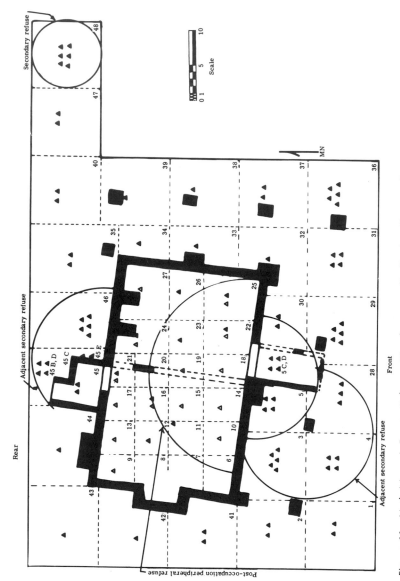

Figure 16. Nath Moore's Front—Tobacco Pipe fragment distribution (Structural Unit S 10, Brunswick Town, Lot 29). Solid symbol = total from yard and burned ash layer to floor; open symbol = above burned ash layer; symbol = I–25 frequency.

64

THE PUBLIC HOUSE-TAILOR SHOP (S25)

The Public House–Tailor Shop (S25) was found to be a six-room structure in a row house plan (Figure 17), built against the wall of the lot. Burned floor joists just below the floor level and the sockets in the foundation wall for these clearly indicated the floor level of this building. However, in the destruction of the building and the salvaging of materials, the actual floor level was destroyed.

Excavation of the easternmost room revealed a construction ditch cutting through a midden deposit located in the depression at the southeast corner caused by the slope of the hill at this point. This discovery indicated that midden had been deposited in this area prior to the construction of this easternmost room. Since a central chimney was located between the two easternmost rooms, it appeared that these two rooms may have been constructed after the four others. A check of the foundation wall at the juncture of these two rooms with the westernmost four rooms revealed a seam in the stonework, verifying this observation. For this reason the bottom layers inside Room 6 contained refuse originally thrown from rooms 1 through 4.

This fact is clearly seen in the distribution of ceramics shown in Figure 18, where a higher concentration of ceramics is obvious in the southeast corner of the ruin resulting from the midden discarded there prior to construction of the eastern two rooms. The ceramic distribution reveals a heavy deposit over the lot wall at the east end of the building, as well as along the end of the structure. This midden deposit was over 3 feet deep to the south of the lot wall in squares 16 through 18. Since this refuse deposit was beyond the private lot—over the lot wall—a higher bone ratio is seen here, giving this deposit more of a peripheral refuse character than an adjacent one, even though the midden is adjacent to the rear of the ruin.

A second concentration of refuse lying outside the lot wall at the rear of the fourth room, plus the fact that a stone landing of cobblestones was located here, suggests a doorway into the building at this point. Not considering the landing, but using the Brunswick Pattern, the prediction of an entryway here would be warranted. The contrast between the ceramics found inside the lot at the front of the structure and the refuse disposal area behind the building is remarkable.

An important point regarding the few fragments of annular and blue-painted pearlware shown in this ruin is the fact that they were found in a context clearly suggesting their presence prior to the time the structure burned in 1776. This finding is in keeping with evidence now appearing from military sites indicating the presence of this type of pearlware at this time period (South 1974: 4,163–166).

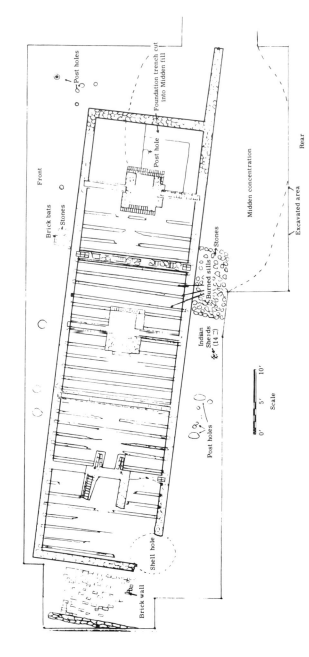

Figure 17. Plan of the Public House and Tailor Shop—field drawing (Excavation Unit S 25, Lot 27, Brunswick Town, N.C., 1732–1776).

66

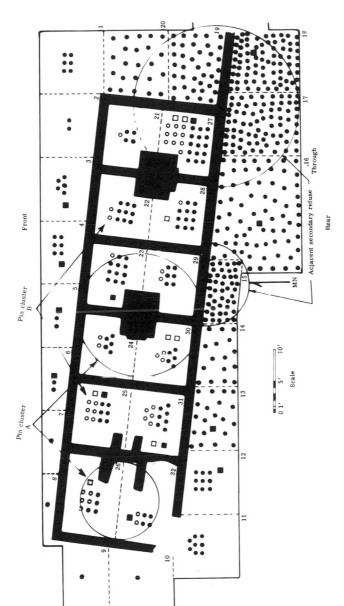

Figure 18. Plan of the Public House and Tailor Shop—Ceramics (S 25, Brunswick Town, N.C., ca. 1732–1776). Ceramics through Creamware and Pearlware Plus; ●■ (total from yard and below burned floor joists); ○□ (above joists); symbol = 1–25 frequency.

The distribution of pins and beads can be studied in Figure 19, which illustrates a contrast between the western five rooms and the eastern Room 6. These objects found below the floor joists apparently fell between floorboards when the floor was intact, or were dropped after the floor rotted and a sand floor was in use, though no evidence of the latter could be seen in the form of a specific surface layer. Some larger tailoring objects, such as scissors and buckles, stretch the limits of imagination to suggest they also fell through cracks in the floor, unless of course rotten floorboards were involved. This is entirely a possibility, however, since sand surrounded the burned floor joists on each side, a situation conducive to producing rot.

The dramatic contrast between the pins and beads in rooms 1–5 with the virtual absence in Room 6 resulted in the field interpretation that Room 6 must have been used for merchandising the objects sewn together in the five other rooms. This interpretation still would appear to be as good as any to account for the lack of pins and beads in this room. A floor without wide cracks in Room 6 would also account for this phenomenon.

The possibility arose, therefore, that perhaps the sand around the floor joists was hauled in from elsewhere after the floorboards rotted in the rooms, in order to provide a level sand floor on which to work. When the structure burned, therefore, the remaining parts of the joists would have become burned as well. If such an alternative was indeed the case for these rooms, then the absence of pins, etc. in the sixth room might be caused by sand having been brought from a different area to this room, whereas sand from a tailoring shop area may have been brought into the remaining five rooms.

With this somewhat fanciful alternative in mind, therefore, questions regarding the ratios of various artifact types found in these rooms can now be asked. If the ratio between pins and beads, for instance, resulted from tailoring activity elsewhere than in the rooms of this structure, there is no conceivable reason for that ratio to remain the same for pins in relation to beads found in the refuse deposit behind the ruin. In other words, if the ratio of beads to pins remained the same inside the ruin as compared with that in the refuse deposit, they may well have originated from the same behavioral activity inside the structure and not elsewhere.

Chi-square comparison of beads to pins inside and outside the ruin revealed a .50 level of significance, suggesting that there is little difference between the ratios inside the structure compared with the refuse deposit. This result suggests that the tailoring objects inside the structure are to be considered as primary de facto artifacts (usable artifacts lost in their place of use, not intentionally discarded).

The question then arises as to whether there is a different pin and bead loss within the five remaining rooms that might reflect different

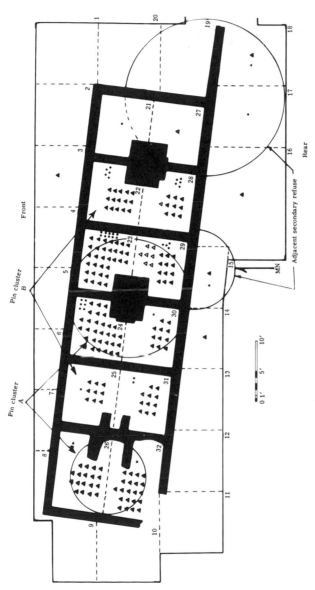

Figure 19. Plan of the Public House and Tailor Shop—Pins and Beads (S 25, Brunswick Town, N.C., ca. 1732–1776). Pins and Beads ▲● (total from yard and below burned floor joists) △○ (above joists; symbol = 1–25 frequency).

69

Artist's interpretive drawing of the Public House—Tailor Shop.

tailoring activities. In order to seek an answer the x^2 values for artifacts from various rooms need to be examined. Total frequencies are presented as follows:

	Room 1	Room 2	Room 3	Room 4	Room 5	Room 6
Pins	967	473	1053	1283	585	1
Beads	87	37	159	308	229	2
Tailoring, Buckles	41	36	40	43	37	27

Looking at the pin frequencies from the rooms, we see a similarity between rooms 1, 3, and 4, with rooms 2 and 5 having smaller totals. The first set of rooms has been designated as Pin Cluster A (rooms 1, 3, and 4), and the other as Pin Cluster B (rooms 2 and 5) (Figure 19). Room 6, of course, is what we have designated as a merchandizing, sales room, or office.

A low x^2 value for tailoring and buckles (hooks and eyes, scissors, bale seals, thimbles, and buttons), indicates no significant difference for these artifacts among the six rooms, suggesting regularity in the processes responsible for these tailoring objects in these rooms. When we drop the "sales room" from the group the similarity between the remaining five rooms is remarkable. The regularity of this patterning, compared with the difference seen for pins, suggests similar activities related to tailoring were carried out in all five rooms, but some factor involving pins results in a clustering of rooms 1, 3, and 4, and rooms 2 and 5. Perhaps activity in rooms 2 and 5 related primarily to the basic tailoring activity of cutting, which would not involve the use of pins. The activity in rooms 1, 3, and 4, may have involved sewing, the second half of the tailoring process, a process in which a number of pins are involved.

These suggestions are supported when we compare the ratio of pins to tailoring objects plus buckles in rooms 1, 3, and 4. Again a low χ^2 value reveals no significant difference in these rooms in the ratio of pins to tailoring objects and buckles. The same is true for rooms 2 and 5. The same is *not* true when rooms from Pin Cluster A are compared with rooms from Pin Cluster B, significant differences then being revealed.

The uniformity of tailoring objects for all six rooms is illustrated in Figure 20, with a far higher ratio of such objects in the refuse deposit than was the case with pins and beads. Comparison of this Figure 20 with Figure 19 clearly reveals why the S25 ruin was interpreted as a tailor shop activity area when contrasted with tailoring objects seen in Figure 10 at the domestic S7 ruin.

The dramatic contrast seen for the distribution of pins inside the S25 ruin compared with those found in the refuse deposit to the south of the lot wall is reversed with the wine bottle distribution (Figure 21). The wine bottle fragments inside the ruin virtually match the frequency for the front yard, with a heavy concentration in the refuse deposits. This fact suggests that when wine bottles were broken inside the building they were cleaned up and thrown into the refuse pile, with only the smaller fragments remaining inside, lost in the sand layer of the floor, or swept through holes in the floor. The fact that somewhat large pieces were sometimes involved inside the building suggests that the wooden floor was allowed to rot, after which a sand floor was used. The wine bottle distribution seen in Figure 21 certainly typifies the Brunswick Pattern in the contrast between the refuse dump area, the entrance, and the front yard.

Tobacco pipe fragments reveal a similar pattern to that seen for wine bottles, with a major concentration centering on the midden deposit areas (Figure 22). Nails, a major architectural class of artifacts, are relatively uniformly distributed throughout the immediate area of the ruin, with fewer in the front yard and a heavy concentration in the refuse deposits (Figure 23). Again, as we have seen for other artifact classes, sample squares taken at the rear of the structure, inside the structure, and in the front yard will reveal contrasting frequencies that have potential predictive value for determining information about an historic site through sampling prior to undertaking total excavation.

The bone frequency distribution seen in Figure 24 clearly reflects the Brunswick Pattern phenomenon, with a somewhat heavier concentration

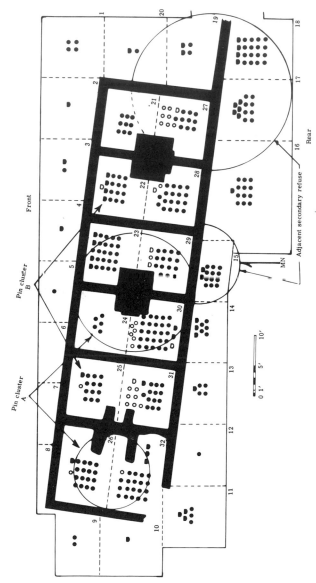

Figure 20. Plan of the Public House and Tailor Shop—Tailoring objects (S 25 Brunswick Town, N.C., ca. 1732–1776). Tailor objects (scissors, hook & eye, bale seals, thimbles, and buttons ● ○ and Buckles (◖▷ solid symbols are total from yard and below burned floor joists; open symbols are above joists); symbol = one object.

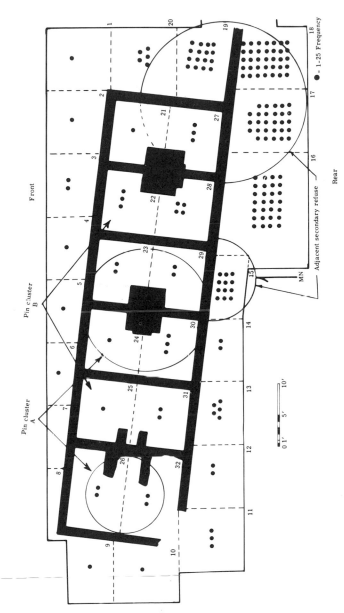

Figure 21. Plan of the Public House and Tailor Shop—Wine Bottle fragments (S 25, Brunswick Town, N.C., ca. 1732–1776).
● = 1–25 frequency.

73

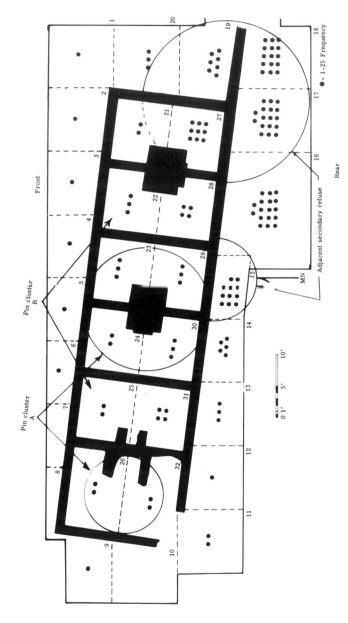

74

Figure 22. Plan of the Public House and Tailor Shop—Tobacco Pipe fragments (S 25, Brunswick Town, N.C., ca. 1732–1776). ● = l–25 frequency.

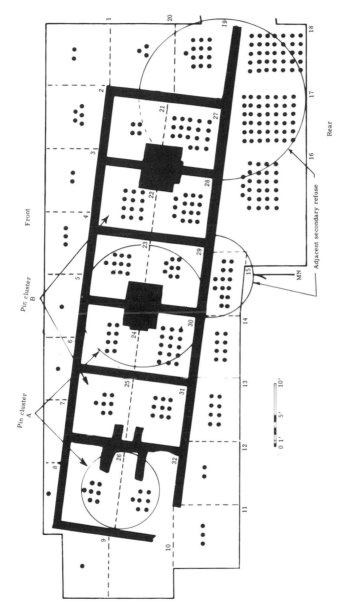

Figure 23. Plan of the Public House and Tailor Shop—Nail distribution (S 25, Brunswick Town, N.C., ca. 1732–1776). Symbol = l–25 frequency.

75

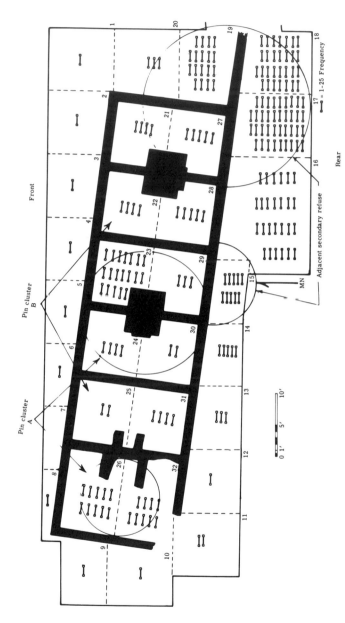

Figure 24. Plan of the Public House and Tailor Shop—Bone fragments (S 25, Brunswick Town, N.C., ca. 1732–1776). ▬—▯ = 1-25 frequency.

in rooms 1 and 4. When the bone from these two rooms is compared with the total of all tailoring objects including pins, no significant difference in the ratios for the two rooms is seen in the x^2 comparison. This suggests a similar behavioral activity regarding these two rooms in the Pin Cluster A rooms. However, beyond suggesting that those working in the tailor shop may have met in these rooms to have lunch, the significance of this information is not clear.

In this chapter we have examined some of the artifact classes from three Brunswick Town ruins with the view of abstracting some comparative information from frequency variability, while demonstrating the Brunswick Refuse Disposal Pattern. This study has concentrated on the entire artifact frequencies from all proveniences rather than conducting an analysis of various levels and features. Such an approach can be used to abstract general quantitative data from historic site excavations such as these. Once such general control over historic site data is accomplished we can begin to examine more specific questions regarding behavioral meaning in the regularity and variability demonstrated in the archeological record.

Suggestions for the use of the Brunswick Pattern have been made in this study, among which is the prospect of reliable prediction from sampling on historic sites. I have long resisted sampling as opposed to total excavation, but if we first totally excavate a number of historic site ruins toward conducting analyses, such as these demonstrated here from excavations conducted in the 1950s, we can begin to sample with some degree of expectation that our projections may be relatively accurate. Such predictive control of the data cannot come, however, without the quantification analysis approach urged in this book. This prediction is addressed to the empirical data base and relates to the relationship between pattern revealed through sampling and that revealed through total excavation of a ruin. In either case deductive explanation does not enter the scene until we ask why the pattern we witness is as it is and invent explanations to account for it. These hypotheses must then be tested with new data.

The Brunswick Pattern is mainly applicable, it is thought, to sites of British-American, or British colonial, origin. There is some evidence to indicate that German-American settlements such as at Bethabara, N.C., the Moravian settlement begun in 1753, that the Brunswick Pattern of refuse disposal does not apply (South 1972). Richard Carrillo (1975), in comparing a German-American with a British-American ruin has found marked contrasts in quantity and distribution of associated artifacts. This suggests that the Brunswick Pattern will not apply to German-American sites, the Germans being inordinately neat compared with the British-Americans. This proposition needs further testing.

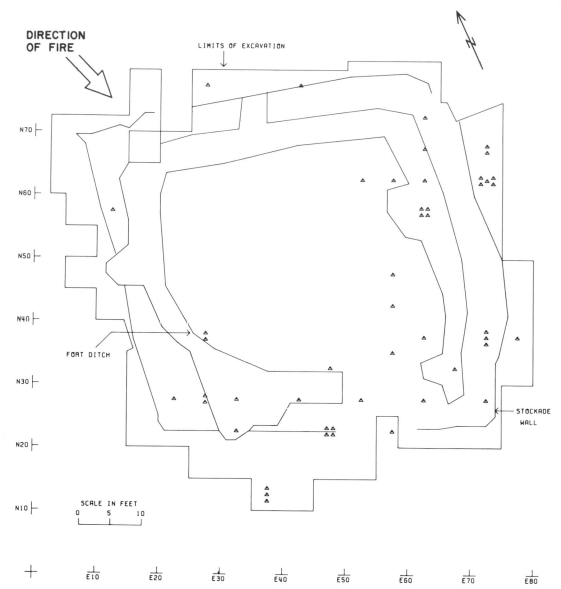

Figure 25.   Mound Summit of Fort Watson 38CRI—distribution of Flattened Lead Balls. Distribution of rifle balls indicates tower was located north of the stockade. Δ = 1 Ball.

The study of artifact distribution illustrated here is only one of the many approaches to pattern recognition that can be undertaken on historic sites by archeologists concerned with asking questions of their data that can be answered only through such a framework. It is hoped that pattern recognition through such methods of quantification will be used by those excavating historic sites.

Leland Ferguson (1975a, b) has demonstrated that a number of artifact types relating to domestic and personal functions are distributed in a different area from military ordnance artifacts, at the site of Fort Watson, S.C. Fort Watson was occupied for four months in 1780–1781, and was built on top of an Indian mound. It fell to Americans under General Francis Marion after a tower was constructed allowing sharpshooters to fire over the stockade wall into the fort. Ferguson's detailed analysis of the association and distribution of all artifact types inside the fort allowed four major interpretations to be made.

1. Activity areas relating to military and personal behavior were discovered.
2. There was a clear demonstration of the use of the tea ceremony on the mound.
3. There was a statistically significant correlation between creamware and pearlware ceramic types, including annular pearlware, clearly demonstrating the occurrence of this type at the 1781 time period.
4. The distribution of flattened lead balls shot by the Americans using rifles (weight and rifling being used to classify these as opposed to the British balls), was along only two sides of the fort interior, making it possible to locate the tower from which the sharpshooters were firing. This information was not previously known from historical documentation.

The distribution of the flattened lead balls shot by the Americans is shown in Figure 25, taken from Ferguson's report (1975a).

This simple and lucid explanation of artifact distribution demonstrates well the value of articulating field methods with questions appropriate to the archeological context. Against a background of decades of excavating fort sites with little more than catalogs of relics to show for the effort, Ferguson's quantification and distribution analysis appears as an

Interpretive sketch of Fort Watson, S.C., during the Revolution.

extremely sophisticated study. To fulfill the responsibility to the data each archeologist has, such studies must become routine.

REFERENCES

Carrillo, Richard, Joseph C. Wilkins, and Howell C. Hunter
  1975   Historical, Architectural, and Archeological Research at Brattonsville (38YK21), York County, South Carolina. *Research Manuscript Series* No. 76. Institute of Archeology and Anthropology, University of South Carolina, Columbia.
Ferguson, Leland G.
  1975a   Analysis of Ceramic Materials from Fort Watson, December 1780–April 1781. *The Conference on Historic Site Archaeology Papers 1973* **8.** Institute of Archeology and Anthropology, University of South Carolina, Columbia.
  1975b   Archeology at Scott's Lake, Exploratory Research, 1972, 1973. *Research Manuscript Series No. 68.* Institute of Archeology and Anthropology, University of South Carolina, Columbia.
Schiffer, Michael B.
  1972   Archaeological Context and Systemic Context. *American Antiquity* **37:**156–165.
South, Stanley A.
  1958   Excavation Report, Unit S10, Lot 29, Brunswick Town, North Carolina: Nath Moore's Front 1728–1776. Manuscript on file with North Carolina Department of Cultural Resources, Raleigh.
  1959   Excavation Report, Unit S7, Lot 71, Brunswick Town, North Carolina: The Hepburn—Reonalds House 1734–1776. Manuscript on file with North Carolina Department of Cultural Resources, Raleigh.
  1960   Excavation Report, Unit S25, Lot 27, Brunswick Town, North Carolina: The Public House-Tailor Shop 1732–1776. Manuscript on file with North Carolina Department of Cultural Resources, Raleigh.
  1967   The Paca House, Annapolis, Maryland. Manuscript on file with the Institute of Archeology and Anthropology, University of South Carolina, Columbia.
  1971   Archeology at the Charles Towne Site (38CH1) on Albemarle Point in South Carolina. Manuscript on file with the Institute of Archeology and Anthropology, University of South Carolina, Columbia.
  1972   Discovery in Wachovia. Manuscript on file with the Institute of Archeology and Anthropology, University of South Carolina, Columbia.
  1974   Palmetto Parapets. *Anthropological Studies No. 1.* Institute of Archeology and Anthropology, University of South Carolina, Columbia.

Archeological links to an apothecary shop.

The Carolina
Artifact Pattern

THEORETICAL CONSIDERATIONS

Through the study of frequency variations in the archeological record, the archeologist gains some degree of appreciation for the dynamic conditions in the context of which his static facts were generated. In the search for explanations of past lifeways, the reflected dynamics, and an accurate statement of culture history, historical archeologists have depended heavily on historical documentation, and have generally neglected quantification analyses directed at discovering patterned culture processes reflected in the material by-products of patterned human behavior. The strong resistance to such studies is partly due to the fact that there has been little demonstration of the value of quantification in pattern recognition for interpreting the remains of past human behavior from historic sites.

This study will concentrate on the delineation of a Carolina Artifact Pattern through frequency variations in artifacts from a number of historic sites of British colonial origin in the Carolinas. This pattern will then be tested against data from other sites to provide clues for its use on such sites generally. The patterns contained within the data from historic sites can be related to the historical information known about the function of the sites, a situation not possible with sites where the function is not a given. Therefore, military sites, village sites, plantation sites, frontier sites, and industrial sites might well be used as variables known from historical sources, against which archeological patterning is projected. This might reveal that although documentation indicates considerable variability in the function of certain sites, archeological patterning may be seen to remain unvarying when one classification is used, and perhaps seen to vary dramatically when the data are classified differently. This advantage is combined with that presented by historic artifacts themselves, some of which have a clear indication of functional use as a result of the archeologist's familiarity with the objects from his own culture.

From this perspective, therefore, the historical archeologist concerned with pattern recognition has an advantage over his colleagues working with prehistoric patterning in that some of the information he seeks is available as a given. He can select a group of known domestic house ruins from varying areas and known cultures, such as those from British-American communities, German-American communities, French-American communities, and Spanish-American communities, and abstract the patterning from each group and make comparisons. He might also examine a group of frontier fort sites to determine the covariation of patterns resulting from such occupation.

As he examines the variables, the archeologist may express the pattern he sees as a timeless, spaceless law, predictive of other cases. His postulates may well not be verified by empirical data, and he must then turn to both the historical and archeological records for further examination in order to isolate other variables. This process of data manipulation, this free exploration of the regularity and variation in the archeological record, is a major part of pattern recognition aimed at understanding the dynamics of past cultural systems. It is this process of pattern recognition, the search for "regularities on varying levels," emphasized by Steward (1955) and the "great pulsations" of Kroeber (1952), that will be the concern in this chapter as the Carolina Pattern is abstracted from the static archeological record.

In studying pattern variability in the static by-products of human behavior from historic sites many questions arise. For instance, what predictable regularities exist between a domestic dwelling of the mid-eighteenth-century in Virginia and one in South Carolina, as seen in the frequency relationships of the artifact groups recovered from an excavation of the sites? Can the frequency of material remains from activity in the kitchen of an eighteenth-century dwelling be seen to be similar to the frequency of such a group of objects from a dwelling a few miles away at the same period of time? Will the artifact frequency ratios resulting from domestic activities of food preparation in relation to architecturally related artifacts such as nails, window glass, hinges, etc., be the same as those from a military site of the same time period? If there are cultural processes whereby behavioral patterns are stamped on participants in a British colonial way of life, would the by-products from such behavior also be seen to be patterned in a predictable manner? Would the pattern vary with the length of time the structure was occupied? Through quantification studies, questions such as these can be examined.

It does not take a trained archeologist or a knowledge of how to analyze data quantitatively to be able to recognize a potter's kiln waster dump and come to the conclusion that it does not represent a typical domestic dwelling. Nor is such knowledge necessary to be able to identify from the furnaces and slag that a smithing operation and not a domestic dwelling is represented by a ruin containing such specialized activity by-products. Functional interpretation of historic ruins containing such information appears obvious. Considerable emphasis has been placed on such special sites by historical archeologists because there is always a need for more understanding of early industries. However, this emphasis on the unique has resulted in a lack of adequate descriptive data relating to the average domestic dwelling of the eighteenth century which was not devoted to an activity more specialized than providing an environment for raising a family. Very little has been said about these, for to do so requires comparison of artifacts based on quantification analysis.

Questions not so easily answered are those centering on the patterned regularity among artifact groups relating to household activities that may have been almost universal on British colonial occupation sites. The basic question is, what does any observed variation mean? Questions on the specific level are: How many tailoring objects can be expected from a mid-eighteenth-century domestic household midden? What is the percentage ratio of arms use to all other artifact classes on an eighteenth-century site of British colonial occupation? Will the arms group of artifact classes (musket balls, gunflints, gun parts, etc.) vary dramatically between domestic household middens and those from military occupations of the same time period? Will frontier sites reveal different artifact group ratios from sites located closer to the source of supply? Questions such as these cannot be answered without resorting to quantification analysis of comparable data for pattern recognition.

Other questions of equal importance are those centering on the behavioral activity represented by the presence of small quantities of specific artifacts in association with others. The presence or absence of certain objects may well reveal a behavioral activity set associated with only one activity, such as a crucible, a silversmith's anvil, and hammer. These are specialized activity by-products, but not so readily obvious as a set of such data reflecting a major craft or industrial activity. The relationship between heavy ceramic serving ware and teaware can only be determined through quantification. The pattern range for any such variables will depend on intersite comparisons, from which predictable empirical data ranges can be established. The examination of data for the isolation of such pattern on an intersite level is the purpose of this chapter. This will be done by abstracting from several Carolina sites a Carolina Artifact Pattern. This pattern will be tested against other data, and the applicable range of the Carolina Pattern will be explored.

Postulates Relating to the Carolina Artifact Pattern

A basic assumption is that each household in an eighteenth-century British colonial society represents a system within a much larger system of complex variables, with the larger system imposing on each household a degree of uniformity in the relationships among its behavioral parts. This uniformity is expected to be revealed in various classes of cultural remains. The quantity of remains resulting from any behavioral activity would not necessarily parallel the importance placed on the activity within the cultural system but would have a definite relationship to the ramains of other activities. It is these relationships among the by-products of human behavior that might be expected to reveal regularity when compared on an intersite basis. The degree of curation, recycling, repair, and ease of breakage are only a few variables relating to the ratios seen among the by-products of behavior recovered by the archeologist. Gold coins, or pocket watches, for instance, were so highly curated that these items are seldom seen in archeological contexts. On the other hand, Jew's-harps are almost universally present on eighteenth-century sites, no doubt due in part to the fact that once the central vibrating spring was broken loose from the frame it was difficult for the owner to replace or to recycle the remains by putting the frame to another use. A wine bottle, once broken, is not something likely to be recycled. Porcelain bowls and cups, however, may well be repaired with rivets, as was delft at Fortress Louisbourg, Nova Scotia, reflecting the value placed on these items by the owners (South 1968). Variables such as these must all be considered in determining the role any class or group of artifact by-products may have had in the systemic context (Schiffer 1972). Our concern here, however, is with examining the ratios between artifact groups with the view of establishing certain broad regularities or pulsations of culture process against which any deviation from such regularity can be contrasted as reflecting behavior somewhat different from expected margins.

These postulates regarding broad culture process are related to the assumption that a British family on the way to America in the eighteenth century would bring a basic set of behavioral modes, attitudes, and associated artifacts that would not vary regardless of whether their ship landed at Charleston, Savannah, or Philadelphia. This tendency toward uniformity is so strongly reflected in the archeological record that historical archeology has yet to *predictively* define whether the by-products are the result of an upper class gentleman or those of a lower status laborer.

The basic postulate here is the assumption that there was a patterned casting off of behavioral by-products around an occupation site that might be viewed as a per capita, per year contribution to the archeological record. Since a middle class laborer in Charleston would contribute his per capita, per year procurement–use–breakage–discard record in a ratio similar to his counterpart in Savannah or Philadelphia, some uniformity in the record would certainly be expected.

Without knowing the extent of this regularity it is difficult to point with assurance to any variability that may distinguish the truly unique, unusual or specific behavior. As a result, historical archeology reports appear as a never ending flow of unique situations reported as unique events. Under such a research format no site is ever seen or interpreted as being just like another site, since ranges for patterned regularity are unexplored and unknown. This lack of a polar nucleus of regularity is a result of the virtual absence of quantification analyses on comparable, complete sets of artifact data from excavated historic sites.

Such regularity does indeed exist, and steps must be taken to define it before much progress can be made toward elevating historical arche-

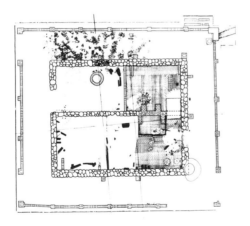

The plan drawing of Russellborough, the Governor's home at Brunswick Town.

ology from a study of the unique to a study of lawful regularities of culture.

In this study we are dealing with the entire collection of artifacts recovered from an occupation site, not selected proveniences. Specific areas of a site may reveal differences in artifact frequencies relating to the behavioral activities that took place in those areas. However, since many sites would have been occupied for decades, or perhaps a century or more, repeated use of the same area for different functions may well result in the artifact relationships from that area reflecting anything but a clear view of the activity that took place at any moment in time. Demonstrating from the archeological record that a single activity with resulting by-products took place in a particular area is often no easy task. More often, the debris around a house can be expected to reflect generalized rather than specific activities from the artifact ratios recovered.

This is not to say that there will not be differential discard activities revolving around the disposal of secondary refuse; there certainly will be. However, given the British colonial cultural system, generalizing archeological formation processes will tend to produce similar artifact ratios when artifact groups are compared, unless, of course, special behavioral activities skew the general picture.

In summary then, we might express postulates to the effect that: (1) British colonial behavior should reveal regularities in patterning in the archeological record from British colonial sites; and (2) specialized behavioral activities should reveal contrasting patterns on such sites. These patterns will be recognized through quantification of the behavioral by-products which form the archeological record.

THE METHOD OF ABSTRACTING THE CAROLINA ARTIFACT PATTERN

Any pattern should derive from comparable samples of consistently gathered data. A broad range of sites of the eighteenth century would be ideal, representing a wide area of British colonial occupation, as well as a variety in the type of occupation represented as revealed in historical documents. However, published reports for sites that have been totally excavated and for which all the classes of artifacts have been tabulated by the archeologist are rare, due to a general lack of interest in artifact frequency relationship studies.

In 1960 a model based on frequency relationships of artifact classes was constructed from data I had recovered from the Brunswick Town, N.C., ruins, and at that time I could locate no comparable artifact lists that were complete because the major historic sites excavated at that time in Virginia and elsewhere had a policy of not quantifying fragments. As a result, a general pattern was not published due to a lack of comparable data. Instead, the ceramic distributions were abstracted and published (South 1962) along with an appeal to colleagues to begin publishing quantification analyses for the goal of building a general body of such data for comparative studies. (See also Appendix A in Chapter 7 of this book.)

The Carolina Pattern is abstracted from only five sites, which is only a small increase over that available to me in 1960. However, I am not intimidated by this small sample because the pattern will be refined by others as new questions are asked. To continue to wait for more data comparable to that with which we are dealing may take more years of excavation. As Flannery (1972: 107) has so well expressed it, "To be useful a model need only organize a body of disorganized data in such a way that hypotheses can conveniently be tested, accepted, modified or rejected."

One of the problems immediately faced when quantification studies are undertaken utilizing all artifact classes is obtaining collections of excavated data recovered under comparable conditions. My 1960 efforts at obtaining data that had been systematically screened at least through a one-quarter inch mesh were met with a variety of reactions from colleagues, including the view that screening was a barbaric method of approaching an historic site, and that every object, including seed beads should be located with the trowel. There was also a too-frequent disdain for controlled screening, and an aversion to recording artifact data by means of counting fragments of wine bottles and ceramics. This situation forced a reliance on my own data recovery techniques for any model I might hope to construct that would have a general applicability.

All the sites used in the model were excavated by me, or under my supervision, and all were subjected to sifting by one-quarter inch mesh screen, with periodic testing of each provenience with a one-eighth inch mesh screen and window screen in order to determine whether seed beads, straight pins, or other small objects were present. At Brunswick Town, when the tailor shop ruin was discovered, this procedure allowed for the sifting of all soil through window screen mesh for maximum recovery of small tailoring objects such as seen beads. This method of adapting the size of screen to the demands of the site was used with all sites contributing to the pattern.

The five collections used to define the pattern were taken from two totally excavated ruins at Brunswick Town, N.C., two midden deposit samples at Fort Moultrie, S.C., and a secondary midden deposit in a cellar hole at Cambridge, Ninety Six, S.C. The artifact counts from these ruins vary from more than 2000 to more than 42,000. These collections are considered to be "reasonably comparable samples."

The primary comparability criteria used were that the collections represent a wide variety of human behavior, and that they cover at least 100 years of time. Other, more specific attributes of the collections are:

Collection Attributes

1. Large collection from totally excavated sites (Brunswick)
2. Large collection from sampled site (Fort Moultrie)
3. Examples of domestic occupation (Brunswick and Cambridge)
4. Example of site on which specialized activity occurred (Brunswick)
5. Examples of secondary midden immediately adjacent to ruin in the yard (Brunswick)
6. Example of secondary midden discarded in the ruin after the occupation of the structure had ceased (Brunswick and Cambridge)
7. Example of secondary midden deposited at a place removed from the immediate vicinity of the occupants discarding the refuse (Brunswick, Cambridge and Fort Moultrie)
8. Examples of midden resulting from domestic occupation (Brunswick and Cambridge)
9. Examples of midden resulting from military occupation (Fort Moultrie)
10. Examples of midden resulting from public occupation (Brunswick)
11. A collection representing a wide variety of activities reflecting human behavior (Brunswick, Fort Moultrie, and Cambridge)
12. Collections recovered in a controlled manner using screens to recover small specimens (Brunswick, Fort Moultrie, and Cambridge)
13. Collections from which total artifact counts were available, no selectivity of artifacts on the basis of value judgments having been made regarding the curation of the objects (Brunswick, Fort Moultrie, and Cambridge)
14. Collections covering at least 100 years (ca.1728–ca.1830) in combined time of occupation represented (Brunswick, Cambridge, and Fort Moultrie)
15. Collections from sites distributed over some spatial distance (Brunswick, N.C., coastal; Fort Moultrie, S.C., coastal; Cambridge, S.C., inland)

With these attributes in mind the following excavated collections were used in defining the Carolina Artifact Pattern.

The Cambridge Cellar at Ninety Six, S.C., during excavation.

The Cambridge Cellar at Ninety Six, S.C., after excavation.

The Provenience

1. Brunswick Town, N.C., The Public House–Tailor Shop (S25), occupied ca. 1732–1776. Excavated by Stanley South in 1960 (South 1960). A six-room row house foundation probably used as a public house or inn prior to 1732, and apparently as a tailor shop sometime after that time. It was burned in 1776. Total artifact collection used.
2. Brunswick Town, N.C., Nath Moore's Front (S10) occupied ca. 1728–1776. Excavated by Stanley South in 1958 (South 1958). A two-room foundation that was apparently a residence until it was burned in 1776. The ruin was used as a refuse dump area until ca. 1830. Total artifact collection used.
3. Fort Moultrie, S.C., the American Midden Deposit (CH50A), occupied 1775–ca. 1794. Excavated by Stanley South in 1973 (South 1974). The midden deposit thrown over the parapet wall onto the berm of the fort, primarily between 1775 and 1780, with some few items deposited there as late as ca. 1794. Sample trenches were cut to locate the fort, and the artifacts from this deposit in these trenches were used.
4. Fort Moultrie, S.C., the British Midden Deposit (CH50B), occupied 1780–1782. Excavated by Stanley South in 1973 (South 1974). The midden deposit from the British occupation was thrown into the fort moat. The contents of the moat where it was crossed by the exploratory trenches were used.
5. Ninety Six, S.C., a Cambridge Cellar Deposit (GN5-224,225), occupied ca. 1783–ca. 1800. Excavated by Steven G. Baker in 1972 (Baker 1972). The small, single-room cellar was used as a secondary midden deposit area by someone probably living nearby after the structure above this cellar was torn down. The deposit probably accumulated from ca. 1800 to ca. 1820. The total deposit in the cellar was used.

Artifact Classification

The artifact classes used in this study are based on the type and class designations assigned in 1960 (South 1962) and have been found to be useful, with changes occurring primarily at the type level as knowledge accumulated. The following (Table 3) illustrates the increasingly generalized type-ware-class-group classification used in this study.

This study is concerned primarily with the class and group levels; later chapters focus on the more specific type level of classification and analysis. Types are often distinguished from other types by a single attribute, though several attributes may well be used. Often, decorative motifs involving color, embossing, and technique are used. Wares are

TABLE 3

Artifact Classification Format

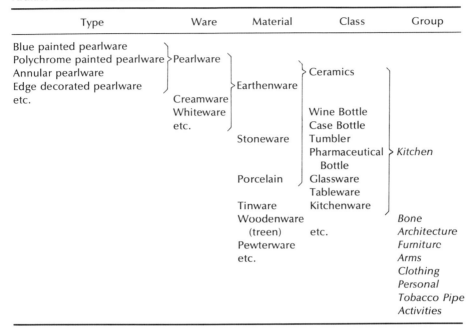

Type	Ware	Material	Class	Group
Blue painted pearlware Polychrome painted pearlware Annular pearlware Edge decorated pearlware etc.	Pearlware Creamware Whiteware etc.	Earthenware Stoneware Porcelain Tinware Woodenware (treen) Pewterware etc.	Ceramics Wine Bottle Case Bottle Tumbler Pharmaceutical Bottle Glassware Tableware Kitchenware etc.	Kitchen Bone Architecture Furniture Arms Clothing Personal Tobacco Pipe Activities

defined by attributes remaining constant across types, as in the example in Table 3, pearlware is defined by the paste, hardness, and cobalt in the lead glaze (producing a bluish glaze). The material classification refers to artifacts on the basis of the material of which they are composed, with ceramics being classified into three divisions on the basis of hardness of paste.

The classes are based on form and sometimes function, with 42 classes being used in this study (Table 4). These classes have been combined into nine groups, including bone. The groups are based on functional activities related to the systemic context reflected by the archeological record.

The organization of data along these classificatory lines should produce results varying with the level of generalization at which the analysis takes place. It is expected that broader cultural processes will likely be revealed at the group level of generalization due to the functional relationship between the group and generalized behavioral activity in the cultural system. Comparison at the type or style level of classification is expected to reveal answers to questions about nationalistic or ethnic origin, trade routes, culture contact, and idiosyn-

In addition to their role in helping the archeologist to understand the processes of culture artifacts are useful in interpreting past lifeways.

cratic behavior, depending on the questions being asked (for a discussion relevant to this point, see Binford 1962).

Some of the classes used in this study could well be broken into types for specific analysis on the type level. For instance, Class 6 (Table 4), Glassware,[1] combines stemmed glass, decanter glass, and glass dishes. One might argue that, functionally, glass dishes have little connection with the wine drinking ceremony suggested by wine glasses and decanters. Such questions of functional relevance can be answered if a study involving frequency relationships between these types is undertaken, in which case the Class 6, Glassware, can be broken down as: 6A—stemmed wine glass; 6B—stemmed compote glass; 6C—engraved decanter glass; 6D—plain decanter glass; 6E—small glass dishes, etc. The relevance of such a classification to questions being asked is the critical point here.

Another point relating to functional relevance of an artifact class with the groups used here is that many types and some classes can well function in different contexts, and regardless of the juggling of types and

---

[1] Classes are given initial capitalization; groups are initially capitalized and italicized; types are lower case.

TABLE 4

Artifact Classes and Groups

Class no.		Class name
		Kitchen Artifact group
1.	Ceramics	(over 100 types)
2.	Wine Bottle	(several types)
3.	Case Bottle	(several types)
4.	Tumbler	(plain, engraved, enamelled)
5.	Pharmaceutical Type Bottle	(several types)
6.	Glassware	(stemmed, decanter, dishes, misc.)
7.	Tableware	(cutlery, knives, forks, spoons)
8.	Kitchenware	(pots, pans, pothooks, gridiron, trivets, metal teapots, water kettles, coffee pots, buckets, handles, kettles, etc.)
		Bone group
9.	Bone Fragments	
		Architectural group
10.	Window Glass	
11.	Nails	(many types)
12.	Spikes	
13.	Construction Hardware	(hinges, pintles, shutter hooks and dogs, staples, fireplace backing plates, lead window cames, etc.)
14.	Door Lock Parts	(doorknobs, case lock parts, keyhole escutcheons, locking bolts and brackets)
		Furniture group
15.	Furniture Hardware	(hinges, knobs, drawer pulls and locks, escutcheon plates, keyhole surrounds, handles, rollers, brass tacks, etc.)
		Arms group
16.	Musket Balls, Shot, Sprue	
17.	Gunflints, Gunspalls	
18.	Gun Parts, Bullet Molds	
		Clothing group
19.	Buckles	(many types, shoe, pants, belt)
20.	Thimbles	(several types)
21.	Buttons	(many types)
22.	Scissors	
23.	Straight Pins	
24.	Hook and Eye Fasteners	
25.	Bale Seals	(from bales of cloth)
26.	Glass Beads	(many types for wearing or sewing onto clothing)
		Personal group
27.	Coins	
28.	Keys	
29.	Personal Items	(wig curlers, bone brushes, mirrors, rings, signet sets, watch fobs, fob compass, bone fan, slate pencils, spectacle lens, tweezers, watch key, and other "personables")

TABLE 4 (Continued)

Class no.		Class name
		Tobacco Pipe group
30.	Tobacco Pipes	(ball clay pipes, many types)
		Activities group
31.	Construction Tools	(plane bit, files, augers, gimlets, axe head, saws, chisels, rives, punch, hammers, etc.)
32.	Farm Tools	(hoes, rake, sickle, spade, etc.)
33.	Toys	(marbles, jew's-harp, doll parts, etc.)
34.	Fishing Gear	(fishhooks, sinkers, gigs, harpoons)
35.	Stub-stemmed Pipes	(red clay, short stemmed tobacco pipes)
36.	Colono-Indian Pottery	(or types clearly associated with the historic occupation)
37.	Storage Items	(barrel bands, brass cock, etc.)
38.	Ethnobotannical	(nuts, seeds, hulls, melon seeds)
39.	Stable and Barn	(stirrup, bit, harness boss, horseshoes, wagon and buggy parts, rein eyes, etc.)
40.	Miscellaneous Hardware	(rope eye thimble, bolts, nuts, chain, andiron, tongs, case knife, flatiron, wick trimmer, washers, etc.)
41.	Other	(button manufacturing blanks, kiln waster furniture, silversmithing debris, etc., reflecting specialized activities)
42.	Military Objects	(swords, insigna, bayonets, artillery shot and shell, etc.)

classes the archeologist may undertake to clarify the situation, he will find someone who will point out that "all pharmaceutical type bottles were not used to hold medicines. Some were used to hold oil of peppermint, spices, seasoning, etc." This is obviously true, just as gunflints were used on both civilian and military weapons, and here we have included them under *Arms* rather than under "Military Objects" in the *Activities* group. Since virtually any class of artifacts can be seen to possibly serve a variety of purposes within the past cultural context, it is foolhardy to attempt to arrive at a classification that has no exceptions. For this reason the artifact classes used here are considered adequate for a wide range of historic sites. There is nothing wrong, of course, in expanding the list to more than 42 classes in the face of a research design demanding such an addition. However, for comparison with the pattern presented here, this classification system should be used.

Artifact Classes and Groups

The *Bone*, *Furniture*, and *Tobacco Pipe* groups consist of a single artifact class, and in this sense are not entirely comparable to the more

A necessary first step in the processing of archeological materials.

generalized groups made up of a number of classes. The *Bone* group is not included in the model since it requires specialized analysis, and is not the same type of by-product of human behavior represented by the other groups. The *Tobacco Pipe* group would be expected to fall under *Activities,* but was kept as a separate group due to the high frequency of this class of artifact usually found on historic sites, and the desire to determine the variability involved in what might be expected to be a highly variable artifact group compared to others.

The Colono-Indian Pottery, Class 36, might functionally be included under the *Kitchen* group, but is kept under *Activities* due to the expected variability of this class of artifact, and its role in indicating Indian contact. Other changes may well be suggested, as was pointed

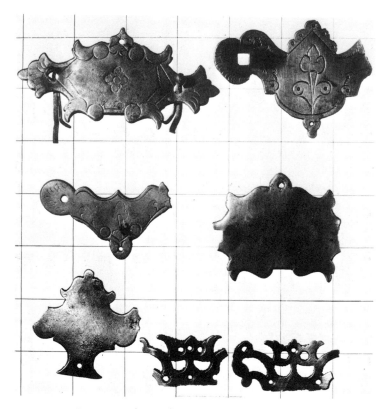

Brass escutcheon plates from the Furniture Hardware class.

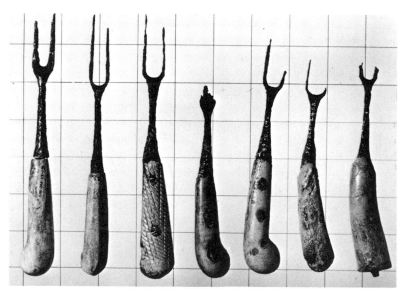

Bone handled forks from the Tableware class.

out previously, but juggling of artifact types, classes and groups will not eliminate the fact that many artifacts are used in several contexts.

The *Kitchen Artifact* group is expected to display little intersite varia-bility when compared with other groups due to the uniformity assumed to be involved in the patterned acquisition, preparation, serving of food and the breakage of associated items of material culture, and the discard of such by-products in a frequency patterned manner.

The *Kitchen Artifact* group might well be seen as artifact classes centered primarily on subsistence activities, but a group entitled "Subsistence" would include any artifacts such as farm tools, storage items, etc., resulting in a far broader group than that we have termed *Kitchen Artifacts*. The term "kitchen" is appropriate in that the classes involved not only reflect behavioral activity primarily centered on the kitchen, but they also characterize midden deposits thrown from British colonial kitchens.

The *Activities* group would be expected to display considerable

Brass padlocks. Photos such as this taken in the field are a valuable means of establishing a record of small finds.

internal variability between classes, reflecting greater behavioral variation than the *Kitchen* group centered on the preparation of food, due to the wider range of activities represented.

The *Architecture* group is quite different from the group of artifact classes resulting from discard of items from the kitchen. These items can be the result of loss of nails and spikes during construction of buildings, or the remains left after such structures are torn down, burned, or abandoned, or they could result from intentional discard along with kitchen midden. This group represents those items most often not intentionally discarded, but directly related to the architecture on a site.

The *Arms* group might be expected to remain relatively stable in that arms are a highly curated object, and the number of by-products resulting from the use, maintenance, and repair might well be fairly consistent on a per capita per year basis. Conjectures as to the relationship of such by-products between civilian and military sites can well be made assum-

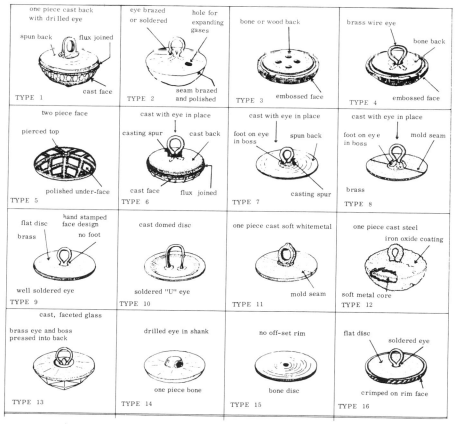

Artifact attribute description is an early step in the archeological process.

Military buttons with regimental numbers are specific historical as well as archeological documents.

ing a more rigid military code of behavior relative to arms. However, an argument can be made that such a situation might produce more by-products associated with arms through better maintenance and discard of worn-out parts, and an equal argument suggesting that less careless loss of musket balls and shot would take place due to greater regimentation. It is best to let the data speak in such cases rather than to become involved in excessive hypothesis formulation based primarily on speculation.

The *Clothing* group of artifact classes relates to the manufacture and use of clothing. Pattern such as we are considering should be able to define the expected norm for clothing objects to be found on eighteenth-century occupation sites, and should single out those contrasting frequencies representing excessive clothing-related activities such as might be seen in a tailor shop ruin.

In a similar way the classes in the *Activities* group should reveal specific behavioral activities through the higher than normal frequency for one or more classes. Such deviation from the ranges defined by the pattern might allow for the interpretation of an industry, a craft activity, or trade with the Indians. Before such behavioral variables can be pinpointed as being "beyond normal margins," pattern defining the frequency range for each artifact group must be determined to allow a better understanding of what might be seen as "normal."

The Empirical Artifact Profiles for Five Carolina Sites

After the five Carolina sites were selected, and the artifact classes and groups defined, the next step in the recognition of a Carolina Pattern was to construct the empirical artifact profiles by determining the percentage relationship between artifact groups. These artifact profiles are depicted in Table 5.

By comparing the percentage relationship of the *Kitchen artifact* group for all five sites the range is seen to be from 51.8% to 64.6%, a range of only 12.8%. The *Architecture* group of artifacts covers a range of only 15.2%. What this immediately indicates is that there is regularity between artifact groups among these sites.

Adjusting the Empirical Artifact Profiles

When comparing the percentages for each artifact group in the above artifact profiles, it becomes apparent that there are five instances where the percentage for an artifact group varies dramatically from that for the other sites. We can then ask "Why?" If the cause can be seen as the result of specialized behavior, then these variables may take on significance in identifying such behavior through contrasting frequencies. Such contrasts would then need to be removed from a pattern resulting from generalized, nonspecific activities.

The Tailor Shop Adjustment (Brunswick S25)

The *Clothing* group from the Public House–Tailor Shop ruin at Brunswick Town reveals a 13.1% ratio, which is far higher than that for the remaining ruins (Table 5). The thousands of clothing- related items from this ruin clearly reveals its function as a clothing producing shop or factory, and the higher percentage of this group of clothing artifacts reflects this contrast with the other four ruins.

Another group out of keeping with the other ratios is the *Arms* group which is three times the percentage of that for the next highest ruin. This is the result of 1228 small shot found in association with the thousands of

TABLE 5

Empirical Artifact Profiles for Five Carolina Sites

							Site						Total
	Brunswick S25		Brunswick S10		Cambridge 96		Ft. Moultrie A		Ft. Moultrie B			
Group	Count	%	Count	%	Count	%	Count	%	Count	%			Total
Kitchen	22,479	52.9	6795	51.8	12,854	64.6	4185	60.1	1208	56.9			47,521
Architecture	9620	22.6	4116	31.4	5006	25.2	1510	21.7	344	16.2			20,596
Furniture	83	.2	82	.6	35	.2	6	.1	2	.1			208
Arms	1262	3.0	45	.3	27	.1	39	.6	20	.9			1393
Clothing	5574	13.1	72	.6	1069	5.4	136	1.9	69	3.3			6920
Personal	71	.2	20	.2	108	.5	4	.1	4	.2			207
Tobacco Pipes	2830	6.7	1829	13.9	349	1.8	167	2.4	50	2.4			5225
Activities	578	1.3	159	1.2	432	2.2	916	13.1	425	20.0			2510
	42,497	100.0	13,118	100.0	19,880	100.0	6963	100.0	2122	100.0			84,580

103

tailoring objects inside the Public House–Tailor Shop (S25) ruin. This association suggests that these shot may have had a function other than in the context of arms, perhaps as weight sewn into draperies to allow them to hang properly. Draperies are not clothing, but tailoring objects have been included here under the *Clothing* group. An alternate interpretation such as this is suggested by the fact that there is not a proportional increase in gunflints, gun parts, and other arms related artifact classes accompanying the increase in shot. The dramatic increase in *Clothing* group artifacts covaries with the increase in shot, suggesting a similar functional explanation may be involved. For this reason these 1228 shot have been removed from inclusion in the *Arms* group for the S25 ruin.

These two adjustments are the only ones made to the S25 ruin, resulting in the lowering of the total artifact count to 35,695. However, rather than totally eliminating the *Clothing* group count the 3% represented by this group for the remaining four sites can be used to arrive at a projected *Clothing* group figure of 1070, 3% of 35,695. This brings the *Clothing* group for the S25 ruin in line with the frequencies for the remaining sites for the purpose of expressing the pattern exclusive of the tailor shop bias.

The Fort Moultrie Adjustment (Fort Moultrie A & B)

The 13.1% *Activities* group for the American Fort Moultrie (A) and the 20.0% for the British Fort Moultrie (B) are dramatically higher than the 1.5% average for the remaining three sites seen in the above empirical artifact profiles (Table 5). This fact would suggest that specialized activity may be involved, as revealed by the by-product of such activity. The list of artifact class frequencies for these deposits, given in the appendix to this chapter, reveals that 94% of the *Activities* group artifacts from the American Fort Moultrie (A) midden are composed of Colono-Indian Pottery (No. 36), and bone button blanks (No. 41), being by-products of specialized activities. The British midden deposit at Fort Moultrie (B) is composed of 88% of these artifact classes also. When we remove these specialized behavioral by-products the new percentage ratios are very close to those for the remaining three sites (Table 6). These are the only adjustments made to the empirical artifact profiles to express the pattern from these five sites as the Carolina Pattern.

Table 6 reflects these adjustments:

The Wide Range within the Tobacco Pipe Group

The 13.9% figure for the *Tobacco Pipe* group in Brunswick Ruin S10 suggests the need for an adjustment in this group also, since this seems

TABLE 6

Adjusted Site Profiles with Known Deviant Samples Removed *i.e.*, **Tailor Shop, Button Industry, and Colono-Indian Pottery**

	Brunswick S25		Brunswick S10		Cambridge 96		Ft. M. (A)		Ft. M. (B)		Total
	Count	%	Count	%	Count	%	Count	%	Count	%	Count
Kitchen	22,479	61.1	6795	51.8	12,854	64.6	4185	68.6	1208	69.2	47,521
Architecture	9620	26.2	4116	31.4	5006	25.2	1510	24.8	344	19.7	20,596
Furniture	83	.2	82	.6	35	.2	6	.1	2	.1	208
Arms	34*	.1	45	.3	27	.1	39	.6	20	1.2	165
Clothing	(1070)**	3.0	72	.6	1069	5.4	136	2.2	69	4.0	2416
Personal	71	.2	20	.2	108	.5	4	.1	4	.2	207
Tobacco Pipes	2830	7.7	1829	13.9	349	1.8	167	2.7	50	2.9	5225
Activities	578	1.5	159	1.2	432	2.2	55***	.9	48***	2.7	1272
	36,765	100.0	13,118	100.0	19,880	100.0	6102	100.0	1745	100.0	77,610

* less #16, 1228 small shot, which may have had a tailoring function.
** less 4504 tailoring items; 3% of the total without *Clothing* was projected here to adjust for the tailor shop bias.
*** less specialized behavioral activity revealed by No. 36 (Colono-Indian Pottery), and No. 41, Bone Button Blanks from a button "industry."

105

quite high compared with the ratio seen in the remaining four ruins. However, this artifact group is actually a class kept separate because it was expected to vary widely between ruins depending on the pipe smoking habits of the occupants represented by the archeological record. No independent explanation for the wide variability can be suggested other than variability in behavioral habit; therefore, this group has not been adjusted beyond the range suggested by the empirical artifact profiles.

THE CAROLINA ARTIFACT PATTERN

Using the above empirical data from the five Carolina sites, with the adjustments indicated, and determining the mean percentage for each artifact group, the Carolina Artifact Pattern is seen to be as shown in Table 7.

Examining the Carolina Artifact Pattern for Intrasite Stability

Before testing the Carolina Artifact Pattern using data beyond that used in its construction, it can be examined relative to the internal, intrasite comparison between various areas of a site. Given an undisturbed site it might be assumed that the scatter of midden associated with a ruin mirrors the garbage disposal practices of the occupants. If extensive postoccupation disturbance has occurred around an historic ruin to alter this record, an invalid interpretation may well result unless the archeologist carefully reveals, identifies, and interprets the strata, features, layers, and levels with which he is working relative to the artifacts and the cultural and noncultural formation processes that have produced that record (Schiffer and Rathje 1973).

The Brunswick Town Public House–Tailor Shop (S25) ruin is an ideal one to use in such an examination of the intrasite stability of the Carolina Artifact Pattern because it has seen little disturbance through subsequent occupation since it was destroyed by fire in 1776. Consequently we might expect the artifacts to be positioned as the result of uses by the occupants of the structure from ca. 1732 to 1776. From a distribution of ceramics throughout the area of the S25 ruin it is seen (Figure 26) that there was a dramatic contrast between the scatter of ceramics and associated midden in the front yard of the structure as compared with the major deposit of midden found behind the building, clearly reflecting the garbage disposal behavior patterns of the occupants.

We are interested in learning about the artifact frequency relationships that exist between the groups of artifact classes composing the

TABLE 7

The Carolina Artifact Pattern

Artifact group	Mean %	% Range
Kitchen	63.1	51.8–69.2
Architecture	25.5	19.7–31.4
Furniture	.2	.1– .6
Arms	.5	.1– 1.2
Clothing	3.0	.6– 5.4
Personal	.2	.1– .5
Tobacco Pipes	5.8	1.8–13.9
Activities	1.7	.9– 2.7
	100.0	

refuse deposited in such a differential manner around this ruin. We might expect this difference in the quantity of midden from the front to the rear of the ruin to possibly reflect differences in the kinds of behavior conducted in these areas. If, however, the relationship between groups of by-products was behaviorally dictated in a rigid manner, and if over a period of years a general deposit representing a range of activities accumulated around a structure as well as in a nearby midden deposit, we would expect the frequency relationships between artifact groups in any area to remain relatively stable as a result. In order to compare the front with the rear at the S25 ruin in relation to the Carolina Artifact Pattern we will examine the *Kitchen* and *Architecture* groups from eight squares in the front yard of the ruin and three midden deposit squares (16–18) at the rear of the structure. This comparison is made in the following (Table 8).

From this table it becomes apparent that there is little difference between the *Kitchen* and *Architecture* groups' percentages from the front and the rear of the Public House–Tailor Shop (S25), and these vary little from the total adjusted ruin figures or from the Carolina Artifact Pattern at the individual square level; however, some differences are to be seen. Squares 3, 4, and 5 fit the range of the Carolina Artifact Pattern, with Squares 1 and 6 falling outside the predicted range. However, 1 and 6 fall within the 95% confidence interval for binomal distribution (Steel and Torrie 1960: 456–457), and can thus be considered as being within the expected range for the Carolina Artifact Pattern, the apparent lack of fit being attributable to the low artifact counts involved in these squares.

The only square falling outside the range of the Carolina Artifact Pattern and outside the 95% confidence interval for binomal distribution, is Square 7 and 8, having a total artifact count of only 33. However, when

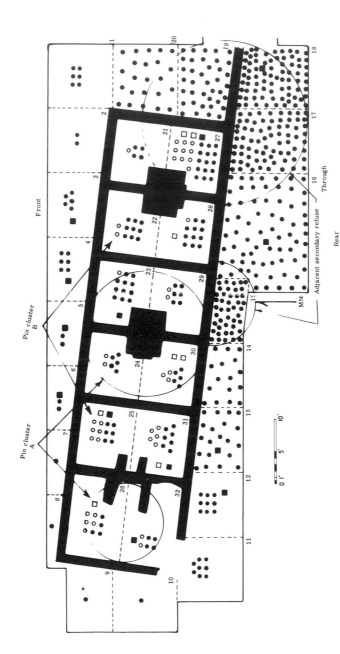

Figure 26. Plan of the Public House—Tailor Shop—Ceramic distribution (S 25, Brunswick Town, N.C., ca. 1732–1776). Ceramics through Creamware ● ○ Pearlware plus ■ □ (solid symbols are total from yard and below burned floor joints, (open symbols are above joists); symbol = 1-25 frequency.

TABLE 8

Comparison of the *Kitchen* **and** *Architecture Groups* **at the Brunswick Public-House–Tailor Shop (S25) to Determine the Degree of Intrasite Stability**

Group	Sq. 1	Sq. 2	Sq. 3	Sq. 4	Sq. 5	Sq. 6	Sq. 7 and 8	
Squares in the Front Yard of the Public House–Tailor Shop (S25) at Brunswick Town, N.C.								
Kitchen	70.8	29.8	65.7	66.6	66.7	80.4	87.9	
Architecture	21.3	64.9	24.3	24.7	18.7	11.7	12.1	
Total %	92.1	94.7	90.0	91.3	85.4	92.1	100.0	
Artifact count	221	194	215	244	64	47	33	Total: 1018
Number of Artifact classes Represented in the Sample	12	11	18	16	11	9	3	

	Percentage for the total of the above 8 squares at Brunswick Town S25		
Kitchen	61.8	686	
Architecture	29.9	332	Number of artifact classes represented in the total sample: 25
Total %	91.7		
Artifact count		1018	

	Squares in the Rear Midden Area of the Public House–Tailor Shop (S25), Brunswick Town		
	Squares 16–18 combined		
Kitchen	62.1	8427	
Architecture	25.2	3423	Number of artifact classes represented in the total sample: 34
Total %	87.3		
Artifact count		11,850	

	Percentage for all artifacts from the Public House–Tailor Shop (S25) (adjusted for tailoring)		
Kitchen	61.1	22,479	
Architecture	26.2	9620	Number of artifact classes represented in the total sample: 39
Total %	87.3		
Artifact count		32,099	

	Percentage for these groups for the Carolina Artifact Pattern		
Kitchen	63.1	47,521	
Architecture	25.5	20,596	Number of artifact classes represented in the total sample: 41
	88.6		
Artifact count		68,117	

all data from this area are combined, the result is within the predicted range for the Carolina Artifact Pattern, and close to the mean.

The implications of this examination are interesting in that regardless of the quantity of midden deposited around the ruin, the relationships seen in the Carolina Artifact Pattern are maintained. This outcome suggests that in midden deposits scattered around a ruin over a period of years a generalizing process is in effect resulting in similar artifact ratios at the level of the artifact group with which we are dealing. This situation opens possibilities for sampling of historic site ruins, with the sample seen to reveal the same basic artifact ratios as those resulting from the use of all artifacts recovered from the ruin, regardless of the concentration of midden involved. This finding suggests that only areas of specialized activity are likely to reveal profiles deviating from the general site relationships. Many more such examples will need to be explored before reliable strategies are in hand for partial, as opposed to total, excavation. It is through such quantification analyses as this that a body of reliable data can be accumulated on which prediction can be based.

It should be kept in mind that we are dealing with artifact group relationships, a generalized level of analysis designed to define broad regularities. At the artifact class level, far more variability can be expected, and specific areas of specialized activity can very likely be defined through pattern recognition. The scatter of nails around a ruin as opposed to the scatter of ceramic or wine bottle fragments may well reveal dramatic contrasts not reflected at the artifact group level of analysis.

The earlier examination of the Carolina Artifact Pattern frequency relationships (Table 8) has revealed considerable stability within a site (S25), from the level of the 10-foot square containing fewer than 100 artifacts, to areas of the site with 1000 artifacts, to midden deposits with 10,000 artifacts, to the entire ruin with more than 30,000 artifacts, all of which closely relate to the Carolina Artifact Pattern frequencies based on more than 68,000 artifacts. This stability throughout the various levels of generalization from the 10-foot square to five Carolina sites scattered over hundreds of miles in space, within 100 years in time, suggests that the regularity demonstrated here is of no fickle nature but reflects a basic patterning resulting from patterned human behavior in the British colonial system.

Identification of Activity Variability Through Contrast with the Carolina Artifact Pattern

In the earlier examination of intrasite stability, only the front and rear yard areas of the Public House–Tailor Shop (S25) were compared with the Carolina Artifact Pattern and found to be in conformity with it. In this examination of the patterned relationships we will use Squares 22 through 26, these being the northern half of the rooms from which the many tailoring objects were recovered. These data are seen in the following (Table 9).

TABLE 9

Comparison of Areas at the Public House-Tailor Shop (S25) at Brunswick Town for Identification of Activity Variability through Artifact Group Frequencies

	(Sq. 1–8) front yard	(Sq. 16–18) rear midden	(Sq. 22–26) inside rooms	(All squares) total ruin	Carolina Pattern	S25 Adjusted Profile
						****
Kitchen	61.8	62.1	21.3	52.9	63.1	61.1
Architecture	29.9	25.2	16.7	22.6	25.5	26.2
Furniture	.4	.3	.1	.2	.2	.2
Arms	.2	.3	11.1*	3.0	.5	.1
Clothing	1.0	.7	45.8**	13.1***	3.0	3.0
Personal	—	.1	.2	.2	.2	.2
Tobacco Pipes	4.8	8.9	3.6	6.7	5.8	7.7
Activities	1.9	2.4	1.2	1.3	1.7	1.5
	100.0	100.0	100.0	100.0	100.0	100.0

    * The high percentage of shot inside the rooms increases with the dramatic increase in *Clothing* group artifacts, suggesting a function relating to clothing manufacture.

    ** The contrast between the frequency of *Clothing* group artifacts inside the rooms with the frequency seen to the front and rear of the ruin, reveals the activity (tailoring) carried on inside this structure in contrast to the occupation "norm" profile outside the ruin, thus pinpointing the specific area of the specialized tailoring activity on the site.

    *** When the frequencies for outside the ruin are combined with those from inside for a combined ruin total, the *Arms* and *Clothing* groups still are revealed as contrasting variables when compared with the Carolina Artifact Pattern.

    **** When the artifact profile is adjusted by removing the small shot from the *Arms* group, and adjusting the *Clothing* group to the 3.0% level based on the frequencies for the other four model sites, the Adjusted Artifact Profile closely matches the profiles for the area outside the ruin, as well as the Carolina Artifact Pattern.

This table reveals a contrast between Squares 22–26 inside the ruin and those in the yard outside the structure. This area inside the ruin is at marked variance with the percentage relationships for the Carolina Pattern, 45.8% of all artifacts being in the *Clothing* group. This lack of conformity to the Carolina Artifact Pattern reflects the specialized activity revealed by the tailoring by-products inside these rooms. Note that the front and rear yard *Clothing* and *Arms* groups do not reflect more than normal frequencies. The high percentage of shot inside the rooms increases with the dramatic increase in *Clothing* group artifacts, suggesting a function relating to tailoring for these objects. If the shot is related to a nontailoring function there is no evidence here to suggest such an interpretation.

When the total artifact count for the entire ruin is used, the high ratio of tailoring objects inside the ruin makes an impact on the resulting profile, revealing *Arms* and *Clothing* as significant variables in contrast with the Carolina Artifact Pattern. The model has thus revealed that this ruin represents a specialized activity (tailoring), and when various areas of the site are compared as we have done here, the interior of the structure is seen as the specific area involved in this activity, whereas the area of the yard and the midden deposit reflects no such specialization.

With comparative data such as these available, archeologists should be better equipped to interpret the tailoring objects they recover from historic ruins. They will be able to know that from the empirical range of the Carolina Artifact Pattern, their *Clothing* group should fall somewhere between .6 and 5.4% of all artifact groups for "normal" activity, but if their Clothing group percentage falls above the limit of the Carolina Pattern, interpretive statements regarding specialized tailoring activity may well be made. Without such control of the data they may well suggest that the "large number" of buttons and pins, scissors, thimbles, etc. recovered from the ruin reveal specialized tailoring activity, but such subjective statements will become increasingly suspect as others ask of the data, "What percentage does this 'large number' represent relative to other artifact groups?" If the answer is within the .6% to 5.4% range of the Carolina Artifact Pattern there is no basis on which to suggest that the "large number" should be interpreted as specialized behavioral activity in the past cultural system. The Carolina Pattern should be particularly useful in those borderline cases when the archeologist has difficulty determining whether there is a more than "normal" tailoring activity or not. The S25 Brunswick ruin was dramatically revealed as a tailor shop, even by subjective standards. Others may not be so obvious, and here the Carolina Pattern should be of particular value.

It is through the use of syntheses such as the Carolina Artifact Pattern that reliable statements can begin to be made about human activity in the past from the patterning observed by archeologists. Until such abstracting of patterns is a primary concern of archeologists, the statements emerging from excavators of archeological sites will continue to be oriented toward the specific, the unique, the artistic, and particularistic, projected through the lens of subjectivity.

TESTING THE CAROLINA ARTIFACT PATTERN

The degree to which the Carolina Artifact Pattern is to be seen throughout the area dominated by British colonial culture can be determined by turning to the reports from such sites having complete artifact lists and there finding the percentages for the artifact groups in the Carolina Pattern. Unfortunately such reports are difficult to find. Many reports deal only with the outstanding artifacts recovered from the site, whereas others concentrate on those unique and rare items, emphasizing description, origin, maker, and the period of manufacture. Others discuss trade routes and other implications of the artifact data.

In spite of the fact that some agencies have been involved in excavating historic sites for decades, little data exist with which to make comparison using the Carolina Artifact Pattern, due to an approach based on an antiquantification attitude. Such programs usually emphasize the quality of past lifeways through listing of individual specimens or groups of specimens, with no concern for how many fragments of each class of artifact are present, the concern being with reconstructing whole forms by fastening fragments together. This approach is antithetic to that used in constructing the Carolina Artifact Pattern, and unfortunately it has dominated the field of historical archeology to the extent that rarely does an historical archeologist address himself to a systematic statement of the frequency relationships existing between artifact classes and groups. This is in spite of the fact that he cannot help but observe that in site after site he finds that ceramics and wine bottles make up the bulk of his data, and that of the 40 or so artifact classes with which he deals, 8 kitchen-related classes invariably constitute from one-half to two-thirds of all artifacts when frequency of fragments is used as a means of comparison.

With an antiquantification bias, however, one doesn't ask questions that can be answered only through quantification studies. Some agencies have been excavating historic sites for decades and have produced no quantification studies of their own, yet they will not allow such studies of their data to be undertaken by others. This "dog in the manger" attitude is regrettable when we are concerned about potentiallly valuable archeological information.

From the above comments it should be apparent that the search for data comparable to the five sites in the Carolina Artifact Pattern was not one productive of a great deal of success. If such data are around I hope they will be compared with the Carolina Artifact Pattern or other patterns delineated here for helping to define the perimeters as well as the nationalistic, ethnic, and behaviorally dictated limitations these patterns may have.

One body of useful archeological data was discovered in Edward Jelks' report on his excavations at Signal Hill, Newfoundland (1973). A problem with this report is that it offered an ideal opportunity for conducting quantification analyses, but none were conducted. The artifacts from various ruins and areas of the site were tabulated, and thus offered an opportunity for comparison with the data from the Carolina Artifact Pattern. This report came as a refreshing contrast to so many historical archeology reports in that it was apparent that Jelks believed that quantification was a necessary step in the archeological process, and because of this a comparison with my data could be made. There were problems to be ironed out, but these posed no major obstacle; rather, they allowed for the testing of a concept of projection or simulation of missing data based on the Carolina Artifact Pattern.

Testing the Carolina Artifact Pattern with Data from Signal Hill, Newfoundland

If the artifact group relationships from the ca. 1800–1860 military occupation at Signal Hill, Newfoundland, were found to fall within the empirical range of the Carolina Artifact Pattern its applicability could be expanded 40 years beyond the data from which the pattern was derived. This later time for the Signal Hill data might well result, however, in a lack of conformity with the Carolina Pattern, perhaps suggesting temporal limits in the nineteenth century. If such were the case, however, a major change in cultural behavior affecting the artifact relationships would be seen as likely responsible for any major disconformity in the artifact groups.

Two major Signal Hill, Newfoundland, ruins were chosen for testing against the Carolina Pattern, the Lower Queen's Battery Area, and Structure 11 (Jelks 1973: 102, 114). A third test was the use of the entire artifact collection from all ruins at the Signal Hill Site.

1. Signal Hill, Newfoundland, Lower Queen's Battery Area, ca. 1800–1860. Excavated by Edward B. Jelks in 1965–1966 (Jelks 1973). British colonial military site. Referred to here as Signal Hill 4 (from Jelks' Table 4).
2. Signal Hill, Newfoundland, Structure 11, ca. 1800–1860. Excavated by Edward B. Jelks in 1965–1966 (Jelks 1973). British colonial military site. Referred to here as Signal Hill 9 (from Jelks' Table 9).
3. Signal Hill, Newfoundland, ruins represented by Jelks' Table 4 through 10. ca. 1800–1860. Excavated by Edward B. Jelks in 1965–1966 (Jelks 1973). British colonial military site. Referred to here as Total Signal Hill.

Rather than itemizing the case bottles, and pharmaceutical bottles as was done with my data, Jelks had a classification he termed "Miscellaneous Bottles," and this was assigned to my Class 5. Rather than having separate classification for tumblers, dishes, stemmed glass, etc., Jelks used a term "Miscellaneous Glass," and I have placed this tabulation under my Class 6. There was an absence of Class 8 (Kitchenware) in the Signal Hill inventories, and these may have been placed by Jelks under Class 40 (Miscellaneous Hardware). These details posed no major problem, the only effect being perhaps to decrease the *Kitchen* group percentage and to raise the *Activities* group percentage slightly.

Adjusting the Signal Hill, Newfoundland Data for the Absence of Nails

A major problem was posed by the total absence of any listing of nails from the Signal Hill site. Nails are a major Architectural group class, along with window glass, and their absence would seriously affect the results of any comparison with the Carolina Pattern, producing an *Architecture* group percentage that was artifically low. The question arose as to whether nails were indeed used at Signal Hill, or whether this was the result of a lack of data recovery techniques sufficiently rigorous to recover nails (which would have posed serious difficulties in using any of this data), or whether this was the result of an attitude that nails were relatively unimportant. It seemed that the mass of nails usually recovered from an historic site would eliminate the possibility of their merely having been overlooked in the tabulation of artifacts.

An answer as to the case of the missing nails was needed before the Signal Hill data could be considered as comparable to that upon which the Carolina Pattern was based. On checking with the curators of the artifacts from Signal Hill it was learned that there were indeed nails there, several boxes of them, but they had never been cataloged or counted. The problem then became one of either asking for a count of nails, or devising a means of projecting a nail count into the Signal Hill data that would have a reasonable expectation of being in the neighborhood of a count of those nails actually recovered. Such an answer was found in the ratio between nails and the total for the Architecture group for the five sites used in the Carolina Pattern.

The ratio between nails and the total artifact count for the *Architecture* group for the five Carolina Pattern sites was determined, and the average ratio was found to be 82.8% for nails, with 17.2% remaining for other architectural artifacts. This was done as follows:

Class 11	S25	S10	96	Ft.M. (A)	Ft.M. (B)	Average %
Nails	8095	3098	3707	1398	302	
	$\frac{8095}{9620} = 84.1$	$\frac{3098}{4116} = 75.3$	$\frac{3707}{5006} = 74.1$	$\frac{1398}{1510} = 92.6$	$\frac{302}{344} = 87.8$	82.8
Architecture group total	9620	4116	5006	1510	344	
Nails (X)	= 82.8					
Other	= 17.2					
	100.0					

Using this information based on the ratios from the Carolina Pattern the projected nail count can be inserted into the Signal Hill data. If the Signal Hill data are dramatically at odds with the Carolina Pattern, this projection of nails based on the Carolina Pattern will not alter that fact. If, however, the Signal Hill relationships between artifact groups are much the same as those from the Carolina Pattern, the insertion of this projected nail count will merely allow this similarity to be properly reflected.

Determining the projected Nail count for Signal Hill #4 (Queen's Battery Area)

Projected Nail count = X= 82.8   17.2X = 82.8(180)
Other =   180   = 17.2   17.2X = 14904
                                              X = 866 (projected Nail count)

Determining the projected Nail count for Signal Hill #9 (Structure 11)

Projected Nail count = X= 82.8   17.2X = 82.8(324)
Other =   324   = 17.2   17.2X = 26827
                                              X = 1560 (projected Nail count)

Determining the projected Nail count for the total Signal Hill site

Projected Nail count = X= 82.8   17.2X = 82.8(1103)
Other = 1103   = 17.2   17.2X = 91328
                                              X = 5310 (projected Nail count)

Comparison of the Signal Hill, Newfoundland, Data with the Carolina Pattern

With the projected nail count for the three sets of data from Signal Hill in hand, a comparison of percentages for the artifact groups can be made with the Carolina Pattern means and its empirical ranges (Table 10).

From this comparative test of the Carolina Pattern against data from other British colonial ruins at Signal Hill, Newfoundland, it is quite apparent that the pattern is correctly predictive of artifact group ratios at Signal Hill within the range of the sites used to abstract the pattern. When the total artifact data from Signal Hill is used the *Activities* group is seen to be .2% higher than the pattern range. When the *Activities* group classes are examined to determine the possible cause for this slight increase over the expected, the 58 bone button blanks of Class 41, or the 70 military objects of Class 42, or the 89 toys of Class 33 are likely variables involved in this increase. If either of these is removed from the total for the *Activities* group, or if all three are removed, the new percentage in any case falls within the predicted pattern range.

The point here is that the Carolina Pattern has acted to focus attention of the archeologist on the artifact classes within the *Activities* group, allowing him to state from artifact relationships alone that this site is somewhat different from the Carolina Pattern possibly with regard to military activity, a bone button disc "industry", or the activity of children. He will know that in other classes of artifacts the Signal Hill data are not unique at all compared to the Carolina Pattern. Eventually

TABLE 10

Comparison of the Signal Hill Artifact Profiles with the Carolina Pattern

Artifact group	Signal Hill		Carolina Pattern		% deviation from Carolina Pattern Range
	Count	%	Mean	Range	
Comparison of the Signal Hill #4 (Lower Queen's Battery) with the Carolina Artifact Pattern					
Kitchen	3188	63.2	63.1	51.8–69.2	0
Architecture	180				
Projected Nails	(866) 1046	20.7	25.5	19.7–31.4	0
Furniture	—	—	.2	.1– .6	−.1
Arms	23	.5	.5	.1– 1.2	0
Clothing	59	1.2	3.0	.6– 5.4	0
Personal	8	.2	.2	.1– .5	0
Tobacco Pipes	605	12.0	5.8	1.8–13.9	0
Activities	116	2.2	1.7	.9– 2.7	0
	5045	100.0	100.0		
Comparison of the Signal Hill 9 (Structure 11) with the Carolina Artifact Pattern					
Kitchen	5795	61.3	63.1	51.8–69.2	0
Architecture	324				
Projected Nails	(1560) 1884	19.9	25.5	19.7–31.4	0
Furniture	—	—	.2	.1– .6	−.1
Arms	5	.1	.5	.1– 1.2	0
Clothing	443	4.7	3.0	.6– 5.4	0
Personal	11	.1	.2	.1– .5	0
Tobacco Pipes	1082	11.5	5.8	1.8–13.9	0
Activities	228	2.4	1.7	.9– 2.7	0
	9448	100.0	100.0		
Comparison of the total Signal Hill Data (Jelks' Tables 4–10) with the Carolina Artifact Pattern					
Kitchen	14188	57.2	63.1	51.8–69.2	0
Architecture	1103				
Projected Nails	(5310) 6413	25.8	25.5	19.7–31.4	0
Furniture	—	—	.2	.1– .6	−.1
Arms	57	.2	.5	.1– 1.2	0
Clothing	652	2.6	3.0	.6– 5.4	0
Personal	36	.1	.2	.1– .5	0
Tobacco Pipes	2762	11.1	5.8	1.8–13.9	0
Activities	720	2.9	1.7	.9– 2.7	+.2
	24828	100.0			

he may, through a specific frequency relationship study of the toys, button blanks, and military insignia compared with those from other sites, pinpoint the specific class of artifacts most deviant and therefore most functionally unique to the occupants of Signal Hill. Without the Carolina Pattern of similar synthesized data, he would have little reliable means of making a suggestion that one artifact class might reflect activity beyond expected margins for similar sites of the period.

THE APPLICABLE RANGE OF THE CAROLINA ARTIFACT PATTERN

The successful fit of the Signal Hill, Newfoundland, data to the Carolina Pattern suggests applicability for British colonial sites far beyond those on which the pattern was derived. Skeptics may well argue that five sites are far too few on which to base such a model, and three sets of data from a single site are certainly not sufficient proof of the stability of the patterning seen. I agree that more data are certainly needed, but it is also apparent to me that the behavioral regularities revealed by the patterned by-products from these eight sites do not represent eight "coincidences." It is also apparent that all British colonial sites will not be seen to fit the empirical ranges proscribed by the Carolina Pattern. This being the case, we certainly would like to know within what ranges future data might be expected to fall. The best way to answer this question is to deal with artifact group relationships as we have done here for comparison with the Carolina Pattern with a view of determining which types of sites fit the empirical ranges of the pattern and which do not. Broad predictions based on the eight cases examined here would certainly not be wise. However, we can predict the ranges within which there is a 95% chance that the *next* set of data might fall. Using the data from the Carolina Pattern plus the two Signal Hill ruins, I used the following formula derived from Mendenhall (1971: 275–276). The example here is for the *Kitchen Artifact* group. In using this formula we are assuming that the normal distribution approximates the binomal data with which we are working, since we are using large samples.

$$\bar{X} \pm t_{.05} \; \sigma \sqrt{1 + \frac{1}{n}}$$

where

$\bar{X}$ = % mean for the artifact group (62.8)
$t_{.05}$ = 2.447 (df = 6 for the 7 sites) (Hodgman 1960: 251)
σ = standard deviation for the artifact group
n = 7 (5 pattern sites and 2 Signal Hill ruins)

The predicted range for the *Kitchen* group can be derived as follows:

Site	Site % $- \bar{X}$ $=$	$(\bar{X} - X)$	$(\bar{X} - X)^2$
S25	61.1–62.8	−1.7	2.89
S10	51.8–62.8	−11.0	121.00
96	64.6–62.8	1.8	3.24
Ft.M. A	68.6–62.8	5.8	33.64
Ft.M. B	69.2–62.8	6.4	40.96
S.Hill 4	63.2–62.8	.4	.16
S.Hill 9	61.3–62.8	−1.5	2.25
			204.14

$$7{-}1 = 34.023 = \sigma^2$$
$$\sigma = 5.833$$

$$\bar{X} \pm t_{.05}\sigma \sqrt{1 + \frac{1}{7}}$$

$$62.8 \pm (2.447)(5.833)(1.069)$$

$$62.8 \pm 15.258$$

Predicted applicable range for the Carolina Pattern *Kitchen* group = 47.5 to 78.0.

This expands the 51.8 to 69.2 empirical range for the Carolina Pattern but provides an expected range within which there is a 95% chance the next set of data might fall. The above procedure was used for each of the artifact groups with the following results (Table 11).

Although the predicted ranges shown here are statistically related only to the next set of data, they may provide a suggested range for sites having the same patterning as the model. Only future comparative application of new data to the Carolina Pattern can determine the extent to

TABLE 11

Predicted Range for the Next Site

Artifact group	Carolina Pattern mean	Suggested range (pattern + S.Hill)	7 site mean	Standard deviation for the 7 sites
Kitchen	63.1	47.5 to 78.0	62.8	5.83
Architecture	25.5	12.9 to 35.1	24.0	4.24
Furniture	.2	0 to .7	.2	.20
Arms	.5	0 to 1.5	.4	.40
Clothing	3.0	0 to 8.5	3.0	1.96
Personal	.2	0 to .6	.2	.13
Tobacco Pipes	5.8	0 to 20.8	7.5	5.06
Activities	1.7	.1 to 3.7	1.9	.67

which this suggestion is applicable. The more narrow empirical range may well be found to be applicable to many sites or, more likely, the broader trial range suggested by the above table may correctly reflect future data.

The empirical ranges of the pattern will certainly be a more sensitive indicator for archeologists comparing their frequencies with the Carolina Pattern, and when the empirical range for any artifact group is exceeded by the new data, the archeologist should determine in what groups and classes this difference lies and what this difference means in behavioral terms. If new data fall beyond the suggested broader ranges, there is certainly more reason to expect an explanation of such variation from the Carolina Pattern. Such a difference merely means that the new data need to be examined comparatively, a prime function of the pattern. As stated earlier, the function of the Carolina Pattern is to provide a basis for comparison of future data from historic sites with the goal of identifying regularity and variability reflecting human behavior. If future data indicate that the Carolina Pattern is not correctly predictive for most eighteenth-century British colonial sites, then this will be exciting news, for to demonstrate that such is the case, the quantification analysis procedures seen here must be used and that means the Carolina Pattern will have served historical archeology well.

An ever present consideration is going to be comparability of data. The more rigorously the data are collected for obtaining a complete sample the better chance we will have of obtaining data with behavioral significance. Data not so collected can hardly be expected to offer comparability with the Carolina Artifact Pattern.

The multinomial nature of the data with which we are concerned is also a fact to be kept in mind. As one artifact group increases due to a behavioral cause, a relative decrease will occur elsewhere, and the archeologist's attention may be drawn to the decrease in some groups rather than to the increase in another caused by the variable involved. If architectural artifacts are seen to exceed those from the kitchen, does this mean an increase in architectural classes or a decrease in kitchen related artifacts; and which of the classes are involved? The Carolina Pattern should help in clarifying such situations, and this is the subject of a following chapter.

Measuring Relative Variability within the Carolina Pattern

From the ranges for the artifact groups of the Carolina Pattern, it is apparent that some artifact groups have a far greater degree of variability than others. Because we are concerned primarily with the dispersion reflected by the empirical range of the Carolina Pattern, the amount of variability within an artifact group is of interest primarily as it is seen to mirror stability or variability in the cultural system responsible for the archeological record. The determination of the coefficient of variation is useful in reflecting the standard deviation in relation to the size of the mean. If the coefficient of variation is a small percentage, the mean is evidently a representative figure and the items of the universe are closely clustered (McMillen 1952: 297–298). The coefficient of variation (V) is expressed by McMillen as follows:

$$V = \frac{\sigma}{M} \times 100$$

The coefficient of variation for the eight artifact groups for the seven sites is determined as follows (Table 12):

From these comparisons the *Kitchen* and *Architecture* groups are found to be most stable on an intersite basis for the seven sites involved. *Furniture* and *Arms* reflect a high degree of variability. This finding suggests that behavior resulting in by-products of kitchen related activities and artifacts architecturally related is far less sensitive in intersite comparisons than furniture- and arms-related by-products. Part of what we are seeing here is no doubt the difference in the quantities involved. This being the case, those groups having low frequencies will be most sensitive to small variations such as the presence or absence of two or three objects. Such groups will also be most sensitive to the lack of controlled data recovery, especially when the objects making up the group are small, such as pins, seed beads, hooks and eyes, and small shot. The small frequencies of some groups as reflected in the Carolina Pattern are, however, no less important as reflectors of past behavior than those groups having greater quantities. The small ranges revealed by the Carolina Pattern for some groups are realities for which the archeologist must develop the techniques for interpreting. Sensitivity to these realities will require a revolution in thinking within historical archeology.

TABLE 12

The Coefficient of Variation for 7 Sites

	σ	$\div$ M (mean)	$\times$ 100	=	V (coefficient of variation)
Kitchen	5.83	62.8	$\times$ 100	=	9.28
Architecture	4.24	24.0	$\times$ 100	=	17.67
Furniture	.20	.2	$\times$ 100	=	100.00
Arms	.40	.4	$\times$ 100	=	100.00
Clothing	1.96	3.0	$\times$ 100	=	65.33
Personal	.13	.2	$\times$ 100	=	65.00
Tobacco Pipes	5.06	7.5	$\times$ 100	=	67.67
Activities	.67	1.9	$\times$ 100	=	35.26

A Law of Behavioral By-Product Regularity

The patterned regularity in the by-products of human behavior has been demonstrated through the Carolina Pattern, reflecting a uniformity in eighteenth-century British colonial behavior on the sites studied. This demonstration of regularity in artifact-group frequency proportions is contrasted with variability reflecting specialized behavioral activities such as military activity, a bone button "industry," contact with Indians, and a tailor shop. The demonstration of this regularity and variability has illustrated the process of pattern recognition through quantification, a major goal of this chapter.

The expression of the regularities seen in the Carolina Pattern can be seen as an empirical generalization in the form of a law of behavioral by-product regularity, constituting a basic assumption of this study.

A Law of Behavioral By-Product Regularity: The by-product of a specified activity has a consistent frequency relationship to that of all other activities in direct proportion to their organized integration.

A specific example of the relationship between the by-products of a specified activity and the level of organized integration can be seen in the following examination of floor space in relation to *Architecture* group artifacts.

The Relationship of Floor Space to Architecture Group Artifacts

The by-product regularity predicted by the above law should certainly be revealed when the architecturally related artifacts with which a structure is fastened together are compared with artifacts from similar structures. This assumes a generally uniform quantity of nails, hinges, spikes, glass, etc., would be involved in relation to the size of the structure.

The Brunswick Town, N.C., ruins we have used in this study have a similar occupation history and were all burned at the same time, in 1776. They also have the comparative advantage of having stone foundations, and therefore the square footage for each ruin can be determined. Due to these similarities the three Brunswick Town ruins appeared to offer an ideal opportunity to test these ideas. Since virtually all artifacts were recovered and the square footage of the ruins was known, the ratio of square footage to *Architectural* group artifacts was hypothesized to fall within a narrow range if the assumed patterning was indeed present. The following (Table 13) illustrates the ratios involved.

The similarity of these ratios certainly suggests that there is some validity to the proposition of a patterned relationship between the artifacts with which a structure is put together and the size of that structure. Since archeologists deal with the remains of structures, among

TABLE 13

The Ratio of Floor Space to *Architecture* Group Artifacts from Three Ruins at Brunswick Town, N.C.

Hepburn-Reonalds House (S7)	Public House–Tailor Shop (S25)	Nath Moore's Front (S10)
(2-room cellar and porch)	(6-room row house style)	(2-room cellar and porch)
Floor space (sq. ft.) $\div$ $\dfrac{Architecture}{\text{group total}}$ = Ratio	Floor space (sq. ft.) $\div$ $\dfrac{Architecture}{\text{group total}}$ = Ratio	Floor space (sq. ft.) $\div$ $\dfrac{Architecture}{\text{group total}}$ = Ratio
638 $\div$ 3953 = (.16)	1400 $\div$ 9620 = (.15)	726 $\div$ 4116 = (.18)

S7 = .16
S25 = .15
S10 = .18

which are the architectural hardware from the building, they should be concerned with such ratios. Under properly controlled conditions of data recovery it is conceivable that prediction as to the size of a structure (and thereby to the number of occupants it may have held) can eventually be made from *Architecture* group artifact frequencies *in the absence of architectural data revealing the size of the structure!* Such are the avenues opening to the archeologist who bases his research on concepts such as those outlined here.

If quantification data were available for all the historic sites excavated during the past quarter of a century in Virginia, Maryland, Pennsylvania, Florida, and elsewhere, a massive body of data would be in hand for comparison with the Carolina Pattern. For example, if systematic quantification of data from excavations in Virginia had been carried out, a "Virginia Pattern" for seventeenth- and eighteenth-century sites could easily be delineated as we have done for the Carolina Pattern, but such an approach was not used, and therefore this valuable data may never be available. The fact that British colonial sites of the same time period exhibit great regularity in their artifact relationships "from Montserrat to Michigan" (Noël Hume 1973: vii) has been recognized but has not been archeologically demonstrated through quantification analysis delineating this pattern. Other archeologists must either accept such observations on faith, as religious dogma must be accepted on faith through reference to "authority," or await a time when scientific archeology is applied to sites in order for a "Virginia Pattern" to be defined for comparison with the Carolina Pattern. The same can be said regarding historical archeology done in other states as well, relative to a "Pennsylvania Pattern," a "Maryland Pattern," or a "Florida Pattern." Some of these areas have had archeologists who are antiquantification in attitude, while some have overtly supported quantification analysis but have failed to delineate pattern. As regrettable as the data comparison gap is in historical archeology, the light of scientific archeology is beginning to break through cracks in the particularistic barrier to understanding. The revolution toward the use of the scientific cycle in archeological research on historic sites has begun, and as a result more comparable data will begin to surface.

The question remains as to what type of sites will fall into the predicted range of the Carolina Pattern. The pattern was derived from sites both domestic and military in nature, and they have in common the fact that they are in the mainstream of a colonial cultural system. That system was British colonial in origin, even though the Cambridge and Brunswick S10 ruins contain materials dating to 1830. The application of the pattern to the Signal Hill data suggests that the phenomena we are dealing with is certainly not limited to the Carolina area from which the pattern was derived, and that its temporal applicability extends at least as late as ca. 1860.

Explanation of *why* the Carolina Pattern exists on British colonial sites is to be found in the examination of hypotheses directed at cultural processes in the British colonial system. These hypotheses would focus on questions such as the logistics of the British distributive system, the production system, discouragement or encouragement of colonial manufacture and self-sufficiency by the British power structure, British expansionist and empire-building policies, status-enforcing rituals, and role-regulating mechanisms. The archeological patterning resulting from such processes would be expected to vary between British-American, German-American, French-American and Spanish-American occupations, reflecting variability in these cultural systems. Patterning would also vary with the functional role of the site in the social system. The role of historical documentation in controlling these and other variables while archeological pattern is defined and compared is the major role of the historical record in the future of historical archeology. By controlling for variability relating to national origin, distributive systems, status, and function through documents providing the basis for classification of historic sites, and then delineating the patterns from such sites through archeology, we will eventually develop the ability to interpret cultural processes from historic site patterns without dependence on historical control. When we achieve this level of archeological sophistication we can apply this knowledge to sites for which there is no historical control—prehistoric sites, for instance. This is the exciting promise historical archeology holds for the future: this potential for contributing to method refinement and theory building in archeology generally.

During the delineation and testing of the Carolina Pattern a serious violation of the ranges predicted by the pattern was found to occur with some sites for which comparable data were available. This deviation was seen in three frontier sites of the French and Indian War Period, far removed from the established sources of supply such as characterized Brunswick, Fort Moultrie (Charleston), and Cambridge, from which the Carolina Pattern was derived. These sites were therefore used to define a Frontier Pattern, which contrasts dramatically with the Carolina Pattern. This Frontier Pattern and the variables relating to it are the subject of the next chapter.

APPENDIX

The artifact class frequencies for the Carolina Pattern are included here for use in comparative studies.

Artifact Class Frequencies

Artifact class no. and description	Brunswick (S25) Site		Brunswick (S10) Site		Brunswick (S7) Site	
	Count	%	Count	%	Count	%
Kitchen group						
1. Ceramics	16,288		4618		2521	
2. Wine Bottle	3895		1753		841	
3. Case Bottle	445		29		56	
4. Tumbler	768		100		190	
5. Pharmaceutical	473		45		35	
6. Glassware	431		191		38	
7. Tableware	122		35		11	
8. Kitchenware	57		24		10	
Total *Kitchen*	22,479	52.9	6795	51.8	3702	45.2
9. Bone	(5497)		(519)		(222)	
Architecture group						
10. Window Glass	1261		838		1396	
11. Nails	8095		3098		2466	
12. Spikes	162		123		50	
13. Construction Hdwe.	78		52		35	
14. Door Lock Parts	24		5		6	
Total *Architecture*	9620	22.6	4116	31.4	3953	48.3
15. *Furniture* group	83	.2	82	.6	18	.2
Arms group						
16. Balls, Shot, Sprue	1228		13		11	
17. Gunflints, Spalls	22		17		1	
18. Gun Parts	12		15		—	
Total *Arms*	1262	3.0	45	.3	12	.1
Clothing group						
19. Buckles	62		16		14	
20. Thimbles	16		1		—	
21. Buttons	225		43		7	
22. Scissors	33		2		1	
23. Straight Pins	4398		3		—	
24. Hook and Eye	9		2		—	
25. Bale Seals	4		2		—	
26. Glass Beads	827		3		2	
Total *Clothing*	5574	13.1	72	.6	24	.3

Artifact Class Frequencies   (Continued)

Artifact class no. and description	Brunswick (S25) Site		Brunswick (S10) Site		Brunswick (S7) Site	
	Count	%	Count	%	Count	%
Personal group						
27. Coins	29		7		3	
28. Keys	14		3		1	
29. Personal	28		10		—	
Total *Personal*	71	.2	20	.2	4	.1
30. *Tobacco pipe* group	2830	6.7	1829	13.9	374	4.6
Activities group						
31. Construction Tools	13		13		8	
32. Farm Tools	6		3		—	
33. Toys	11		9		1	
34. Fishing Gear	6		3		1	
35. Stub-stemmed Pipes	1		9		—	
36. Colono-Indian Pottery	231		—		12	
37. Storage Items	158		40		53	
38. Botanical	9		4		4	
39. Horse Tack	3		10		2	
40. Misc. Hardware	140		68		15	
41. Other	—		—		—	
42. Military Objects	—				—	
Total *Activities*	578	1.3	159	1.2	96	1.2
TOTAL (without Bone)	42,497	100.0	13,118	100.0	8183	100.0

Artifact Class Frequencies

Artificial class no. and description	Ft. Moultrie Site A		Ft. Moultrie Site B		Cambridge Site 96, S.C.	
	Count	%	Count	%	Count	%
Kitchen group						
1. Ceramics	1217		269		8751	
2. Wine Bottle	2213		754		2123	
3. Case Bottle	363		51		201	
4. Tumbler	114		30		714	
5. Pharmaceutical	261		87		873	
6. Glassware	3		10		57	
7. Tableware	10		4		116	
8. Kitchenware	4		3		19	
Total *Kitchen*	4185	60.1	1208	56.9	12,854	64.6
9. Bone	(4057)		(1020)		(11,187)	
Architecture group						
10. Window Glass	31		10		1189	
11. Nails	1398		302		3707	
12. Spikes	72		26		61	
13. Construction Hdwe.	9		5		34	
14. Door Lock Parts	—		1		15	
Total *Architecture*	1510	21.7	344	16.2	5006	25.2
15 *Furniture* group	6	.1	2	.1	35	.2
Arms group						
16. Balls, Shot, Sprue	11		7		12	
17. Gunflints, Spalls	26		7		9	
18. Gun Parts	2		6		6	
Total *Arms*	39	.6	20	.9	27	.1
Clothing group						
19. Buckles	10		4		40	
20. Thimbles	—		—		9	
21. Buttons	122		62		236	
22. Scissors	—		—		11	
23. Straight Pins	—		—		760	
24. Hook and Eye	2		3		—	
25. Bale Seals	2		—		1	
26. Glass Beads	—		—		12	
Total *Clothing*	136	1.9	69	3.3	1069	5.4

Artifact Class Frequencies **(Continued)**

Artificial class no. and description	Ft. Moultrie Site A		Ft. Moultrie Site B		Cambridge Site 96, S.C.	
	Count	%	Count	%	Count	%
Personal group						
27. Coins	—		—		4	
28. Keys	2		1		11	
29. Personal	2		3		93	
Total *Personal*	4	.1	4	.2	108	.5
30. *Tobacco pipe* group	167	2.4	50	2.4	349	1.8
Activities group						
31. Construction Tools	1		5		10	
32. Farm Tools	—		—		2	
33. Toys	1		—		21	
34. Fishing Gear	1		—		1	
35. Stub-stemmed Pipes	—		—		30	
36. Colono-Indian Pottery	617		141		62	
37. Storage Items	20		29		45	
38. Botanical	—		4		34	
39. Horse Tack			—		43	
40. Misc. Hardware	27		9		104	
41. Other	244		236		—	
42. Military Objects	5		1		—	
Total *Activities*	916	13.1	425	20.0	432	2.2
TOTAL (without Bone)	6963	100.0	2122	100.0	19,880	100.0

Artifact Class Frequencies

Artifact class no. and description	Signal Hill Site (4)		Signal Hill Site (9)		Signal Hill total Site (4–10)	
	Count	%	Count	%	Count	%
Kitchen group						
1. Ceramics	2548		4715		10,779	
2. Wine Bottle	439		689		2303	
3. Case Bottle	—		—		—	
4. Tumbler	—		—		—	
5. Pharmaceutical	65		190		383	
6. Glassware	131		191		691	
7. Tableware	5		10		32	
8. Kitchenware	—		—		—	
Total *Kitchen*	3188	63.2	5795	61.3	14,188	57.2
9. Bone	(??)		(??)		(??)	
Architecture group						
10. Window Glass	180		324		1103	
11. Nails (Projected/ Model)	(866)		(1560)		(5310)	
12. Spikes	—		—		—	
13. Construction Hdwe.	—		—		—	
14. Door Lock Parts	—		—		—	
Total *Architecture*	1046	20.7	1884	19.9	6413	25.8
15. *Furniture* group	—	—	—	—	—	—
Arms group						
16. Balls, Shot, Sprue	2		1		13	
17. Gunflints, Spalls	2		4		6	
18. Gun Parts	19		—		38	
Total *Arms*	23	.5	5	.1	57	
Clothing group						
19. Buckles and chin strap leaves	14		11		26	
20. Thimbles	—		—		—	
21. Buttons	45		431		625	
22. Scissors	—		—		—	
23. Straight Pins	—		—		—	
24. Hook and Eye	—		—		—	
25. Bale Seals	—		1		1	
26. Glass Beads	—		—		—	
Total *Clothing*	59	1.2	443	4.7	652	2.6

Artifact Class Frequencies **(Continued)**

Artifact class no. and description	Signal Hill Site (4)		Signal Hill Site (9)		Signal Hill total Site (4–10)	
	Count	%	Count	%	Count	%
Personal group						
27. Coins	5		2		15	
28. Keys	—		—		—	
29. Personal	3		9		21	
Total *Personal*	8	.2	11	.1	36	.1
30. *Tobacco Pipe* group	605	12.0	1082	11.5	2762	11.1
Activities group						
31. Construction Tools	—		—		—	
32. Farm Tools	—		—		—	
33. Toys	24		14		89	
34. Fishing Gear	—		—		—	
35. Stub-stemmed Pipes	—		—		—	
36. Colono-Indian Pottery	—		—		—	
37. Storage Items	—		—		—	
38. Botanical	—		—		—	
39. Horse Tack	—		—		—	
40. Misc. Hardware	85		156		503	
41. Other	—		49		58	
42. Military Objects	7		9		70	
Total *Activities*	116	2.2	228	2.4	720	2.9
TOTAL (without Bone)	5045	100.0	9448	100.0	24,828	100.0

Artifact Class Frequencies

Artifact class no. and description	Brunswick (S25) Site Square 1		Brunswick (S25) Site Square 2		Brunswick (S25) Site Square 3	
	Count	%	Count	%	Count	%
Kitchen group						
1. Ceramics	142		44		117	
2. Wine Bottle	20		13		27	
3. Case Bottle	—		1		2	
4. Tumbler	8		1		1	
5. Pharmaceutical	—		—		2	
6. Glassware	—		—		4	
7. Tableware	—		—		—	
8. Kitchenware	—		2		4	
Total *Kitchen*	170	70.8	61	29.8	157	65.7
9. Bone	(14)		(7)		(8)	
Architecture group						
10. Window Glass	6		19		15	
11. Nails	36		114		37	
12. Spikes	7		5		5	
13. Construction Hdwe.	2		—		1	
14. Door Lock Parts	—		—		0	
Total *Architecture*	51	21.3	133	64.9	58	24.3
15. *Furniture* group	—	—	—	—	2	.8
Arms group						
16. Balls, Shot, Sprue	—		—		—	
17. Gunflints, Spalls	—		—		—	
18. Gun Parts	—		—		2	
Total *Arms*	—	—	—	—	2	.8
Clothing group						
19. Buckles	—		1		—	
20. Thimbles	—		—		—	
21. Buttons	3		—		1	
22. Scissors	1		—		—	
23. Straight Pins	—		—		3	
24. Hook and Eye	—		—		—	
25. Bale Seals	—		—		—	
26. Glass Beads	—		—		—	
Total *Clothing*	4	1.7	1	.5	4	1.7

Artifact Class Frequencies   (Continued)

Artifact class no. and description	Brunswick (S25) Site Square 1		Brunswick (S25) Site Square 2		Brunswick (S25) Site Square 3	
	Count	%	Count	%	Count	%
Personal group						
27. Coins	—		—		—	
28. Keys	—		—		—	
29. Personal	—		—		—	
Total *Personal*	—	—	—	—	—	—
30. *Tobacco Pipe* group	10	4.1	7	3.4	11	4.6
Activities group						
31. Construction Tools	—		—		1	
32. Farm Tools	—		—		—	
33. Toys	—		—		—	
34. Fishing Gear	—		—		—	
35. Stub-stemmed Pipes	—		—		—	
36. Colono-Indian Pottery	2		—		—	
37. Storage Items	3		3		1	
38. Botanical	—		—		3	
39. Horse Tack	—		—			
40. Misc. Hardware	—					
41. Other	—		—		—	
42. Military Objects	—		—		—	
Total *Activities*	5	2.1	3	1.4	5	2.1
TOTAL (without Bone)	240	100.0	205	100.0	239	100.0

Artifact Class Frequencies

Artifact class no. and description	Brunswick (S25) Site Sq. 4		Brunswick (S25) Site Sq. 5		Brunswick S25 Site Sq. 6		Brunswick S25 Site Sq. 7 and 8	
	Count	%	Count	%	Count	%	Count	%
Kitchen group								
1. Ceramics	155		42		34		29	
2. Wine Bottle	6		4		4		—	
3. Case Bottle	—		—		1		—	
4. Tumbler	4		1		—		—	
5. Pharmaceutical	3		1		—		—	
6. Glassware	4		—		1		—	
7. Tableware	2		—		—		—	
8. Kitchenware	4		2		1		—	
Total *Kitchen*	178	66.6	50	66.7	41		29	87.9
9. Bone	(23)		(2)		(5)		(7)	
Architecture group								
10. Window Glass	10		3		4		—	
11. Nails	53		11		2		1	
12. Spikes	3		—		—		3	
13. Construction Hdwe.	—		—		—		—	
14. Door Lock Parts	—		—		—		—	
Total *Architecture*	66	24.7	14	18.7	6	11.7	4	12.1
15. *Furniture* group	1	.4	1	1.3	—		—	—
Arms group								
16. Balls, Shot, Sprue	—		—		—		—	
17. Gunflints, Spalls	—		—		—		—	
18. Gun Parts	—		—		—		—	
Total *Arms*	—	—	—	—	—	—	—	—
Clothing group								
19. Buckles	1		—		—		—	
20. Thimbles	—		—		—		—	
21. Buttons	—		1		—		—	
22. Scissors	—		—		—		—	
23. Straight Pins	—		—		—		—	
24. Hook and Eye	—		—		—		—	
25. Bale Seals	—		—		—		—	
26. Glass Beads	—		—		—		—	
Total *Clothing*	1	.4	1	1.3	—	—	—	—

Artifact Class Frequencies   (Continued)

Artifact class no. and description	Brunswick (S25) Site Sq. 4		Brunswick (S25) Site Sq. 5		Brunswick S25 Site Sq. 6		Brunswick S25 Site Sq. 7 and 8	
	Count	%	Count	%	Count	%	Count	%
Personal group								
27. Coins	—		—		—		—	
28. Keys	—		—		—		—	
29. Personal	—		—		—		—	
Total *Personal*	—	—	—	—	—	—	—	—
30. *Tobacco Pipe* group	16	6.0	3	5.9	3	5.9	—	—
Activities group								
31. Construction Tools	—		—		—		—	
32. Farm Tools	2		—		—		—	
33. Toys	—		—		—		—	
34. Fishing Gear	—		—		—		—	
35. Stub-stemmed Pipes	—		—		—		—	
36. Colono-Indian Pottery	—		—		—		—	
37. Storage Items	2		1		1		—	
38. Botanical	—				—		—	
39. Horse Tack	—		—		—		—	
40. Misc. Hardware	1		—		—		—	
41. Other	—		—		—		—	
42. Military Objects	—		—		—		—	
Total *Activities*	5	1.9	1	2.0	1	2.0	—	—
TOTAL (without Bone)	267	100.0	51	100.0	51	100.0	33	100.0

Artifact Class Frequencies

Artifact class no. and description	Brunswick S25 Site Front, Sq. 1–8		Brunswick S25 Site Back, Sq. 16–18		Brunswick S25 Site Inside, Sq. 22–26	
	Count	%	Count	%	Count	%
Kitchen group						
1. Ceramics	563		5477		1117	
2. Wine Bottle	74		2239		171	
3. Case Bottle	4		104		46	
4. Tumbler	15		183		67	
5. Pharmaceutical	6		159		74	
6. Glassware	9		215		21	
7. Tableware	2		32		34	
8. Kitchenware	13		18		7	
Total *Kitchen*	686	61.8	8427	62.1	1537	21.3
9. Bone	(66)		(2265)		(526)	
Architecture group						
10. Window Glass	51		811		126	
11. Nails	254		2551		1045	
12. Spikes	23		36		20	
13. Construction Hdwe.	4		15		11	
14. Door Lock Parts	—		10		4	
Total *Architecture*	332	29.9	3423	25.2	1206	16.7
15. *Furniture* group	4	.4	35	.3	10	.1
Arms group						
16. Balls, Shot, Sprue	—		29		803	
17. Gunflints, Spalls	—		12		1	
18. Gun Parts	2		2		0	
Total *Arms*	2	.2	43	.3	804	11.1
Clothing group						
19. Buckles	2		33		11	
20. Thimbles	—		4		1	
21. Buttons	5		28		57	
22. Scissors	1		3		4	
23. Straight Pins	3		23		2663	
24. Hook and Eye	—		1		6	
25. Bale Seals	—		—		—	
26. Glass Beads	—		4		570	
Total *Clothing*	11	1.0	96	.7	3312	45.8

Artifact Class Frequencies (Continued)

Artifact class no. and description	Brunswick S25 Site Front, Sq. 1–8		Brunswick S25 Site Back, Sq. 16–18		Brunswick S25 Site Inside, Sq. 22–26	
	Count	%	Count	%	Count	%
Personal group						
27. Coins	—		1		9	
28. Keys	—		—		3	
29. Personal	—		—		—	
Total *Personal*	—	—	1	.1	12	.2
30. *Tobacco Pipe* group	53	4.8	1212	8.9	260	3.6
Activities group						
31. Construction Tools	1		1		5	
32. Farm Tools	2		2		—	
33. Toys	—		2		3	
34. Fishing Gear	—		1		1	
35. Stub-stemmed Pipes	—		—		1	
36. Colono-Indian Pottery	2		132		13	
37. Storage Items	12		37		24	
38. Botanical	3		—		2	
39. Horse Tack			3		1	
40. Misc. Hardware	2		23		41	
41. Other	—		—		—	
42. Military Objects	—		—		—	
Total *Activities*	22	1.9	333	2.4	91	1.2
TOTAL (without Bone)	1110	100.0	13,570	100.0	7220	100.0

REFERENCES

Baker, Steven G.
  1972   A House on Cambridge Hill: An Excavation Report. *Research Manuscript Series No. 27*. Institute of Archeology and Anthropology, University of South Carolina, Columbia.
Binford, Lewis R.
  1962   Archaeology as Anthropology. *American Antiquity* **28** (No. 2):217–225.
Flannery, Kent V.
  1972   Culture history versus cultural process: A debate in American archaeology. In *Contemporary archaeology*, Edited by Mark P. Leone. Carbondale and Edwardsville: Southern Illinois University Press.
Hodgman, Charles D. (Editor)
  1960   *C.R.C. standard mathematical tables*. Cleveland, Ohio: Chemical Rubber Publishing Co.
Jelks, Edward B.
  1973   Archaeological Explorations at Signal Hill, Newfoundland, 1965–1966. *Occasional Papers in Archaeology and History, No. 7*. Ottawa: National Historic Sites Service, Department of Indian Affairs and Northern Development.
Kroeber, A. L.
  1952   *The nature of culture*. Chicago: University of Chicago Press.
Mendenhall, William
  1969   *Introduction to probability and statistics*. Belmont, California: Wadsworth.
  1971   *Introduction to probability and statistics. Second edition.* Belmont, California: Wadsworth.
McMillen, Wayne
  1952   *Statistical methods for social workers*. Chicago: University of Chicago Press.
Nöel Hume, Ivor
  1973   Preface—Five Artifact Studies. *Colonial Williamsburg Occasional Papers in Archaeology* **1**:vii–viii. Colonial Williamsburg Foundation. Charlottesville: University Press of Virginia.
Schiffer, Michael B.
  1972   Archaeological Context and Systemic Context. *American Antiquity* **37**:156–165.
Schiffer, Michael B., and William L. Rathje
  1973   Efficient exploitation of the archeological record: Penetrating problems. In *Research and theory in current archeology*, edited by Redman, Charles L. New York: John Wiley.
South, Stanley A.
  1958   Excavation Report, Unit S10, Lot 29, Brunswick Town, North Carolina: Nath Moore's Front 1728–1776. Manuscript on file with North Carolina Department of Cultural Resources, Raleigh.
  1959   Excavation Report, Unit S7, Lot 71, Brunswick Town, North Carolina: The Hepburn-Reonalds House 1734–1776. Manuscript on file with North Carolina Department of Cultural Resources, Raleigh.
  1960   Excavation Report, Unit S25, Lot 27, Brunswick Town, North Carolina: The Public House and Tailor Shop 1732–1776. Manuscript on file with North Carolina Department of Cultural Resources, Raleigh.
  1962   The Ceramic Types at Brunswick Town, North Carolina (1960). *Southeastern Archaeological Conference Newsletter* **9:** (No. 1):1–5.
  1968   Archaeological Evidence of Pottery Repairing. *The Conference on Historic Site Archaeology Papers 1967* **2,** Part 1:page 62.

1974   Palmetto Parapets. *Anthropological Studies No. 1*. Institute of Archeology and
       Anthropology, University of South Carolina, Columbia.
Steel, Robert G. D., and James H. Torrie
1960   *Principles and procedures of statistics*. New York: McGraw-Hill.
Steward, Julian H.
1955   *Theory of culture change*. Urbana: University of Illinois Press.

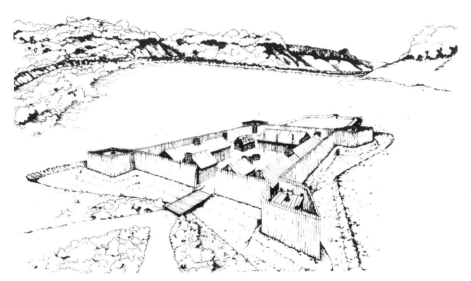

An artist's rendering of Fort Prince George, S.C.

The Frontier
Artifact Pattern

DEFINING THE PATTERN

In this chapter I will define the pattern of artifact relationships seen in three documented frontier sites, and compare this Frontier Artifact Pattern with the Carolina Artifact Pattern. I will also examine data that reveal pattern not matching either of these.

In the process of abstracting pattern from the 41 classes of artifacts used in the study, a cluster analysis was used to determine the extent to which sites were related by virtue of frequency. The computer program is known as the Hierarchical Clustering Program of the OSIRIS statistical package. The sites used were the five sites of the Carolina Pattern, plus the two Signal Hill, Newfoundland, ruins (Jelks 1973), and a Brunswick Town (S7) ruin known as the Hepburn-Reonalds House (South 1959), as well as a study of artifacts from Spalding's Lower Store (PU-23) from Putnam County, Florida (Lewis 1969).

The cluster analysis revealed that the Brunswick Town ruins S25 and S10, and the Cambridge 96 site, were related at the .94 proximity level (Figure 27). These are all domestic sites. The Fort Moultrie collections were related at the .98 proximity level, and the Signal Hill ruins were virtually identical, at a .998 level. These are all military sites, with a proximity level of .90 for all four sites. There is some suggestion here of a domestic versus a military clustering, but since both the military and domestic sites cluster at a level of .85, this was considered sufficiently high for including both types of sites in a Carolina Pattern.

The sites we are concerned with in this chapter are seen on the right in Figure 27, the Brunswick (S7) ruin, and the Spalding's Store site. These sites are related at a .97 level of proximity, but are distant from the seven

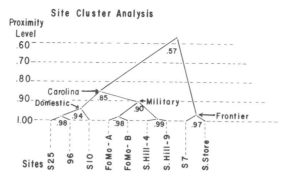

Figure 27.   Site cluster analysis.

European trade goods had a major impact on American Indians. (After a 1762 drawing by Sir Joshua Reynolds of the Cherokee Warrior Ostenaco)

other sites, related at only the .57 level. It is these sites and two others like them that we will be concerned with here, none of which fit the Carolina Pattern.

The Sites

The four sites for which data were available represent a dramatic contrast to the Carolina Pattern sites, all having an inverse ratio between the *Kitchen* and *Architecture* groups. Three of these were frontier sites dating from the 1750s and 1760s, and these were used to abstract the Frontier Pattern. A summary of the site information follows:

1. Spalding's Lower Store, Putnam County, Fla. (PU-23), ca. 1763–present. Excavated by students of John M. Goggin, and reported by Kenneth E. Lewis, Jr. in 1969 (Lewis 1969). A British trading post site.
2. Fort Ligonier, Pa., 1758–1766. Excavated by Jacob L. Grimm, 1960–1965 (Grimm 1970). A British anti-Indian fort site of the French and Indian War period.
3. Fort Prince George, S.C. (PN-1), ca. 1753–ca. 1769. Excavated by John D. Combes in 1966–1968 (Combes n.d.). A French and Indian War British anti-French fort and Cherokee trading post site.
4. Brunswick Town, N.C., The Hepburn-Reonalds House (S7), occupied ca. 1734–ca. 1776. Excavated by Stanley South in 1959 (South 1959). A two-room, combination dwelling and shop, ruin of a structure that was burned in 1776.

The Empirical Artifact Profiles

The artifact group relationships for the three frontier sites are seen in Table 14. In tabulating the Fort Ligonier data only those artifacts usually seen on archeological sites were used. The many shoes, belts, wooden objects, etc. that were recovered on this site are somewhat unusual and would have served to skew the data in a manner not comparable to the other sites with which we were dealing.

Adjusting the Fort Prince George Profile for Cherokee Pottery

From the empirical percentage relationship profiles seen here it is apparent that the most deviant percentage is that for the *Activities* group from Fort Prince George. When the artifact classes for this group are examined, the 2583 Cherokee Indian sherds are the obvious reason for this 26.4% figure. The presence of this quantity of Cherokee pottery on the site is understandable since a major function of Fort Pringe George was Indian trade (John Combes, personal communication). This being

Contrasting cultures clashed when Highlanders met the Cherokee in the French and Indian War on the Carolina Frontier.

TABLE 14

Empirical Artifact Profiles for Three Frontier Sites

	Fort Ligonier, Pa.		Fort Prince George, S.C.		Spalding's Lower Store, Fla.		
	Count	%	Count	%	Count	%	
Kitchen	5566	25.6	1679	16.8	5789	34.5	
Architecture	12,112	55.6	4252	42.6	7222	43.0	
Furniture	44	.2	6	.1	51	.3	
Arms	1820	8.4	471	4.7	227	1.4	
Clothing	833	3.8	70	.7	51	.3	
Personal	99	.4	9	.1	10	.1	
Tobacco Pipes	411	1.9	851	8.5	2343	14.0	
Activities	893	4.1	2633	26.4	1077	6.4	
	21,778	100.0	9971	100.0	16,770	100.0	Total: 48,519

TABLE 15

Adjustment for Removing Known Deviant Sample, i.e., Cherokee Pottery

	Fort Lignonier, Pa		Fort Prince George, S.C.		Spalding's Lower Store, Fla.		
	Count	%	Count	%	Count	%	
Kitchen	5566	25.6	1679	22.7	5789	34.5	
Architecture	12,112	55.6	4252	57.5	7222	43.0	
Furniture	44	.2	6	.1	51	.3	
Arms	1820	8.4	471	6.4	227	1.4	
Clothing	833	3.8	70	1.0	51	.3	
Personal	99	.4	9	.1	10	.1	
Tobacco Pipes	411	1.9	851	11.5	2343	14.0	
Activities	893	4.1	50	.7 (less no. 36)	1077	6.4	
	21,778	100.0	7388	100.0	16,770	100.0	Total: 45,936

the case, it would be unreasonable to build into a frontier model this bias for Class 36, so we will remove it. With this single adjustment the relationships shown in Table 15 are seen.

The Frontier Artifact Pattern

The Frontier Artifact Pattern can be derived by averaging the percentages for each artifact group for these three sites. The range within which there is a 95% chance of the next set of data falling is then determined (Mendenhall 1971: 275–276). Only three sites are involved, and the range was found to be far larger than that seen for the Carolina Pattern (see Table 16).

TABLE 16

Adjusted Frontier Pattern Mean and Range, with Standard Deviation and Predicted Range for the Next Site

Artifact group	Mean %	Pattern range %	σ	Predicted range (95%)
Kitchen	27.6	22.7–34.5	6.15	10.2 to 45.0
Architecture	52.0	43.0–57.5	7.88	29.7 to 74.3
Furniture	.2	.1– .3	.10	0 to .5
Arms	5.4	1.4– 8.4	3.60	0 to 15.6
Clothing	1.7	.3– 3.8	1.85	0 to 6.9
Personal	.2	.1– .4	.17	0 to .7
Tobacco Pipes	9.1	1.9–14.0	6.39	0 to 27.1
Activities	3.7	.7– 6.4	2.87	0 to 11.8
	100.0			

COMPARING THE FRONTIER PATTERN WITH THE CAROLINA PATTERN—ISOLATING VARIABLES

The Inverse Ratio of the Architecture and Kitchen Artifact Groups

The most apparent contrast between the Carolina Pattern and the Frontier Pattern is the inverse ratio between the *Architecture* and *Kitchen* groups. This results in the contrast seen in Figure 28. The empirical pattern ranges do not overlap, and at the expanded, predictive range for the next set of data there is only a 5% overlap for the *Architecture* group. In Figure 28 the Brunswick, Hepburn-Reonalds House (S7) ruin is seen in its marginal position at the outer perimeter of the predictive range of the Frontier Pattern. This site did not fit the range of either pattern, and more will be said later of the marginal position of this ruin relative to the sites used to define the pattern.

Figure 28 also illustrates the hypothesized position of a "pure" kitchen midden and of a newly finished, burned house in order to point out some of the variables with which we are concerned relative to these patterns. A house newly finished that burned prior to occupation, and was thereafter abandoned, would reveal a total architectural emphasis compared with discarded refuse. A building used as a lawyer's office, in which no serving of food took place, or an industrial activity area, might also reveal a similar situation, as would a dwelling around which no refuse was allowed to be thrown due to the idiosyncratic behavior of the occupant compared with refuse disposal practices at neighboring dwellings. The variable we are dealing with here is the degree of organized integration of the artifacts within the system.

It should be noticed that the total percentage for *Kitchen* and *Architecture* artifact classes averages 88.6% in the Carolina Pattern, as seen on the comparative intersite Table 17, and 79.6 for the Frontier Pattern (Table 16). It is the interplay of these two variables, sometimes resulting in the reversal of their positions as seen in the Carolina Pattern, that results in the Frontier Pattern. When we question the cause of this reversal, an increase in by-products associated with architecture in frontier situations can be suggested. This might result from a shorter occupation period for each architectural unit on the frontier than in the settlements not on the frontier, thus increasing the *Architecture* group artifacts in relation to secondary midden deposits of Kitchen group artifacts.

An alternative can be postulated regarding a decrease in *Kitchen* group artifacts in relation to *Architecture* group artifacts resulting from the remoteness of the frontier from the source of supply. This alternative might be paralleled by a decrease in the number of artifact classes making up the *Kitchen* group.

These and other alternative postulates directed at explaining the pat-

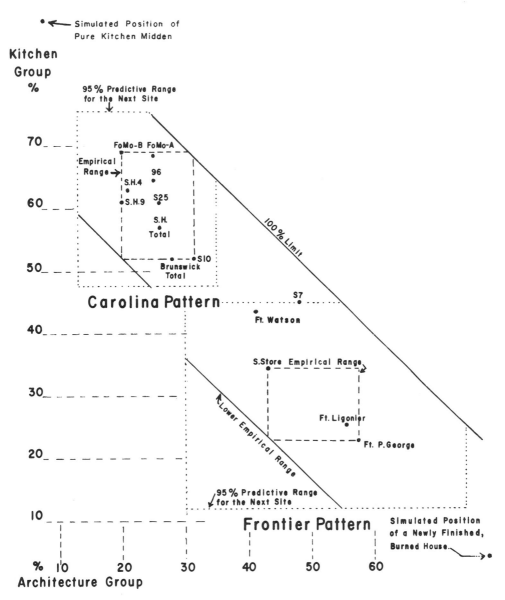

Figure 28.   The empirical and predictive pattern ranges for *Kitchen & Architecture Artifact* groups.

terning seen on frontier sites can be tested through excavations on historically known frontier sites. Our concern here, however, is with the examination of the classes making up the groups. By isolating each class as a variable, clues to cause of the inversion of the *Architecture* and *Kitchen* groups of artifacts can become available through this pattern

TABLE 17

Comparison of the *Kitchen* and *Architecture* Artifact Groups for Intersite Stability

Percentage relationship of the two groups from Cambridge, Ninety-Six, S.C.

Kitchen	64.6	12,854	
Architecture	25.2	5006	Number of artifact classes represented in total sample: 38
Total %	89.8		
Artifact count:		17,860	

Relationships from the American occupation of Fort Moultrie, South Carolina (adjusted for button industry and Indian pottery)

Kitchen	68.6	4185	
Architecture	24.8	1510	Number of artifact classes represented in total sample: 31
Total %	93.4		
Artifact count:		5695	

Relationships from the British occupation of Fort Moultrie, South Carolina (adjusted for button industry and Indian pottery)

Kitchen	69.2	1208	
Architecture	19.7	344	Number of artifact classes represented in total sample: 30
Total %	88.9		
Artifact count:		1552	

Comparison relationships from Lower Queen's Battery, Signal Hill, Newfoundland Jelks' Table 4 (adjusted for nails)

Kitchen	63.2	3188	
Architecture	20.7	1046	Number of artifact classes represented in total sample: 18
Total %	83.9		
Artifact count:		4234	

Comparison relationships from Structure 11, Signal Hill, Newfoundland Jelks' Table 9 (adjusted for nails)

Kitchen	61.3	5795	
Architecture	19.9	1884	Number of artifact classes represented in total sample: 19
Total %	81.2		
Artifact count:		7679	

Relationships for all artifacts from Signal Hill, Newfoundland Jelks' tables 4 through 10

Kitchen	57.2	14,188	
Architecture	25.8	6413	Number of artifact classes represented in the total sample: 20
Total %	83.0		
Artifact count:		20,601	

Mean percentage relationship from the Carolina Pattern for comparison

Kitchen	63.1	47,521	
Architecture	25.5	20,596	Number of artifact classes represented in total sample: 41
Total %	88.6		
Artifact count:		68,117	

148

recognition process. In the case of *Architecture* and *Kitchen* group artifacts three major variables are involved: Ceramics, Wine Bottles, and Nails.

Nails, Ceramics, and Wine Bottles

In order to determine which of these variables has the greatest influence on producing a higher *Architecture* group ratio on frontier sites, all three classes must first be removed from the total artifact count for each site. The remaining figure is the "working total" to be used as a devisor with the nail, ceramic, or bottle count from each site to produce a ratio for each variable in relation to the "working total." This procedure for the three variables is shown in Table 18.

With these ratios in hand the relationship between the variables nails, ceramics, and wine bottles can be compared as seen in Figure 29. The Wine Bottle class ratios reveal a stable relationship on eighteenth- and early nineteenth-century sites, regardless of whether a domestic or frontier site is involved. The Fort Moultrie collections representing British and American military occupation at the Revolutionary War period, however, have a dramatic increase in the ratio of wine bottles present. This should not be interpreted as a dramatic increase in the consumption of spirits by the military at this time period, though this is certainly one possibility. It may merely reflect that there was a greater availability of wine in bottles rather than in barrels during this period at Fort Moultrie, during both the British and American occupations. This increase will certainly need to be kept in mind in studies of artifact relationships from sites of the Revolutionary war period, both military and civilian, in order to accumulate more data relating to the implications suggested by the increase seen here. Since the wine bottle ratio remains steady across domestic and frontier sites in both patterns, this artifact class is certainly not a contributor to the variability we are concerned with here.

The ceramic ratios seen in Figure 29 for eighteenth-century domestic sites are much higher than those for sites of the Frontier Pattern or for the Fort Moultrie military occupations. This may well reflect the closeness of the domestic sites to supply lines compared with the greater difficulty of transporting ceramics to the frontier. This does not mean that frontier sites did not have ceramics. On the contrary, teaware—as opposed to heavyware—has been found to be a major type of ceramic ware on frontier military sites (Ferguson 1975; South 1972: 99) related no doubt not only to the strength of the tea ceremony in the culture, but perhaps to the greater ease of transportation as well (Roth 1961). This is suggested by the fact that at the Revolutionary War British field encampment site at Fort Watson, S.C., the ratio of teaware types to heavyware

TABLE 18

Ratios for Nails, Ceramics and Wine Bottles

	Determination of Nail Ratio					
Site	Adjusted site total	−	Variables: Ceramics, Nails, Wine Bottle	=	Working total	Nail total	Ratio (Nails ÷ working total)
Spalding's Store	16,770	−	11,469	=	5301	7157	1.35
Fort Ligonier	21,778	−	14,077	=	7701	9013	1.17
Fort Prince George	7388	−	5263	=	2125	3875	1.82
Fort Moultrie (A)	6102	−	4828	=	1274	1398	1.10
Fort Moultrie (B)	1745	−	1325	=	420	302	.72
Brunswick (S7)	8183	−	5828	=	2355	2466	1.05
Brunswick (S25)	36,765	−	28,278	=	8487	8095	.95
Brunswick (S10)	13,118	−	9469	=	3649	3098	.85
Cambridge (96)	19,880	−	14,581	=	5299	3707	.70

	Determination of Ceramic Ratio				
Site	Ceramics	÷	Working total	=	Ratio
Spalding's Store (SS)	2796	÷	5301	=	.53
Fort Ligonier (FL)	3170	÷	7701	=	.41
Fort Prince George (FPG)	764	÷	2125	=	.36
Fort Moultrie (A)	1217	÷	1274	=	.96
Fort Moultrie (B)	269	÷	420	=	.64
Brunswick (S7)	2521	÷	2355	=	1.07
Brunswick (S25)	16,288	÷	8487	=	1.92
Brunswick (S10)	4618	÷	3649	=	1.26
Cambridge (96)	8751	÷	5299	=	1.65

	Determination of Wine Bottle Ratio				
Site	Wine Bottle	÷	Working total	=	Ratio
Spalding's Store, Fla. (SS)	1516	÷	5301	=	.28
Fort Ligonier, Pa. (FL)	1894	÷	7701	=	.24
Fort Prince George, S.C. (FPG)	624	÷	2125	=	.29
Fort Moultrie, S.C., American (A)	2213	÷	1274	=	1.74
Fort Moultrie, S.C., British (B)	754	÷	420	=	1.79
Brunswick, N.C., Hepburn-Reonalds (S7)	841	÷	2355	=	.36
Brunswick, N.C., Tailor Shop (S25)	3895	÷	8487	=	.46
Brunswick, N.C., Nath Moore (S10)	1753	÷	3649	=	.48
Cambridge, S.C., Ninety Six (96)	2123	÷	5299	=	.40

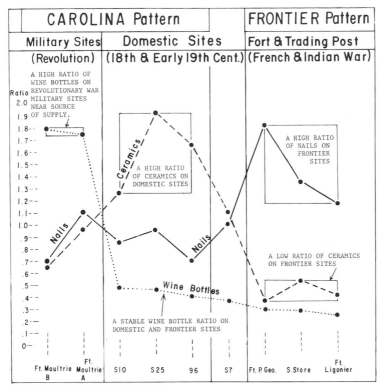

Figure 29. Comparison of Carolina and Frontier Patterns for three artifact classes in relation to all other artifacts.

types was three to one, and the frequency of teaware to heavyware was two to one; whereas at the site of Fort Moultrie, close to the Charleston supply center, the frequency of heavyware to teaware was three to one, the reverse of that at Fort Watson (Ferguson 1975a; South 1974: 177).

The nail ratios can be seen to be higher on sites with the Frontier Pattern (Figure 29) compared with the Carolina Pattern sites. With this information available, it becomes apparent why there is an inverse ratio between the *Kitchen* and *Architecture* groups, resulting in the Carolina and Frontier Patterns. The increase in nails on frontier sites tends to produce a higher *Architecture* group ratio, whereas at the same time there is a decrease in ceramics on frontier sites acting to produce a lower *Kitchen* group ratio. These variables working in opposite directions within the *Kitchen* and *Architecture* artifact groups produce the inverse ratios between the Carolina and Frontier Patterns.

The Wine Bottle class, on the other hand, remains relatively stable except at the Fort Moultrie site, where its dramatic increase is sufficiently

Oriental Porcelain Teacups from the Oeconomie Store at the Moravian Settlement at Bethabara, N.C.

strong to result in a high *Kitchen* group ratio, placing the Fort Moultrie site collections within the framework of the Carolina Pattern in spite of the inverse ratio it produces between the Wine Bottle and Ceramic classes. More will be said about these variations between artifact classes in the next chapter.

We must keep in mind in reference to the inverse ratio of *Kitchen* to *Architecture* groups, that Fort Prince George and Fort Ligonier represent only samples of the total sites, though Fort Prince George was completely excavated inside the fort. It is possible that if forts such as these are totally excavated, the resulting relationships will appear more like the Carolina Pattern than is now the case, since we may have a skewed picture from the forts used to define the Frontier Pattern. This skewness may result from a high *Architecture* to *Kitchen* ratio existing inside the fort, whereas another ratio may result if all the midden in the moat were available, which is not the case. We must be prepared, therefore, for the possible revealing of different percentage relationships for artifact groups from totally excavated frontier forts than for those Frontier Pattern relationships seen here. Only more data from questions asked through excavation of known frontier sites will answer these questions.

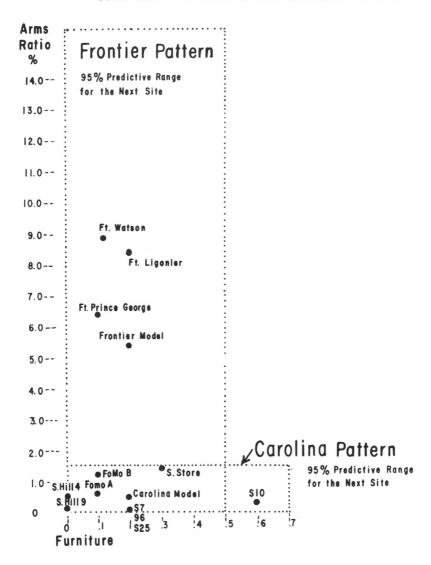

Figure 30. Stability and variability in Furniture and Arms group ratios in relation to the Carolina and Frontier Patterns. Note that the military sites from the Frontier Pattern far exceed the others in the ratio of Arms Group artifacts, while remaining within the Carolina Pattern ratio range in the Furniture group. This illustrates the stability of the Furniture group ratio across all types of sites, contrasted with the increase in Arms group artifacts on frontier military sites of the French and Indian War Period. No such increase is seen at the later military sites of Fort Moultrie and Signal Hill, Newfoundland. Note that the Frontier Pattern Spalding's Store trading post site falls within the Carolina Pattern range.

Contrasting the *Arms* **and** *Furniture* **Groups in the Carolina and Frontier Patterns**

Another comparison of variability and stability reflected in artifact ratios can be seen in comparing the *Arms* and *Furniture* groups (Figure 30). The *Furniture* group ratios are tightly clustered for all sites from both patterns between the range of 0 and .3%, with the exception of the S10 site. This demonstrates a high degree of consistency between the sites relative to the *Furniture* group of artifact classes.

The *Arms* group, however, is seen to reflect a similar tight range between 0 and 1.5% for all sites except the two fort sites in the Frontier Pattern. These British military sites of the French and Indian War period have a significantly higher ratio of *Arms* group artifacts compared to all other sites, including the Revolutionary War military garrisoned sites of Fort Moultrie and the nineteenth-century military garrisoned sites at Signal Hill, Newfoundland. These data suggest that garrisoned forts of the late eighteenth and early nineteenth centuries may not reveal a higher ratio of *Arms* group artifacts in their middens than do domestic sites of the same time period. The French and Indian War period military sites and the more temporary military outpost encampments however, are likely to reveal a far higher ratio of such artifacts than domestic sites. Such trial generalizations require comparison data on a far broader base than is now available. It is hoped that archeologists will begin to quantify their data under conditions that will allow for comparisons to be made with the Carolina and Frontier Patterns. Such comparisons will contribute toward less subjective interpretations of past human behavior from archeological data than is now common.

THE HEPBURN-REONALDS HOUSE (S7), A DEVIANT FROM THE CAROLINA AND FRONTIER PATTERNS

From the position of the Brunswick Town Hepburn-Reonalds House (S7) ruin on the *Architecture* and *Kitchen* group graph in Figure 28, it can be seen that this ruin falls outside the empirical range of both patterns. Since the ruin is located in a central position in Brunswick Town, it can hardly be interpreted as a frontier site. The group relationships for this site are shown in Table 19.

The slightly inverted, almost equal percentages for the *Kitchen* and *Architecture* groups results in this percentage profiles' not fitting either the Carolina or the Frontier Patterns. From a comparison of the nail ratios in Figure 29, the S7 ruin appears to be in line with the other ruins in the Carolina Pattern. The Wine Bottle class is also in keeping with the ratios seen for both patterns, thus eliminating this variable as the one responsible for the problem. The Ceramics class, however, is lower than the other ratios for domestic sites, and this variable would seem to be responsible for the equalizing effect between the *Kitchen* and *Architecture* artifact groups.

TABLE 19

Artifact Group Relationships for the Hepburn-Reonalds House (S7)

Artifact group	Count	%
Kitchen	3702	45.2
Architecture	3953	48.3
Furniture	18	.2
Arms	12	.1
Clothing	24	.3
Personal	4	.1
Tobacco Pipes	374	4.6
Activities	96	1.2
Totals:	8183	100.0

Ruin of the Hepburn-Reonalds House (S7) at the British colonial settlement of Brunswick, N.C.

Another clue to the cause for the deviation of the S7 ruin from the pattern norms lies in a comparison of the total artifact count from the three Brunswick ruins—more than 42,000 for S25, more than 13,000 for S10, but only slightly more than 8,000 for the S7 ruin. Apparently the garbage disposal practices at the S7 ruin differed somewhat from those at the other ruins, resulting in less midden distributed around the structure. This might have some effect on the distributions, particularly if there was a selectivity involved and only certain types of midden were discarded near the house, while others were discarded elsewhere. Some evidence for this exists in the fact that only 31 artifact classes are represented at the S7 ruins, but 38 and 39 classes were recovered from the S10 and S25 ruins, respectively.

We assume that the patterning seen here does indeed mirror the behavior of the occupants. The fact that it is different brings our attention to it with a number of questions, one being whether we can determine what area of the site is responsible for the disconformity with which we are concerned. In order to explore this question the frequency relationship between the artifacts from five squares in the front yard (Sq. 21–25), can be compared with a similar area at the rear of the structure (Sq. 7 14). These areas can be seen in Figure 31, which illustrates the distribution of nails by square throughout the area of the ruin.

By comparing the frequencies for the groups of artifact classes by area, the archeologist can undertake a more detailed examination on the square level until the entire site is dissected square by square. However, the reader will not be subjected to this entire process, only the highlights being presented here. Table 20 presents these comparative data:

TABLE 20

Comparison of Frequency Relationships from Various Areas of the Brunswick Town S7 Ruin with the Carolina Pattern

Artifact group	The Front Yard (Sq. 21–25)		The Rear Patio Area Midden (Sq. 7–14)		Square 11 midden area		Carolina Pattern
	Count	%	Count	%	Count	%	%
Kitchen	784	66.4	1582	39.1	358	39.1	63.1
Architecture	252	21.3	2300	56.8	513	56.1	25.5
Furniture	3	.3	6	.1	3	.3	.2
Arms	4	.3	4	.1	0	0	.5
Clothing	3	.3	8	.2	4	.4	3.0
Personal	0	0	1	.1	1	.1	.2
Tobacco Pipes	130	11.0	119	2.9	25	2.7	5.8
Activities	5	.4	27	.7	11	1.2	1.7
	1181	100.0	4047	100.0	915	100.0	100.0

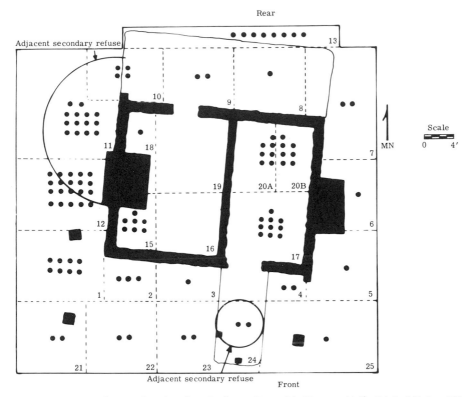

Figure 31. Foundation Plan for the Hepburn–Reonalds House—Nails (Unit S 7, Lot 71). Symbol = I–25 frequency.

The front yard squares can be seen to fall well within the range of the Carolina Pattern, as did the areas in the yard around ruin S25, examined earlier. However, the rear yard squares reveal the inverse ratio seen in the ratios for the entire ruin, but on a more extreme basis. When the single square 11, where the major concentration of midden was recovered, is examined, the same ratios appear. The problem clearly lies with the rear area of the house near the patio where the midden concentration was found. In this area an unusually large ratio of *Architectural* group artifacts contrasts with the low *Kitchen* group ratio, apparently resulting primarily from a decrease in the ceramic ratio as seen in Figure 29.

Because the front yard of the structure reveals a typical Carolina Pattern percentage relationship profile, and the rear yard reverses that ratio between the *Kitchen* and *Architecture* groups, it is tempting to suggest that quantities of structural materials were stored in the area to the rear of this ruin, resulting in the increase in *Architecture* group artifacts such as nails. However, the architecturally related artifacts do not seem to be present in unusually high frequencies, leaving the decrease in ceramics as the primary variable thought to be responsible for the problem of deviation at this ruin. As we have indicated, other artifact classes decrease here also, so a single variable is hardly responsible.

The explanation could be, as we have suggested, in variability in the individualized refuse disposal practices at this site. A fact to consider is that the kitchen for this building was not excavated, being located some distance away from this structure. If secondary refuse from the kitchen was discarded primarily around the kitchen, the variation we see here may be the result. If this is true, then a decrease in bone fragments discarded around this ruin should be expected and as we will see in the following chapter, this is exactly the case, supporting the interpretation of special behavioral activity regarding the discard of refuse adjacent to the house. A short occupation span would also produce a higher *Architecture* to *Kitchen* group ratio, with a virtual absence of *Kitchen* group artifacts anticipated. The use of a structure as an office, or shop, or industrial activity with a minimum of domestic activity would also produce a high *Architecture* to *Kitchen* group ratio. In such cases the lack of organized integration between the architecture and by-products from the kitchen becomes noticable as an inconsistent frequency relationship in the patterns. This example has direct applicability to the empirical generalization we have stated previously as "A Law of Behavioral By-Product Regularity."

ARTIFACT PATTERN AT FORT WATSON, S.C.

Another example of a site that has a pattern not fitting either the Carolina or Frontier Pattern is the British Fort Watson located on top of an Indian Mound at the Scott's Lake site, S.C. (Ferguson 1975b). Fort Watson was occupied by British troops for four months in 1780–1781. It was not a domestic site, nor was it strictly a frontier site, though it was somewhat removed from any concentrated settlement. It functioned as a protection for the supply line, and therefore was primarily an outpost serving a military function at the time of the Revolution. A battle was fought at the site, and American forces captured the fort using rifles fired from a high tower overlooking the fort on top of the mound.

Table 21, showing artifact group relationships, was furnished by Leland Ferguson for the purpose of comparison with the Carolina and Frontier Patterns.

Comparing the diagnostic *Kitchen* and *Architecture* group percentages with those from the sites in the Carolina and Frontier Patterns reveals that Fort Watson falls midway between these patterns (Figure 28). This in itself is interesting in that it places Fort Watson in a similar relationship to these patterns as the Brunswick S7 ruin. The dra-

TABLE 21

The Artifact Group Profiles from the Mound Summit at Fort Watson, S.C., at the Scott's Lake Site

Artifact group	Topsoil		Features		Total	
	Count	%	Count	%	Count	%
Kitchen	609	46.3	18	15.5	627	43.8
Architecture	553	42.0	42	36.2	595	41.6
Furniture	16	1.2	3	2.6	19	1.3
Arms	90	6.8	38	32.8	128	8.9
Clothing	16	1.2	7	6.0	23	1.6
Personal	2	.2	0	0	2	.1
Tobacco Pipes	17	1.3	1	.9	18	1.3
Activities	13	1.0	7	6.0	20	1.4
	1316	100.0	116	100.0	1432	100.0

matic variable at Fort Watson is the *Arms* group of artifacts, which is the highest of any of the frontier sites from which the Frontier Pattern was derived. This is shown in Figure 30.

Table 21 contrasts the artifacts from the topsoil zone with those taken from features. The features are considered as representing the period of the battle more directly than the topsoil zone. This being the case it is interesting to notice that the *Arms* group percentage is 32.8, a dramatic indication of the importance of arms-related activity during the final period the site was occupied. In contrast to the frontier sites from which the Frontier Pattern was abstracted, Fort Watson alone was involved in a battle. The high *Arms* group artifact percentage appears to reflect this fact. However, in order to clearly demonstrate the fact of a battle having occurred, the ratio of distorted (through impact) rifle balls and shot to nondistorted musket balls and swan shot would likely be a better indicator. The percentage of rifle balls distorted through impact at Fort Watson is 62.2%, while those not distorted (apparently lost by the British while loading) is 37.8%. At military sites where battles were not involved we would postulate a far different ratio, with nondistorted balls in the majority. Unfortunately the classification of lead balls and shot along these lines was not conducted at Fort Ligonier and Fort Prince George, so comparison in this direction cannot be made at this time.

Ferguson's data from Fort Watson do suggest that the recognition of whether a battle took place on a site can be derived through a classification of musket balls, rifle balls, and shot on the basis of whether or not they have been distorted through having been fired. The Fort Watson data also suggest that Revolutionary War period military outpost encampment sites such as this may well not fit either the Frontier or Carolina Patterns when compared on the basis of the *Kitchen* and *Archi-*

tecture group artifact percentages. The Fort Watson pattern seen here may well represent what might be found to be a Revolutionary War Military Outpost Pattern in contrast to the Frontier and Carolina Patterns. It could also be found to be more specific, representing instead, a Revolutionary War Military Battle Pattern representing sites on which a battle occurred.

When such pattern is defined, explanation will be required to account for the pattern, either in terms of a battle, supply lines, logistic base, military supply, types of arms available, etc. The emphasis in this book is on pattern recognition, but to discover the fact that pattern exists is not the goal of archeology. Merely to point out variability and stability, pattern and redundancy is not to explain why these differences in the static archeological record exist. Only when we can explain the differences we see are we going to understand culture and how it works. A basic first step in this direction, however, is pattern recognition.

APPENDIX

The artifact class frequencies for the Frontier Pattern are included here for use in comparative studies.

Artifact Class Frequencies

Artifact class no. and description	Ft. Prince George Site (38PN1) S.C.		Ft. Ligonier, Pa. Site		Spalding's Store, Fla. Site	
	Count	%	Count	%	Count	%
Kitchen group						
1. Ceramics	764		3170		2796	
2. Wine Bottle	624		1894		1516	
3. Case Bottle	139		—		896	
4. Tumbler	32		—		—	
5. Pharmaceutical	75		—		504	
6. Glassware	1		395		12	
7. Tableware	6		85		7	
8. Kitchenware	38		22		58	
Total *Kitchen*	1679	16.8	5566	25.6	5789	34.5
9. Bone	(2644)		(44,547)		(8214)	
Architecture group						
10. Window Glass	240		1863		28	
11. Nails	3875		9013		7157	
12. Spikes	126		916		29	
13. Construction Hdwe.	8		297		8	
14. Door Lock Parts	3		23		—	
Total *Architecture*	4252	42.6	12,112	55.6	7222	43.0

Artifact Class Frequencies   (Continued)

Artifact class no. and description	Ft. Prince George Site (38PN1) S.C. Count	%	Ft. Ligonier, Pa. Site Count	%	Spalding's Store, Fla. Site Count	%
15. *Furniture* group	6	.1	44	.2	51	.3
Arms group						
16. Balls, Shot, Sprue	393		1338		102	
17. Gunflints, Spalls	40		345		86	
18. Gun Parts	38		137		39	
Total *Arms*	471	4.7	1820	8.4	227	1.4
Clothing group						
19. Buckles	18		27		11	
20. Thimbles	—		5		1	
21. Buttons	33		516		34	
22. Scissors	5		3		2	
23. Straight Pins	—		237		2	
24. Hook and Eye	1		2		—	
25. Bale Seals	2		—		—	
26. Glass Beads	11		43		1	
Total *Clothing*	70	.7	833	3.8	51	.3
Personal group						
27. Coins	2		31		—	
28. Keys	1		3		5	
29. Personal	6		65		5	
Total *Personal*	9	.1	99	.4	10	.1
30. *Tobacco Pipe* group	851	8.5	411	1.9	2343	14.0
Activities group						
31. Construction Tools	8		19		5	
32. Farm Tools	3		8		3	
33. Toys	1		11		2	
34. Fishing Gear	—		—		1	
35. Stub-stemmed Pipes	—		1		1	
36. Colono-Indian Pottery	2583		—		167	
37. Storage Items	6		42		832	
38. Botanical	—		—		—	
39. Horse Tack	24		180		6	
40. Misc. Hardware	4		103		60	
41. Other	—		359		—	
42. Military Objects	4		170		—	
Total *Activities*	2633	26.4	893	4.1	1077	6.4
TOTAL (without Bone)	9971	100.0	21,778	100.0	16,770	100.0

Artifact Class Frequencies (Continued)

Artifact class no. and description	Brunswick, S7, Rear Site Sq. 7–14		Brunswick, S7, Front Sq. 21–25		Brunswick, S7, Midden Sq. 11	
	Count	%	Count	%	Count	%
Kitchen group						
1. Ceramics	1181		638		288	
2. Wine Bottle	222		77		57	
3. Case Bottle	24		6		11	
4. Tumbler	105		50		29	
5. Pharmaceutical	20		7		2	
6. Glassware	28		1		—	
7. Tableware	1		5		—	
8. Kitchenware	1		—		—	
Total *Kitchen*	1582	39.1	784	66.4	358	39.1
9. Bone	(51)		(2)		(16)	
Architecture group						
10. Window Glass	1037		78		180	
11. Nails	1229		168		327	
12. Spikes	19		3		1	
13. Construction Hdwe,	14		3		5	
14. Door Lock Parts	1		—		—	
Total *Architecture*	2300	56.8	252	21.3	513	56.1
15. *Furniture* group	6	.1	3	.3	3	.3
Arms group						
16. Balls, Shot, Sprue	3		4		—	
17. Gunflints, Spalls	1		—		—	
18. Gun Parts	—		—		—	
Total *Arms*	4	.1	4	.3	—	—
Clothing group						
19. Buckles	5		2		3	
20. Thimbles	—		—		—	
21. Buttons	3		—		1	
22. Scissors	—		1		—	
23. Straight Pins	—		—		—	
24. Hook and Eye	—		—		—	
25. Bale Seals	—		—		—	
26. Glass Beads	—		—		—	
Total *Clothing*	8	.2	3	.3	4	.4

Artifact Class Frequencies   (Continued)

Artifact class no. and description	Brunswick, S7, Rear Site Sq. 7–14		Brunswick, S7, Front Sq. 21–25		Brunswick, S7, Midden Sq. 11	
	Count	%	Count	%	Count	%
Personal group						
27. Coins	—		—		—	
28. Keys	1		—		1	
29. Personal	—		—		—	
Total *Personal*	1	.1	—	—	1	.1
30. *Tobacco Pipe* group	119	2.9	130	11.0	25	2.7
Activities group						
31. Construction Tools	6		1		1	
32. Farm Tools	—		—		—	
33. Toys	—		—		—	
34. Fishing Gear	1		—		—	
35. Stub-stemmed Pipes	—		—		—	
36. Colono-Indian Pottery	8		2		6	
37. Storage Items	8		—		3	
38. Botanical	—		—		—	
39. Horse Tack	—		—		—	
40. Misc. Hardware	4		2		1	
41. Other	—		—		—	
42. Military Objects	—		—		—	
Total *Activities*	27	.7	5	.4	11	1.2
TOTAL (without Bone)	4047	100.0	1181	100.0	915	99.9

REFERENCES

Combes, John D.
  n.d.   The Archeology at Fort Prince George. Manuscript in preparation. Institute of Archeology and Anthropology, University of South Carolina, Columbia.
Ferguson, Leland G.
  1975a   Analysis of Ceramic Materials from Fort Watson, December 1780–April 1781. *The Conference on Historic Site Archaeology Papers 1973* **8.** Institute of Archeology and Anthropology, University of South Carolina, Columbia.
  1975b   Archeology at Scott's Lake, Exploratory Research, 1972, 1973. *Research Manuscript Series No. 68.* Institute of Archeology and Anthropology, University of South Carolina, Columbia.

Grimm, Jacob L.
  1970 Archaeological Investigation of Fort Ligonier 1960–1965. *Annals of the Carnegie Museum, 42.* Pittsburgh.
Jelks, Edward B.
  1973 Archaeological Explorations at Signal Hill, Newfoundland, 1965–1966. *Occasional Papers in Archaeology and History, No. 7.* Ottawa: National Historic Sites Service, Department of Indian Affairs and Northern Development.
Lewis, Kenneth E.
  1969 The History and Archeology of Spalding's Lower Store (PU-23), Putnam County, Florida, M.A. thesis, Department of Anthropology, University of Florida, Gainesville.
  1973 An Archaeological Consideration of the Frontier. *Papers in Anthropology* **14,** No. 1. Graydon H. Doolittle and Christopher Lintz, eds. Department of Anthropology, University of Oklahoma, Norman.
  1975 The Jamestown Frontier: An Archaeological View of Colonization, Ph.D. dissertation, Department of Anthropology, University of Oklahoma. University Microfilms, Ann Arbor, Michigan.
Mendenhall, William
  1971 *Introduction to probability and statistics.* Second Edition. Belmont, California: Wadsworth.
Roth, Rodris
  1961 Tea Drinking in 18th-Century America: Its Etiquette and Equipage. *Contributions from the Museum of History and Technology.* Paper 14. Washington, D.C.: Smithsonian Institution.
South, Stanley A.
  1959 Excavation Report, Unit S7, Lot 71, Brunswick Town, North Carolina: The Hepburn-Reonalds House 1734–1776. Manuscript on file with North Carolina Department of Cultural Resources, Raleigh.
  1972 Evolution and Horizon as Revealed in Ceramic Analysis in Historical Archeology. *The Conference on Historic Site Archeology Papers, 1971* **6:**71–116.
  1974 Palmetto Parapets. *Anthropological Studies No. 1.* Institute of Archeology and Anthropology, University of South Carolina, Columbia.

Glassware—one of the eight artifact classes in the Kitchen Artifact group.

Exploring
Analytical
Techniques

EXAMINING THE *KITCHEN* ARTIFACT PATTERNS

After almost a half-century of various kinds of digging on historic sites, justified by varying rationales, there are as a result certain questions that can be answered. Unfortunately, there are other problems that are no nearer a solution now than before all this activity began. Some artifact types have been described and some classes have been established. Artifact types can sometimes be placed in a chronological framework relative to a manufacture period for those types. As a result, historical archeologists are anxious to pass this information on to others less informed, and reports of excavations on historic sites emphasize the chronological placement of the relics recovered, too often ending with that.

Some other questions that can be answered by the historical archeologist are: Was this a pottery making site? Was this a glasshouse site? Was this a printshop? Was this a blacksmith shop? Was this an iron foundry? The historical archeologist's "skill" at interpreting the remains from the past allows him to identify, for example, the kilns, wasters, furnaces and slag, printer's type and crucibles as the by-products of such specialized past activities. He can also interpret the function of wells, privies, smokehouses, fireplaces, and springhouses.

Questions he cannot so readily answer after a half-century of effort are: Were women present on this site? Was this a domestic or a military occupation? Was a battle fought on this site? Was this a trading post or a frontier home? Was this a tavern or the governor's home? What impact on the archeological record did women and children have? Can we tell from the archeological record whether the occupants of the site were participants in a German-American cultural system or a British-American system? Does this collection of artifacts represent the cultural by-products of activity by slaves, or by the master of the plantation? Was this ruin once the home of a wealthy gentleman planter or his servant? Is this ruin a typical mid-eighteenth-century dwelling, and if not, in what way is it different from the multitude of other domestic dwellings of the period? What does this difference mean when interpreted in the cultural system of which it was once a part? Does the increase in tailoring objects from 5% in one ruin to 13% in another indicate that one was a domestic dwelling while the other was a tailor shop? The list could be made even more lengthy, but the point we are making is that if we are to make more progress in the next half-century than we did in the last there must be a fundamental, revolutionary change in thinking, design, and method in historical archeology. The change should be aimed toward answering these elementary questions. In asking the question the revolution has begun.

We must begin asking what to some may seem to be impertinent, irrelevant questions in order that pertinent and relevant answers can emerge. Once the questions are asked, methods relevant to them must be developed for collecting the appropriate data. This chapter will explore only a few of the methodological tools being developed toward answering such questions. I will examine artifact classes in the *Kitchen* group and derive from them a Kitchen Artifact Pattern. In a similar manner, I will explore the classes of artifacts by deriving simple ratios for pattern recognition. Finally, I will provide an example of pattern recognition using probate inventories, and will compare these to pattern in the archeological record.

The Kitchen Artifact Class Pattern

In the same manner that the Carolina and Frontier Patterns were derived, the individual artifact groups can be broken down into their constituent classes to allow for comparison and isolation of variables on the class level. The *Kitchen* artifact group will be used here as an example of this procedure to point the way toward the delineation of specifically sensitive pattern on the artifact class level. The relationship of Kitchen Artifact Classes from several sites is seen in Table 22.

The remarkable similarity of the percentage for Ceramics is seen for the domestic sites, with the relationship between Ceramics and Wine Bottle classes indicating patterning within the grouped sites (Table 22). The grouped sites can be compared by determining the mean for each artifact class to reveal Kitchen Artifact Class Patterns (Table 23).

The ratio between Ceramics and Wine Bottle classes is the most critical for determining the variation in these types of sites. If these patterns were based on 15 or 20 sites, their predictive value would be far firmer than is now the case. However, the domestic group of four sites is extremely regular and should prove a good pattern for comparison of the ratios of these eight artifact classes with new site data.

The Signal Hill ruins have three classes of artifacts missing from the tabulation, those missing probably having been counted under other classificatory headings. This results in a higher ratio of Ceramics than would likely be the case had these three classes of artifacts been included as separate units. It is suspected that if this were done, the Signal Hill data would fall far closer to the Domestic mean, rather than "distorted" as it appears here.

The artifact classes reveal a greater sensitivity to variability than do the groups when classes are missing from the tabulation. In cases where there has been a tendency of the archeologist to lump artifacts under

TABLE 22

The Relationship of Kitchen Artifact Classes from Several Sites

| | Domestic Sites | | | | | | | |
| | Brunswick (S25) | | Brunswick (S10) | | Brunswick (S7) | | Cambridge (96) | |
Class	Count	%	Count	%	Count	%	Count	%
1. Ceramics	16,288	72.5	4618	68.0	2521	68.1	8751	68.1
2. Wine Bottle	3895	17.3	1753	25.8	841	22.7	2123	16.5
3. Case Bottle	445	2.0	29	.4	56	1.5	201	1.6
4. Tumbler	768	3.4	100	1.5	190	5.1	714	5.6
5. Pharmaceutical	473	2.1	45	.7	35	1.0	873	6.8
6. Glassware	431	1.9	191	2.8	38	0	57	.4
7. Tableware	122	.5	35	.5	11	.3	116	.9
8. Kitchenware	57	.3	24	.3	10	.3	19	.1
Total	22,479	100.0	6795	100.0	3702	100.0	12,854	100.0

| | Distorted Domestic Sites (from lack of complete data) | | | |
| | Signal Hill (4) | | Signal Hill (9) | |
Class	Count	%	Count	%
1. Ceramics	2548	79.9	4715	81.3
2. Wine Bottle	439	13.8	689	11.9
3. Case Bottle	0	0	0	0
4. Tumbler	0	0	0	0
5. Pharmaceutical	65	2.0	190	3.3
6. Glassware	131	4.1	191	3.3
7. Tableware	5	.2	10	.2
8. Kitchenware	0	0	0	0
Total	3188	100.0	5795	100.0

TABLE 22 (Continued)

| | Revolutionary War Military | | | |
| | Ft. Moultrie (A) | | Ft. Moultrie (B) | |
Class	Count	%	Count	%
1. Ceramics	1217	29.1	269	22.3
2. Wine Bottle	2213	52.9	754	62.4
3. Case Bottle	363	8.7	51	4.2
4. Tumbler	114	2.7	30	2.5
5. Pharmaceutical	261	6.2	87	7.2
6. Glassware	3	.1	10	.8
7. Tableware	10	.2	4	.3
8. Kitchenware	4	.1	3	.3
Total	4185	100.0	1208	100.0

| | Frontier Sites | | | | | |
| | Ft. Ligonier (FL) (distorted) | | Ft. Prince George (FPG) | | Spaldings Store (SS) | |
Class	Count	%	Count	%	Count	%
1. Ceramics	3170	57.0	764	45.5	2796	48.3
2. Wine Bottle	1894	34.0	624	37.2	1516	26.2
3. Case Bottle	0	0	139	8.3	896	15.5
4. Tumbler	0	0	32	1.9	0	0
5. Pharmaceutical	0	0	75	4.4	504	8.7
6. Glassware	395	7.1	1	.1	12	.2
7. Tableware	85	1.5	6	.3	7	.1
8. Kitchenware	22	.4	38	2.3	58	1.0
Total	5566	100.0	1679	100.0	5789	100.0

catchall classes such as "Miscellaneous Glass," "Miscellaneous Hardware," "Miscellaneous Iron," and "Miscellaneous Artifacts," the group level of comparison allows such lumping to be accommodated far better than does the more specific class level of comparison we are concerned with here.

The high ratio of Wine Bottle to Ceramics at Fort Moultrie, seen in Table 23, was identified in the last chapter as the variable contrasting Fort Moultrie with the domestic and frontier groups of sites. Whether this phenomenon will be seen to represent pattern on military sites of the Revolutionary War period generally will have to await other data designed to answer this question through quantification.

A detailed discussion of the variability in all classes will not be undertaken here, but the Case Bottle Class 3, which has a mean of 1.4% on the domestic sites but jumps to 6.5% and 7.9% on military and

TABLE 23

The Kitchen Artifact Class Patterns

Artifact class	Domestic (S25, S10, S7, 96)	Distorted Domestic (Signal Hill 4, 9)	Revolutionary War military (Ft. Moultrie)	Frontier (FL, FPG, SS)
1. Ceramics	69.2	80.6	25.7	50.3
2. Wine Bottle	20.6	12.9	57.7	32.5
3. Case Bottle	1.4	0	6.5	7.9
4. Tumbler	3.9	0	2.6	.6
5. Pharmaceutical	2.6	2.6	6.7	4.4
6. Glassware	1.5	3.7	.4	2.5
7. Tableware	.5	.2	.2	.6
8. Kitchenware	.3	0	.2	1.2
Total	100.0	100.0	100.0	100.0

frontier sites, is certainly a significant difference reflecting frontier and/ or military contrast in activity. This could well be the result of the ease of transporting such square bottles in cases (thus the name Case Bottle) to frontier locations in contrast to transporting the round Wine Bottles to such remote areas.

Pharmaceutical type bottles also show a decided increase on military and frontier sites, possible reflecting a greater need for, and use of, medicines in frontier situations as opposed to domestic life. As limited as this data base is, the patterns revealed are provocative of postulates directed at further pattern recognition, and explanation of the patterning through hypotheses focused on the past cultural system. Further pattern can be abstracted by isolating variables through comparison of simple ratios.

ISOLATING VARIABLES THROUGH COMPARISON OF SIMPLE RATIOS

The Ceramic Ratio

The ceramic ratio is determined by subtracting the total for ceramics from the entire artifact count for the site, and dividing the ceramics by the resulting artifact total. The resulting ceramic ratios for eleven sites can then be grouped by similar ratios into three site groups: domestic sites, Signal Hill, Newfoundland, sites, and military-frontier sites as shown in Table 24.

The implication here is that domestic site ceramic ratios may be

TABLE 24

The Ceramic Ratios for 11 Sites

Site	Ceramics	÷	Adjusted total less Ceramics	=	Ceramic ratio	=	Resulting site grouping
Brunswick S25	16,288	÷	20,477	=	.79		
Brunswick S10	4618	÷	8500	=	.54		= Domestic sites
Brunswick S7	2521	÷	5662	=	.44		
Cambridge 96	8751	÷	11,129	=	.79		
Signal Hill 4	2548	÷	2497	=	1.02		
Signal Hill 9	4715	÷	4733	=	1.00		= Signal Hill sites
Ft. Moultrie A	1217	÷	4885	=	.25		
Ft. Moultrie B	269	÷	1476	=	.18		
Ft. Ligonier	3170	÷	18,608	=	.17		= Military-Frontier sites
Ft. Prince George	764	÷	6624	=	.11		
Spalding's Store	2796	÷	13,974	=	.20		

expected to fall within the .44 to .79 range, with military-frontier sites in the .11 to .25 range when the ceramic ratio is used as an index.

The Signal Hill sites pose a problem in that they are clearly on the opposite end of the scale from the military-frontier sites, yet Signal Hill was a nineteenth-century military site. This being the case it is suspected that the Signal Hill ceramic ratio of 1.00 may well foretell this ratio as an index for nineteenth-century military sites. In order to test this proposition comparable data from nineteenth-century military sites can be compared using the ceramic ratio as an index. With the great interest in such sites in the western states, such comparative data should be available from those archeologists willing to undertake the basic task of quantitative analysis of data recovered under controlled conditions.

The Colono-Indian Pottery Ratio

In the above examination of the ceramic ratio from various sites, the Fort Prince George, S.C., site adjusted total was used, as was that for the Brunswick S25 for tailoring, and the Fort Moultrie collections for Colono-Indian pottery (Noël Hume 1962; South 1974). The Fort Prince George adjustment was necessary owing to the presence of 2583 Cherokee Indian pottery fragments recovered along with the other artifacts of European and Indian origin. The pottery was not, strictly speaking, Colono-Indian, but complicated stamped and plain wares of the eighteenth century, another reason for eliminating them from our model. The presence of Cherokee Indian pottery is no surprise since the fort was designed to protect and encourage trade with this nation.

With these facts in mind it should be interesting to see what the ceramic ratio for Fort Prince George would be if this Colono-Indian Class 36 were transferred to Class 1 (Ceramics) and added to that total. This would be done under the assumption that in situations where Colono-Indian pottery is present on a site, it reflects a need not otherwise met and a high percentage of Indian or Colono-Indian pottery might be assumed to reveal not only Indian contact but kitchen-related activity along with other ceramics. The best expression of this variability is seen in the Colono-Indian Pottery ratio.

Before comparing these ratios, we will add the Ceramics and Colono-Indian totals for Fort Prince George to see what the resulting ratio reveals in relation to the ratios for the other types of sites. The 2583 Cherokee sherds added to the 764 sherds of European origin at Fort Prince George results in a ceramic ratio of .50. When we compare this with the ratios for ceramics from the other sites we find that it falls easily within the range for the domestic sites (Table 24). Using the ceramic ratio (including Cherokee pottery) as the only criterion results in the classification of Fort prince George as a Carolina Pattern site, not a Frontier Pattern site. In other words, the shortage of European ceramics at Fort

Behavioral patterns of past lifeways are revealed through analysis of the static archeological record.

Prince George on the Carolina frontier appears to have been compensated for by utilization of Cherokee pottery.

This situation reveals the wisdom of placing Colono-Indian pottery as a class within the *Activities* group rather than with European ceramics as a separate class under the *Kitchen* group. It is best to classify the Fort Prince George site by means of the Frontier Pattern as a frontier site, *then* examine the Colono-Indian to European ceramics ratio by the means used here. This procedure allows this variable to be isolated, helping us to understand the relationship between Indians and colonists through the archeological record.

In this same regard, the Fort Ligonier site should be examined for the relationship revealed by the archeological record between the Indians and the occupants of the fort. The Indian objects recovered from Fort Ligonier are prehistoric and unrelated to the historic occupation of the site (Grimm 1970: 170). Therefore, no Colono-Indian ratio can be determined. When we ask why this contrast to the Fort Prince George site existed (at the same time period) we are struck by the fact that historical control data indicate a friendly trade relationship at Fort Prince George, whereas Fort Ligonier functioned entirely as an anti-Indian stronghold (Combes n.d.; Grimm 1970)

In view of this fact, the dramatic contrast between the Cherokee pottery at Fort Prince George and the absence of contemporary Indian pottery at Fort Ligonier is most interesting. The archeological data alone would suggest trade and contact with Indians at Fort Prince George and the absence of behavior reflecting such friendly relations and culture contact at Fort Ligonier. This is exactly what the historical documents suggest was the case.

Before examining the manner in which the Colono-Indian Pottery Ratio Index separates the various sites with which we are concerned, a comment on the Fort Moultrie middens should be made. Colono-Indian pottery was one of the classes used to adjust these site totals, since a considerable quantity of this ware was recovered from both the British and American occupations (South 1974). When we add the Colono-Indian pottery totals to the ceramic totals for Fort Moultrie, we find that the resulting ratios are .38 for the American midden at the site (A), and .28 for the British midden (B). These increased ratios do not have the dramatic impact seen at Fort Prince George but do raise the American midden ratio to within a few points of the lowest ratio in the domestic group of sites. Again, the need not met by European ceramics at Fort Moultrie was apparently being filled, or was being attempted to be filled, by Indian ceramics. The presence of Colono-Indian pottery in such large quantities at Fort Moultrie (about 40% of all ceramics) has been interpreted as resulting from behavior of enlisted men, whose usual equipment was not ceramics, but wooden bowls and/or tin cups and plates, the officers being the carriers of ceramics in the latest fashion from Europe (South 1974; Ferguson 1975). Both the British and Americans had Indians with them at Fort Moultrie. By subtracting Colono-Indian pottery from the total artifact count from various sites, the Colono-Indian pottery ratio is determined as shown in Table 25.

This Colono-Indian Pottery Ratio has divided the sites into three groups, those domestic sites having a small amount of Indian pottery, those frontier and domestic as well as nineteenth-century military sites having no Indian pottery, and those frontier sites having far more Indian contact, as suggested by the contrasting ratios of Colono-Indian Pottery. These ratios may well serve as indices for determining the relative degree of friendly Indian contact as revealed by the single variable Colono-Indian Pottery or pottery contemporary with the site being studied. As we have seen suggested by the contrasting data from Fort Ligonier and Fort Prince George, basic policy regarding trade as opposed to warfare may be reflected in the behavioral by-product Colono-Indian pottery and/or contemporary Indian pottery recovered from historic sites.

The Military Ratio

The artifact class most sensitive to determining the difference between a military and a domestic or nonmilitary frontier site is Class 42, Military Objects. This class is composed of military insignia, artillery objects, swords, bayonets, etc. As we have seen, the *Arms* group of artifact

TABLE 25

Colono-Indian Pottery Ratios for 11 Sites

Site	Colono-Indian Pottery	÷	Total artifacts less Colono-Ind.	=	Colono-Ind. ratio	
Brunswick S25	231	÷	36,534	=	.006	Some Indian contact on domestic sites
Brunswick S7	12	÷	8171	=	.001	
Cambridge 96	62	÷	19,818	=	.003	
Brunswick S10	0	÷	13,118	=	0	No Indian contact revealed
Signal Hill 4	0	÷	5045	=	0	
Signal Hill 9	0	÷	9448	=	0	
Ft. Ligonier	0	÷	21,778	=	0	
Ft. Moultrie A	617	÷	6346	=	.10	Frontier sites with far greater Indian contact than domestic sites
Ft. Moultrie B	141	÷	1981	=	.07	
Ft. Prince George	2583	÷	7388	=	.35	
Spalding's Store	167	÷	16,603	=	.01	

classes, which includes musket balls, gunflints, gunparts, etc., can be used to distinguish frontier-military sites from trading posts and domestic sites, but it did not distinguish between these and the military sites at Fort Moultrie and Signal Hill. Using the Military Object Class 42, a military ratio can be seen as in Table 26.

This military ratio for Class 42 appears to be a positive index for identification of a military versus a nonmilitary site, in spite of the small ratios involved. This variable is far more critical in this respect than the *Arms* group, which includes items used both in a military and a nonmilitary context.

The Nail Ratio

In the previous chapter we examined the nails and found that a high ratio can be expected on frontier sites compared with domestic sites, and the details of that procedure will not be repeated here. However, the implications of a nail increase on frontier sites call for explanatory postulates. The domestic sites involved in this study all represent considerable periods of occupation, around 50 years in most cases, whereas the frontier sites, mostly forts, represent less than a decade. There was a greater period of time for generalization and integration of activity by-products on domestic sites as opposed to frontier sites, which might well be a major factor in pattern variability between domestic and frontier sites.

TABLE 26

The Military Object Ratio for 11 Sites

Site	Military objects	÷	Adjusted total less military	=	Military ratio	Resulting site grouping
Brunswick S25	0	÷	36,765	=	0	No military activity revealed on domestic sites
Brunswick S10	0	÷	13,118	=	0	
Brunswick S7	0	÷	8183	=	0	
Cambridge 96	0	÷	19,880	=	0	
Signal Hill 4	70	÷	5038	=	.01	Military activity revealed on all known military sites
Signal Hill 9	9	÷	9439	=	.0009	
Ft. Moultrie A	5	÷	6097	=	.0008	
Ft. Moultrie B	1	÷	1744	=	.0006	
Ft. Ligonier	170	÷	21,608	=	.008	
Ft. Prince George	4	÷	7384	=	.005	
Spalding's Store	0	÷	16,770	=	0	No military activity revealed on trading post site

What we may be seeing, therefore, is the result of a great amount of construction activity in a relatively small area (inside the walls of a fort), thus concentrating the architectural by-products within narrow spatial bounds. Add to this a short occupation period in which by-products of activities can accumulate in this small area. Add to this the likelihood that in frontier-military situations, midden would not be allowed to accumulate indiscriminately around the structures inside the fort. Add to this the fact that in domestic situations such as Brunswick Town, no such military prohibition existed. The result may be that the archeologically revealed record might well show a high nail ratio in relation to other artifacts.

We have listed these postulates in the framework of an assumption, that we can historically demonstrate that the sites from which the pattern was derived are frontier sites. However, the contrast in the inverse ratio between *Kitchen* and *Architecture* group artifacts seen on domestic and frontier sites may not be due to the domestic versus the frontier type of site at all. This contrast might well be the result of the variable of time of occupation, suggested as a postulate in the earlier discussion. This postulate could be tested by excavation of historically documented structures known to have been occupied for a short time. The results might reveal patterning such as that seen at the Brunswick S7 ruin, with a high *Architecture* to *Kitchen* artifact ratio. Such testing should help to reveal the extent to which time was a critical variable in the differences in pattern we are seeing between frontier and domestic sites of the same time period. The goal of such studies is, of course, to isolate the variables responsible for the patterning we delineate in the static archeological record. In so doing, we gain a better understanding of cultural processes and how they work.

An artifact class relating to *Architecture* is Construction Tools in Class 31. An increase in these on frontier sites might be expected to parallel an increase in nails, because increased architectural activity ratios might well be accompanied by an increase in breakage and loss of tools relating to construction.

The Construction Tool Ratio

Although small numbers are involved in the Construction Tool Class 31, the ratios may still be expected to reflect variation in behavior on domestic versus frontier sites, where behavior might well be expected to vary. The Signal Hill site did not include a classification allowing separation of construction tools, so comparison could not be made with that site. The average ratio for the four domestic sites at Brunswick and Cambridge can be compared with the average for the two military frontier sites, Fort Ligonier and Fort Prince George. The frontier average for Construction Tools, Class 31, was four times that of the domestic sites, a ratio increase paralleling that for nails on the frontier. This parallel increase in these artifact classes relating to construction activity certainly warrants attention when comparative studies of historic site data from comparable sites are undertaken.

The Wine Bottle Ratio

The wine bottle ratios were also examined in the past chapter, and contrasted with nails and ceramics. The ratio of wine bottles to other artifacts was seen to be quite stable for domestic and frontier sites, but increased considerably on the Fort Moultrie site. As was suggested earlier, this may reflect the increase in use of bottled spirits during the Revolutionary War period compared with the use from barrels. The closeness to the source of supply may also be involved. An obvious first attempt at interpretation may be the postulate eventually demonstrated to be the case, namely, that both the British and Americans drank a lot at Fort Moultrie. The contrast at Fort Moultrie is certainly fascinating, but equally significant is the stability of the wine bottle ratio across the domestic and frontier sites (Figure 29). Further pattern recognition such as demonstrated here can contribute to answering these questions.

Explanation of the variability we are examining in this chapter must come through testing of hypotheses directed at behavioral variability, such as implied by the postulate stated above that "soldiers drank a lot." If this in indeed found to be the behavioral cause of the increase in the wine bottle ratio on military sites of the Revolutionary War period, then we have still to ask why. We still must cross the "why threshold" of the hypothetico-deductive method to enter the theory building arena. Hypotheses directed at explanation of this phenomenon would question the role of the male on the frontier; the role-specific, ego-indulgent activity in military behavior contrasted with multiple options of domestic life. These would need to be examined in a context of the logistics of distribution on the colonial frontier.

Questions such as these can be asked through the hypothetico-deductive method of science as pattern, such as we have been concerned with in this book, is being delineated from the archeological record. Our primary concern here has been to demonstrate the tools the archeologist has at his disposal for exploring the statics of the archeological record for abstracting the dynamics of past cultural systems represented by that record. A vital part of that tool kit is the conceptual theory set the archeologist carries with him throughout the archeological process. Without this he may find himself particularistically involved with mere things, a collector of relics from the past rather than a manipulator of ideas about man's past and his unique attribute, culture, its dynamic processes and how they work.

The Bone Ratio as an Indicator of Adjacent and Peripheral Secondary Midden

Analysis of archeological bone from historic sites can determine which animals were being utilized, which imported, which obtained locally, and which used for specific behavioral functions such as button making. We concentrate here on the fragments of bone "garbage" discarded on historic sites. We assume bone discard behavior can be monitored by ranking pieces of refuse on an "odorimetric" scale. For example, those odorous remains of refuse, such as bone, would be discarded farther from the structure whereas those less odorous items such as a broken plate, dish, or sweepings from the floor would be thrown nearby, beside the back door or off the end of the porch, front or back, to become scattered throughout the yard by pigs, dogs, chickens, and children. Under these conditions, a higher ratio of bone to artifacts thrown from the house would be found at a distance peripheral to the structure, whereas that refuse thrown adjacent to the house would have a low bone-to-artifact ratio.

The midden-filled cellar hole at Cambridge at Ninety Six, S.C., is an example of what we have termed a peripheral secondary midden, the refuse having been thrown there by someone living nearby, not by the occupants of the structure represented by the cellar. A fort moat would be a good example of peripheral midden since a moat filled with refuse is an obvious result of behavior designed to remove such trash from the immediate vicinity of the occupied area of the fort. It is expected that artifacts recovered from inside a fort will reveal a far lower bone-to-artifact ratio than midden thrown into the moat, where a high bone-to-artifact ratio would result from attempts to get the refuse beyond the occupied area as far as possible without going too far out of one's way.

The refuse allowed to accumulate inside a military fort would be relatively slight compared to that likely to be found in the moat, and within this accumulation the ratio of bone to artifacts would be small. These factors, as has been pointed out before, may well result in an inversion of the frequencies of the *Kitchen* and *Architecture* artifact groups if only the inside of the fort is excavated. A similar situation may be expected at domestic sites where middens adjacent to dwellings would be expected to have a low bone content compared with those peripheral middens farther from the house, in a gully, a marsh, or abandoned well, privy, or cellar hole.

To test these postulates, we can examine the bone ratio from the ruins used in this study (Table 27).

The highest bone ratios are seen for the frontier and fort sites, as well as the Cambridge 96 cellar hole. All three domestic Brunswick Town, N.C., ruins have lower bone ratios than any of the frontier or military sites. The Brunswick (S25) Tailor Shop ruin also has a low bone ratio in all

TABLE 27

The Bone Ratio

Site		Bone fragments	Adjusted total less bone	Bone ratio	
	Ft. Ligonier	44,547	21,778	2.04	High bone ratio indicating a *peripheral* secondary midden is involved. (Range: .36 to 2.04)
	Ft. Prince George	2644	7388	.36	
	Ft. Moultrie A	4057	6102	.66	
	Ft. Moultrie B	1020	1745	.58	
	Spalding's Store	8214	16,770	.49	
	Cambridge 96	11,187	19,880	.56	
	Brunswick S25	5497	36,765	.15	Low bone ratio indicating an *adjacent* secondary midden is involved. (Range: .03 to .17)
	Brunswick S10	519	13,118	.04	
	Brunswick S7	222	8183	.03	
Sq. 1–8	Brunswick S25 Front Yard	66	1110	.06	
Sq. 16–18	Brunswick S25 Rear Yard	2265	13,570	.17	
Sq. 22–26	Brunswick S25 Inside Ruin	526	7220	.07	
Sq. 21–25	Brunswick S7 Front Yard	2	1181	.002	Extremely low bone ratio indicating adjacent secondary midden; parallels a decrease in *Kitchen* artifacts. (Reflecting special antirefuse disposal behavior around this structure.) (Range: .002 to .02)
Sq. 7–14	Brunswick S7 Rear Yard	51	4047	.01	
Sq. 11	Brunswick S7 Midden Area	16	915	.02	

three areas examined. The midden area behind the tailor shop, however, has a slightly higher ratio than that inside or in front of the structure, due perhaps to the "over-the-wall" situation seen at this structure, allowing some peripheral midden to be thrown outside the lot over the lot wall. This still does not bring the bone ratio high enough to match those high peripheral ratios seen on the frontier and military sites, or at the Cambridge 96 cellar.

The Brunswick S7 ruin, which revealed so low a percentage of *Kitchen* artifacts compared with the *Architecture* group was of interest in that it was hypothesized that this was the result of special antirefuse disposal behavior around this ruin, and a very low adjacent secondary midden ratio would support this interpretation. The ratios seen at the Brunswick S7 ruin are indeed the lowest for any site in this study, indicating a different behavioral patterning was probably involved at this structure, producing this effect on the archeological record.

The low bone ratio at the Brunswick Town ruins certainly indicates

Peripheral secondary refuse in a cellar hole at Bethabara, North Carolina.

that the artifact-loaded peripheral middens were never excavated at these structures, probably having been thrown over the high bank across the street from the ruins. Using this ratio the archeologist may well judge whether he has located and excavated the major secondary midden represented by the high bone ratio peripheral midden. This ratio may well be used in cases where test squares are used to attempt to locate the architectural area of an historical ruin. Those test squares having peripheral ratios might be those containing the best representative collection of artifacts from the site, but the architectural remains of the structure itself should be found in those areas having an adjacent bone ratio.

Although the bone variability allows the identification of an adjacent as opposed to a peripheral secondary midden deposit, it is anticipated that the number of classes of artifacts reflected in either type of deposit would remain relatively the same. This is based on the assumption that over a period of years there will be a blending effect tending to erase all but the most dramatic differences in by-product clusters reflecting specialized activity areas; thus most artifact types and classes will eventually be found distributed around the structure through this generalizing process of refuse disposal. If this is the case the same general number of artifact classes should be found in peripheral deposits as found in adjacent areas. The average number of artifact classes for the adjacent midden sites is 32.25, whereas that for the peripheral midden sites is 33.50, revealing that bone is apparently the primary variable for distinguishing an adjacent from a peripheral midden deposit.

Summary of Ratio Comparison

Some of the many possibilities of isolating variables on historic sites have been explored here through the use of simple comparison of artifact ratios. The broad base for such comparison lies in the Carolina Pattern and the Frontier Pattern, but examination of specific behavioral variability reflected in artifacts is most effectively seen on the level of artifact class ratios, some of which we have examined here. Any artifact class tabulated in the manner done here can be examined for information it may contain relative to identifying and understanding variability and regularity in the archeological record.

Other classes of artifacts not examined here can be explored for clues to past human behavior, such as Toys, Class 33, a class recovered from all sites except two, representing domestic, military, frontier and trading post sites. This class could be considered as indicating the presence of women and children, but is this a valid assumption? Why are "whizzers," Jew's-harps, and marbles frequently found on military camp sites of both the British and American Revolutionary War forces (Calver and Bolton 1970)? Do these artifacts represent children, and thereby women, or do these items merely reflect the youth of some of the soldiers on both sides during the Revolution? It very well may reflect behavior among adults at that time period; behavior no longer practiced among adults today. Marbles, or taws, for instance, may have evolved from a game played by adults and children to a game played primarily by children, and today, to a game played by hardly anyone. The forms of the game, no doubt, have changed considerably, many varieties being known to most people only a few years ago but unrecognized by children of today.

Questions such as these call for coordinated research between the historical archeologist, the historian, the folklorist, and the social historian for effective interpretation of the information revealed by the archeologist. The groups and classes used here dictate to a degree the results of our comparisons, and we realize that ratio comparisons on the artifact type and attribute level will be more sensitive yet in answering some questions. Quantification studies based on them should be used to gain a greater command of the broader patterns revealed at the group and class level.

In working with folklore specialists, social historians, and other specialists we may find that in order to understand a past cultural system, the classification of marbles, Jew's-harps, and "whizzers" as artifacts in a class called "Toys" is not acceptable procedure. This may become apparent *if* we learn that in the eighteenth century "whizzers" were used for gambling, marbles for witchcraft ceremonies, and Jew's-harps for making music and thus better classified under "recreation," "religion," and "musical instruments." The point is that classification may vary with the questions being asked, because many artifacts functioned in different ways in different contexts in past cultural systems.

SUMMARIZING VIEWPOINT—THE FLAX HACKLE EXAMPLE

The many contexts within the cultural system in which a single artifact can occur are well illustrated by the case of the lowly flax hackle. The hackle was an instrument made of a number of sharp headless nails fastened through a tin-wrapped board. It was used to comb flax fibers in preparation for spinning into linen yarn. It functions in the "technomic" sense as an instrument for combing flax, or for combing hair for making wigs (Binford 1962: 219; South 1968: 224). It is seen by the archeologist as a rusting pile of what appears to be headless nails. If he is unfamiliar with the hackle he may well identify the remains as a pile of headless nails. When the hackle was an artifact in the "systemic context" (Schiffer 1972), it had the initials of a betrothed couple and their betrothal date, as well as a decorative tulip shaped by nail holes punched into the tin band around the wooden base. In the historian's eyes, surviving examples of this type are documents subject to genealogical search to establish the name the initials represent. As a betrothal gift, however, the hackle symbolized the fulcrum in the balance of labor involved in producing clothing for the family, the man growing, retting, and breaking the flax to the point where the fibers were combed. Then the woman took over, combing, spinning, weaving, and sewing until a garment was complete. This symbolic connotation of the cooperative division of labor between the sexes had the hackle functioning as a "socio-technic" object in the system, "articulating individuals one with another into cohesive groups capable of efficiently

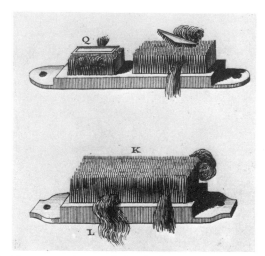

Hackles are used to comb flax for linen and hair for wigs.

maintaining themselves and . . . manipulating the technology (Binford 1962: 219)." In the betrothal ceremony focused on the hackle, and in its symbolic context, it is an "ideo-technic" artifact symbolizing "the ideological rationalizations for the social system and . . . [providing] the symbolic milieu in which individuals are enculturated, a necessity if they are to take their place as functional participants in the social system (Binford 1962: 219–220)."

In the antique store the hackle becomes a piece of merchandise to be sold because it is "old." In this context it takes on new symbolism, one in which the mere fact of age is important, both to the seller and to the buyer. In this "relic merchandising" or business context, the past "technomic," "socio-technic," or "ideo-technic" functions of the hackle are irrelevant; it is primarily seen as a curiosity, and as merchandise. However in this latter context the hackle is still a part of a system, but with changed symbolic meaning. As a museum object it functions in an educational context, serving to recall to mind the "technomic" function it once served in the past, and if the curator is perceptive, its past symbolic and betrothal gift aspects may be emphasized, in order to effect a "confrontation with the past."

The woman using a modern version of a hackle in a fashionable wig shop to comb swatches of hair has no knowledge that she is using the same instrument and making the same motions as those used in preparing flax. In the art museum, hung by the original hole used to fasten it to a bench and festooned with a complex hanging of macramé, the hackle becomes part of a work of art to be admired for its role in a composition having nostalgic overtones. When the show is over, a visit to the artist's shop finds him combing flax with the hackle part of his masterpiece, having been caught up in a national "return to the soil" movement involving the replication of the entire flax growing, retting, breaking, combing, spinning, weaving, and sewing process. In this renaissance the hackle again takes on the same literal "technomic" function, but now after 200 years the system is different, the reasons for the function are different, and the complex of performance variables is different, even though the task performance is the same. The hackle continues to function in the system, however, in whatever context the imagination of man can dream up.

To return to the archeologist who found the pile of what he cataloged as a set of headless nails, what can he interpret from the data he has unearthed? First, he must identify the "nails" as a hackle. The task facing him now in regard to interpreting the hackle in terms of the past cultural system is the same that faces him for virtually all of the artifacts he uncovers. He could tack onto his report the story just related from the "vast corpus of material already published on the subject," as Noël Hume has urged us to do, and thus attempt to arrive at a "confrontation with the past." In so doing he makes his report a clothes horse of history draped with a few archeological specifics (Noël Hume 1968: 104).

His alternative is to view the hackle as a contribution toward understanding culture process. His careful study of associations relating to the hackle may reveal the pointed iron spindle and other artifacts associated with spinning and weaving flax into linen. In this context he is addressing himself to the functional associations on the "technomic" level. He must look beyond his ruin, however, to find the broader answers he is seeking. In doing this he may find that more hackles in archeological context

The hackle may function in technological, social, and ideological contexts.

have been reported from Pennsylvania than any other area, in association with artifact frequencies fitting the "Pennsylvania German Colonial Artifact Pattern" (yet to be developed). He may discover that a secondary concentration of hackles in archeological context has been reported from Virginia and North Carolina Piedmont. From these quantification-distribution comparisons he is now about ready to suggest what is beginning to appear as a correlation with historical data relating to a German-American migration out of Pennsylvania into the Carolinas. He may then suggest that if this proposition is true, there may be a correlation between the soils, temperature, and rainfall, in relation to the requirements for successful flax growing, and the archeological data he has at his command. He may also suggest that in areas where soils are poor, such as coastal zones, no hackles would be expected, and available data from Brunswick Town and other colonial sites in this zone could be used to support such a postulate, no hackles having been found on such sites. By now it may have become apparent that hackles are to be recovered on German-American sites identified by the Pennsylvania Pattern, but not found associated with sites fitting the Carolina Pattern. At his point prediction might be made with considerable expectation that examination of empirical data will verify expectations and validate the postulates upon which predictions were stated. The pattern recognized, questions of causal processes can be asked.

Assuming that this hypothetical projection of pattern relating to flax

The Ruin of the Doctor's Laboratory at the Moravian Settlement at Behabara, N.C.

hackles is demonstrated, and assuming that similar patterning of other artifacts indicating a high degree of self-sufficiency in German-American settlements during colonial times is also demonstrated, such a situation could likely be expressed as a "law." The testing of the "law" through new data collection would follow, and finally the threshold of the hypothetico-deductive method would be crossed by asking why the pattern was as it was observed to be. The hypotheses would be directed at examining the German-American colonial idea of encouraging self-sufficiency, and the British-American colonial idea of discouraging self-sufficiency, as well as propositions examining the British-American and the German-American distributive systems for supplying the American colonies. Other hypotheses might examine the tulip motif found on flax hackles, locally made pottery, and many other objects in the German-American areas. These hypotheses might ask:

1. Why does the tulip appear on German-American artifacts?
2. What is the relationship between the concept of self-reliance and the tulip motif?
3. What is the relationship between the tulip motif and the five doctrines of Calvinism affirmed at the Synod of Dort in 1618–1619 held by the Reformed Church of Netherlands, each of which began with a letter in the word "tulip"[1] (Hall 1965; Kingdon 1973)?
4. Did the "tulipomania" of 1638 relate to the Reformed Church doctrines affirmed in 1618 (Evans 1931: 79)?
5. Is there a connection between the attitude of self-sufficiency reflected by the artifacts from German-American communities and the individualistic philosophy fostered by Calvinist doctrine as opposed to the more conservative, authoritarian-based principles of Lutheranism? Is the tulip primarily a Calvinist-based motif?
6. What laws, relating to motifs such as the tulip and its connection to religious ideology, can be formulated from such motif patterns derived from historic site archeology?
7. What hypotheses can we deduce for explaining pattern based on the knowledge gained from such a tulip motif study?
8. Can the laws derived from such a combined archeology and archival study be projected through hypotheses and testing for explanation of prehistoric motifs?

Such hypotheses, once stated in the hypothetico-deductive framework, would be tested with new data. The intent here is not to go through such a procedure, but merely to cite an example of how such historic site data can be dealt with for arriving at some degree of under-

---

[1] Theocentrism, Unconditional predestination, Limited atonement, Irrestibility of Grace, Perseverance of the saints.

standing of past cultural processes. The flax hackle is only one of the many artifacts that could be similarly dealt with.

Thus through continuous observation, analysis, synthesis, questioning, and testing through the scientific cycle, the archeologist can arrive at laws relating to culture process as seen through data from sites of the historic period. In the case of the flax hackle, a great deal depends on establishing whether flax hackles are objects to be found more in one area than in another, and this can be done only through an awareness of the problems raised by each class of data, artifacts, architecture, features, frequencies, and associations. Such an approach demands a similar frame of reference for revealing culture process to be used by archeologists excavating historic sites in America, so that comparable data can be made available. With each archeologist excavating his site as though it were a particularistic, unique phenomenon, this visionary projection appears, at times, as a remote dream. However, processual archeology has its dreamers, its missionaries, and its prophets. For the most effective pursuit of laws of culture process that directed past human behavior, everyone must get into the act.

The significant point here is that the archeologist must work with the record remaining from the complex social system that produced that record, and a first step toward understanding something about the laws under which that system operated comes with an understanding of the pattern in the data at hand, be it flax hackles or Jew's-harps. That pattern will be revealed through quantification analysis, regardless of the classificatory system used as a tool to abstract the pattern from the data. In other words, horseshoes could be combined with ceramics in a study designed to reveal pattern, and pattern would be revealed.

If consistent covariation exists between this horseshoe-ceramic class and a class made up of wine bottles and nails, then it matters not what the archeologist's preconceived notions are about the relationship between ceramics, horseshoes, wine bottles, and nails; the reality of the pattern and the predictive value of this knowledge is what is archeologically important. By examining other variables such as floor space, relative position of various buildings on the site, the source of water, the relationship of high ground to marsh, the location of the kitchen, barn, roads, and the refuse disposal practices of the occupants, the archeologist may discover other covariables. With this information he may begin to understand the pattern in terms of his site. When he expands his view to other sites and other areas, again looking for regularity and variability, he may begin to address himself to the system of which his site is a part. This approach removes the archeologist's preconceptions as to the meaning inherent in the artifacts themselves and directs him toward ascertaining their relevance in a broader context.

Quantification analyses of archeological data can be done on the level of the group, the class, the type, or on specific attributes in order to determine pattern reflective of past human behavior. This can be done under almost any classificatory scheme toward discovering pattern reflecting culture process. Historical archeologists have leaned on historical data to allow them to interpret the "true" meaning of "whizzers," marbles, and Jews-harps, when the meaning lies in the questions he asks and in the relevance of the data he collects toward answering these questions. If classifying ceramics and horseshoes in the same artifact class is relevant to the question being asked, then the archeologist by all means should do this to get at answers. He should not imply, however, that his classification is the end result being sought in archeology (Stone 1974), when it is merely a convenience toward asking specific questions of the data. If we merely classify attributes, types, classes, and groups without a research design justifying such a procedure, then we are merely placing artifacts into pigeon holes.

As we learn more about the patterning in the archeological record, and the processes that caused this patterning, we will certainly revise our classification schemes. We will be asking questions relating to the critical variables responsible for trade, status, the expanding frontier, socio-economic level, national and ethnic origins, plantation economy, the industrial revolution, and changing life styles.

The analyses such as we have conducted here are certainly only a beginning, raising as many new questions as providing answers to other ones, but questions are the beginning of the scientific cycle. For instance, examining the relationship between seventeenth-century settlement along major river systems as revealed by maps of the period, and the points at which the deep water channel touches high ground, in relation to the class status of individuals located at such points, is certainly worthwhile. Questions regarding population studies of historic sites from artifacts recovered in relation to the square footage excavated could be asked by using historical data indicating the number of occupants in a structure for a known period of time; excavation of the ruin would yield artifacts recovered from known square footage areas, and from these data eventual per-capita-per-year-per-square-foot indices could be developed from which predictions could be made. Testing and continual evaluating of variables would eventually produce a body of reliable data.

Perhaps these are audacious and impertinent questions, but merely to continue to insist, as some have done in the past, that answers to such questions are impossible to abstract from historic sites through archeological procedures is counterproductive. Isolating variables as we have done here, in order to understand the processes reflected by human behavior through the archeological record, is a first step in archeological analysis. Historical archeology is caught in the wave of an archeological revolution in theory, method, and research design leading toward archeological science. Archeologists must either ride the crest of the scientific wave or "wipe out," falling victim to the internalized, particularistic undertow.

EXPLORING INVENTORY PATTERN FOR COMPARISON WITH ARCHEOLOGICAL PATTERN

In deriving the Carolina and Frontier Patterns the archeological record has been used. The question arises as to the relationship between the archeological patterns and historical inventories of past household goods. It should be clear from the summary presented in the previous section that analysis of archeological patterning is not done with the view of satisfying our preconceptions about past cultures by imposing our expectations, as programmed into us by our own culture, on the data.

The recognition of pattern in the archeological record is certainly not a process designed to allow us to reconstruct past inventories. It does behoove us, however, to have an understanding of the relative degree to which the archeological record represents, even in a gross manner, an inventory of the system of which it was once a part. Ceramics and wine bottles in their fragmentary state constitute the major artifacts, along with nails, used on British colonial sites examined in this study. Silver forks, gold coins, and pewter objects are seldom seen on archeological sites, yet we know from surviving documents that such objects were indeed a part of the British colonial system. These highly curated objects,

Historical documentation and the static archeological record are patterned by-products of past cultural systems.

when inventoried by the participants in the culture, would certainly represent a ratio different from the one for fragments of the same objects in an archeological context.

In this section, Carolina inventories for the same time period as that represented by the Carolina Pattern will be used to derive an Inventory Pattern. The differences between these patterns will be examined for developing transformation indices that will allow a statement to be made contrasting what *was* there in the system to what *is* there in the archeological context.

This goal could best be accomplished with the help of a computer. A data base exists in the form of probate records providing inventories for many areas during the past 300 years. Studies are under way toward programming such data into computer banks for use in asking many questions. However, this study will be designed primarily to be compatible with the archeological patterns we have examined so that a direction can be explored, rather than to present a definitive pattern based on such a project as that outlined earlier.

The Method of Abstracting the Inventory Pattern

The *North Carolina Wills and Inventories* volume by Grimes (1912) was used as a source for the eighteenth-century inventories used in this study. The first 25 pages of the "Inventories" section (pp. 469–494) were used to obtain a sample of wills for North Carolina. A seventeenth-century inventory from South Carolina was also used (Salley 1944: 25), which was made when John Foster and Capt. Thomas Gray dissolved their partnership in a store in 1672, at Charles Towne, S.C. A Maryland inventory of Thomas Jenings (South 1967) was also used in comparison with the Carolina data.

In tabulating the objects listed in the inventories, items likely to leave no archeological record, such as books, cloth, clothing, table cloths, napkins, chairs, tables, salt, and grain were not listed. Those items of furniture listed as having drawers were counted as a single item under the assumption that the drawer might well have brass hardware. Objects clearly capable of leaving an archeological record were tabulated, such as pewter plates, basins, dishes, bottles, forks, spoons, knives, tongs, hammers, hinges, kettles, spits, andirons, and pothooks. No consideration in this study was given to the value of the estate being inventoried, nor was any attempt made to evaluate the social status of the individuals involved, their economic level, or profession. Our primary concern was with a tabulation of objects within the artifact classes used in developing the Carolina Pattern.

Questions of socio-economic level, etc., can well be asked using inventories from individuals for whom historical data are available in order to determine which artifact variables covary with the known information. Such studies constructed on inventories from a wide area, using selected classes of individuals based on controlled attributes for selection, should provide information of value in comparison with artifact inventory profiles constructed from archeological excavations. Such studies should be based on a close parallel between the types of data listed in the inventory and that from the archeological context. The critical factor in such comparisons will be the transformation of pattern from the archeological record to the systemic inventory. The exploration of this factor is the purpose of the following study.

The 13 inventories chosen for comparison were used in the Hierarchical Clustering Program of the OSIRIS statistical package in order to arrive at a computer clustering of the inventories based on the frequency relationships between the 41 classes of artifacts. The results of this clustering are seen in Figure 32. Six inventories are seen to cluster at the .94 level of significance, and these were chosen for illustration.

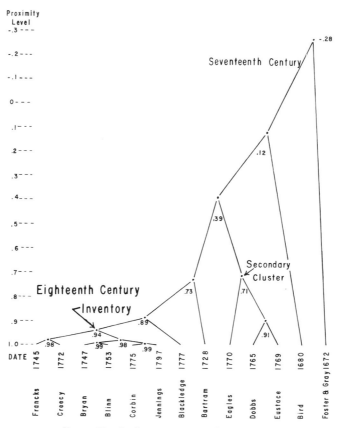

Figure 32. Probate inventory cluster analysis.

A second cluster at the .71 level is seen for the inventories of Richard Eagles (a Cape Fear landowner), Governor Arthur Dobbs (Royal Governor of North Carolina), and Dr. John Eustace (Figure 32). In examining these three inventories for clues as to why they differ from other inventories, joining with the primary cluster at a level of only .39, we see that the *Clothing* group for Dr. Eagles is unusually high (Table 28) because of 480 mohair buttons, that Governor Dobbs' *Personal* group is extremely high because of 230 gold and silver coins, and that Dr. John Eustice's *Activities* group is high due to 73 surgical tools.

If we had a sample of inventories numbering in the hundreds, for which historical research had provided data for division of the inventories into postulated status groupings before such a cluster analysis was conducted, differences and clusterings such as we see here would allow the abstraction of pattern having status predictive value. In the case of these three inventories, we do not know what the relationship between these men might have been relative to status within the system, but it is interesting to note that merely in the titles of the men accompanying the inventories we have clues to the socio-economic level for at least two of the individuals involved. However, individuals in the .94 cluster may well have had equal status within the Carolina colonial system with which we are concerned. We will ignore these questions for the moment since our problem does not involve status but rather the determination of an Inventory Pattern based on the mean of the six inventories correlating at the .94 proximity level, for use in comparison with the Carolina Artifact Pattern.

Two inventories are dramatically contrastive with the others, and these are the two seventeenth-century examples (Figure 32). These examples suggest that if we had available many seventeenth-century inventories, a radically different pattern might be revealed to contrast with that cluster of eighteenth-century inventories at the .94 level. Identification of such pattern by those having access to seventeenth-century data should be undertaken.

The Eighteenth-Century Inventory Pattern

The artifact counts and percentage relationships for the eight artifact groups in our classification are seen in Table 28 for the six inventories we will use for constructing the Inventory Pattern. In addition to these eight artifact groups, we have added a pewter class to illustrate the many classes of material objects that were in the cultural system but seldom in any numbers in archeological contexts. When we derive the mean for each of the percentages for each artifact group, the resulting Inventory Pattern is seen in Table 29.

It is interesting to note that the percentage relationship of the *Kitchen*

TABLE 28

Eighteenth-Century Probate Inventories Clustering at the .94 Proximity Level[a]

Artifact group	Martin Francks 1745		Levy Creecy 1772		William Bryan 1747	
	Count	%	Count	%	Count	%
Kitchen	208	49.8	255	52.3	251	62.7
Architecture	0	0	0	0	0	0
Furniture	5	1.2	8	1.6	5	1.3
Arms	4	.9	4	.8	12	3.0
Clothing	2	.5	8	1.6	0	0
Personal	8	1.9	6	1.2	7	1.8
Tobacco Pipes	0	0	0	0	0	0
Activities	118	27.8	158	32.5	93	23.2
Pewter	80	18.8	49	10.0	32	8.0
Totals	425	99.9	488	100.0	400	100.0

Artifact group	Daniel Blinn 1753		Mrs. Jean Corbin 1775		Thomas Jenings 1797	
	Count	%	Count	%	Count	%
Kitchen	175	59.9	298	60.7	470	63.8
Architecture	0	0	0	0	0	0
Furniture	5	1.7	4	.8	13	1.8
Arms	3	1.0	4	.8	7	.9
Clothing	4	1.4	2	.4	0	0
Personal	5	1.7	16	3.3	35	4.7
Tobacco Pipes	0	0	0	0	0	0
Activities	68	23.3	156	31.8	188	25.5
Pewter	32	11.0	11	2.2	24	3.3
Totals	292	100.0	491	100.0	737	100.0

group of artifact classes is very close in both the archeological and the inventory means. Groups such as the *Architecture* group however, reveal a contrast because the inventories don't mention these construction-related artifact classes. The *Activities* group is also much higher in the Inventory Pattern than in the Carolina Pattern as is the *Personal* group. The Pewter class is represented by a percentage of 8.9 in the inventories, but is absent from the archeological pattern. The higher percentages seen in the Inventory Pattern are thought to reflect the curation of these objects in the cultural system, resulting in their appearing in higher frequencies in the inventory than in the archeological context.

The absence of artifacts from the inventories that are found in

TABLE 28   (Continued)

	Richard Eagles 1770		%	Gov. Arthur Dobbs 1765		%
	Count			Count		
Kitchen	1285		42.8	549		62.0
Architecture	522		17.4	0		0
Furniture	11		.4	14		1.6
Arms	160		5.3	0		0
Clothing	608	(480 mohair buttons)	20.3	7		.8
Personal	80	(62 coins)	2.7	245	(230 coins)	27.7
Tobacco Pipes	0		0	0		0
Activities	310		10.3	38		4.2
Pewter	26		.8	33		3.7
Total	3002		100.0	886		100.0

	Dr. John Eustace 1769		
	Count		%
Kitchen	558		84.5
Architecture	0		0
Furniture	6		.9
Arms	7		1.0
Clothing	1		.2
Personal	15		2.3
Tobacco Pipes	0		0
Activities	73	(surgical tools)	11.1
Pewter	0		0
Total	660		100.0

[a] The inventories used here are from Grimes 1912, pages: Francks, 494; Creecy, 481; Bryan, 480; Blinn, 476; Corbin, 482; Eagles, 486; Dobbs, 484; Eustace, 490. The Jenings inventory is from South 1967, p. 203.

considerable quantities in the archeological context, such as *Architecture* and *Tobacco Pipe* artifacts, reflects the fact that nails, window glass, and tobacco pipes were not considered a part of the inventory, except perhaps in unusual cases not seen in these six examples.

If we can consider, for purposes of illustration, that the Inventory Pattern is reflective of the patterning seen in the cultural system, and the ratio between the percentages for the Inventory Pattern and the Carolina Pattern mirrors a degree of curation, then it would be possible to construct a curation-transformation ratio from this information. This step might allow a statement to be made about the historical inventory represented by an archeological artifact collection on the basis of the ratio difference between the Inventory Pattern and the Carolina Artifact

TABLE 29

Inventory Pattern from Six Inventories of the Eighteenth Century Compared with the Carolina Pattern

	Mean %	Range	Carolina Artifact Pattern
Kitchen	58.2	49.8–63.8	63.1
Architecture	0		25.5
Furniture	1.4	.8– 1.8	.2
Arms	1.2	.8– 3.0	.5
Clothing	.6	0– 1.6	3.0
Personal	2.4	1.2– 4.7	.2
Tobacco Pipes	0		5.8
Activities	27.3	23.2–32.5	1.7
(Pewter)	8.9	2.2–18.8	0
	100.0		100.0

Pattern. The application of the curation-transformation ratio to archeological data (Cambridge 96) for deriving an interpreted historical inventory is shown in Table 30.

This curation-transformation ratio procedure has been used to express the artifacts from the Cambridge 96 ruin in terms of the Inventory Pattern to produce an intepreted Cambridge historical inventory percentage profile. This percentage profile inventory is not intended to represent a literal inventory of the goods from the occupants of the home from which the Cambridge midden was thrown. Rather, it is an interpretive tool intended to make the archeologist aware of the fact that the 25% of all artifacts he recovered from the ruin he excavated, represented by the *Architecture* group, were not likely to have been included in inventories. He should also be aware of the fact that the archeologically revealed .5% of all artifacts, represented by the *Personal* group, was likely to represent 5.8% in inventories of material culture made by those participants in the system represented by the archeological record. This percentage is a figure 12 times (curation-transformation ratio) that seen in the archeological record. Similarly the *Activities* group artifacts are mentioned in inventories 16 times more frequently than the fragmentary remains of such activities in the archeological record.

These contrasts relate to the degree of curation of personal items such as watches, gold, and silver and to the fact that once architectural hardware becomes a part of a structure, its frequency ratios to other artifacts is far more likely to be revealed by the archeologist than by a study of the inventories. Tobacco pipes leave a far more impressive

TABLE 30

Application of the Curation-Transformation Ratio to Data from Cambridge, 96, S.C.

Artifact group	Inventory pattern mean	÷	Carolina Pattern	=	Curation-Transformation ratio	×	Cambridge 96 count	=	Ratio-Adjusted Cambridge count	Interpreted historical inventory for Cambridge	Cambridge artifact % profile for comparison
Kitchen	58.2	÷	63.1	=	.9	×	12,854	=	11,569	52.2	64.6
Architecture	0(.1)*	÷	25.5	=	.004	×	5006	=	20	.09	25.2
Furniture	1.4	÷	.2	=	7.0	×	35	=	245	1.1	.2
Arms	1.2	÷	.5	=	2.4	×	27	=	65	.3	.1
Clothing	.6	÷	3.0	=	.2	×	1069	=	214	1.0	5.4
Personal	2.4	÷	.2	=	12.0	×	108	=	1296	5.8	.5
Tobacco Pipes	0(.1)*	÷	5.8	=	.017	×	349	=	6	.02	1.8
Activities	27.3	÷	1.7	=	16.0	×	432	=	6912	31.2	2.2
(Pewter)	8.9	÷	0	=	8.9	×	0	=	(1809)**	8.2	0
	100.0		100.0				19,880		22,136	99.9	100.0

* Insert .1 when zero
** When artifact count equals zero, insert the appropriate percentage (8.9) of the total ratio-adjusted count (20,327 × .089 = 1809)

197

record in archeological context than in the lists provided by those participants in the past cultural system who were listing only those things that had particular significance to them from an inventory point of view. Use of the curation-transformation ratio tool suggested here should help in attempts to discover laws governing behavior in past cultural systems.

In this study, we have compared whole objects on the one hand with fragments on the other, a procedure that makes absolutely no difference when our primary purpose is to compare these kinds of data sets. The archeologist happens to work with fragments; the compiler of inventories is tabulating whole objects. Both types of data are material remains of past cultural systems. Inventory records are highly fickle due to the many variables involved in compiling the inventories, but regularities can be discovered that are pertinent to the analyses that archeologists are making, provided inventory studies are designed to answer the kinds of questions archeologists are asking. Too often there is a wide gap separating the studies being done by those dealing with probate records and those quantification studies being carried out by archeologists looking for laws of culture process. Both types of data are rich sources for deriving pattern in the reconstruction of past cultural systems. Too often the probate records are used merely as a means for answering historical questions. Archeologists are beginning to utilize historical documents from the point of view of abstracting data similar to that recovered from the earth in the form of fragments. Both records are fragmentary, but both can yield complementary data sets for discovering laws directing human behavior.

REFERENCES

Binford, Lewis R.
   1962   Archaeology as Anthropology. *American Antiquity* **28** (No. 2):217–225.
Calver, William Louis, and Reginald Pelham Bolton
   1970   *History written with pick and shovel.* New York: The New York Historical Society.
Combes, John D.
   n.d.   The Archeology at Fort Prince George. Manuscript in preparation. Institute of Archeology and Anthropology, University of South Carolina, Columbia.
Evans, Joan
   1931   *Pattern.* Oxford: Oxford University Press.
Ferguson, Leland G.
   1975   Analysis of Ceramic Materials from Fort Watson, December 1780–April 1781. *The Conference on Historic Site Archaeology Papers 1973* **8**. Institute of Archeology and Anthropology, University of South Carolina, Columbia.
Grimes, J. Bryan (Editor)
   1912   *North Carolina wills and inventories.* Raleigh, N.C.: Edwards and Broughton.
Grimm, Jacob L.
   1970   Archaeological Investigation of Fort Ligonier 1960–1965. *Annals of Carnegie Museum 42,* Pittsburgh.

Hall, Basil
  1965   Synod of Dort. *Encyclopaedia Britannica* **7:**p. 600. Chicago: Encyclopaedia Britannica.

Kingdon, Robert M.
  1973   Determinism in theology: Predestination. In *Dictionary of the history of ideas,* edited by Philip P. Wiener. New York: Scribner's.

Noël Hume, Ivor
  1962   An Indian Ware of the Colonial Period. *Quarterly Bulletin* **17,** No. 1, Charlottesville: Archeological Society of Virginia.
  1968   Historical Archaeology in America. *Post-Medieval Archaeology* **1:**104–105.

Salley, A. S. (Editor)
  1944   *Records of the Secretary of the Province and the Register of the Province of South Carolina 1671–1675.* Columbia: Historical Commission of South Carolina.

Schiffer, Michael B.
  1972   Archaeological Context and Systemic Context. *American Antiquity* **37:**156–165.

South, Stanley A.
  1967   The Paca House, Annapolis, Maryland. Prepared for Contract Archaeology, Inc. On file at Historic Annapolic, Inc., Alexandria, Virginia.
  1968   The Lowly Flax Hackle. *Antiques* **94** (No. 2):224–227.
  1974   Palmetto Parapets. *Anthropological Studies No. 1.* Institute of Archeology and Anthropology, University of South Carolina, Columbia.

Stone, Lyle M.
  1974   Fort Michilimackinac 1715–1781. *Publications of the Museum.* East Lansing: Michigan State University.

Large storage jars reflect a totally different function than most other Ceramic forms.

Revealing
Culture Process
through the
Formula
Concept

THE HORIZON PHENOMENON REVEALED IN CERAMIC ANALYSIS IN HISTORICAL ARCHEOLOGY

INTRODUCTION

In this chapter the quantification approach used in the previous chapters is climaxed through the demonstration of pattern recognition in the context of chronology. This study will examine the relationship between the manufacture period of ceramic types found on British-American sites and the occupation period for the sites on which type-fragments are found. We will present data indicating that on eighteenth-century sites there is a high correlation between the dates of ceramic manufacture and the period of site occupation. We will also look at the effectiveness of ceramic analysis based on presence and absence as compared to quantification of fragments of ceramic types. The horizon phenomenon as reflected in analysis of ceramics from historic sites will also be examined through British ceramics and Spanish majolica.

Terms

Attributes are those observable criteria, primarily technological or stylistic, by which a ceramic type has been defined, including shape, paste, hardness, design, decoration, color, and glaze. A *type* refers to pottery defined by one or more key attributes. With historic site ceramics a type is often distinguished on the basis of a single attribute. (See Clark 1968: 134, for a discussion of attribute and artifact systems.) *Form* is a generalized term referring to the physical shape of an object,

201

such as a teapot or teacup form. *Function* deals with the use that the form was designed to serve (Longacre 1970: 132). *Evolutionary dynamics* may be seen in the change of form through time.

Type Manufacture Date and Deposition Date

In historical archeology, the period during which artifacts were manufactured can be arrived at through documents, paintings, and patent records. The beginning date for the manufacture of a type may depend on the innovative action of one individual acting to introduce an additional attribute which is subsequently used to establish a type. The green glaze of the Whieldon-Wedgwood partnership developed in 1759, for instance (Noël Hume 1970: 124–125) quickly went out of production, providing us with a known beginning manufacture date and an end manufacture date probably no later than 1775. In many cases the end manufacture date cannot be fixed with the degree of accuracy of that of the beginning date. The point midway between the beginning and end manufacture dates would be the median manufacture date, an important date for the purpose of this study. As Noël Hume points out, "The trick is to be able to date the artifacts . . . (1970: 11)." The knowledge of manufacture dates for artifacts is an invaluable aid in the determination of occupation dates for historic sites. This is not to say that the manufacture date and the occupation date are the same, but rather that there is a connection between the two in that the manufacture date provides a *terminus post quem*, "a date after which the object must have found its way into the ground (Noël Hume 1970: 11)." This is, as Noël Hume points out, "the cornerstone of all archaeological reasoning." However, there are those who believe there is such a slight connection between the date of manufacture and the date of deposition of ceramic type specimens on historic sites that they view as error any attempts to fix the occupation of sites by association of ceramics with the known date of manufacture (Dollar 1968: 41–45). A major concern of this chapter is to present data revolving around the artifact manufacture date and the artifact deposition date.

Another major conviction here is that changing ceramic form through time is useful in dating. Twenty years ago I emphasized that evolutionary theory is the basic framework of archeology (South 1955). This chapter is also anchored in the assumption that evolution of form is basic to the culture process and is the foundation for the "cornerstone of all archaeological reasoning" of which Noël Hume speaks in his discussion of *terminus post quem*.

Horizon

Through the excavation of a variety of eighteenth-century historic sites I have become convinced that groups of ceramic types from different ruins of the same time period are similar enough to allow them to be used in determining periods of site occupation. This seems to be so regardless of whether the site is a remote frontier fort, a Cherokee village, a congested port town house, or a mansion. This conviction has resulted in the development of analytical tools for use in determining the occupation dates for eighteenth-century British-American sites. These tools are useful and reliable when used on sites of varying functions over a broad area (Maryland, North Carolina, South Carolina). The reason for this is suggested in the horizon concept (Willey and Phillips 1958: 31–34), where the horizon is defined as "*a primarily spatial continuity represented by cultural traits and assemblages whose nature and mode of occurrence permit the assumption of a broad and rapid spread. The archaeological units linked by a horizon are thus assumed to be approximately* contemporaneous." This phenomenon of a broad and rapid spread of groups of contemporaneous ceramic types in the eighteenth century is examined through the tools described in this chapter.

The Unimodal Curve

The popularity of ceramic types is seen to represent a unimodal curve that had an inception (beginning manufacture date), a rise to a peak and a decrease to extinction (end manufacture date). This basic assumption is expressed by Dunnell (1970) based on concepts outlined by Rouse, Ford, Phillips and Griffin: "The distribution of any historical or temporal class exhibits the form of a unimodal curve through time. The rationale for this assumption is that any idea or manifestation of an idea has an inception, a rise in popularity to a peak, and then a decrease in popularity to extinction (p. 309)." An example of this concept is seen in Mayer-Oakes' study of illumination methods used in Pennsylvania between 1850 and 1950 as cited by James A. Ford in *A quantitative method for deriving cultural chronology* (Washington: 1962, Figure 6).

THE PROBLEM

In the seventeenth century, British-American settlements were relatively few and far between compared with those of the eighteenth century, and population density was considerably less. As a result there are fewer seventeenth-century sites for archeologists to examine. This paucity, plus few historical references to the manufacture dates of ceramics, limits our knowledge of seventeenth-century ceramics.

We do know that the lower-class seventeenth-century household had a much greater dependence on pewter, leather, and wooden trenchers and other vessel forms and less daily use of ceramics than did the gentry. From the ruins of the mansions of the seventeenth century, we would therefore expect to find ceramics more abundantly represented than from ruins of the lower class homes (Noël Hume 1970: 24; personal communication, Oct. 26, 1971). This status difference is *not* seen in ceramics from archeological sites in the eighteenth century.

The limits of our present knowledge of seventeenth-century ceramic manufacture dates and the temporally significant attributes within certain wares has resulted in a broader manufacture time span being assigned in comparison with the eighteenth century where short manufacture periods can be assigned to a number of marker types. For this reason a comparison of manufacture dates with site occupation may well reveal less correlation than such a comparison made with data from eighteenth-century sites. We might at first be inclined to interpret this discrepancy as a time lag phenomenon, and indeed some time lag may well be involved in that, with less use of ceramics in the lower class seventeenth-century homes, less breakage would naturally be expected to occur, resulting perhaps in a greater percentage of older ceramic types finding their way into the midden deposits. In the upper class homes, however, we would expect more ceramics and a closer correlation between manufacture dates and site occupation dates due to more frequent use of ceramics in the home. However, as for the time it took barrels of ceramics to make the trip from Britain to America aboard a vessel, there was no appreciable difference between the seventeenth and eighteenth centuries. In either case it was a relatively rapid process.

Ceramic types found on colonial sites are well enough known from documents and kiln site excavations that an approximate beginning and ending manufacture date can be assigned to ceramic types within certain limits of variability. Each of these ceramic types is seen to represent a unimodal curve through time as the type was introduced, reached a peak of popularity and then was discontinued. The median date for the ceramic types is the point midway through the duration of its period of manufacture. When the median date for a group of ceramic types is known, the types can be arranged so as to represent a chronology based on the median dates. Since such a chronology is based on documented periods of manufacture it is seen as an historical chronology, not a relative one such as those derived from stratigraphy and seriation on prehistoric sites. In constructing such a chronology, ceramic types such as locally made wares of unknown manufacture duration periods, or coarse English earthenwares of unknown periods of manufacture are not included for the obvious reason that they will contribute nothing to the chronology. If coarse earthenware and local wares of known periods of manufacture are present, they are most certainly to be used as valuable additions to the chronology model. Given this model, British ceramic

British Ceramics and Wine Bottle fragments in a drainage tunnel at the Governor's House at Brunswick, N.C.

types can be arranged in an historical chronology on the basis of the median known manufacture date, and this chronology accurately reflects the change in ceramic forms through time. Colonial French and Spanish ceramics could also be arranged in a similar historical chronology provided the manufacture dates were known for the ceramic types. Once the approximate beginning and ending manufacture dates of groups of historic artifact types such as wine bottles, wine glass, tobacco pipes, and buttons are established, these too can be used to construct historical chronologies of formal change through time that in turn can be used to arrive at the duration of occupation of historic sites.

Eighteenth-century English ceramics were manufactured in groups of several types at a time, some types having a shorter manufacture span than others. They were available in several types at the factories and groups of types were exported to British-American ports. A limited number of these ceramic types were available on order through agents

Overglaze enamelled Chinese export Porcelain Type 26.

in Britain or through American outlets. Among those types available to the colonist was Chinese porcelain which took its place along with British ceramic types in the colonial American home. The purchasers of these ceramic types were no farther than a few days or weeks at the most from the remote frontier of the colonies, thus the possibility was present for the rapid distribution of ceramic types over a broad area (Noël Hume 1970: 25). This broad and rapid spread of a limited number of ceramic types at one time can be described as a horizon in which the cultural traits are approximately contemporaneous (Willey and Phillips 1958: 31–34). Thus eighteenth-century historic site ceramics can be seen to represent a series of horizons in sequence.

Ceramic types manufactured in a short duration are excellent temporal markers for determining the approximate brackets for the accumulation of the sample, allowing an interpretation to be made regarding the occupation period of the historic site. Such short-period types can be used effectively on a presence and absence basis as clues to sample accumulation. An important consideration here is that a ceramic type specimen cannot appear on a site prior to the beginning manufacture date for the type, thus creating a temporal relationship between the manufacture date and the occupation of the site by those who used and broke the ceramic objects.

Regarding broken ceramics we can state a number of postulates. The cultural use patterns of the eighteenth century were such that not long after ceramic types arrived in the home in a town or frontier fort, breakage began to occur. The broken ceramic types were discarded and older types broken along with the most recent acquisitions resulted in a number of types becoming associated in the midden deposits. Although a few heirloom pieces would be broken along with a few of the most recent acquisitions, the majority of the fragments would represent those most in use during the occupation of the site. Those few most recent acquisitions would provide the clue for placing the end date on the deposit. From these postulates we can state that *an approximate mean date for the ceramic sample representing occupation of an eighteenth-*

century British-American site can be determined through the median manufacture dates for the ceramic types and the frequency of the types in the sample. With these problems in mind we will construct tools for use in ceramic analysis.

THE TOOLS

The Chronological Model for Constructing the Analytical Tools

The first step in constructing ceramic analysis tools is to build a chronological model upon which the tools can be based. An excellent example of the potential of historic site data in this regard is the use of hole measurement of tobacco pipestems by Harrington (1954) for arriving at an approximate date of the accumulation of the sample and the expression of this by Binford (1961) in terms of a regression line formula. The pipestem analysis tool as well as our ceramic analysis tools and other constructions built on a chronological framework is based on the dynamics of formal change through time.

Any unique combination of attributes constituting a type that has become extinct represents a time capsule having a median date that can be fixed as an approximate point in time, provided the beginning and ending dates can be reasonably determined. If a series of overlapping ceramic types with known median dates can be determined historically and refined archeologically, we have a temporal scale by which we can fix a collection of ceramic types in time. If this scale is established through occurrence or frequency seriation, as is the case with prehistoric artifact types and classes, the seriation can be viewed as a gross chronology, verifiable only through carefully controlled stratigraphic studies designed to accompany the seriation, or through radiocarbon dating (Dunnell 1970: 315). However, if previously dated groups of attributes representing historical stylistic types are used, such as Dethlefsen and Deetz (1966) have done with dated New England gravestones, there is a positive historical chronology involved that provides a more direct framework with which to work. In their study, Dethlefsen and Deetz demonstrated variation in time and space because they were dealing with an artifact form that was a locally manufactured folk object. With the present ceramic study, however, a standardized factory product with a known manufacture period is involved, thus eliminating local variation. Therefore, with known historically based typologies such as those found in historical archeology, a specific chronology can be constructed in a manner not possible on the prehistoric level. Historical archeologists are only beginning to explore the possibilities offered by this unique quality of their historic site data toward the examination of cultural problems.

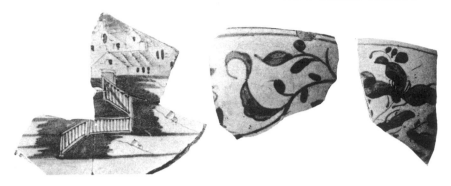

Decorated Delftware Type 49.

Historic site archeologists have constructed typologies of ceramics based on the references available to them and on their own observation, and these have been dealt with in temporal terms with varying degrees of success. Some have seen the numerous historic types and the accompanying documents as a confusing situation, and one not to be improved by attempts at typology and seriation of historic artifacts (Dollar 1968: 14). Meanwhile, others have continued to define the diagnostic criteria for recognition of ceramic types in time and space with emphasis on those attributes of color, surface finish, design, decoration, and form by means of which delineation of types can be accomplished. One of the leaders in the field of English ceramics has been Ivor Noël Hume, chief archeologist at Colonial Williamsburg. Before the publication of his book *A guide to artifacts of Colonial America* (1970), he and others were exposed to some criticism for what was seen as a lack of concern for artifact description based on specific criteria (Cleland and Fitting 1968). With the publication of this book, however, it is clear that Noël Hume is concerned with the determination of specific ceramic attributes that have significance in time and space. A book incorporating a definitive typology for English ceramics is still to be written. Meanwhile Noël Hume's book, along with basic ceramic references, enables the archeologist to make an acquaintance with the ceramic types found on British-American sites. Noël Hume does not use quantification based on ceramic fragments from archeological sites, but prefers to use vessel shape along with presence and absence in his analysis. Some of us, on the other hand, have utilized specific attributes of ceramic types as Noël Hume has done and also have used frequency occurrence of the fragments as well as presence and absence.

With the present available information on ceramic types, both descriptive and temporal, the historical archeologist should be able to take the next step in the archeological process. For years to come we will continue to be concerned with description in historical archeology, as

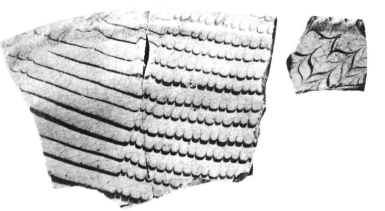

Lead Glazed Slipware (Combed Yellow) Type 56.

we should be, but we should not lose sight of the fact that this is not the goal, only the means toward understanding something about culture. Lewis Binford has quoted Sherwood L. Washburn, a physical anthropologist, concerning this point:

> The assumption seems to have been that description (whether morphological or metrical), if accurate enough and in sufficient quantity, could solve problems of process, pattern, and interpretation. . . . But all that can be done with the initial descriptive information is to gain a first understanding, a sense of problem, and a preliminary classification. To get further requires an elaboration of theory and method along different lines [Binford and Binford 1968:26; after Washburn 1953:714–715].

It is time to construct hypotheses and tools with which to deal with historic site data. Descriptive typology, temporally anchored in history, is available for a number of classes of historic site artifacts. This descriptive base will be refined as more information becomes available. However, for illustrating the analytical tools in this paper we have confined ourselves to Noël Hume's criteria as seen in *A guide to artifacts of Colonial America* and through personal communication with him and Audrey Noël Hume.

The procedure used to construct the model was to select 78 ceramic types based on attributes such as form, decoration, surface finish, and hardness with the temporal dates assigned by Noël Hume for each type. These were given type numbers and classified according to the type of ware (Table 31), with page numbers following the types discussed in Noël Hume's book. Since Noël Hume has spent a lifetime attempting to define and delimit the attributes and temporal brackets for the manufacture of English ceramic types, his manufacture dates can be assumed to be based on the historical and archeological documents available to him

TABLE 31

The Ceramic Types Used to Construct the Analysis Tools[a]

Type number	Date range	Median date	Ceramic type name and page reference
			Porcelain
5.	c.1800–1830	1815	Canton porcelain (262).
7.	c.1790–1825	1808	Overglaze enamelled China trade porcelain (258, 261).
26.	c.1660–1800	1730	Overglaze enamelled Chinese export porcelain (261).
31.	c.1745–1795	1770	English porcelain (137).
39.	c.1660–1800	1730	Underglaze blue Chinese porcelain (257).
41.	c.1750–1765	1758	"Littler's Blue" (119–23) (on white salt-glazed stoneware, porcelain, and creamware).
69.	c.1574–1644	1609	Chinese porcelain, underglaze blue, Late Ming (257, 264).
			Stoneware
Brown			
1.	c.1820–1900+	1860	Brown stoneware bottles for ink, beer, etc. (78–79).
46.	c.1700–1810	1755	Nottingham stoneware (Lustered) (114).
52.	c.1700–1775	1738	Burslem "crouch" pale brown stoneware mugs.
53.	c.1690–1775	1733	Brown salt-glazed mugs (Fulham) (111–13).
54.	c.1690–1775	1733	British brown stoneware (excluding 1, 52, 53) (112–114).
66.	c.1620–1700	1660	Deteriorated Bellarmine face bottles (one dated example to the 1760's) (56–57).
74.	c.1550–1625	1588	Bellarmine, brown salt-glazed stoneware, well molded human face (55–57).
75.	c.1540–1600	1570	Rhenish brown-glazed sprigged, mould-decorated, Cologne type stoneware (277–79).
Blue, gray			
44.	c.1700–1775	1738	Westerwald, stamped blue floral devices, geometric designs (284–85).
58.	c.1650–1725	1668	Sprig molding, combed lines, blue and manganese decorated Rhenish stoneware (280–81).
59.	c.1690–1710	1700	Embellished Hohr gray Rhenish stoneware (284).
77.	c.1700–1775	1738	Westerwald chamber pots (148, 281).
White			
16.	c.1740–1765	1753	Moulded white salt-glazed stoneware (115).
24.	c.1765–1795	1780	Debased "Scratch blue" white salt-glazed stoneware (118).
30.	c.1755–1765	1760	Transfer printed white-salt-glazed stoneware (128).
34.	c.1744–1775	1760	"Scratch blue" white salt-glazed stoneware (117).
40.	c.1720–1805	1763	White salt-glazed stoneware (excluding plates and moulded) (115–17).
41.	c.1750–1765	1758	"Littler's blue" (119–23) (on white salt-glazed stoneware, porcelain, and creamware).

TABLE 31   (Continued)

Type number	Date range	Median date	Ceramic type name and page reference
43.	c.1740–1775	1758	White salt-glazed stoneware plates (115–17).
48.	c.1715–1775	1745	Slip-dipped white salt-glazed stoneware (114–15).
55.	c.1720–1730	1725	"Scratch brown or trailed" white salt-glazed stoneware (117).
Other			
3.	c.1813–1900	1857	Ironstone and granite china (131).
27.	c.1750–1820	1785	"Black basaltes" stoneware (121–22).
28.	c.1763–1775	1769	Engine-turned unglazed red stoneware (121).
37.	c.1690–1775	1733	Refined red stoneware, unglazed, sprigged (120–21).
50.	c.1732–1750	1741	Ralph Shaw, brown, slipped stoneware (118–19).

Earthenware

Type number	Date range	Median date	Ceramic type name and page reference
Slipware			
56.	c.1670–1795	1733	Lead glazed slipware (combed yellow) (107, 134–36).
63.	c.1650–1710	1680	North Devon ograffito slipware (104–05).
67.	c.1612–1700	1656	Wrotham slipware (103–04).
68.	c.1630–1660	1645	"Metropolitan" slipware (103).
70.	c.1610–1660	1635	Red marbelized slipware (North Italian) (77).
73.	c.1580–1625	1603	Wanfried slipware (139).
Refined			
2.	c.1820–1900+	1860	Whiteware (130–31).
6.	c.1795–1890	1843	Mocha (131).
29.	c.1740–1780	1760	"Jackfield" ware (123).
33.	c.1759–1775	1767	Green glazed cream-bodied ware (124–25).
36.	c.1740–1770	1755	"Clouded" wares, tortoiseshell, mottled glazed cream-colored ware (123).
42.	c.1740–1775	1758	Refined agate ware (132).
51.	c.1725–1750	1738	"Astbury" ware, white sprigged and trailed (123).
78.	c.1790–1840	1815	Luster decorated wares.
Coarse			
35.	c.1750–1810	1780	Coarse agate ware (excluding doorknobs) (132).
38.	c.1745–1780	1763	Iberian storage jars (143).
47.	c.1720–1775	1748	Buckley ware (132–33, 135).
61.	c.1650–1775	1713	North Devon gravel tempered ware (133).
Tin-enamelled			
21.	c.1775–1800	1788	Debased Rouen faience (141–42) (c.1755 on French sites).
32.	c.1730–1830	1780	Pedestal-footed type delft ointment pot (204–05).
45.	c.1700–1800	1750	Everted rim, plain delft ointment pot (204–05).
49.	c.1600–1802	(1650)	(17th cent.)
		(1750)	(18th cent.) Decorated delftware (105–11).

TABLE 31   (Continued)

Type number	Date range	Median date	Ceramic type name and page reference
57.	c.1750–1800	1775	Plain delft wash basins.
60.	c.1710–1740	1725	Mimosa pattern delft (108–11).
62.	c.1620–1720	1670	English delftware (blue dash chargers) (108–09).
64.	c.1630–1700	1665	Cylindrical delft ointment pots (109, 203–10).
65.	c.1640–1800	1720	Plain white delftware (109).
71.	c.1620–1775	1698	Delft apothecary jars (monochrome).
72.	c.1580–1640	1610	Delft apothecary jars and pots (polychrome) (203).
76.	c.1660–1800	1730	Delft chamber pots (146–47).
Creamware			
8.	c.1790–1820	1805	"Finger-painted" wares (polychrome slip on creamware or pearlware) (132).
14.	c.1780–1815	1798	"Annular wares" creamware (131).
15.	c.1775–1820	1798	Lighter yellow creamware (126–28).
18.	c.1765–1810	1788	Overglaze enamelled hand painted creamware.
22.	c.1762–1820	1791	Creamware (125–26).
23.	c.1765–1815	1790	Transfer printed creamware (126–28).
25.	c.1762–1780	1771	Deeper yellow creamware (126–28).
41.	c.1750 1765	1758	"Littler's blue" (119–23) (on white salt-glazed stoneware, porcelain, and creamware).
Pearlware			
4.	c.1820–1840	1830	Underglaze polychrome pearlware, directly stenciled floral patterns, bright blue, orange, green, pinkish red (129).
6.	c.1795–1890	1843	Mocha (131).
8.	c.1790–1820	1805	"Finger-painted" wares (polychrome slip on creamware or pearlware) (132).
9.	c.1800–1820	1810	Embossed feathers, fish scales, etc. on pearlware (131).
10.	c.1795–1840	1818	"Willow" transfer-pattern on pearlware (130).
11.	c.1795–1840	1818	Transfer-printed pearlware (128–30).
12.	c.1795–1815	1805	Underglaze polychrome pearlware (129).
13.	c.1790–1820	1805	"Annular wares" pearlware (131).
17.	c.1780–1820	1800	Underglaze blue hand painted pearlware (128–29).
19.	c.1780–1830	1805	Blue and green edged pearlware (131).
20.	c.1780–1830	1805	Undecorated pearlware.

a From Hume, Ivor Noël, *A guide to artifacts of Colonial America,* New York: Knopf, 1970; updated in a Conference with Noël Hume, October 1971.

at the time the book was written. These dates were recently revised in a conference with him. It should be emphasized that in arriving at the median manufacture date, Noël Hume's generalized "1770s" was expressed as 1775 for the model, and that he frequently uses "about" and "around" and "c." to indicate that he is generalizing. The variation introduced by our conversion of these qualifying statements as definite dates is seen to be a relatively minor one when we consider the scale of the model we are building. In this study, we are dealing with the ceramic types often seen on colonial sites in the English tradition and comparable chronological models need to be constructed for sites reflecting French or Spanish tradition. This is illustrated by debased Rouen faience (type 21) which is found on French sites to date around 1755, whereas on English sites it dates some 20 years later (Noël Hume 1970: 141), clearly demonstrating the need for separate models for different cultural traditions.

Type 49, decorated delftware, has a time span of 200 years (Table 31). A median manufacture date of 1650 was assigned for use when the site is obviously of the seventeenth century, and a date of 1750 for use when associated types are from the eighteenth century. This is the only adjustment from the true median manufacture date used in this study. Some types have a long time period of manufacture, such as types 26, 39, and 65, and because of this they should not be used when applying the method presented here.

The chronological tool being constructed here might be extended through the nineteenth century by anyone interested in extending its temporal application. It should also be kept in mind that additional types can be added by the archeologist, provided the manufacture dates for such types are known. Thus the degree of refinement of the tool is dependent upon the degree of sophistication of the archeologist's ceramic knowledge. Because of this it might be argued that the more knowledgable archeologist may find he has little use for the analytical tools outlined here. The extent of the usefulness of the tools presented here is yet to be determined, but they have proved highly useful and

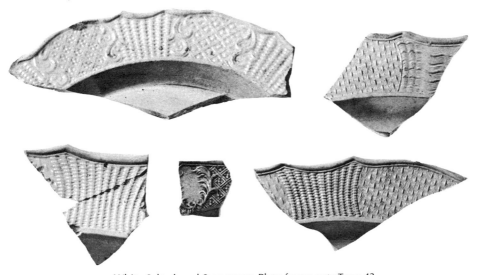

White Salt-glazed Stoneware Plate fragments Type 43.

reliable in many applications to date. For the archeologist who has a reasonable knowledge of the ceramic types involved the tools presented here may well assist him in interpreting the occupation period of historic sites.

The Tools—Visually Interpreting the Occupation Period of the Site from a Sample Using Manufacture Duration Dates and Presence and Absence

Once the unimodal curve representing the duration of manufacture for each ceramic type in a sample from a site is plotted on a time line as a bar, and the type bars are arranged one above the other in a graphic manner, it is possible to see at a glance the limits for the duration of manufacture for all ceramic types. For instance, in Figure 33, we see that most of the bars for the Charles Towne Site (38CH1) include a time span from 1580 to 1725. Immediately we can see that this surely indicates a relationship between the manufacture date and the occupation of the site. To demonstrate otherwise would take some doing. However, we are interested in narrowing the temporal bracket, and a method I have used for a number of years involves placing a vertical bracket to the left and right on the ceramic bar graph, with the resulting time span between being the *interpreted* period, inside of which the occupation of the site took place. The placing of the left bracket is determined by choosing the point at which at least half of the ceramic type bars are touching or intersecting the bracket. The right bracket is placed generally using the same rule; however, it must be placed far enough to the right to at least touch the beginning of the latest type present. An exception to this is surface collections from sites revealing multiple occupation periods as revealed in a gap or discontinuity between the ceramic bars of the first occupation period and those of the later period. In such cases brackets for both occupations must be placed (see Goudy's Post, GN3, and Fort Prince George, PN1, in Figure 33). Using this method, we can place the brackets for Site 38CH1 at 1650 and 1700, which happens to include the known historic date of the site from 1670 to 1680 (South 1971a). This is a tool that has proved most useful through the years in arriving at an interpreted occupation date for a site from ceramics from historic sites. It should be pointed out that this is entirely a presence–absence approach.

The time period can be narrowed further in some instances by consideration of the ceramic types conspicuously absent from the sample. For instance, the Goudy's Trading Post cellar hole from site 38GN1–5 (Figure 33) has a bracket date range from 1740 to 1775, which can be narrowed when we realize that absent from the sample are types manufactured during the 1750s and 1760s usually present on sites of the 1760s (types 27, 33–36, 41, 42). If creamware (type 22) was present, we would have to leave the bracketed date at 1775. In the absence of it as

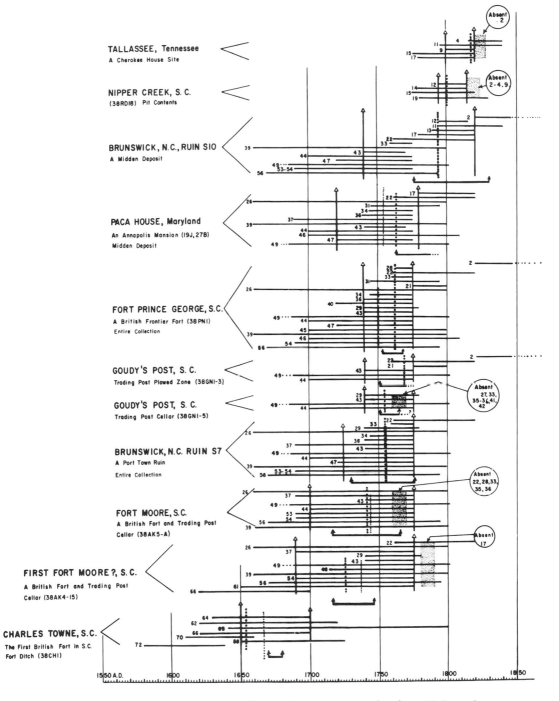

Figure 33. Application of the analysis tools. The Ceramic analysis data from 11 sites using interpretive occupation brackets, presence and absence, and the mean Ceramic date formula compared to the documented site occupation period. 9— Ceramic Type 9 manufacture period; ⋀⋀ visually interpreted occupation period brackets; ⦙ mean Ceramic formula date; ⦙ Pipestem data; ▦ area of absent types for interpreting an occupation end date; ⌐___⌐ documented occupation period for the site.

well as other types of the 1760s, we can assign an occupation date from approximately 1740 to the early 1760s for the cellar hole. This dating matches well the historical information that the site was occupied in 1751 and was attacked in 1760 by Cherokee Indians who burned most of the buildings (South 1971b). This bracketing from ceramics alone is seen to work well in arriving at an occupation period for historic sites with known dates of occupation, and since this is the case we have used it in the same manner on sites of unknown historic dates, such as Cherokee Indian village sites. This is basically a *terminus post quem* approach also using marker type absence to interpret an end occupation date.

It should be clear that in a sealed archeological deposit, the beginning manufacture date for the latest type present gives us a date after which the deposit was made. This is the traditional *terminus post quem*. The interpretive tools we are now discussing are designed to assist us in going beyond merely determining the date of the fill, and allowing us to make an interpretation as to the occupation period reflected by the ceramics in the deposit. This information is not based solely on the latest ceramic type present, but is interpreted through the frequency of other ceramic types. We should keep in mind the nature of the deposit, which may have an important bearing on our interpreted occupation brackets. For instance, if the cellar fill is an accumulation of secondary midden thrown from another house over a long period of time we would expect a result different from that if the cellar hole was filled at one moment in time using displaced soil and refuse collected from other areas of the site. In either case, the fill would have no bearing on the structure represented by that particular cellar hole. The significance of any interpreted occupation period based on ceramics depends on the provenience from which the ceramic sample came. Regardless of whether the ceramic sample came from a pit or a cellar hole, or is the total of all sherds recovered from a site, an interpreted occupation period represented by the sample can be determined.

On sites such as Brunswick Town, Fort Prince George, Goudy's Trading Post, Fort Moore, and Charles Towne there has been little occupation since the eighteenth-century period use of these sites. In high density urban occupation areas, there may well be continuous occupation to the present. Because of this, it would be necessary to isolate features from high density sites and deal with these so as to reduce the effect of later ceramic types. On sites such as Brunswick, Fort Moore, and Fort Prince George every sherd from the site can be included in our sample and still allow an interpreted occupation period relative to the eighteenth century. We should keep in mind that in discussing occupation periods represented by ceramics we are dealing with cultural generalities and not historical specifics. For instance, our occupation periods interpreted from ceramics as revealed on the chart in Figure 33 vary from 15 years in duration to 80 years, but we should also notice that these brackets most often do include the known historic occupation period for the sites.

Similar versions of this interpretive tool have long been used by some historic site archeologists for arriving at an approximate occupation period for their sites. However, a drawback is that it does not take frequency into consideration, and a single sherd of creamware (type 22), for instance, has the same weight as 500 sherds of white salt-glazed stoneware in determining the approximate temporal range for the sample. Consideration of frequency of occurrence would certainly place the relationship between the types in a more valid perspective than presence or absence alone. In order to consider both presence or absence and frequency in the determination of our approximate occupation period, we have devised a formula useful in arriving at a mean ceramic date for a group of ceramic types from an historic site. This date can then be used with the historical data, or with *terminus post quem* dates to arrive at an interpreted occupation period represented by the sample. This date can also be compared with mean pipestem dates, as well as with other artifact data to arrive at an interpretation of the site occupation period.

The Tools—The Mean Ceramic Date Formula Using Presence–Absence and Frequency

The mean manufacture date for the group of British ceramic types from an eighteenth-century historic site, taking into consideration the frequency of occurrence of fragments of the types, can be determined by a mean ceramic date frequency formula as follows:

The mean ceramic date, Y, is expressed:

$$Y = \frac{\sum\limits_{i=1}^{n} X_i \cdot f_i}{\sum\limits_{i=1}^{n} f_i}$$

where

X_i = the median date for the manufacture of each ceramic type
f_i = the frequency of each ceramic type
n = the number of ceramic types in the sample.

The median manufacture date for each ceramic type in the sample is determined from the documents, and in this study we have derived this from the book by Noël Hume (1970) and through personal communication with him. This information is seen in the list of ceramic types in Table 31. In order to use the formula, the archeologist places the sherd count for each type in a column beside the median date and these are multiplied, producing a third column which is a product of the median date times the frequency of occurrence. The sum of the frequency column is divided into the sum of the product column, producing the mean ceramic date for the sample. Although this frequency-adjusted manufacture date might be assumed to have nothing to do with the occupation date for an historic site, we will see that there is a remarkable degree of similarity between the mean ceramic date derived from use of the formula and the historically known median occupation date of the eighteeenth-century historic sites on which it has been used.

APPLICATION OF THE TOOLS

Applicability

The mean ceramic date formula is designed as a tool expressing the frequency relationship of ceramic types of known manufacture period in terms of a mean ceramic date. In this respect it is similar to the Binford (1961) and Hanson (1971) formula for dating tobacco pipestems. The beauty of these formulas is the fact that anyone can pick up a set of drills and proceed to measure a sample and arrive at a mean pipestem bore size from which a mean date for the accumulation of the sample can be determined. The mean ceramic date formula is not as easily applied because the user must know something about British ceramic types before he can determine a mean ceramic date from a group of types. If he has little understanding of the attributes for separating the 78 types used in the model he will not get far in arriving at a meaningful mean ceramic date from the formula. For the formula to be used, therefore, it is necessary to have a knowledge of ceramic types, which can be gained from the many references available. This reference work must be combined with a familiarity with the archeological specimens. A knowledge of the ceramic type attributes cannot be overemphasized for there are far too many meaningless descriptions appearing in the historic site literature now in spite of the availability of numerous excellent sources to act as guides for learning. Historical archeology is plagued by reports revealing no interpretation of any kind—historical, anthropological, cultural, or archeological—to justify a catalog publication of objects. To use the mean ceramic date formula, the archeologist should have more than a passing knowledge of the ceramic types with which he deals. Some archeologists may prefer to deal primarily with a *terminus post quem* date for a deposit and feel they have no need for a median date such as the formula provides. Others may find it useful in the interpretation of site occupation periods.

The Sample

The size of the sample cannot always be controlled by the archeologist due to the fact that only seven sherds may be recovered from a feature from which he wishes to apply his ceramic analysis tools. He should remember, however, that a sample of that size would be somewhat less reliable than one of a much larger size. The nature of the sample would most certainly also have a bearing on the date that results from any interpretive analysis of the ceramics. For instance, a sloppily excavated cellar hole where poor contextual control was maintained by the archeologist might contain fragments of creamware or ironstone that fell into the hole during excavation from layers outside the actual contents of the cellar fill, or were carelessly thrown into the bag by an irresponsible worker. These fragments would result in a much later date being assigned to the feature than would have been the case had these one or two fragments not been allowed to intrude upon the sample from the context of the cellar. The importance of tight provenience control in the field cannot be overemphasized (unless the reasons for the control are not understood by the practitioner and an unnecessarily expensive and fruitless nit-picking approach is used to no effectual end, as is too frequently witnessed on historic sites). A large, tightly controlled sample is desirable, regardless of the length of time a site was occupied. In the absence of a large sample, however, the tools described here can still be used but the reliability might naturally be expected to be less.

Instead of the frequency occurrence based on individual sherds by ceramic type as we have done in this study, quantification by type and form could as well be used, and in some instances where form is a critical attribute, a more refined temporal bracket may result. It is through an analysis of form (teacups, saucers, plates, platters, and mugs) that this writer feels that certain important cultural differences may be reflected. Our present study is concerned, however, with ceramic type analysis as a reflector of the occupation period of historic sites.

The Technique of Application of the Visual Bracketing Tool to Historic Site Ceramic Samples

In Figure 33, 11 sites have been plotted with the following information graphically shown. The duration of manufacture of each ceramic type has been plotted as a bar against a time line. The known historic occupation period is plotted as a heavy horizontal bar with arrows indicating the approximate beginning and end dates as determined from the documents. The visual bracket for the interpretive occupation period of the site is plotted as two vertical lines that touch at least half of the ceramic type bars on both ends. The mean ceramic date for the site sample derived from the use of the ceramic date formula is plotted as a vertical line of large dots, with the pipestem date represented as a vertical line of small dots. The influence of absent ceramic types within a zone where they are usually found on historic sites is plotted as a shaded area of dots. This allows the interpreted occupation date to be narrowed in some cases.

The Technique of Application of the Mean Ceramic Date Formula to Historic Site Ceramic Samples

An example of this process is illustrated by unit S7, in the ruined town of Brunswick, N.C. This ruin was a stone lined cellar located on lot 71 in Brunswick (South 1959b). The records reveal that the structure was probably standing by 1734 and was burned in 1776. The collection of ceramic material from the entire ruin was used as the sample. The historic date would bracket the period from 1734 to 1776, with a median historic date of 1755 (Table 32).

It is interesting to note that the mean ceramic date derived from the formula is only 3.4 years from the median historic date of 1755 for the ruin. As we will see, this is more than a coincidence. The mean ceramic date seldom deviates from a range of ±4 years from the known median

TABLE 32

Using the Formula with Ceramics from the Brunswick Hepburn-Reonalds Ruin (S7)

Ceramic type	Type median (X_i)	Sherd count (f_i)	Product
22	1791	483	865,053
33	1767	25	44,175
34	1760	32	56,320
36	1755	55	96,525
37	1733	40	69,320
43	1758	327	574,866
49	(1750)	583	1,020,250
44	1738	40	69,520
47	1748	28	48,944
53, 54	1733	52	90,116
56	1733	286	495,638
29	1760	9	15,840
		1960	3,446,567 ÷ 1960 = 1758.4

The mean ceramic date formula

$$Y = \frac{\sum_{i=1}^{n} X_i \cdot f_i}{\sum_{i=1}^{n} f_i}$$

$$Y = \frac{3,446,567}{1960} = 1758.4$$

historic date for those examples involved in this study. The pipestem date for this ruin using the Binford formula (1961) is 1756, revealing a close relationship between historic, ceramic, and pipestem dates. (See Appendix B for the application of the mean ceramic date formula to samples from several historic sites.)

Ceramic Analysis of Samples from Historic Sites
Charles Towne (38CH1), The First English Fortification in South Carolina

Each of the 11 sites on the chart (Figure 33) can be discussed to reveal various aspects seen in refining a temporal bracket for the occupation of a site through ceramics using the methods outlined here. Our discussion will follow the chronological chart from bottom to top (Figure 33), beginning with the fortification ditch dug by the first Charles Towne settlers in South Carolina in 1670 and abandoned by 1680, providing a median historic date of 1675 (South 1971a). The bracketing tool reveals a date from 1650 to 1700, a date that includes the historic occupation period. Attempting to narrow this date by means of the mean ceramic date formula produces a date of 1654.4 some 21 years prior to the known historic median date. This difference may well reflect our present knowledge of the ceramic types from which the mean date was derived. It may also reflect a time lag caused by the latest items not being present in the households at Charles Towne when the first settlers arrived in 1670. This gap may also relate to the fact that far more references are available to leather and wooden trenchers being in the town than ceramics, revealing, perhaps, less daily use of ceramic items, and thus less breakage (South 1971a). In this case the breakage that did occur would reveal a greater time lag than is seen on eighteenth-century sites where ceramics came into more daily use, and breakage. This hypothesis needs to be checked by the use of the mean ceramic date formula on more seventeenth-century sites of known occupation dates. This time lag may well be found to be a factor on any seventeenth-century site, in which case the formula can be altered to take this into consideration once enough data are at hand from seventeenth-century sites. The pipestem date from this feature is also too early, being 1667 (Hanson 1971: 2), again possibly reflecting a true time lag situation with artifacts in the seventeenth century. From this site we see an exception to the high reliability seen in the use of the mean ceramic date formula on sites of the eighteenth century. Noël Hume has pointed out that on seventeenth century sites of the wealthy class he has found many ceramic types represented and little evidence of time lag, whereas on the ruins of the less affluent there are definitely fewer ceramic types present, thus revealing a socioeconomic distinction not seen to exist on sites of the eighteenth century (Noël Hume, personal communication 1972).

The First Fort Moore? (38AK4-15), An Eighteenth-Century Frontier Fort and Trading Post

The second site is a cellar hole of a timber and clay structure with a clay chimney, located on the bank of the Savannah River at the historic site of Fort Moore, S.C. The first Fort Moore was built in 1716, and a second one was ordered built in 1747; the site went into private hands in 1766 (Polhemus 1971). This site was excavated during the summer of 1971 by Richard Polhemus, Assistant Archeologist of the Institute of Archeology and Anthropology at the University of South Carolina. Using the bracketing method, we can see that the site was likely occupied between 1700 and 1775. The mean ceramic date formula produces a date of 1726.1, not far from the historic median date of 1732 for the first Fort Moore. The presence of creamware (two sherds of type 22 in the top layer of the cellar), but the absence of pearlware (type 17), does not allow us to narrow the date bracket using absence (shaded area of the graph). The Hanson pipestem formula produces a date of 1730.9. These early dates within the known historic range for the occupation of the first Fort Moore allow us to interpret this cellar and this area of the site as likely that for the first Fort Moore. Even though creamware is present in the top layer of fill, providing us with a *terminus post quem* date for the final filling of the cellar, the frequency of types of the earlier period is such that a first Fort Moore period of occupation is interpreted as being represented by the ceramic sample.

Fort Moore (38AK5-A), An Eighteenth-Century Frontier Fort and Trading Post

One hundred yards away from the cellar just discussed another cellar of the same type of construction was excavated some years ago, and the material was stored at the Institute of Archeology and Anthropology at the University of South Carolina. The bottom two feet of this cellar fill were used in the ceramic analysis, which contained the large majority of the ceramics present. The bracketing bars reveal a likely date of 1700 to 1775 for the occupation of the site. However, the fact that there is an absence of types 22, 28, 33, 35, and 36, usually seen on sites of the 1760s and 1770s, this range can be narrowed to include the period from 1700 to the early 1760s. The mean ceramic date formula produced a date of 1741.7 and the pipestem date was 1744.16. The mean ceramic date is virtually the same as the known median historic date of 1741 for the total occupation period of Fort Moore from 1716 to 1766.

From the use of the bracketing and mean ceramic date tools on the Fort Moore site, it was possible to separate a ceramic sample of a cellar that likely represented the entire occupation of Fort Moore, from a cellar with a ceramic sample interpreted as representing the occupation period of the first Fort Moore. An interesting point here is that the cellar having the earliest mean ceramic date has creamware present in the fill, whereas the cellar without creamware has a later mean ceramic date, the reverse of what one might interpret from presence–absence alone. This illustrates the potential value of the mean ceramic date in such instances, particularly when supported by the same relationship between the pipestem dates as seen here. This does not mean we ignore the *terminus post quem* date indicated by creamware for the final fill of the cellar. It does mean that we are giving consideration to the mass of the ceramics rather than to the latest type in the sample (perhaps represented by a single sherd), when it comes to interpreting the major occupation period represented by the collection.

Brunswick Town, North Carolina, A Colonial English Port Town

We have discussed this ruin previously and found the historic median to be 1755, the mean ceramic date to be 1758.4, and the mean pipestem date to be 1756. Other Brunswick Town ruins demonstrate the following comparison between the historic median and the ceramic formula mean:

S15 historic median date   1751.0
    ceramic formula date 1746.4
    pipestem date   1748.0

N1 historic median date   1754.0
    ceramic formula date 1750.1

S2 historic median date   1754.0
    ceramic formula date 1749.0
    pipestem date   1748.0

S18 historic median date   1769.5
    ceramic formula date 1776.2
    pipestem date   1756

Goudy's Trading Post at Fort Ninety Six, South Carolina (38GN1-3 and 38GN1-5)

Goudy's Trading Post at Ninety Six, S.C., was begun in 1751 and was attacked and burned in 1760 (South 1971b). Preliminary excavation revealed a small cellar hole with some eighteenth-century objects in the top surface of the fill. The cellar is yet to be excavated. Only four ceramic types and a total of seven sherds were recovered, but these were used to attempt to date the deposit using the tools under discussion here. The median historic date is 1756, with a mean ceramic date of 1754.6, an impressive match using only seven sherds. However, without the known historic date we can establish a duration, using our bracketing tool, of from around 1740 to 1775. In the absence of types 27, 33–36, 41, 42 (representing the types likely to be present if the sample dated from the 1760s), and also using the mean ceramic formula date of 1754.6, we could say that the deposit represents an approximate date range of from around 1744 to the early 1760s, impressively close to our 1751 to 1760 historic data. We have arrived at this date using the ceramic analysis tools here under discussion, and not our historic data.

The surface layer and plowed soil zone of Goudy's Trading Post site revealed creamware, which was absent from the cellar hole sample. This sample was designated 38GN1-3, and has an historic occupation date of unknown length after the first occupation of 1751 and the fire of 1760. From the mean ceramic date formula we determine a date of 1769.3, and with this and our known beginning date of 1751 as half of our date range, we can conjecture a date from 1751 to around 1787 for the period represented by the sample, because *if we know the mean date and one end date* we can interpret the approximate position of the opposite bracket. It should be noted that one sherd of whiteware was found on the site in the plowed soil (type 2), and because of the absence of pearlwares, this fact clearly reveals a disconformity between it and the other ceramic types, reflecting a post-1820 occupation and not a continuous one.

Fort Prince George, South Carolina (38PN1), A British Military Post on the Cherokee Frontier

Fort Prince George was built by Governor Glen of South Carolina in 1753, and the last reference to it is in 1768 when it was abandoned (Combes n.d.). The median historic date is 1761. The site was dug by John Combes, then assistant director of the Institute of Archeology and Anthropology, University of South Carolina. The ceramic sample includes all sherds recovered from the entire site. From the bracketing technique of the ceramic type bars we arrive at a date of around 1745 to 1775 for the site. The mean ceramic date formula reveals a mean date of 1763.0, and the pipestem date is 1750.14 (Hanson 1971:2). In this case the mean ceramic formula date is much closer to the median date for the site than is the pipestem date. Without the known historic date we might take our interpreted end date of 1775 and the mean ceramic formula date of 1763, and conjecture a date bracket of from 1751 to 1775, again not far removed from the known occupation of 1753 to 1768.

The Paca House, Annapolis, Maryland (19J,27B), A Town House Mansion

The Paca House was built in 1763 by William Paca, signer of the Declaration of Independence, and is still standing and in the process of being restored. Archeological work was carried out there in 1967 by this writer (through a contract with Contract Archaeology, Inc.) and two eighteenth-century midden deposits were discovered still relatively undisturbed

(South 1967). These were combined for this analysis. The median historic date for the sample is not known, but the context in which the midden was found indicates that it was among the earliest midden thrown from the house after it was constructed in 1763. The presence of creamware and one piece of pearlware, however, indicates that the midden received material at least as late as the 1780s. The mean ceramic formula date for the deposit is 1763.1. The left and right bracketing lines fall at 1720 and 1780, and using the mean ceramic date of 1763, we can narrow our interpreted date range to 1748 to 1780.

The Secondary Refuse Deposit at Nath Moore's Front (S10) at Brunswick Town

Nath Moore's Front in Brunswick Town (S10) was burned in 1776 (South 1958) and the interior of the stone foundation wall for the cellar was used as a garbage dump for some years afterward; in fact, judging from the whiteware present, it was used into the 1830s. The last reference to anyone living in Brunswick was in the early 1830s. The median historic date for the dump would be 1803. Using the vertical brackets we arrive at a date of from 1740 to 1820. The mean ceramic date is found to be 1794.0, not too far from the historic median date of 1803. An interesting feature of this ceramic profile is the continuation of the overlapping ceramic-type bars throughout the period of the Revolution into the early decades of the nineteenth century.

The Nipper Creek Site (38RD18), South Carolina

No historical information is available on this pit, which was located in a bulldozed area of an Archaic Indian site. The brackets point to a short time span from 1795 to 1815, with a mean ceramic formula date of 1801.3. The absence of types of the 1815–1835 period indicate that this ceramic sample can be interpreted as representing an occupation period from around 1795 to about 1810.

Tallassee, A Nineteenth-Century Cherokee Indian? House Site in Tennessee

The historic information available on this site indicates that it was transferred from Indian to white hands in the early nineteenth century (Richard Polhemus, personal communication 1971). Other than this no information is available, except that a quantity of Cherokee ceramic types was found associated with the house ruin, suggesting possible Indian occupants.

The mean ceramic formula date was found to be 1818.1. In the absence of type 2 we would interpret a date bracket of from 1800 to 1820 as the likely range for the occupation represented by the sample.

Additional Cherokee Indian Village Sites Not Shown in Figure 33—The Rock Turtle Site (38PN4), An Eighteenth-Century Indian Village Site

One hundred yards from the site of Fort Prince George, a Cherokee Indian village site (38PN4) was tested and revealed ceramic types producing a mean ceramic formula date of 1749.7 and a Hanson pipestem date of 1756.36. There is no historic data associated with the site other than its close association with Fort Prince George and the eighteenth-century Cherokee town site of Keowee (Combes n.d.).

Toxaway (380C3), An Eighteenth-Century Cherokee Indian Village Site

This Indian village site was excavated by John Combes. The absence of creamware, and the presence of pearlware and nineteenth-century stoneware clearly reveal a nineteenth-century occupation distinct from the eighteenth-century occupation represented by white salt-glazed stoneware and combed yellow slipware. For this reason two dates were determined for this site, 1735.8 for the eighteenth-century ceramics, and 1855.4 for the nineteenth-century ceramics. This is an excellent example of two occupation periods clearly revealed through the absence of a major ceramic type, in this case creamware. If creamware were present to bridge the temporal gap, there would be no archeological justification for separating the ceramic groups for obtaining separate mean dates, since there would be a continuous sequence of types represented.

A Discussion of the Reliability of the Ceramic Analysis Tools

The measure of the reliability of the temporal bracketing and mean ceramic formula analyses is the degree of correlation between the interpreted dates and the known historic dates for the particular site. Prehistorians do not have such a readily available check on their chronologies and seriations. As we have seen with the individual samples from various historic sites, the bracketing and mean ceramic tools, along with presence–absence consideration, allow a relatively high percentage of correlation between the interpreted and the historically known dates. Table 33 illustrates the comparison between the historical bracket and median date, and the visual bracketing tool and the mean ceramic formula date for those sites in this study. The correlation between the historical median date for a site and the mean ceramic formula date is seen to be quite high in most instances (see Appendix B). What is needed now is more application of the tools to determine the limits of reliability on broader frames of reference for time and space.

TABLE 33

Comparative Table of Ceramic Analysis Data

Site	Historical date range	Bar graph date range	Historical median date	Mean ceramic formula date	Years away from historical median with quantification	Pipestem date	Formula date without quantification	Years away from historical medium without quantification	Site name
38CHI	1670–1680	1650–1685	1675	1654	(21)	1667	1661	(14)	Charles Towne
38AK4-15	1716–1747	1725–1775	1732	1726	(6)	1731	1736	(4)	1st Ft. Moore
38AK5-A	1716–1766	1725–1775	1741	1742	(1)	1744	1738	(3)	Ft. Moore
S7	1734–1776	1740–1775	1755	1755	(0)	1756	1749	(6)	Brunswick
38GN1-5	1751–1760	1745–1775	1756	1755	(1)	—	1752	(4)	Goudy's Post
38GN1-3	1751– ?	1740–1775	—	1769		—			Goudy's Post
38PN1	1753–1768	1740–1775	1761	1763	(2)	1750	1755	(6)	Ft. Prince George
Paca (19J, 28B)	1763– ?	1750–1780	—	1763		1753			Paca House
S10	1776–1830	1740–1820	1803	1794	(9)	—	1773	(30)	Bruns. Dump
38RD18	?	1795–1805	?	1801		—			Nipper Creek
Tallassee	c.1800– ?	1800–1815	?	1818		—			Tallassee
S18	1763–1776	1740–1775	1770	1776	(6)	1751	1753	(17)	Brunswick
S15	1726?–1776	1740–1775	1751?	1746	(5)	1748	1755	(4)	Brunswick
N1	1731–1776	1740–1775	1754	1750	(4)	—	1746	(8)	Brunswick
S2	1731–1776	1740–1775	1754	1749	(5)	1748	1757	(3)	Brunswick
38PN4	18th cent.	1750–1775	?	1750		1756			Rock Turtle
38OC3	18th cent.	1725–1780	?	1736		—			Toxaway
					(39)[a]			(85)[b]	

[a] Average years from historical median with quantification: (4).
[b] Average years from historical median without quantification: (8).

227

To judge the role of quantification in the mean ceramic date formula between the known historical median date and the formula date, we substituted the frequency of one for each of the ceramic types and thereby nullified the effect of quantification on the date derived from the formula. This step reduced the formula to a presence–absence tool, and by comparing the date thus determined with the ceramic formula date, we can see which is closer to the historical median. This comparison can be seen on the chart in Table 33. This process reveals a slight advantage in reliability when using quantification as opposed to presence–absence alone. This advantage can be seen by comparing the number of years difference from the historical median of the formula dates with and without the consideration of frequency. Using frequency only, one date is as much as 9 years from the known historical median for the occupation of the site; without considering frequency, two of the 10 sites are 17 and 30 years distant from the known historical median. The average deviation from the historical median date using frequency is only 4 years, whereas the average deviation without consideration of frequency is 8 years, or twice that when frequency is considered. Our conclusion from this is that frequency consideration appears to have a refinement advantage over presence–absence when used with the mean ceramic date formula.

From this average of 4 years variation from the known historic median occupation for the 10 eighteenth-century sites in this study we can suggest that when frequency is considered, the mean ceramic date derived can be accompanied by an average deviation of ±4 years on sites of the eighteenth century. As the ceramic collection from a larger number of sites are examined with this formula, this plus or minus factor can be refined as the data indicate. Without using frequency by type, thus utilizing the formula strictly on a presence–absence basis, a ±8 years should be added to the mean ceramic date thus derived. When we statistically compare the standard deviation for the data now available, we find that instead of the simple ±4 years average deviation mentioned here the standard deviation is 4.56 years for formula dates from known median occupation dates.

We will now look at the one seventeenth-century site represented in this study, the Charles Towne fortification ditch (38CH1). The deviation here between the known median date of 1675 and the ceramic formula dates with and without consideration of frequency is 21 and 14 years respectively. This is a dramatic contrast to the 10 eighteenth-century sites for which the median historical manufacture dates are known. At present this gap seems to be a result of possibly two factors, lack of knowledge of seventeenth-century ceramic types and manufacture dates, and a possible status factor. Noël Hume has found seventeenth-century upper class mansions have more ceramics represented than do the lower class homes of that period but has not found this to be so in the eighteenth century (Noël Hume 1970: 25; and personal communication, 1972). It appears that the lower class seventeenth-century homes may well have had a greater time lag represented in ceramics than the mansions did.

The rapid distribution of ceramics from the factory to British-American ports and the subsequent journey to the frontier resulted in the horizon phenomenon in both the seventeenth- and eighteenth-century periods. This will probably best be demonstrated through analysis of ceramics from the more affluent seventeenth-century homes, but such a status difference is yet to be demonstrated through ceramics from eighteenth-century British-American sites. On the eighteenth-century sites included in this study, the high correlation between the mean ceramic manufacture date derived from the formula and the historic median date for the occupation of the site is a clear demonstration of the horizon phenomenon.

In instances where we might have wanted more precision in the tool, we can sometimes see a possible explanation due to a small sample. The Paca House midden, for example, had only 46 sherds, and a probable historical range for the deposit of from 1763 to around 1780 when the house was sold to a new owner, producing a median date of around 1771, some 8 years later than the formula date of 1763 plus or minus 4 years. However, if no historical data were available our slightly "too early" mean ceramic date would still be only 8 years away from the actual date.

It is hoped that more such formulas will be forthcoming with which to deal with historic site data, with buttons, beads, wine bottles, and glasses all contributing their individual chronologies and mean artifact dates suitable for comparison with the mean ceramic date and brackets, pipestems, and coins, but this only as introduction to the examination of questions of broader scope.

The apparent success of the methods discussed here is thought to be due to the fact that with colonial artifacts we are dealing with a historical chronology reflecting cultural process, just as we would be doing with a study of motifs from a collection of dated coins from the same cultural tradition. The coins are indicators of the historical as well as the cultural process, and reflect the temporal occupation span for a site just as we have seen ceramics to do. For instance, at Brunswick Town the documented duration of the site was from 1725 until it was burned in 1776. The coins from the ruins of houses burned at that time date from 1696 to 1775. The coins from all ruins including those occupied after the Revolution into the 1830s date to 1820. Thus coins are used along with ceramics to help fix dates for historic site occupation. However, they are not often found in quantity sufficient for them to be a major tool. They can provide auxiliary data as historically fixed documents.

In order to help understand what the use of the mean ceramic date formula does, we might visualize each sherd as having imprinted on it the median manufacture date, equivalent to finding a dated coin for each sherd. The formula allows us to deal with this wealth of dates represented by each sherd found on the site and arrive at an interpreted date representing the mean of all the median dates represented by the sherds.

INTERPRETIVE SUMMARY

In this study we have concentrated on the similarity between groups of eighteenth-century ceramic types as found on colonial English historic sites over a wide area and of varying functions. We have suggested that this focus is possibly due to the horizon nature of the ceramic groups in the eighteenth century and to the fact that the ceramic types reflect culture change through time. We have not dealt with the important differences between ceramic forms as reflectors of functional or socioeconomic factors at work within the culture. The potential of such a study has been pointed out by Stone (1970) and others regarding porcelain as an index of status. Miller and Stone (1970) have also indicated that ceramic analysis offers great potential in studies of sociocultural change, status and social level and functional interpretations. The study of ceramic types, which we have used in this paper as indicators of site occupation periods reflecting the cultural horizon concept, does not negate the study of ceramic forms as more sensitive indicators of status and function within the culture. Although ceramic analysis by type can be demonstrated to vary but relatively little from a port town such as Brunswick and the frontier forts of the same period, thus providing us with a valuable temporal tool for use on eighteenth-century sites, an analysis of the same ceramic fragments using form might well reflect status or cultural pattern of a different sort. At the 1970 meeting of the Society for Historical Archaeology, Garry Stone presented a paper illustrating the high percentage of ceramic forms relating to the tea drinking ceremony at the frontier outpost of Fort Dobbs, N.C. In the present study, of the 19 ceramic types present at the frontier site of Fort Prince George, 10 were represented by the presence of teapots, teacups or saucers, tending to support the observations made by Stone in North Carolina regarding the extension of the tea ceremony to the far corners of the colonial frontier (Roth 1961). The emphasis on form as opposed to type, reflecting perhaps an emphasis on function as compared to time can be seen in the manner in which archeologists approach their data. Noël Hume, for instance, classifies and catalogs his ceramics by quantification by form of various types present, whereas I have always used quantification by fragments of ceramic types present. Analysis by form would seem to be a more sensitive indicator of function and possible socioeconomic level, whereas that by type is useful for discovering the kind of cultural information dealt with in this present study. Thus the manner in which we classify our data relates directly to the questions we are asking.

Other points dealing with this subject should be mentioned. Ceramic analysis should consider such factors as absence, which may well correlate with documents, such as the period from about 1640 to 1680 when the English were barred from Chinese ports, an embargo that had a definite effect on the import of Chinese porcelain during this period (Noël Hume 1970: 257). The absence of porcelain in the collection from the Charles Towne deposits of 1670–1680 is therefore no surprise. Another point is that from the first Fort Moore of the early eighteenth century, fewer ceramic shapes were present dealing with the tea ceremony than were found on the later frontier forts in the area. This difference in ceramic shape between these eighteenth-century forts may reflect the greater popularity of the tea ceremony from the mid-eighteenth century on as opposed to its popularity in the early part of the century (Roth 1961).

In 1970, Garry Stone found an association between porcelain and the more affluent in the inventories he studied, and we surely need more studies of this type from the historical perspective. Such associations must now be demonstrated in archeological collections. Miller and Stone (1970: 100) have also suggested that archeologists "should be able to establish the relative socioeconomic level of a population and define any major status differences which existed at a site by means of the distributional analyses of ceramics." Comparison of French and English ceramics at Michilimackinac was done by Miller and Stone with interesting differences observed. Cleland (1970: 122) has mentioned that differences in ceramics from two row houses have been interpreted as reflecting social status of the occupants. He suggests that this interpretation can validly be made in the absence of specific historical data for the row houses themselves. This is certainly true provided the demonstration of status related artifacts and relationships is carefully delineated in the research strategy for the study. Through postulates controlled by historical documentation of the status of the occupants of a structure, and through quantified relationships demonstrated for status related artifacts and other data from the ruins of such a structure, status related pattern should indeed be revealed. Through historical control of status as suggested here and through archeological control of artifact frequencies, understanding of status indicators should be developed through the pattern recognition procedures emphasized throughout this book.

Functional interpretations from historic site ruins are also often frustratingly unsatisfactory. With kiln sites, furnaces, and other specialized structures the interpretation becomes obvious as the data are revealed. However, with the town ruins of Bethabara, N.C., for instance, maps of 1760 and 1766 revealed the intended use for each structure at that time (the tailor shop, kitchen, pottery shop, business manager's house, the doctor's laboratory, the apothecary shop, and blacksmith shop, the millwright's house, the gunsmith shop, and the tavern) but when excavation was complete not a single structure could be interpreted from the archeological data as to its correct function except the pottery shop of Gottfried Aust. This was identifiable from the clay wedging floor and the kiln waster dump. Function, therefore, is not an interpretation easily arrived at by the archeologist. It is most effectively approached through the pattern recognition procedures outlined in previous chapters. A variable at Bethabara should be emphasized, and that is that it was a German-American colonial town, with dramatically different artifact relationships and refuse disposal behavior than was present at the British American colonial town of Brunswick

In this study we have seen that eighteenth-century British-American sites of varied functions, from port town ruins to town house mansions to frontier forts and Indian villages have similar groups of ceramic types present at similar periods of time. This has been interpreted in terms of the horizon concept (Willey and Phillips 1958: 31–34). The time required for the spread of the cultural material representing the horizon is a factor to be considered, as Willey and Phillips point out. Therefore, an approximate contemporaneity is involved. With our historic ceramics used in this study we are dealing with a class of objects that originated, for the most part, in England, and were brought into America aboard vessels to ports such as Charleston, Savannah, Boston, New York, and Philadelphia, and from these centers were distributed to inland sites. This distribution was often quite rapid, being only as long as it took a man on horseback to ride the distance from the port town where the limited collection of ceramic types was available, to his frontier destination at Fort Prince George, Goudy's Trading Post, or Fort Moore. A few months at the most might have been involved, so that within a few weeks after a ship arrived in a port town, teacups, teapots and saucers of white salt-glazed stoneware or "clouded" polychrome painted cream-colored ware could easily have been used by an Indian to pour a cup of the "black drink" at the Cherokee town of Keowee opposite Fort Prince George. Such ceramic types and forms are found in Cherokee midden deposits, and whether they reached the Cherokee nation by way of

Philadelphia or Charleston is immaterial when we consider that in either case the journey would take but a few weeks at the most. Thus the argument that considerable time lag must have been involved for English ceramic types to reach the various remote corners of the colonial frontier is a more difficult position to support than that dispersal of goods was a relatively rapid process. If the latter were so, then we can understand why a great deal of uniformity would exist among ceramic types from sites of the same time period, regardless of the fort, port, or Indian village function of the site on which the ceramics were used.

Documents from port records may well reveal that certain colonial ports received ceramic goods from different English ports, thus theoretically introducing another variable into the picture. However, as Cleland has said (1970: 122), "These are historic facts that are really irrelevant to the interpretation of the archaeological data." For example, if the historical documents were to reveal that Charleston did not receive any Oriental porcelain in the eighteenth century, this discovery would not alter the percentage relationships of this type from the sites in this study, or the applicability of the mean ceramic data formula, or the interpretation of the data in terms of the horizon concept. It would point to questions centering on transportation and supply routes relative to the sites in this study, questions that might well be examined under a different research design from that used here.

From this examination of our postulates we can see that the bracketing and mean ceramic date formula tools have proved of value in producing a time bracket for eighteenth-century sites that correlates well with the historically known occupation periods. From this correlation the validity of our postulates has tended to be confirmed to the limits of our present data. More use of these and similar tools on a broader scope should now be undertaken in similar studies if we are to gain the most from our archeological data.

We have demonstrated the process of pattern recognition in a temporal context. We have seen that the phenomenon involved is that described by Willey and Phillips (1958) as the horizon concept. In demonstrating the regularity of the pattern and expressing this as an empirical generalization in terms of the horizon concept, we still have not explained the phenomenon in terms of the processes of culture. This can be done by stating hypotheses relating the horizon concept to processes at work in the British-American colonial cultural system, postulating the mechanism whereby these are related, and presenting arguments of relevance within a research design directed at the collection of new data. This hypothetico-deductive method follows the pattern recognition procedures demonstrated in this book to complete the scientific cycle.

The testing of the tools presented here should be carried out through a controlled variable procedure such as examining sites with the same mean ceramic formula date for type frequency variance in order to better understand the role played by such variance. Another test could use sites with similar, documented functions but with different mean ceramic formula dates in order to explore the variability in ceramic forms.

Hypotheses for explaining the horizon phenomenon demonstrated in this study would center on the distributive system of the British colonial empire. The variability we have seen on the frontier contrasted with domestic sites not on the frontier might well be explained by means of the logistics of the distribution of goods from the British empire to the colonies.

The horizon phenomenon we have studied here might be visualized in terms of a continuous line of ships from Britain to the colonies throughout the eighteenth century. Such a condition would be required to produce the broad and rapid spread of goods characterized by the horizon. The hypothesized "Pennsylvania German-American Pattern" mentioned in a previous chapter (in which a high ratio of self-sufficiency artifacts are expected to be present), would contrast dramatically with the British-American pattern. Such contrasting patterns would suggest a continuous line of ships was *not* involved in supplying the German-American colonies. From such archeological data suggestions as to the relative size of the supply fleets involved in British and German colonization efforts could be made, and from the contrast between artifact patterns reflecting self-sufficiency, statements regarding the difference in empire building and colonization being carried out by Britain and Germany could be hypothesized and tested.

For example, we might hypothesize that the horizon phenomenon on British-American sites is a result of a dependence on British ships bringing supplies, whereas German American colonies such as the Moravian settlements were designed to be self-supportive and independent. Historical documentation could be used to check the validity of such an hypothesis invented to account for the archeologically demonstrated horizon phenomenon. The documents would reveal that the early English settlement at Jamestown and the earlier effort in North Carolina were so dependent on supplies from the mother country that they virtually starved to death when the expected supply ships did not arrive. This policy was continued in later years as well, to which the historical documentation and the horizon phenomenon both attest. The Moravian colonization was based on the assumption of self-sufficiency, and postulates directed at the future excavation of sites from such occupation in Pennsylvania and elsewhere would suggest that the archeological record will most certainly reveal this in pattern comparison. (For references for the above, see Harrington 1962; Noël Hume 1963; Fries 1968.)

Questions relating to the production systems, expansionist systems, and exploitation systems of nations can also be explored from patterned archeological data in studies in which certain variables are held constant through historical documentation, variables such as time of occupation, national origin of occupants, source of supply, and function of the site. By thus controlling site structure, site content, and site temporal context, the archeologist can begin to focus on explanation of cultural phenomena.

The historical archeologist is in the unique position of being able, through archival records, to control certain variables while delineating archeological patterning, an advantage not possible in the absence of documentation. Historical archeology is in the fortunate position of having a tremendous potential for contributing to method and theory building in archeology generally. Through the pattern recognition procedures emphasized in this book the first steps in this direction can be taken.

Historical archeology has now matured to the point where it should begin to explore this potential rather than continuing to crowd bookshelves with descriptive catalogs of systematized relic collecting devoid of any redeeming analytical or interpretive value. Historical archeologists have a challenge and a responsibility to abstract order through analysis of their data and to assign meaning to the data. "From the pages of the earth, the historical archeologist gathers bits and pieces representing past human activity and relates these to the shreds and patches surviving as the worn documents and faded words of history. From this collection of essentially meaningless, unique fragments of the past, he abstracts the order, and strives to press a meaning" (South 1969: 30). Too often we stop with description of the bits and pieces and the relation of these to the documentary shreds and patches without attempting to abstract the order and discover the meaning. Historical archeologists should more frequently take that next step from data to theory, a step so clearly stated by Hempel (1966: 15):

> The transition from data to theory requires creative imagination. Scientific hypotheses and theories are not *derived* from observed facts, but *invented* in order to account for them. They constitute guesses at the connections that might obtain between the phenomena under study, at uniformities and patterns that might underlie their occurrence.

In this chapter we have made guesses at some of the connections and uniformities we have observed from historic site ceramics. If our guesses prove valid we have sharpened our theoretical tools (Deetz 1968: 130) for revealing culture process, a basic goal of archeological science.

EXAMINING THE STATISTICAL CONFIDENCE AND CORRELATION OF THE FORMULA

This chapter was originally published in a more detailed form in 1972, after which a number of comments were received by colleagues regarding the statistical confidence and correlation involved in the use of the formula (South, ed., 1972). David South demonstrated that the standard deviation for 12 sites for which data was available at that time was 4.58 years (D. South 1972: 170). He examined the confidence factors for the formula dates and found that there is a 95% chance that approximately 68% of the ceramic formula dates will not be more than ± 7.77 years off from the historic median date (D. South 1972: 173).

Later, a total of 16 sites was available for determining the average number of years the mean ceramic date misses the median occupation date for this larger sample (Appendix B), and this was found to be 1.025 years (South ed., 1972: 217). Based on this average overestimate of one year, the archeologist using the mean ceramic date formula was advised to subtract one year from the mean ceramic date for the maximum statistical correlation between the ceramic date and predicted median occupation date.

Recently, midden deposits from the British occupation of Fort Moultrie, S.C., from 1780 to 1782, and the American occupation from 1775 to 1780, were excavated, and the mean ceramic dates for these deposits were found to be 1781.8 for the British deposit, and 1774.0 for the American deposit (South 1974a: 147). Richard Carrillo used these data, and data from 14 other sites for which detailed frequencies were available as well as known historic occupation periods, as data input for statistically deriving a least squares multiple linear regression equation for the purpose of arriving at a date most accurately predictive of the median occupation date represented by the ceramic sample. The results indicate the optional equation using the mean ceramic date formula is as follows:

The mean ceramic date formula is used to derive an interpreted median occupation date (Z) from the ceramic data. 235.5 years are added to 87% of this date, and this formula adjustment is expressed as:

$$Z = 235.5 + .87Y$$

Using this computer determined equation an R^2 value of .980 was obtained, indicating that 98.0% of the variance of the median occupation date was explained by this equation. The date resulting from this adjusted equation is the best mathematical prediction of the median occupation date represented by the ceramic sample (South 1974a: 147). The standard deviation from this study was 4.56 years.

The Expanding Use of the Formula Concept

In the original version of this chapter I urged archeologists to use the formula concept with other types of data from historic sites and to apply it to data from prehistoric sites as well. The response to this admonition was far greater than was received from my admonition of 1960 that quantification analyses be undertaken with data from historic sites. This quick response is indicative of a receptive climate in archeology to such studies, reflecting the interest on the part of archeologists in methods exploring the methodological frontier toward asking better questions of the data.

Examples of this phenomenon can be seen in Richard Carrillo's paper using the formula concept to examine English wine bottle attributes in relation to a control formed by dated wine bottles (Carrillo 1974). The concept was also used by Roger Grange Jr. in examining protohistoric to historic Pawnee ceramics in the Central Plains (Grange 1974), and he is exploring the use of the formula with clay pipes, bottles, and window glass (paper presented at the sixteenth Conference on Historic Site Archeology: 1975).

Michael Schiffer has used the concept in "Arrangement versus Seriation of Sites: A New Approach to Relative Temporal Relationships," (1975: 254), and in "Several Archaeological Laws" (1973). A healthy ferment in archeology is in progress. These and similar studies are a part of the new wine.

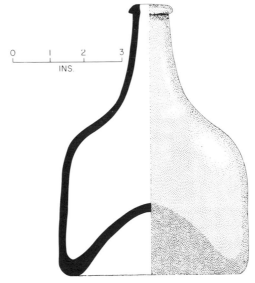

Changing form through time is revealed through temporal control and attribute variability.

THE HORIZON CONCEPT REVEALED IN THE APPLICATION OF THE MEAN CERAMIC DATE FORMULA TO SPANISH MAJOLICA IN THE NEW WORLD

Under the assumption that the horizon phenomenon seen on British-American sites would also be in effect on Spanish-American sites, a study of patterning of Spanish majolica was undertaken. This study was designed to examine the application of the mean ceramic date formula concept to Spanish majolica in the New World based on the data compiled by John M. Goggin (1968).

The manufacture period for various majolica types was not as well known as was the case with British-American ceramics, the ceramic dates having been assigned by Goggin on the basis of known dates of site occupation. As a result a disconformity was found between known occupation dates and the date derived from the use of the mean ceramic date formula. To adjust for this, an index date was assigned to seven majolica types, resulting in a closer conformity between the historical control dates of site occupation and the mean ceramic date derived by use of the formula. This procedure resulted in a majolica pattern seen to be reflective of the horizon concept. This section of this chapter is concerned with demonstrating this process of pattern delineation.

Deriving the Majolica Pattern

The first step in deriving a majolica pattern was to examine Goggin's majolica types and the temporal brackets assigned by him. Twenty-three majolica types were used to determine median dates, and these are shown in Table 34.

Taking the Goggin median date for the majolica types, I used the ceramic formula with eight collections for which there was controlling historic occupation period information.

Where

X_i = the Goggin median date for each majolica type
f_i = the frequency of each majolica type (sherd count)
n = the number of ceramic types in the sample

the mean ceramic date, Y, is expressed:

$$Y = \frac{\sum\limits_{i=1}^{n} X_i \cdot f_i}{\sum\limits_{i=1}^{n} f_i}$$

The eight collections for which historic median occupation dates are known are shown in Table 35, revealing a comparison between the

TABLE 34

Majolica Types with Goggin Dates and South Index Dates

Majolica type reference number	Majolica type name	Goggin date range (ca.)	Reference page number (Goggin 1968)	Goggin median date	South index date
1	Columbia Plain	1493–1650	124	1572	1535
2	Isabela Polychrome	1490–1560	128	1525	1445
3	Yayal Blue on White	1550–1600	130	1575	1532
4	La Vega Blue on White	1525–1575	131	1550	1507
5	Caparra Blue	1500–1560	135	1530	1487
6	Santo Domingo Blue on White	1550–1630	133	1590	1547
7	Ichtucknee Blue on Blue	1550–1650	139	1600	1675
8	Ichtucknee Blue on White	1615–1650	150	1633	
9	San Luis Blue on White	1630–1690	157	1660	
10	Fig Springs Polychrome	1610–1660	154	1635	
11	Blue and Orange Polychr.	1625–1650	166	1638	
12	Puebla Polychrome	1650–1700	180	1675	
13	Puebla Blue on White	1700–1850	194	1775	
14	San Luis Polychrome	1660–1720	169	1690	
15	Abó Polychrome	1650–1700	172	1675	
16	Aranama Polychrome	1750–1800	198	1775	
17	Aucilla Polychrome	1650–1685	163	1668	
18	Tallahassee Blue on White	1635–1700	159	1668	
19	Castillo Polychrome	1685–1704	185	1695	
20	Mt. Royal Polychrome	mid-century	161	1650	
21	Puaray Polychrome	1675–1700	183	1688	
22	San Agustin Blue on White	1700–1730	189	1715	
23	Huejotzingo Blue on White	1700–1900	195	1800	

known historic occupation median date and the ceramic formula date. This comparison reveals that the five earliest sites have a ceramic formula date averaging over 42 years later than the known historic median occupation date. This lack of correlation between formula date and historic occupation date is seen in the graph on the left in Figure 34. The three sites from the seventeenth and eighteenth centuries reveal a reasonable degree of correlation between the historic median occupation date and the formula date, but clearly something must be done to the earlier sites to insure a greater correlation between the two sets of dates.

In order to meet this requirement, an index date was assigned to the first seven majolica types to replace the median date derived from Goggin's data (Table 34). Columbia Plain majolica was assigned an index date 37 years below the Goggin median date, and Isabela Polychrome majolica was assigned an index date 80 years earlier than the Goggin Median Date, with Types 3 through 6 being assigned dates 43 years lower than

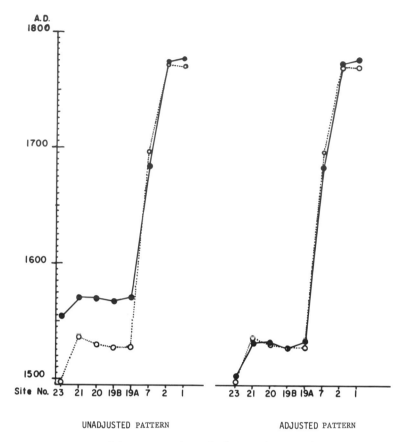

Figure 34. Comparison of the Ceramic formula dates with the median historic dates, using the Goggin median and the index date on Majolica samples from 8 sites. *Unadjusted pattern:* formula dates using Goggin Median for all Majolica types (Ceramic formula date—) and (median historic date . . . .). *Adjusted Pattern:* formula dates using index dates for seven Majolica types.

the Goggin median dates. Type 7, Ichtucknee Blue on Blue, was assigned a date 75 years later than Goggin's Median Date. This was done to bring the seventeenth-century sites into line with the generalized dates assigned by Goggin and recent studies on seventeenth-century sites (Deagan 1972; Milanich 1972).

Taking the assigned index date for the first seven majolica types, and Goggin's median date for the remaining types, I used the mean ceramic date formula to determine a date for use in interpreting the median occupation date represented by the sample. The result of this adjustment is seen in Table 35, with the sherd counts for these eight collections in Appendix C. The sum of the differences between the historic median dates and the formula dates using the Goggin median dates is seen to be

TABLE 35

Comparison of Historic Median Date, Goggin Median Date, and Majolica Formula Date Showing Difference, Mean, and Standard Deviation

Site Reference Number	Site name	Historic median	Goggin median date	Difference	Majolica formula date	Difference	Difference²
1	Falcon, Texas	1770	1777.2	+ 7.2	→→→→→→	+ 7.2	51.84
2	Aranama, Texas	1771	1773.0	+ 3.0	→→→→→→	+ 3.0	9.0
7	San Luis, Fla.	1697	1684.0	− 13.0	→→→→→→	−13.0	169.0
19B	La Vega Vieja, Dom. Rep.	1528.5	1567.8	+ 39.3	1528.5	0.0	0.0
19A	La Vega Vieja, Dom. Rep.	1528.5	1571.3	+ 42.8	1534.0	+ 5.5	30.25
20	Nueva Cadiz, Venezuela	1530.0	1570.2	+ 40.2	1532.5	+ 2.5	6.25
21	Jacagua, Dom. Republic	1536.5	1570.5	+ 34.0	1532.0	− 4.5	20.25
23	Isabela, Dom. Republic	1498.0	1554.9	+ 56.9	1502.8	+ 4.8	23.04
				+210.4		+ 5.5	309.63

$t\alpha/2$ = number used when confidence coefficient desired is x percent and n observations are used

$\bar{Y}$ = sample mean

n = number of observations in the sample

S = standard deviation of the sample

$$\bar{Y} = \frac{\sum_{i=1}^{n} Y_i}{n} = 5.5 \div 8 = .688$$

$$S = \sqrt{\frac{\sum_{i=1}^{n} Y_i^2 - \frac{\left(\sum_{i=1}^{n} Y_i\right)^2}{n}}{n-1}} = \sqrt{\frac{309.63 - \frac{(5.5)^2}{8}}{7}} = \sqrt{43.69}$$

$S = 6.61$

$S^2 = 43.69$

$t\alpha/2 = 2.365$ with a confidence factor of 95% (Weast 1968: A-161)

$\bar{Y} \pm t\alpha/2\, S/\sqrt{n} = .69 \pm (2.365)\,\dfrac{6.61}{\sqrt{8}} = .69 \pm 5.527$

241

plus 210.4 years for the eight collections, whereas using the Index Dates for the first seven majolica types and Goggin's median date for the remaining types produces a sum of differences of only 5.5 years. The comparison between the Goggin median dates and the combination index date and Goggin median date can be seen in the graphs in Figure 34.

With the adjusted pattern producing a sum of differences for the eight collections of only 5.5 years, for an average overestimate of the majolica formula of .69 years above the known median dates, we can have some degree of confidence in the pattern. In order to infer from this small sample the range in which the total population mean might fall, we use the formula (D. South 1972: 165):

$$\bar{Y} \pm t\alpha/2\ S/\sqrt{n}$$

From this (Table 35) we determine that there is a 95% confidence that the total population mean (μ) would fall between 6.217 and −4.837. This, plus the fact that the majolica formula overestimates the known historic median dates by an average of only .69 years, allows us with some confidence to apply the formula to data from sites for which the historic dates are not known but for which there is some relative chronological data derived from seriation and stratigraphy. If the formula replicates the temporal sequence revealed through seriation and stratigraphic excavation, we have additional data to support the validity of the analysis tool.

Application of the Ceramic Formula to Goggin's Stratigraphic Data

At Huejotzingo, Mexico, Goggin has stratigraphic data by 6-inch levels to a depth of 54 inches (Goggin 1968: 99). Application of the ceramic formula to this data revealed the following sequence:

Level in inches	Formula date
0–6	1727.7
6–12	1698.8
12–18	1697.9
18–24	1654.6
24–30	1643.3
30–36	1636.7
36–42	1636.1
42–48	1635.0
48–54	1635.0

Goggin interprets the 24 to 30-inch level as representing an occupation dating around 1650, and the formula date for this level is 1643.3; the level above had a formula date of 1654.6, which is entirely in keeping with Goggin's interpretation. The sherd count by majolica type for each level is seen in Appendix D.

From the Convento de San Francisco, Dominican Republic, Goggin reveals stratigraphic data from levels to a depth of 85 inches (Goggin 1968: 109). Application of the ceramic formula to this data produced the following sequence:

Level in inches	Formula date	Goggin (1968: 113) interpretive date	
0–8	1603.3 ⎫		
8–16	1605.7 ⎬	Post–1800	⎧ "a sudden increase in
16–24	1547.0 ⎭		⎪ European chinaware dating
24–32	1629.3	1750–1800	⎨ from the second half of
32–40	1708.2	1700–1750	⎩ the 18th century [p. 108]."
40–48	1649.8	1650–1700	
48–51	1636.0	1615–1650	
51–59	1557.1	1580–1615	
59–67	1534.5 ⎫		
67–79	1534.8 ⎬	1500–1580	
79–85	1531.7 ⎭		

The seven bottom levels produce a consistent sequence from the second quarter of the sixteenth century to the early eighteenth century. At the 24- to 32-inch level, however, there begins a reversal of ceramic formula dates, clearly reflecting a change in the cultural factors relating to majolica that resulted in the consistent sequence observed in the lower levels. One explanation for this phenomenon could be that the site in the area of this stratigraphic cut was subjected to a cultural use varying dramatically from that represented in the deeper levels of the deposit, resulting in a greater disturbance of the ground in the higher levels. However, another, more likely, explanation is seen in cultural phenomena of a broader scope, such as a dramatic change in the role played by majolica in the culture represented by the deposits above the 32-inch level. The recognition of this fact is seen in Goggin's statement that with the 24- to 32-inch level there was "a sudden increase in European chinaware dating from the second half of the 18th century" (Goggin 1968: 108). This decrease in the importance of majolica in the culture is also reflected in the fact that from the 32-inch level up to the surface, only 32 majolica sherds were recovered, whereas from this level down more than this number were recovered from each level. It is clear then that the ceramic formula has sensitively reflected a cultural phenomenon in terms of a temporal sequence, in the lower levels when majolica was a major cultural item and through a discontinuity of dates in the upper levels when majolica had virtually been replaced by

European ceramics in the eighteenth century. The fact that the ceramic formula dates reflect this phenomenon is an indication of its sensitivity as a research tool. The majolica sherd counts for each level of this stratigraphic excavation are seen in Appendix E.

Application of the Ceramic Formula to Goggin's Seriation

Using seriation Goggin placed collections of majolica from 23 sites in a temporal sequence which he illustrates in his Figure 1 (Goggin 1968; 25–27). The 23 sites have been assigned a reference number according to the sequence revealed by Goggin's seriation. If the majolica ceramic formula is a valid research tool it should replicate the seriation sequence constructed by Goggin. If it can be seen to do this, we have additional support for the formula as a tool for deriving a date of value in interpreting the occupation period represented by the majolica sample from historic sites of the sixteenth, seventeenth and eighteenth centuries. Table 36 reveals the sequence of ceramic formula dates compared with the seriation sequence derived by Goggin, and with the historic median dates.

From this comparison it is evident that there is only a minor difference between the sequence arrived at by Goggin and that resulting from the application of the ceramic formula; the Fig Springs, Fla., site and the Obispo, Venezuela, site are those most out of place in the seriation. The majolica sherd counts for each site in the seriation are seen in Appendix F. The known historic median dates for eight of the collections are also shown in this Table, and as has been pointed out the formula dates overestimate these historic median dates by an average of .69 years, with the greatest discrepancy being the −13 years for the collection from Fort San Luis, Fla. (See Table 35).

A slight difference is seen in the listing of the sites here from that of Goggin, in that there is a 14A and 14B, and a 19A and 19B. This was done as a check against the ceramic formula. Collections 14A and 14B are from Maurica, Venezuela, where Goggin used the majolica from one excavation unit (Rocx 15) as representative of all those excavated (14A). The majolica sample 14B represents the entire collection from all units including Rocx 15. The date for the one excavation unit used by Goggin was 1633.6, and the date for all the majolica from all inits was 1627.2 a difference of only 6.4 years.

A different comparison is seen in collections 19A and 19B, from the La Vega Vieja, Dominican Republic, site. Goggin used 19A, a collection made in 1952, in his seriation. Collections made in 1953 and 1954 are combined and designated 19B. The 1952 collection from the site produced a ceramic formula date of 1534.0, and the combined collections of 1953 and 1954 produced a formula date of 1528.5, only 5.5 years

TABLE 36

Comparison of the Ceramic Formula Dates with Goggin's Seriation[a]

Site reference number and name in Goggin seriation	Ceramic formula date	Historic median date and Goggin comment
1 Falcon Reservoir, Texas	1777.2	1770
2 Aranama, Texas	1773.0	1771
3 Quiburi, Arizona	1770.3	
4 N. Senora de la Leche, Florida	1718.9	
5 Pine Tuft, Florida	1676.0	"probably destroyed 1700–1706"
6 Zetrouer, Florida	1677.3	
7 Fort San Luis, Florida	1684.0	1697
8 Scott Miller, Florida	1676.8	"terminal date ca. 1685"
9 Beaty, Florida	1667.2	"late 17th century"
10 Wright's Landing, Florida	1653.2	"early 1650s"
11 Darien Bluff (Ft. King Geo.), Fla.	1639.1	
12 Mt. Royal, Florida	1633.3	"middle of seriation" [1640?]
13 Fig Springs, Florida	1615.7	"1615–1650 postulated"
14A Maurica, Venezuela (Rocx 15)	1633.6	"between 1620 and 1645"
14B Maurica, Venezuela (All units)	1627.2	"between 1620 and 1645"
15 Punta Mosquito, Venezuela	1620.7	"early 17th century"
16 Obispo, Venezuela	1646.3	"about 1630"
17 Richardson, Florida	1620.2	"ca.1615"
18 Cepicepi, Dominican Republic	1615.9	"ca.1600"
19A La Vega Vieja, Dom. Rep. (1952)	1534.0	1528.5
19B La Vega Vieja, Dom. Rep. (1953–1954)	1528.5	1528.5
20 Nueva Cadiz, Venezuela	1532.5	1530.0
21 Jacagua, Dominican Republic	1532.0	1536.5
22 Juandolio, Dominican Republic	1520.4	"early 16th century"
23 Isabela, Dominican Republic	1502.8	1498.0

[a] Figure 1 in Goggin 1968:25–27.

apart, with 19A's being 5.5 years removed, and 19B the same as the historic median date of 1528.5. The majolica sherd counts for all collections used in the seriation are seen in the Appendix.

Application of the Ceramic Formula to Various Archeological Sites

A number of collections of majolica from various sites were discussed by Goggin that were not used in his seriation. Those for which he had some temporal comment are included here along with the ceramic formula date (Table 37).

Goggin says (1968: 84) that the two samples from Puaray, N.M. apparently represent "two occupations, one previous to the revolt of 1680 and a second in the 18th century." The formula dates support this interpretation.

TABLE 37

Application of Ceramic Formula Date to Various Sites

Site	Ceramic Formula Date	Goggin's Temporal Range and Comments
Awatovi, Arizona	1668.6	1629–1680
Tumacacori, Arizona	1777.1	1701–
Kuaua, New Mexico	1675.0	before 1680
Puaray, New Mexico		
first sample	1678.6	
second sample	1747.7	

Adaes, Texas 1737.6 (Formula Date); 1721–1773 (Goggin's Temporal Range)

Goggin believed that there must have been two settlements represented by this collection because of the presence of types 12 and 15 of the seventeenth century and the presence of 37 fragments of type 13 of the third quarter of the eighteenth century. One settlement he thought would have been "about 1600" and the other during the documented period of 1721–1773 (Goggin 1968: 81). However, the ceramic formula indicates a date only 9.4 years from the known historic median date for the eighteenth century occupation of the site. Types 12 and 15 reveal a ceramic formula date of 1675.0, and types 22 and 13 produce a formula date of 1770.5, which is certainly in keeping with Goggin's interpretation if we divide the collection as Goggin did.

Fox Pond, Florida 1635.1 (Formula Date); 1630–1650 (Goggin's Temporal Range)

Middle Plateau Trading Post, Macon, Georgia 1684.2 (Formula Date); 1690–1710 (Goggin's Temporal Range)

Goggin stated (1968: 79) that this sample of 12 sherds "equates perfectly with the supposed date of the trading post," but the ceramic formula date certainly indicates a date earlier than the middle of Goggin's historic time range. The sherd counts for the majolica in these collections are seen in Appendix G.

The Demonstrated Horizon

The sites from which came the majolica collections used in this study are from a broad area including Georgia, Florida, Texas, Arizona, and

New Mexico, as well as Mexico, Venezuela, and the Dominican Republic. Any patterned relationships existing between majolica types having temporal consistency, such as demonstrated through the application of the ceramic formula in this study, is a clear indication that there was a broad and rapid spread of majolica throughout the area involved in this study. This is expressed in terms of the horizon concept of Willey and Phillips (1958: 31–34).

Summary

In this study we have applied the mean ceramic date formula concept to data compiled by John M. Goggin from Spanish majolica found on sites in the New World (Goggin 1968). It was found that the median date for six sixteenth-century majolica types was too late for producing a ceramic formula date closely approximating the median historic occupation date for the sites for which these dates are known. One seventeenth-century type was seen to have a median date too early to produce formula dates closely approximating Goggin's estimates for seventeenth-century sites. Because of this an index date was assigned to these seven majolica types, and when these dates were used along with Goggin's median ceramic dates for seventeenth- and eighteenth-century sites, the ceramic formula produced dates that are seen to overestimate the known historic median occupation date for the sites by an average of only .69 years.

Using this majolica formula with the stratigraphic date gathered by Goggin, I found that the ceramic formula dates closely replicated the stratigraphic sequence. Applying the ceramic formula to the sites used by Goggin in his seriation chart also produced a close replication of the sequence arrived at by Goggin using traditional seriation methods.

The fact that the majolica formula is seen to work as well as it does within the limits of the Goggin data illustrates that it is likely a reliable means of expressing the Goggin data. This study has used the formula concept with majolica patterning for comparison with data from sites not included in this study and for which there is some chronological control other than majolica. Since Goggin's data were used to construct the formula, the formula cannot then be tested by reference to the same data. Internal consistency between the formula and Goggin's data can be demonstrated, such as we have done with the seriation and stratigraphic data comparisons and comparisons with collections from sites of known occupation periods. Testing, however, in terms of reliability must come through application of the formula to data lying outside that used by Goggin. If subsequent research demonstrates that the formula is invalid for dating majolica collections, then this may reflect an area where the formula was not internally consistent with Goggin's data, or it may represent a need to adjust Goggin's conclusions in the light of new evidence, and thereby the index dates whereby the formula date is derived.

Since the majolica formula is designed to express the Goggin data through statistical means, we are free to manipulate the index dates toward the end of producing consistent ceramic dates from the formula that are in keeping with the Goggin data. It is not necessary, therefore, that the index dates correlate with Goggin's estimates for the time period during which each majolica type was being deposited on occupation sites, so long as the resulting mean ceramic date obtained from the formula is reasonably consistent with the chronology outlined by Goggin. The index date represents, therefore, a functional expedient with unlimited flexibility for use in arriving at ceramic formula dates that can be used, with some degree of reliability, as an interpretive aid in establishing the occupation period represented by majolica samples. The index date is not the median manufacture date such as was used in constructing the mean ceramic date formula for British ceramics in the last section, nor does it represent the period of maximum use of the majolica type to which it is assigned. It is an *index number* designed to produce consistent results from the majolica formula that are internally consistent within the Goggin data. As more data become available specifically dating sites on which majolica is found, with controls other than majolica, the index dates assigned here may well have to be revised to accommodate the new data. Cultural variation may well be found to be reflected in the formula dates, for instance Indian-occupied as opposed to Spanish-occupied sites, where we may find that the formula dates from Indian-occupied sites will be earlier than Spanish-occupied sites of the same time period. As we discover and program new data into the majolica formula, we should eventually have a formula that will be so firmly rooted in research that its reliability will be high enough to allow it to become a basic chronological tool.

When the above point is understood, it should be easily seen how this concept could be applied to prehistoric ceramic sequences for which there is a well-defined series of ceramic types within a relatively short period of time, and for which there is some comparative control, such as dendrochronology or two or three radiocarbon dates. A firmly established seriation such as this, verified by stratigraphic control, could be the basis for constructing a model where index dates were assigned to the various ceramic types using the radiocarbon or cross dating dates as control for the chronology. Once such a model was constructed, the South mean ceramic date formula used in the majolica study and in the study of British ceramics could be applied. The formula dates would first have to be seen to have internal consistency within the sequence used to construct the model, then the formula could be tested by application to site collections in the same area where the ceramic types are found. Once reliability was demonstrated by temporal controls other than those of the ceramics themselves, the formula could be applied with confidence that the resulting mean ceramic date could be used to interpret the occupation period represented by the ceramic collections with perhaps a more sensitive degree of temporal separation than is now enjoyed through traditional seriations. An important application would be in quick relative temporal placement of a site from a surface survey where pottery constitutes the primary data recovered. The application of the formula to prehistoric collections should focus on temporally confined ceramic sequences for the most effective model.

The explanation for the existence of the horizon concept revealed by majolica patterning is to be found in the distributive system in Spanish colonial culture. Wherever Spanish colonial occupation occurred there was a supply of majolica to accompany the period of occupation. This supply had to have been continuous enough to produce the sequence of majolica types seen through time on the sites in this study. Just as British ceramics continued to flow into the corners of the British empire in the eighteenth century through colonization, Spanish majolica continued to occupy an important role in Spanish-American culture throughout the period of colonization in the area involved in this study.

An important factor not dealt with in this study is the distribution of locally made majolica. Distribution studies with this as a variable should be undertaken in order to define other patterns for hypothesis formulation to get at details of explanatory concepts. The concern here has been with pattern recognition expressed as a formula.

The formula approach presented here and in the analysis of ceramics from British-American sites has implications far beyond the use of formulas for analysis of historic ceramics. As was mentioned in the previous section, archeologists are beginning to use this concept in innovative ways to explore data, and it is hoped this trend will continue. Much broader implications are inherent in the formula approach in that if seriations anchored in historical control (such as Goggin's) are valid then we may have some assurance that prehistoric frequency seriations constructed in a like manner might have validity. If the patterns upon which such seriations are based can be seen to be reliably expressed in terms of statistical formulas, then we will have taken the first step toward understanding the culture process represented by the archeological record.

The following is a list of the events in the process of development of the majolica formula, and a paradigm of the role of the formula model in explaining culture process from the archeological record (Figure 35).

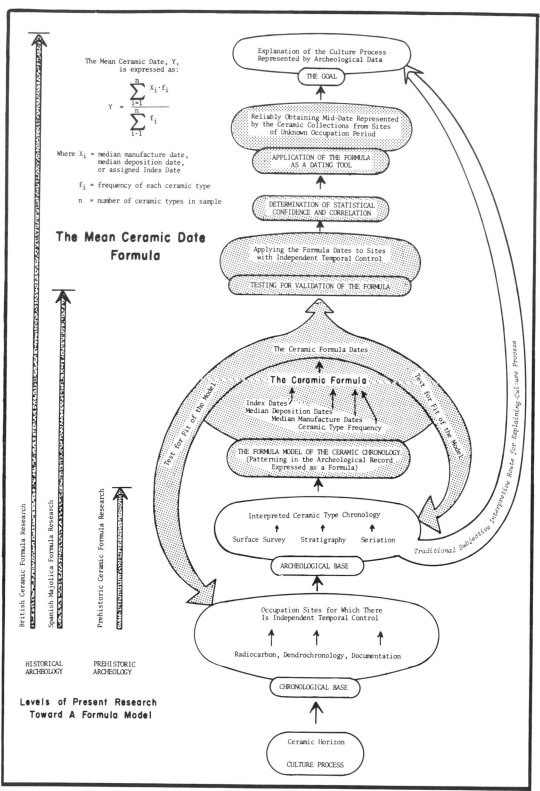

The Mean Ceramic Date, Y, is expressed as:

$$Y = \frac{\sum\limits_{i=1}^{n} X_i \cdot f_i}{\sum\limits_{i-1}^{n} f_i}$$

Where X_i = median manufacture date, median deposition date, or assigned Index Date

f_i = frequency of each ceramic type

n = number of ceramic types in sample

The Mean Ceramic Date Formula

British Ceramic Formula Research

Spanish Majolica Formula Research

Prehistoric Ceramic Formula Research

HISTORICAL ARCHEOLOGY

PREHISTORIC ARCHEOLOGY

Levels of Present Research Toward A Formula Model

Explanation of the Culture Process Represented by Archeological Data

THE GOAL

Reliably Obtaining Mid-Date Represented by the Ceramic Collections from Sites of Unknown Occupation Period

APPLICATION OF THE FORMULA AS A DATING TOOL

DETERMINATION OF STATISTICAL CONFIDENCE AND CORRELATION

Applying the Formula Dates to Sites with Independent Temporal Control

TESTING FOR VALIDATION OF THE FORMULA

The Ceramic Formula Dates

The Ceramic Formula

Index Dates
Median Deposition Dates
Median Manufacture Dates
Ceramic Type Frequency

THE FORMULA MODEL OF THE CERAMIC CHRONOLOGY
(Patterning in the Archeological Record Expressed as a Formula)

Test for Fit of the Model

Test for Fit of the Model

Traditional Subjective Interpretive Route for Explaining Culture Process

Interpreted Ceramic Type Chronology

Surface Survey   Stratigraphy   Seriation

ARCHEOLOGICAL BASE

Occupation Sites for Which There Is Independent Temporal Control

Radiocarbon, Dendrochronology, Documentation

CHRONOLOGICAL BASE

Ceramic Horizon

CULTURE PROCESS

Figure 35. Paradigm of the role of the formula model in explaining culture process from the archeological record.

Sequential Events in Majolica Research

Steps 1 through 14 indicate the extent of present research. Steps 15 through 18 outline the work remaining.

1. Majolica type manufacture period unknown.
2. Majolica types accumulated on occupation sites.
3. Goggin collected majolica from occupation sites of known historic periods.
4. Majolica types were assigned temporal brackets based on occurrence or nonoccurrence on sites of known historic periods.
5. Majolica collected from sites of unknown historic period was used to assign interpreted occupation period for the site.
6. Stratigraphic tests were used to clarify the temporal relationship of majolica types.
7. Seriation was used to aid in determining the temporal position of sites for which no documented period was known.
8. Seriation was used to clarify temporal relationships among majolica types.
9. Sites of known occupation were used as a controlling framework for the seriation.
10. Goggin's majolica median dates were used with South's mean ceramic date formula to test the fit of the formula to majolica data.
11. Index dates were assigned to seven majolica types to adjust the fit of the formula dates to the documented median occupation dates for sites and Goggin's estimates of the occupation period represented by majolica collections from occupation sites.
12. Formula dates were compared with Goggin's stratigraphic test to check for internal consistency of the formula to the strata dates assigned by Goggin.
13. Formula dates were compared with Goggin's seriation sequence of sites based on majolica types.
14. The formula dates were seen to have a high degree of correlation to the median historic occupation dates and with Goggin's estimates of the occupation period represented by the sites from which the majolica samples were recovered.
15. The next step is to test the formula by apply it to majolica samples from sites where there is some independent temporal control: historical documentation, artifact analysis of known artifact types, cross dating of artifact types of known temporal period, dendrochronology or radiocarbon dating.
16. If the formula dates for majolica from many such sites can be statistically demonstrated to have a high degree of correlation with the independent temporal control prediction, then confidence can be placed in the reliability of the formula dates.
17. When this point is reached, the formula can for the first time be reliably used to arrive at a date upon which interpretation can be

		Edward Jones (carpenter)	Cornelius Harnett (Victualor)	Harnett's Inn		Cornelius Harnett's lot wall
PROPERTY OWNER						
DEED DATE +		1731	1732	1732	1732	1732
ORIGINAL LOT NUMBER		120	27	27	27	27
ARCHAEOLOGICAL UNIT NO.		NI	S25*	S25	S25	S13
SHERD PROVENIENCE		TOTAL AREA	INSIDE INN	MIDDEN 0-1.5'	MIDDEN 1.5'-3.3'	MIDDEN PIT
TYPE NO. (1971)						
17	UNDERGLAZE BLUE HAND PAINTED PEARLWARE					
6,13	MOCHA AND ANNULAR PEARLWARE					
2	WHITEWARE					
19	BLUE & GREEN EDGED PEARLWARE					
11,2	TRANSFER-PRINTED PEARLWARE & WHITEWARE					
36	"CLOUDED", "WHIELDON" MOTTLED GLAZED CREAMWARE BURNISHED					
22	CREAMWARE					
—	BRUNSWICK BURNISHED COLONO-INDIAN WARE					
—	BRUNSWICK PLAIN COLONO-INDIAN WARE					
39	CHINESE PORCELAIN					
43,48	WHITE SALT-GLAZED STONEWARE					
45,49	DELFTWARE					
56	COMBED YELLOW LEAD-GLAZED SLIPWARE					
		100%	100%	100%	100%	100%
	SHERD COUNT	200	1736	2730	1453	829

% SCALE
0   25   50

made as to the occupation period represented by the majolica sample from an archeological site.

18. When such reliability is established, we will have demonstrated that the patterning in the archeological record resulting from culture process can be expressed by means of a formula. In so doing, we will have taken a step toward testing some of our assumptions regarding frequency seriation, and toward the further application of the formula concept to prehistoric data. Such an application will allow for a more specific temporal control within an already known general chronology.

APPENDIXES

These appendixes are presented here to provide data for comparative studies using the formula concept of pattern recognition.

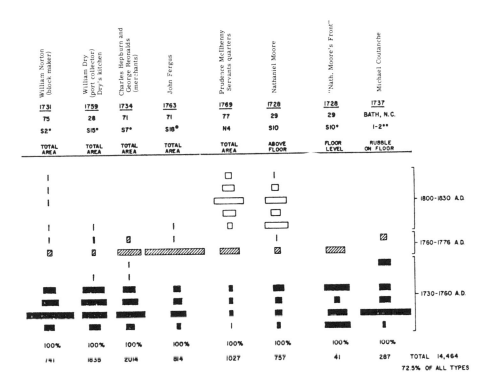

Appendix A*

This chart demonstrates the similarity of percentage relationships between several ruins of similar documented time periods, providing data of value in determining the occupation period of ruins of unknown time periods from a percentage relationship comparison of the ceramic types. The ceramic type numbers used in this study have been added to the original chart.

This chart is presented here to illustrate the visual pattern recognition resulting from plotting the relationships in the form of a bar graph. The formula concept presents the same data in a different manner.

* Percentage relationship of certain ceramic types from several structures at Brunswick Town, N.C., from a paper delivered at the first Conference on Historic Site Archaeology in 1960 by Stanley South entitled "The Ceramic Types at Brunswick Town, North Carolina," *Southeastern Archaeological Conference Newsletter* 1962, **9,** No. 1.

Application of the Mean Ceramic Date Formula to Samples from Historic Sites

Ceramic type	Type median	Sherd count	Product

Charles Towne (38CH1): The first English fortification in South Carolina

64	1665	4	6660
62	1670	13	21,710
65	1720	10	17,200
66	1660	60	99,600
70	1635	62	101,370
58	1668	1	1668
72	1610	1	1610
		151	249,818 ÷ 151 = 1654.4

Historic dates 1670–1680
Historic median date 1675
Mean ceramic date 1654.4
Pipestem date 1667

The First Fort Moore? (38AK4-15): An eighteenth-century frontier fort and trading post

22	1791	2	3582
26	1730	1	1730
37	1733	1	1733
29	1760	1	1760
43	1758	35	61,530
49	(1750)	64	112,000
48	1745	1	1745
39	1730	38	65,740
54	1733	4	6932
56	1733	18	31,194
61	1713	42	71,946
66	1660	39	64,740
		246	424,632 ÷ 246 = 1726.1

Historic dates 1716–1747
Historic median date 1732
Mean ceramic date 1726.1
Pipestem date 1730.9

Fort Moore (38AK5-A)

26	1730	1	1730
37	1733	2	3466
43	1758	13	22,854
49	(1750)	17	29,750
44	1738	4	6952
39	1730	18	31,140
53	1733	3	5199
54	1733	4	6932
56	1733	4	6932
		66	114,955 ÷ 66 = 1741.7

Historic dates 1716–1766
Historic median date 1741
Mean ceramic date 1741.7
Pipestem date 1744.16

APPENDIX B   (Continued)

Ceramic type	Type median	Sherd count	Product
Goudy's Trading Post at Fort Ninety Six, South Carolina (38GN1-3): Plowed zone			
22	1791	7	12,537
21	1788	1	1788
43	1758	2	3516
49	1750	6	10,500
44	1738	1	1738
		17	30,079 ÷ 17 = 1769.3

Historic dates 1751–?
Mean ceramic date 1769.3

Goudy's Trading Post at Fort Ninety Six, South Carolina (38GN1-5): Cellar			
29	1760	2	3520
43	1758	3	5274
49	1750	1	1750
44	1738	1	1738
		7	12,282 ÷ 7 = 1754.6

Historic dates 1751–1760?
Historic median date 1756
Mean ceramic date 1754.6

Fort Prince George, South Carolina 38PN1: A British military post on the Cherokee frontier			
28	1769	2	3538
22	1791	255	456,705
33	1767	1	1767
31	1770	78	138,060
21	1788	12	21,456
26	1730	25	43,250
34	1760	2	3520
36	1755	6	10,530
40	1763	4	7052
29	1760	12	21,120
43	1758	127	223,266
49	(1750)	123	215,250
44	1738	15	26,070
47	1748	2	3496
45	1750	72	126,000
39	1730	68	117,640
46	1755	10	17,550
54	1733	16	27,728
56	1733	21	36,393
		851	1,500,391 ÷ 851 = 1763.0

Historic dates 1753–1768
Historic median date 1761
Mean ceramic date 1763.0
Pipestem date 1750.14

APPENDIX B (Continued)

Ceramic type	Type median	Sherd count	Product
The Rock Turtle Site (38PN4): An eighteenth-century Indian village site			
22	1791	2	3582
33	1767	4	7068
26	1730	1	1730
34	1760	1	1760
36	1755	2	3510
40	1763	1	1763
37	1733	1	1733
41	1758	1	1758
43	1758	23	40,434
49	(1750)	54	94,500
44	1738	5	8690
39	1730	9	15,570
54	1733	3	5199
56	1733	5	8665
		112	195,962 ÷ 112 = 1749.7

Mean ceramic date 1749.7
Pipestem date 1756.36

Brunswick Town, North Carolina (Ruin S15)			
11	1818	1	1818
22	1791	96	171,936
33	1767	37	65,379
26	1730	54	93,420
35	1780	2	3560
42	1758	2	3516
37	1733	23	39,859
29	1760	63	110,880
43	1758	532	935,256
49	(1750)	485	848,750
44	1738	68	118,184
47	1748	52	90,896
39	1730	418	723,140
46	1755	3	5265
53, 54	1733	79	136,907
56	1733	330	571,890
		2245	3,920,656 ÷ 2245 = 1746.4

Historic dates 1726–1759–1776
Historic median date 1751
Mean ceramic date 1746.4
Pipestem date 1748

APPENDIX B (Continued)

Ceramic type	Type median	Sherd count	Product
Brunswick Town, North Carolina (Ruin N1)			
33	1767	3	5310
26	1730	1	1730
34	1760	8	14,080
29	1760	7	12,320
43	1758	64	112,512
49	(1750)	89	155,750
44	1738	6	10,428
47	1748	2	3496
39	1730	17	29,410
53, 54	1733	1	1733
56	1733	14	24,262
		212	371,022 ÷ 212 = 1750.1

Historic dates 1731–1776
Historic median date 1754
Mean ceramic date 1750.1

Brunswick Town, North Carolina (S2)			
11	1818	1	1818
13	1805	3	5415
22	1791	41	73,431
33	1767	4	7068
26	1730	14	24,220
34	1760	4	7040
36	1755	3	5265
37	1733	5	8665
29	1760	12	21,120
43	1758	136	239,088
49	(1750)	373	652,750
44	1738	45	78,210
47	1748	112	195,776
39	1730	103	178,190
53, 54	1733	31	53,723
56	1733	91	57,703
		978	1,709,482 ÷ 978 = 1749.0

Historic dates 1731–1776   Mean ceramic date 1749.0
Historic median date 1754   Pipestem date 1748

APPENDIX B   (Continued)

Ceramic type	Type median	Sherd count	Product
	Brunswick Town, North Carolina (S18)		
11	1818	1	1818
22	1791	558	999,378
33	1767	6	10,602
26	1730	8	13,840
34	1760	11	19,360
36	1755	8	14,040
37	1733	3	5199
43	1758	73	128,334
49	(1750)	137	239,750
44	1738	7	12,165
47	1748	4	6992
39	1730	28	48,440
53, 54	1733	10	17,330
56	1733	15	25,995
		───	───
		869	1,543,243 ÷ 869 = 1776.2

Historic dates 1763–1776   Mean ceramic date 1776.2
Historic median date 1770   Pipestem date 1756

	The Paca House, Annapolis, Maryland 19J, 27B: A town house mansion		
44	1738	4	6952
22	1791	14	25,074
26	1730	2	3460
43	1758	9	15,822
47	1748	3	5244
37	1733	1	1733
49	(1750)	5	8750
39	1730	2	3460
36	1755	1	1755
17	1800	1	1800
31	1770	2	3540
46	1755	1	1755
34	1760	1	1760
		───	───
		46	81,105 ÷ 46 = 1763.1

Historic dates 1763–1780
Mean ceramic date 1763.1

APPENDIX B (Continued)

Ceramic type	Type median	Sherd count	Product
The S10 Dump at Brunswick Town: A post-Revolutionary War dump			
2	1860	45	83,700
12	1805	44	79,420
11	1818	136	247,248
13	1805	32	57,760
17	1800	1	1800
22	1791	17	30,447
33	1767	10	17,670
19	1805	47	84,835
26	1730	13	22,490
43	1758	21	36,918
49	(1750)	16	28,000
44	1738	12	20,856
47	1748	2	3496
39	1730	37	64,010
53, 54	1733	15	25,995
56	1733	15	25,995
		463	830,640 ÷ 463 − 1794.0

Historic dates 1776–1830
Historic median date 1803
Mean ceramic date 1794.0

Tallassee, A nineteenth century Cherokee Indian? House site in Tennessee			
4	1830	28	51,240
11	1818	10	18,180
9	1810	6	10,860
15	1798	5	8990
17	1800	10	18,000
		59	107,270 ÷ 59 = 1818.1

Mean ceramic date 1818.1

Toxaway (380C3): An eighteenth-century Cherokee Indian village site			
48	1745	11	19,195
39	1730	2	3640
56	1733	32	55,456
		45	78,111 ÷ 45 = 1735.8

APPENDIX B   (Continued)

Ceramic type	Type median	Sherd count	Product
	Toxaway, a nineteenth-century occupation		
1	1860	11	20,460
19	1805	1	1805
		12	22,265 ÷ 12 = 1855.4

Mean ceramic date, 18th century = 1735.8
Mean ceramic date, 19th century = 1855.4

	The Nipper Creek Site (38RD18)		
12	1805	29	52,345
14	1798	2	3596
15	1798	30	53,940
19	1805	1	1805
		62	111,686 ÷ 62 = 1801.3

Mean ceramic date 1801.3

APPENDIX B   (Continued)

Comparison of Historic Median and Mean Ceramic Dates for Sixteen Historic Sites

Site	Median historic date	Mean ceramic date	Difference (CD − HD)
Brunswick S7, N.C.	1755.0	1758.5	+3.5
Fort Moore AK4-15, S.C.	1731.5	1730.0	−1.5
Fort Moore AK5-A, S.C.	1741.0	1746.5	+5.5
Ninety Six GN1-5, S.C.	1755.5	1754.6	− .9
Ft. Prince George, S.C.	1760.5	1767.1	+6.6
Brunswick S15, N.C.	1751.0	1750.7	− .3
Brunswick N1, N.C.	1753.5	1752.0	−1.5
Brunswick S2, N.C.	1753.5	1750.4	−3.1
Brunswick S18, N.C.	1769.5	1777.9	+8.4
Brunswick S10, N.C.	1803.0	1801.8	−1.2
Trebell, Va.	1797.0	1797.6	+ .6
Tellico, Tenn.	1800.5	1802.8	+2.3
Ft. Dobbs, N.C.	1759.5	1755.8	−3.7
Ft. Michilimackinac, Mich.	1775.0	1775.4	+ .4
Ft. Michilimackinac, Mich.	1768.5	1769.3	+ .8
Castle Hill, Newfoundland	1762.5	1763.0	+ .5
			+16.4

Mean of the difference $= \dfrac{\sum\limits_{i=1}^{n} Y_i}{n} = 16/\overline{16.4}^{\,1.025} = 1.025$

Standard deviation = 3.489 years

APPENDIX C

Application of the Ceramic Formula to Majolica Collections using the Goggin Median Date and Index Date for Constructing the Majolica Model Formula

Majolica type	Goggin median	Index	Sherd count	Median product	Index product
Site Reference No. 1					
Falcon Reservoir, Texas 1760?–1780? (Goggin 1968: 82)					
13	1775		90	159,750	
17	1800		16	28,880	
22	1715		1	1715	
16	1775		45	79,875	
			152	270,140 ÷ 152 = 1777.2	
Date using Goggin median = 1777.2				Historic median date = 1770	
Site Reference No. 2					
Aranama, Texas 1749–ca. 1793 (Goggin 1968: 82)					
22	1715		25	42,875	
13	1775		293	520,075	
23	1800		30	54,000	
16	1775		25	44,375	
			373	661,325÷ 373 = 1773.0	
Date using Goggin median = 1773.0				Historic median date = 1771	
Site Reference No. 7					
Fort San Luis, Florida 1690–1704 (Goggin 1968: 76)					
14	1690		63	106,470	
12	1675		35	58,625	
19	1695		10	16,950	
15	1675		5	8375	
9	1660		7	11,620	
22	1715		2	3430	
17(?)	1668		1	1668	
			123	207,138 ÷ 123 = 1684.0	
Date using Goggin median = 1684.0				Historic median date = 1697	
Site Reference No. 19B (1953–1954 Collection)					
La Vega Vieja, Dominican Republic 1495?–1562 (Goggin 1968: 29)					
1	1572	1535	149	234,228	228,715
3	1575	1532	27	42,525	41,364
2	1525	1445	7	10,675	10,115
5	1530	1487	11	16,830	16,357
4	1550	1507	8	12,400	12,056
7	1600	1675	1	1600	1675
			203	318,258 ÷ 203 = 1567.8	310,282 ÷ 203 = 1528.5
Date using Goggin median = 1567.8					
Date using index number = 1528.5				Historic median date = 1528.5	

APPENDIX C (Continued)

Majolica type	Goggin median	Index	Sherd count	Median product	Index product
		Site Reference No. 19A (1952 Collection)			
		La Vega Vieja, Dominican Republic 1495?–1562 (Goggin 1968: 28)			
1	1572	1535	442	694,824	678,470
3	1575	1532	17	26,775	26,044
2	1525	1445	4	6100	5780
5	1530	1487	5	7650	7435
7	1600	1675	2	3200	3350
4	1550	1507	4	6200	6028
6	1590	1547	2	3180	3094
			476	747,929 ÷ 476 = 1571.3	730,201 ÷ 476 = 1534.0

Date using Goggin median = 1571.3
Date using index number = 1534.0   Historic median date = 1528.5

		Site Reference No. 20			
		Nueva Cadiz, Venezuela (Ex. 5) 1515–1545 (Goggin 1968: 43)			
1	1572	1535	202	317,544	310,070
3	1575	1532	10	15,750	15,320
5	1530	1487	9	13,770	13,383
2	1525	1445	1	1525	1445
			222	348,589 ÷ 222 = 1570.2	340,218 ÷ 222 = 1532.5

Date using Goggin median = 1570.2
Date using index number = 1532.5   Historic median date = 1530.0

		Site Reference No. 21			
		Jacagua, Dominican Republic 1511–1562 (Goggin 1968: 29)			
1	1572	1535	265	416,580	406,775
3	1575	1532	8	12,600	12,256
2	1525	1445	8	12,200	11,560
4	1550	1507	3	4650	4521
6	1590	1547	2	3180	3094
5	1530	1487	1	1530	1487
			287	450,740 ÷ 287 = 1570.5	439,693 ÷ 287 = 1532.0

Date using Goggin median = 1570.5
Date using index number = 1532.0   Historic median date = 1536.5

		Site Reference No. 23			
		Isabela, Dominican Republic 1493–1503 (Goggin 1968: 24)			
1	1572	1535	61	95,892	93,635
2	1525	1445	34	51,850	49,130
3	1575	1532	1	1575	1532
5	1530	1487	2	3060	2974
			98	152,377 ÷ 98 = 1554.9	147,271 ÷ 98 = 1502.8

Date using Goggin median = 1554.9
Date using index number = 1502.8   Historic median date = 1498.0

APPENDIX D

Application of the Ceramic Formula to Stratigraphic Data at Huejotzingo, Mexico[a]

Level	Majolica type number	Goggin median or South index date	Sherd count	Product	South formula date
0–6"	9	1660	1	1660	
	14	1690	6	10,140	
	12	1675	5	8375	
	15	1675	1	1675	
	17	1668	2	3336	
	13	1775	13	23,075	
	22	1715	6	10,290	
	16	1775	4	7100	
			38	65,651	÷ 38 = 1727.7
6–12"	9	1660	2	3320	
	14	1690	30	50,700	
	12	1675	4	6700	
	15	1675	1	1675	
	13	1775	5	8775	
	22	1715	5	8575	
	23	1800	1	1800	
			48	81,545	÷ 48 = 1698.8
12–18"	10	1635	1	1635	
	9	1660	1	1660	
	14	1690	12	20,280	
	12	1675	1	1675	
	17	1668	1	1668	
	13	1775	3	5325	
	22	1715	1	1715	
			20	33,958	: 20 = 1697.9
18–24"	10	1635	12	19,620	
	9	1660	1	1660	
	14	1690	1	1690	
	17	1668	1	1668	
	13	1775	1	1775	
	22	1715	1	1715	
			17	28,128	÷ 17 = 1654.6
24–30"	10	1635	19	31,065	
	14	1690	2	3380	
	12	1675	1	1675	
	15	1675	1	1675	
			23	37,795	÷ 23 = 1643.3
30–36"	10	1635	28	45,780	
	9	1660	2	3320	
			30	49,100	÷ 30 = 1636.7
36–42"	10	1635	21	34,335	
	9	1660	1	1660	
			22	35,995	÷ 22 = 1636.1
42–48"	10	1635	10	16,350	÷ 10 = 1635.0
48–54"	10	1635	1	1635	÷ 1 = 1635.0

[a] Table 6 in Goggin 1968: 99.

APPENDIX E

Application of the Ceramic Formula to Stratigraphic Data at Convento de San Francisco, Dominican Republic[a]

Level	Majolica type number	Goggin median or South index date	Sherd count	Product	South formula date	Goggin (1968: 113) interpretive date range
0–8″	1	1535	3	4605		
	7	1675	2	3350		
	8	1633	1	1633		
	10	1635	1	1635		
			—			
			7	11,223	÷ 7 = 1603.3	
8–16″	1	1535	4	6140		Post-1800
	10	1635	1	1635		
	13	1775	1	1775		
	14	1690	1	1690		
			—			
			7	11,240	÷ 7 = 1605.7	
16–24″	6	1547	1	1547	÷ 1 = 1547.0	
24–32″	1	1535	6	9210		
	7	1675	2	3350		
	8	1633	1	1633		
	9	1660	1	1660		
	10	1635	1	1635		
	12	1675	1	1675		
	13	1775	1	1775		
	14	1690	4	6760		
			—			
			17	27,698	÷ 17 = 1629.3	1750–1800
32–40″	1	1535	4	6140		
	9	1660	7	11,620		
	10	1635	1	1635		
	11	1638	1	1638		
	12	1675	4	6700		
	13	1775	13	23,075		
	14	1690	9	15,210		
	16	1775	9	15,975		
			—			
			48	81,993	÷ 48 = 1708.2	1700–1750
40–48″	1	1535	10	15,350		
	6	1547	2	3094		
	7	1675	9	15,075		
	8	1633	6	9798		
	9	1660	14	23,240		
	10	1635	12	19,620		
	12	1675	14	23,450		
	13	1775	3	5325		
	14	1690	7	11,830		

APPENDIX E (Continued)

Level	Majolica type number	Goggin median or South index date	Sherd count	Product	South formula date	
	15	1675	1	1675		
	16	1775	1	1775		
	17	1668	2	3336		
	18	1668	2	3336		
	19	1695	1	1695		
			84	138,581	÷ 84 = 1649.8	1650–1700
48–51″	1	1535	17	26,095		
	6	1547	4	6188		
	7	1675	4	6700		
	8	1633	4	6532		
	9	1660	8	13,280		
	10	1635	10	16,350		
	11	1638	1	1638		
	12	1675	2	3350		
	13	1775	12	21,300		
			62	101,433	÷ 62 = 1636.0	1615–1650
51–59″	1	1535	136	208,760		
	2	1445	1	1445		
	5	1487	2	2974		
	6	1547	2	3094		
	7	1675	18	30,150		
	8	1633	7	11,431		
	9	1660	6	9960		
			172	267,814	÷ 172 = 1557.1	1580–1615
59–67″	1	1535	188	288,580		
	2	1445	1	1445		
	3	1532	9	13,788		
	6	1547	1	1547		
			199	305,360	÷ 199 = 1534.5 ⎫	
67–79″	1	1535	34	52,190		
	3	1532	3	4596		
			37	56,786	÷ 37 = 1534.8 ⎬	1500–1580
79–85″	1	1535	26	39,910		
	2	1445	1	1445		
			27	41,355	÷ 27 = 1531.7 ⎭	

[a] Table 12 in Goggin 1968: 109.

APPENDIX F

Application of the Ceramic Formula to Goggin's Seriation Chart[a]

Site reference number	Majolica type number	Goggin median or index date	Sherd count	Product	South formula date	Historic median date and Goggin comment
1	*Falcon Reservoir, Texas 1760?–1780?* (Goggin 1968: 82)					
	(See Appendix C for data)				1777.2	1770
2	*Aranama, Texas 1749–ca. 1793* (Goggin 1968: 82)					
	(See Appendix C for data)				1773.0	1771
3	*Quiburi, Arizona* (Goggin 1968: 91–92)					
	13	1775	670	1,189,250		
	23	1800	11	19,800		
	22	1715	68	116,620		
	16	1775	57	101,175		
			806	1,426,845 ÷ 806 =	1770.3	
4	*Nuestra Senora de la Leche Shrine, Florida* (Goggin 1968: 65)					
	9	1660	2	3320		
	14	1690	18	30,420		
	12	1675	5	8375		
	22	1715	69	118,335		
	13	1775	20	35,500		
			114	195,950 ÷ 114 =	1718.9	
5	*Pine Tuft, Florida ?–ca. 1704* (Goggin 1968: 75)					
	12	1675	401	671,675		
	14	1690	57	96,330		"probably a
	9	1660	19	31,540		mission destroyed
	18	1668	9	15,012		in 1700–1706"
	15	1675	2	3350		
			488	817,907 ÷ 488 =	1676.0	
6	*Zetrouer, Florida ?–1706* (Goggin 1968: 73)					
	12	1675	234	391,950		
	14	1690	92	155,480		
	9	1660	43	71,380		
	15	1675	2	3350		
	19	1675	6	10,170		
			377	632,330 ÷ 377 =	1677.3	
7	*Fort San Luis, Florida 1690–1704* (Goggin 1968: 76)					
	(See Appendix C for data)				1684.0	1697

APPENDIX F   (Continued)

Site reference number	Majolica type number	Goggin median or index date	Sherd count	Product		South formula date	Historical median date and Goggin comment
8	Scott Miller, Florida ?–1706 (Goggin 1968: 75)						
	14	1690	55	92,950			
	12	1675	54	90,450			
	15	1675	42	70,350			
	9	1660	21	34,860			"terminal date . . . perhaps 1685 would be close"
	18	1668	9	15,012			
	17	1668	10	16,680			
	20	1650	1	1650			
			192	321,952	÷ 192 −	1676.8	
9	Beaty, Florida (Goggin 1968: 74)						
	1	1535	3	4605			
	12	1675	23	38,525			
	15	1675	8	13,400			
	17	1668	34	56,712			
	9	1660	17	28,220			
	14	1690	18	30,420			"late 17th century"
	10	1635	5	8175			
	18	1668	2	3336			
			110	183,393	÷ 110 =	1667.2	
10	Wright's Landing, Florida ca. 1650–? (Goggin 1968: 64)						"early 1650s"
	1	1535	4	6140			
	6	1547	1	1547			"just after the middle of the 17th century"
	7	1675	2	3350			
	8	1633	4	6532			
	10	1635	74	120,990			
	9	1660	31	51,460			
	18	1668	5	8340			
	17	1668	2	3336			
	14	1690	8	13,520			
	15	1675	1	1675			
	12	1675	5	8375			
	22	1715	6	10,290			
	13	1775	6	10,650			
	16	1775	1	1775			
			150	247,980	÷ 150 =	1653.2	

APPENDIX F (Continued)

Site reference number	Majolica type number	Goggin median or index date	Sherd count	Product	South formula date	Historical median date and Goggin comment
11	Darien Bluff (Ft. King George), Georgia (Goggin 1968: 78)					
	1	1535	6	9210		
	7	1675	2	3350		
	8	1633	1	1633		
	10	1635	39	63,765		
	9	1660	36	59,760		
			84	137,688 ÷ 84 =	1639.1	
12	Mt. Royal, Florida (Goggin 1968: 70)					
	1	1535	2	3070		
	7	1675	5	8375		
	8	1633	6	9798		
	10	1635	19	31,065		
	18	1668	3	5004		"middle of our
	20	1650?	1	6600		seriation [1640?]"
	6	1547	4	6188		
	9	1660	5	8300		
			48	78,400 ÷ 48 =	1633.3	
13	Fig Springs, Florida (Goggin 1968: 74)					
	1	1535	58	89,030		
	7	1675	43	72,025		
	8	1633	43	70,219		
	10	1635	66	107,910		
	18	1668	17	28,356		"1615–1650
	6	1547	12	18,564		postulated"
	11	1638	2	3276		
			241	389,380 ÷ 241 =	1615.7	
14a	Maurica, Venezuela (Rocx 15) (Goggin 1968: 45–46)					
	1	1535	10	15,350		
	6	1547	2	3094		
	7	1675	24	40,200		
	8	1633	20	32,660		"between 1620 and
	10	1635	13	21,255		1645"
	9	1660	6	9960		
			75	122,519 ÷ 75 =	1633.6	

APPENDIX F (Continued)

Site reference number	Majolica type number	Goggin median or index date	Sherd count	Product		South formula date	Historical median date and Goggin comment
14b	*Maurica, Venezuela* (All units) (Goggin 1968: 46)						
	1	1535	31	47,585			
	6	1547	5	7735			
	7	1675	37	61,975			
	8	1633	31	50,623			"between 1620 and 1645"
	10	1635	35	57,225			
	9	1660	24	39,840			
	18	1668	6	10,008			
			169	274,991	÷ 169 =	1627.2	
15	*Punta Mosquito, Venezuela* (Goggin 1968: 44)						
	1	1535	34	52,190			
	7	1675	51	85,425			
	8	1633	15	24,495			
	10	1635	4	6540			"early 17th century"
	9	1660	7	11,620			
	6	1547	5	7735			
			116	188,005	÷ 116 =	1620.7	
16	*Obispo, Venezuela* (Goggin 1968: 43)						
	1	1535	5	7675			
	8	1633	6	9798			
	7	1675	29	48,575			
	10	1635	10	16,350			"about 1630"
	9	1660	1	1660			
	6	1547	1	1547			
			52	85,605	÷ 52 =	1646.3	
17	*Richardson, Florida* ca. 1606–? (Goggin 1968: 72)						
	2	1445	1	1445			
	1	1535	5	7675			
	7	1675	11	18,425			"about 1615"
			17	27,545	÷ 17 =	1620.2	
18	*Cepicepi, Dominican Republic* (Goggin 1968: 31)						
	1	1535	24	36,840			
	7	1675	34	56,950			
	6	1547	1	1547			(ca. 1600 A.D.)
			59	95,337	÷ 59 =	1615.9	

APPENDIX F (Continued)

Site reference number	Majolica type number	Goggin median or index date	Sherd count	Product	South formula date	Historic median date and Goggin comment
19a	La Vega Vieja, Dominican Republic (1952 Collection)					
	(Goggin 1968: 28) (See Appendix C for data)				1534.0	1528.5
19b	La Vega Vieja, Dominican Republic (1953–1954 Collection)					
	(Goggin 1968: 29) (See Appendix C for data)				1528.5	1528.5
20	Nueva Cadiz, Venezuela (Ex. 5) 1515–1545					
	(Goggin 1968: 43) (See Appendix C for data)				1532.5	1530.0
21	Jacagua, Dominican Republic 1511–1562					
	(Goggin 1968: 29) (See Appendix C for data)				1532.0	1536.5
22	Juandolio, Dominican Republic (Goggin 1968: 30)					
	1	1535	267	409,845		
	2	1445	42	60,690		
	3	1532	6	9192		"early 16th
	5	1487	24	35,688		century"
			339	515,415 ÷ 339 =	1520.4	
23	Isabela, Dominican Republic 1493–1503 (Goggin 1968: 24)					
	(See Appendix C for data)				1502.8	1498.0

[a] Figure 1 in Goggin 1968: 25–27.

APPENDIX G

Application of the Ceramic Formula to Various Archeological Sites

Majolica type number	Goggin median or index date	Sherd count	Product	South formula date	Goggin's temporal range comments
Awatovi, Arizona (Goggin 1968: 90)					
10	1635	14	22890		
9	1660	3	4980		
12	1675	4	6700		
21	1688	4	6752		
19	1695	1	1695		
22	1715	1	1715		
13	1775	3	5325		
		30	50057 ÷ 30 =	1668.6	1629–1680
Tumacacori, Arizona (Goggin 1968: 91)					
13	1775	33	58575		
23	1800	3	5400		
		36	63975 ÷ 36 =	1777.1	1701–

APPENDIX G   (Continued)

Majolica type number	Goggin median or index date	Sherd count	Product	South formula date	Goggin's temporal range comments
		Kuaua, New Mexico (Goggin 1968: 84)			
12	1675	30	50250		
15	1675	2	3350		
		32	53600	÷ 32 =	1675.0 before 1680
		Puaray (Bandelier's Puaray), New Mexico (Goggin 1968: 84)			
12	1675	5	8375		
21	1688	8	13504		
15	1675	13	21775		"two occupations, one
17	1668	1	1668		previous to the revolt of
					1680 and a second in the
		27	45322	÷ 27 =	1678.6 18th century."
Second sample					
15	1675	2	3350		
12	1675	1	1675		
13	1775	8	14200		
		11	19225	÷ 11 =	1747.7
		Adaes, Texas (Goggin 1968: 81)			"two settlements"
12	1675	13	21775 }	= 1675.0	"about 1680"
15	1675	8	13400		
22	1715	3	5145 }	= 1770.5	1721–1773
13	1775	37	65675		
		61	105995	÷ 61 =	1737.6
		Fox Pond, Florida (Goggin 1968: 73)			
1	1535	4	6140		
7	1675	1	1675		
8	1633	21	34293		
6	1547	7	10829		
10	1635	54	88290		
9	1660	36	59760		
20	1650	1	1650		
12	1675	3	5025		
		127	207662	÷ 127 =	1635.1	1630–1650
		Middle Plateau Trading Post, Macon, Georgia (Goggin 1968: 78–79)			
14	1690	6	10140		
12	1675	4	6700		
15	1675	1	1675		
19	1695	1	1695		
		12	20210	÷ 12 =	1684.2	1690–1710

REFERENCES

Binford, Lewis H. and Moreau S. Maxwell
 1961   Excavation at Fort Michilimackinac, Mackinac City, Michigan, 1959 season. Lansing, Michigan: Stone Printing Co.
Binford, Sally R. and Lewis R. Binford
 1968   New perspectives in archeology. Chicago: Aldine.
Carrillo, Richard F.
 1972   English Wine Bottles as Revealed by a Probability and Statistical Analysis: A Further Systematic Approach to Evolution and Horizon in Historical Archaeology. Research Manuscript Series, No. 35. Institute of Archeology and Anthropology, University of South Carolina, Columbia.
 1974   English Wine Bottles As Revealed By a Statistical Study: A Further Approach to Evolution and Horizon in Historical Archeology. The Conference on Historic Site Archaeology Papers 1972, 7:290–317. Institute of Archeology and Anthropology, University of South Carolina, Columbia.
Clark, David L.
 1968   Analytical archaeology. London: Methuen & Co.
Cleland, Charles E.
 1970   Diverse Comments and Sundry Suggestions Concerning Ceramics in Suffolk County, Massachusetts, Inventories 1680–1775: A Preliminary Study with Diverse Comments Thereon, and Sundry Suggestions. Conference on Historic Site Archaeology Papers, Historical Archaeology Forum, 3, Part 2. Institute of Archeology and Anthropology, University of South Carolina, Columbia.
Cleland, Charles E. and James E. Fitting
 1968   The Crisis of Identity: Theory in Historic Site Archaeology. Conference on Historic Site Archaeology Papers, Historical Archaeology Forum, 2, Part 2. Institute of Archeology and Anthropology, University of South Carolina, Columbia.
Combes, John D.
 n.d.   The archeology at Fort Prince George. Manuscript in preparation. Institute of Archeology and Anthropology, University of South Carolina, Columbia.
Deagan, Kathleen A.
 1972   Fig Springs: The Mid-Seventeenth Century in North-Central Florida. Historical Archaeology, 6.
Deetz, James
 1968   Late Man in North America: Archeology of European Americans. The Anthropological Society of Washington. Washington, D.C.: 121–130.
Dethlefsen, Edwin and James Deetz
 1966   Death's Heads, Cherubs, and Willow Trees: Experimental Archaeology in Colonial Cemeteries. American Antiquity 31, No. 4
Dollar, Clyde D.
 1968   Some Thoughts on Theory and Method in Historical Archaeology. Conference on Historic Site Archaeology Papers, Historical Archaeology Forum 2, Part 2:3–30. Institute of Archeology and Anthropology, University of South Carolina, Columbia.
Dunnell, Robert C.
 1970   Seriation Method and Its Evaluation. American Antiquity 35, No. 3
Ford, James A.
 1962   A quantitative method for deriving cultural chronology. Technical Publications and Documents, Department of Social Affairs, Pan American Union.
Fries, Adelaide L.
 1968   Records of the Moravians in North Carolina. 8 vols. North Carolina State Department of Archives and History, Raleigh.

Goggin, John M.
   1968   Spanish Majolica in the New World. *Yale University Publications in Anthropology,* No. 72.
Grange, Roger T. Jr.
   1974   Pawnee Potsherds Revisited: Formula Dating of a Non-European Ceramic Tradition. *The Conference on Historic Site Archaeology Papers 1972* **7**:318–336. The Institute of Archeology and Anthropology, University of South Carolina, Columbia.
   1975   An Extension of the Formula Dating Method in Clay Pipes, Wine Bottles, and Window Glass. *The Conference on Historic Site Archaeology Papers 1975* **10:** (in press). The Institute of Archeology and Anthropology, University of South Carolina, Columbia.
Hanson, Lee H. Jr.
   1971   Kaolin Pipe Stems—Boring in on a Fallacy. *Conference on Historic Site Archaeology* **4,** Part 1.
Harrington, Jean C.
   1954   Dating Stem Fragments of Seventeenth and Eighteenth Century Clay Tobacco Pipes. *Quarterly Bulletin* **9,** No. 1, Archeological Society of Virginia.
   1962   Search for the Cittie of Ralegh. *Archeological Research Series No. 6.* Washington, D.C.: National Park Service, United States Department of the Interior.
Hempel, Carl G.
   1966   *Philosophy of natural science.* Englewood Cliffs, N.J.: Prentice-Hall.
Longacre, William A.
   1970   Current thinking in American archeology. In Current Directions in Anthropology: *Bulletins of the American Anthropological Association* **3** (No. 3, Part 2): 126–138.
Mayer-Oakes, William J.
   1955   Prehistory of the Upper Ohio Valley. *Annals of the Carnegie Museum* **34** (Anthropological Series, No. 2).
Milanich, Jerald T.
   1972   Excavations at the Richardson Site, Alachua County, Florida: An Early 17th-Century Potano Indian Village (with notes on Potano culture change). *Bureau of Historic Sites and Properties, Bulletin No. 2.* Tallahassee: Florida Department of State.
Miller, J. Jefferson and Lyle M. Stone
   1970   *Eighteenth-century ceramics from Fort Michilimackinac.* Washington, D.C.: Smithsonian Institution Press.
Noël Hume, Ivor
   1963   *Here lies Virginia.* New York: Knopf.
   1970   *A guide to artifacts of Colonial America.* New York: Knopf.
Polhemus, Richard
   1971   Excavations at Fort Moore–Savanno Towne (38AK4 and 5). *The Institute of Archeology and Anthropology Notebook* **3** (No.6): 135. The University of South Carolina, Columbia.
Roth, Rodris
   1961   *Tea drinking in 18th-century America: Its etiquette and equipage.* Contributions from the Museum of History and Technology, Paper 14. Washington, D.C.: Smithsonian Institution.
Schiffer, Michael B.
   1973   Several Archaeological Laws. Manuscript on file with Arkansas Archeological Survey, Fayetteville.
   1975   Arrangement versus Seriation of Sites: A New Approach to Relative Temporal Relationships. *The Cache River archeological project: An experiment in Contract archeology;* assembled by Michael B. Schiffer and John H. House. Fayetteville: Arkansas Archeological Survey.

South, David B.
  1972 Mean Ceramic Dates, Median Occupation Dates, Red Ant Hills and Bumble Bees: Statistical Confidence and Correlation. *The Conference on Historic Site Archaeology Papers* **6:**164–174. Institute of Archeology and Anthropology, University of South Carolina, Columbia.
South, Stanley A.
  1955 Evolutionary Theory in Archaeology. *Southern Indian Studies* **7.**
  1958 Nath Moore's Front, Unit S10, 1728–1776. Manuscript on file with State Department of Archives and History, North Carolina, and with the Institute of Archeology and Anthropology, University of South Carolina, Columbia.
  1959a The McCorkall-Fergus House, Unit S18, c.1760–1775. Manuscript on file with State Department of Archives and History, North Carolina, and at the Institute of Archeology and Anthropology, University of South Carolina, Columbia.
  1959b The Hepburn-Reonalds House, Unit S7, 1734–1776. Manuscript on file with State Department of Archives and History, North Carolina, and at the Institute of Archeology and Anthropology, University of South Carolina, Columbia.
  1962 The Ceramic Types at Brunswick Town, North Carolina, *Southeastern Archaeological Conference Newsletter* **9,** No. 1.
  1967 The Paca House, Annapolis, Marylar.d. Manuscript on file with the Institute of Archeology and Anthropology, University of South Carolina, Columbia.
  1969 Exploratory Archaeology at the Site of 1670–1680 Charles Towne on Albemarle Point in South Carolina. *Research Manuscript Series No. 1.* Institute of Archeology and Anthropology, University of South Carolina, Columbia.
  1971a Archeology at the Charles Towne Site (38CHI) on Albemarle Point in South Carolina. Manuscript on file with the Institute of Archeology and Anthropology, University of South Carolina, Columbia.
  1971b Historical perspective at Ninety Six, with a summary of exploratory excavation at Holmes' Fort and the Town Blockhouse. *Research Manuscript Series,* No. 9. Institute of Archeology and Anthropology, University of South Carolina, Columbia.
  1972 Evolution and Horizon As Revealed in Ceramic Analysis in Historical Archaeology. *The Conference on Historic Site Archaeology Papers* **6:**71–116. Institute of Archeology and Anthropology, University of South Carolina, Columbia.
  1972 (Ed) *The Conference on Historic Site Archaeology Papers* **6:**71–116. Institute of Archeology and Anthropology, University of South Carolina, Columbia.
  1974a Palmetto Parapets. *Anthropological Studies No. 1.* Institute of Archeology and Anthropology, University of South Carolina, Columbia.
  1974b The Horizon Concept Revealed in the Application of the Mean Ceramic Date Formula to Spanish Majolica in the New World. *The Conference on Historic Site Archaeology Papers 1972* **7:** 96–122. Institute of Archeology and Anthropology, University of South Carolina, Columbia.
Stone, Garry Wheeler
  1970 Ceramics in Suffolk County, Massachusetts, Inventories 1680–1775—A Preliminary Study with Divers Comments Thereon, and Sundry Suggestions, *Conference on Historic Site Archaeology, Historical Archaeology Forum* **3,** Part 2. Institute of Archeology and Anthropology, University of South Carolina, Columbia.
Washburn, S. L.
  1953 The strategy of physical anthropology. In *Anthropology Today,* edited by Kroeber, A. L. Chicago: University of Chicago Press.
Weast, Robert C.
  1968 *Handbook of chemistry and physics.* Cleveland, Ohio: Chemical Rubber Co.
Willey, Gordon R. and Philip Phillips
  1958 *Method and theory in American archaeology.* Chicago: University of Chicago Press.

Revealing the ruins of the Moravian Town of Bethabara, N.C.

Methodological Considerations

The previous chapters have emphasized the fact that there can be no archeological science without pattern recognition, and pattern cannot be reliably recognized without a quantification approach for identifying regularity and variation in the archeological record. It follows that quantification of poorly observed and inadequately collected data will not lead to reliable pattern recognition and a science of archeology. This chapter emphasizes the importance of careful and efficient observation in the archeological process, the need for classification of the archeological record, and the methodological phases in the archeological process; it also evaluates analysis situations relative to their contribution to the archeological data bank of knowledge. Emphasis is placed on the need for the archeologist to employ a flexible attitude for meeting the demands of the research design while observing the maximum amount of data relating to site structure, site content, and site context (chronology).

THE FUNCTION OF OBSERVATION IN THE ARCHEOLOGICAL PROCESS

Archeological sites are located through surface survey, aerial photography, resistivity and magnetometer survey, topographic mapping and historical documentation, as well as through other survey techniques. Such activity can become so involved that a specialty in such techniques can be developed. From the moment a survey begins and throughout the research, the observation and recording of data is of primary concern to the archeologist. The quality of the observation and

recording process has a direct relationship to the problems the archeologist is attempting to solve. The sophistication of the hypotheses
depends on equally sophisticated field observation for relevant explanation to emerge.

Traditionally archeologists have dealt with features, postholes and
burials, under an implied assumption that "a posthole is a posthole,"
when careful observation reveals a wide variety of attributes of value in
recording and interpreting features for componential analysis. The more
distinctions the archeologist draws between features at the observational
level the more sophisticated his hypotheses can become. The Accokeek
Creek Site is an excellent example of posthole recording resulting in
very limited interpretive data as a result of the lack of distinctions drawn
between the various postholes (Stephenson and Ferguson, 1963: Figure 6).
Here thousands upon thousands of postholes were recorded by Mrs.
Ferguson, but no structures other than a series of palisades could be
identified by Robert Stephenson who analyzed the data. If a variety of
attributes had been used to draw distinctions between the postholes as
they were observed during excavation a number of architectural structures may well have been identified and various components isolated.
Many other reports could be cited revealing similar lack of posthole and
feature recording based on a wide range of attributes observable in plan
at the excavated level of the site. The features illustrated in the chart in
Figure 36 reveal various attributes observable in the field that allow for
separation of features into classes useful in architectural, componential,
functional, and cultural identification.

In observing features for multiattribute recording, a consistent recording technique must be utilized. Consistency requires that the archeologist not record postholes and features in one area when the ground is
powder dry, and others when the ground is moist from a recent rain. In
order to consistently observe features for recording the archeologist
must keep the excavated level moist enough to allow for maximum
observation. This means an ample source of water for wetting down
areas to be observed must be at hand. Fire engines, water wagons,
pumps, and fire hoses have been used to dump thousands of gallons of
water a day on sites I have excavated in order to insure this consistency
of observation and recording of the data. The archeologist cannot hope
to consistently record the archeological record if he cannot observe it,
and yet sites are frequently examined under such dry, baked conditions
that thorough or consistent data cannot possibly be recovered. Under
such conditions the archeologist may well find that his data consist primarily of masonry ruins and other obviously observable features, and he
may come to believe that because of this no postholes nor other features
requiring more sensitive observation are present.

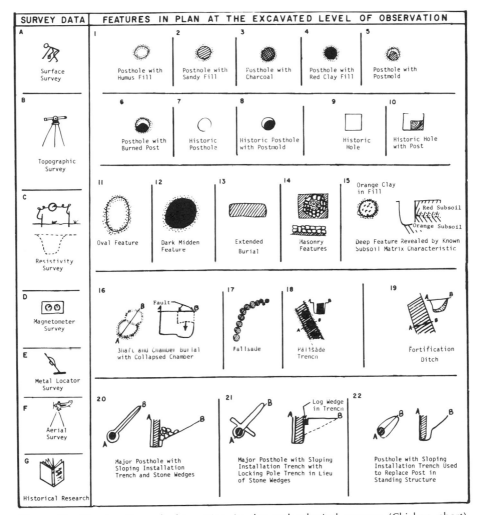

SURVEY DATA	FEATURES IN PLAN AT THE EXCAVATED LEVEL OF OBSERVATION

A — Surface Survey

1. Posthole with Humus Fill
2. Posthole with Sandy Fill
3. Posthole with Charcoal
4. Posthole with Red Clay Fill
5. Posthole with Postmold

B — Topographic Survey

6. Posthole with Burned Post
7. Historic Posthole
8. Historic Posthole with Postmold
9. Historic Hole
10. Historic Hole with Post

C — Resistivity Survey

11. Oval Feature
12. Dark Midden Feature
13. Extended Burial
14. Masonry Features
15. Deep Feature Revealed by Known Subsoil Matrix Characteristic (Orange Clay in Fill, Red Subsoil, Orange Subsoil)

D — Magnetometer Survey

E — Metal Locator Survey

16. Shaft and Chamber Burial with Collapsed Chamber (Fault)
17. Palisade
18. Palisade Trench
19. Fortification Ditch

F — Aerial Survey

G — Historical Research

20. Major Posthole with Sloping Installation Trench and Stone Wedges
21. Major Posthole with Sloping Installation Trench with Locking Pole Trench in Lieu of Stone Wedges
22. Posthole with Sloping Installation Trench Used to Replace Post in Standing Structure (Log Wedge in Trench)

Figure 36. The function of observation in the archeological process (Chicken chart), recording and interpretation of features for componential analysis.

Under dry conditions delicate soil distinctions are always lost, and even features that show up dramatically under moist soil conditions will totally disappear when the sand or clay surface is allowed to dry out. Occasionally, drying may reveal features through more rapid evaporation of moisture from disturbed areas, and some archeologists are coming to rely on this technique in lieu of moist earth observation. However, relying on this technique in lieu of moist earth observation is like preferring braille over visual observation. It can be used but is definitely secondary to primary observation of features in moist soil. Certain areas,

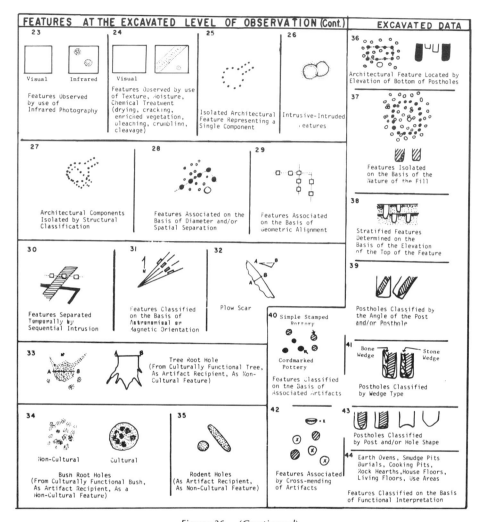

Figure 36.   (Continued)

because of their unique soil conditions, may not lend themselves to moist soil observation, but I believe these cases would be more the exception than the rule.

Once the features are revealed through removal of the plowed soil zone or other overlying soil layer, the surface must be schnitted (cut clean) using trowels or shovels. Scraping or brushing of moist soil only obliterates the data to be observed. When this process of schnitting is completed over an area as large as possible, recording of each posthole and feature should be undertaken immediately by the data recording crew, Photographs, elevations, horizontal position, width and shape of

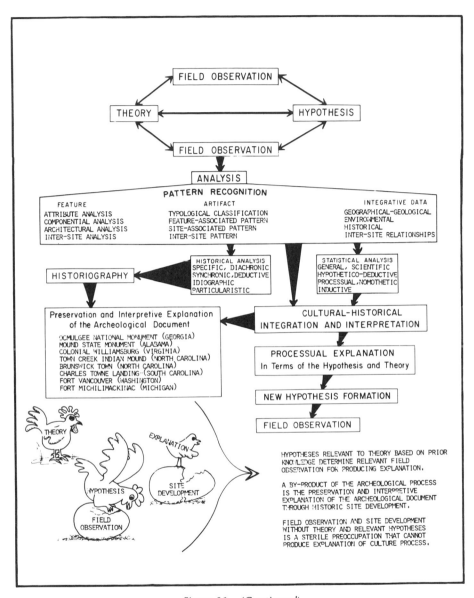

Figure 36.   (Continued)

feature outlines, and the attributes observable in the fill are recorded, with care being taken by the excavators not to add confusion to the scene by footprints and disturbance of this cleaned level. While the recording process is under way, it is often necessary to spray water over the area constantly. A mist of water keeps the soil in good condition for observing and recording the attributes of the features at this level. On the chart in Figure 36, of the 44 types of features listed, 35 can be observed and recorded before any excavation into the features themselves is undertaken, a fact which emphasizes the need for thorough observation and recording at this stage in the archeological process for maximum recovery of data.

A typical posthole visible at the subsoil level is a dark humus filled area from four to eight inches in diameter, with the edge of the original hole no longer a sharp line, but blended by the action of worms (Figure 36: 1). This action of worms is often so extensive that it is difficult to observe just where the original edge of the posthole was located. Unfortunately archeological reports reveal that this type of posthole is most often the only designation assigned, "humus filled posthole." However, some postholes can be seen to have a higher relationship of sandy fill than others, some have a higher percentage of charcoal flecks in the fill than others, and some may contain fragments of daub visible at the excavated level, or perhaps red clay from a collapsed daub-plastered palisade (Figure 36: 2–4).

At the Indian ceremonial center at Charles Towne, S.C., the subsoil matrix was sandy loam, and a clear contrast could be seen between those humus filled postholes and those containing flecks of red clay (interpreted as coming from a clay-plastered palisade). Recording of this observable attribute made possible the location of ceremonial sheds, and the separation of one of the palisades from the two others. Similar posthole and feature attributes can be separated on almost any site on the basis of the relationship of the color and/or texture of the various soils comprising the fill.

Another means of observation and recording of postholes for separating various components is to record the presence of an especially dark humus area within the posthole representing the post itself. Postmolds and burned posts are dramatic attributes for revealing architectural features distinguished from other posthole data (Figure 36: 11–12). Posthole and feature shape, whether oval, round, or irregular is important in determination of associated postholes or pit features.

Because of the recent age of historic postholes, there are fewer worm holes to blend the edge of the feature with the subsoil matrix, and consequently the edges of more recent features are still relatively sharply defined. These features are also easily separated into groups based on the presence of postmolds or surviving posts in the hole (Figure 36: 7–10). The observation that historic period features have less worm-hole blending might be used to form an hypothesis regarding the use of worm hole concentration as a temporal index, similar to taking a blood count. The methodology might involve the use of a small grid for count-

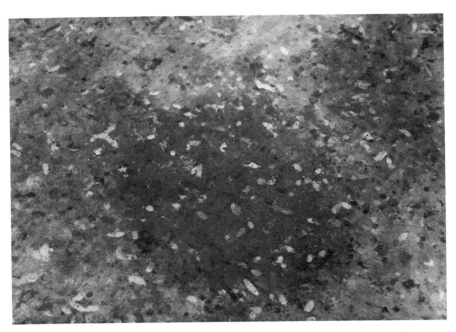

An archeological feature with considerable worm hole blending of the edge.

ing the worm holes, and from this a series of indices could be created for use in comparison with features for which radiocarbon or other dates were known. The technique might have only single site or area applicability but might prove to be a useful method of observation.

Another attribute of the historic period features is the presence of square or rectangular postholes, footing holes and features (Figure 36: 9–10, 13). Such features cannot simply be plotted by a central point with the diameter recorded, as one might do with circular features; rather, three points at least must be recorded to obtain the proper orientation of such angular features. This must be done even if (particularly if) the feature is a small one such as a square posthole only 6 inches on the side. The feature in Figure 36: 10, for instance, requires no less than six measured points for accurate recording. In recording such features for meaningful interpretation a roughly triangulated plotting from grid stakes is not sufficiently precise, and transit and tape, or alidade and tape recording of the most exacting nature should be employed. This caution would seem to be an obvious standard procedure, but careless horizontal plotting of features is often the rule rather than an exception. This is illustrated by the fact that an historic brick ruin measuring 40 by 87 feet on a side cannot be plotted to reveal a measurement of 40.1 by 86.9, and roughly triangulated points from grid stakes do not normally yield this accuracy unless the most exacting care is utilized in controlling the reference points and recording procedures.

Using the square posthole attribute, and the sharply defined, non-worm-blended edge of the features at the site of the Charles Towne Indian cermonial center, we were able to identify a nineteenth-century barn complex and associated fence lines through differential plotting of this type feature in plan, thus isolating these features as a separate component from the Indian occupation of the site.

Archeology of the historic period also reveals characteristic features of masonry, such as wells, footings, and foundation walls. These are accompanied by their construction ditches which must also be plotted and carefully excavated, though many historical archeology reports fail to mention these important features associated with the obvious masonry (Figure 36: 14). Excavation of prehistoric masonry structures such as kivas is often characterized by a failure to excavate beyond a foot from the masonry. This procedure successfully eliminates any chance of discovering any associated features and artifact distributions. Masonry features are accompanied by their construction ditches which must also be carefully recorded and excavated, though many archeology reports even fail

An archeological feature during excavation.

to mention these important features invariably associated with masonry walls (Figure 36: 14).

Sometimes the geology of a site is an aid to the classification of certain features, when the geology is known from previous excavation. For instance, at Town Creek Indian Mound in North Carolina there is an orange clay subsoil underlying the red clay subsoil. As a result of this phenomenon those pits such as burials that were dug into the orange layer and backfilled almost immediately contain flecks of orange clay in the fill (Figure 36: 15). Pits allowed to fill with midden are easily distinguished by the absence of the orange clay flecks. At Town Creek, then, burials can be tentatively identified on the basis of flecks of orange clay in the fill of pits before excavation into the feature is carried out.

Another type of feature that can often be identified before excavation is begun into the contents is the shaft and chamber burial with collapsed chamber (Figure 36: 16). The collapse of the chamber produces a fault line when the chamber drops, allowing the soil above it to sag into the depression. This produces what appears to be a later intrusive pit into an older pit, since the same type of soil is sometimes seen in the collapsed chamber area as that appearing in the plowed soil zone. However, this apparent intrusion of pits can be distinguished from an intrusive pit by the indistinct edge caused by the fault as opposed to an edge caused by digging the burial shaft. Once this type of feature is observed it can be correctly interpreted in most cases before excavation is begun on the shaft and chamber. A noncollapsed shaft and chamber burial cannot be so easily identified. appearing as an oval or round pit. The depth of such pits, however, can sometimes be interpreted from the presence of the deeply lying subsoil flecks in the fill. Many sites have such geological clues valuable for use in pre-excavation interpretation and classification of features.

Linear features, such as lines of palisade posts, palisade trenches with or without the postmolds, and fortification ditches are particularly interesting in that they provide linearity and architectural identity and draw a distinction between areas of the site (Figure 36: 17–19). The width of from 2 to 15 feet for fortification ditches clearly distinguishes them from palisade trenches that may be from 8 to 18 inches in width. Fortification ditches when excavated reveal in profile, and often in plan before excavation, the evidence needed to determine on which side of the ditch the accompanying parapet was located by the position of the subsoil like fill (on the parapet side) in contrast with the darker humus fill (on the side opposite the parapet). This is a characteristic of most fortification ditches, though particular cases may reveal exceptions to this pattern.

Another class of postholes are those with tapering ramp trenches lead-

The archeological features must be kept moist during excavation for proper reading of the soil record.

ing toward the bottom of the hole, resulting from installation of the post. These are usually major posts such as the ball ground poles excavated at Town Creek Indian Mound. These often have stones placed against the post when it was slid into the hole and raised upright to hold it in posi- tion (Figure 36: 20). One of these at Town Creek had no stone wedges, but instead was furnished with a trench at right angle alignment to the installation trench, which I interpreted as representing a seat for a log wedge to support the pole once it was raised into position. This proved to be a functionally valid interpretation in that the same technique was used to advantage when a 45-foot pole was replaced in the original five- and-one-half-foot-deep hole (Figure 36: 21).

An interesting variation of the posthole with an installation trench was found by Leland Ferguson at Earth Lodge No. 2 at the Garden Creek Site in Haywood County, N.C. (Dickens 1970: Figure 20). Wall posts for the earth lodge had tapering trenches toward the inside of the lodge, and Ferguson has interpreted these as having been the result of replacing wall posts while the structure was still standing (Figure 36: 22). If wall posts needed to be replaced in an earth lodge a trench would have to be dug to remove the old post or to insert a new post beneath the wall plate. When similar postholes are seen in excavations of other structures,

A British Revolutionary War redoubt at Charles Towne, S.C., before excavation.

The Charles Towne redoubt after excavation.

the likely function can be interpreted before excavation of the postholes themselves is undertaken. Such postholes are also valuable in defining the structure through drawing a distinction with other postholes not a part of the structure.

There are times when a visual examination of the subsoil level of excavation reveals no features, but when the same area is photographed using infrared photography disturbed humus-bearing features can be observed (Figure 36: 23). Other features can be located on occasion by using the texture of the soil as a clue for separating disturbed from subsoil areas. The variation in moisture content, as has been mentioned, is another clue to observation of disturbances in the subsoil matrix when the direct visual observation is not sufficient. Chemical treatment of the surface of an excavated level is being used to react with humus or residual chemicals in wood or bone to reveal features and burials. This method is also being used to identify rodent holes (Van Der Merwe and Stein 1972: 245). Enriched vegetation over wells and midden deposits is also being used as a survey technique in locating subsurface features. Any of these, or other methods of observation of attributes, can be used to draw a distinction between groups of features for componential analysis (Figure 36: 24).

Some features, through their associations, are immediately identified as a single component representing a single moment in time. Such features are postholes from nonintruded architectural features representing a single structure (Figure 36: 25). Seldom is the archeologist presented with such clear, straightforward situations to interpret. A classic means of separating components on a site is through intrusion of one feature on another, with the intrusive feature being later (Figure 36: 26).

At the Dodd Site in South Dakota, Donald Lehmer (1954) was aided in his interpretation of the components by the fact that rectangular houses were intruded on by later round houses, and though his house floors were stratigraphically one above the other, he could still have isolated the components on the basis of structural classification had the features been on the same level (Figure 36: 27).

Spatial separation of features, along with similar diameters, often allow a number of features to be associated as elements of a single structure (Figure 36: 28). Geometric alignment is a frequently used means for separating architectural components related in time and space. A palisade is a primary example of a geometric alignment of postholes that even the most cavalier observer can recognize immediately. Other more widely spaced postholes are not so easily distinguished and associated. During the historic period square footings, fence post holes, and even landscaping bushes are, through their alignment, associated with property lines and other features of similar period (Figure 36: 29–30, 34).

Linear features such as fortification ditches, palisade trenches and geometrically aligned footings and fence postholes provide excellent componental separation through sequential intrusion (Figure 36: 30).

Similar separation can be accomplished on the basis of observation of features at the excavation level, before the removal of the contents of the features themselves is undertaken with any site where features are carefully observed and recorded according to their distinguishing attributes, then plotted on plan on this basis. If, however, features are recorded only as "postholes, pits, and burials," we can hardly hope for more than a limited separation of components for analysis and interpretation.

Analysis of features on the basis of magnetic-astronomical orientation was reported at the Hatchery West Site (Binford & others 1970), resulting in an impressive cultural interpretation (Figure 36: 31). Trees, bushes, plow scars, and rodent holes are all site features with which the archeologist must deal (Figure 36:32–35). These features can be noncultural or they can act as recipients of artifacts that may have fallen into them when they were open. Plow scars in the subsoil reveal clues to the erosion history of the site. The direction of plowing often provides for clarification of features disturbed by plowing. Some bushes and trees, particularly on historic sites, are cultural in that they were part of a landscaping plan, and for these reasons they are observed and recorded and interpreted along with other observable data on the site. Noncultural features such as geological changes in subsoil characteristics and veining often appear as misleading pseudofeatures that must also be interpreted by the archeologist, if for no other reason than to be able to recognize their noncultural aspect.

So far we have discussed the attributes observable in features in plan at the excavated level. Additional feature attributes can be determined from the excavated features that can be used to classify and associate certain features. At Town Creek Indian Mound in North Carolina Joffre Coe has used the aerial mosaic technique in recording each 10-foot square photographically and joining these to make a master mosaic of every feature on the site. From this exacting record, plus the square sheet data from the square ground area in front of the mound, no structures could be interpreted from the galaxy of postholes in the square ground area. However, in 1956 I used the depth of each excavated posthole as an attribute for recording with a colorcode the various postholes and features and was able to isolate a rectangular square ground shed from the mass of postholes in one area of the square ground (Figure 36: 36).

Bennie Keel (1972: 120–122) used another attribute to accomplish a similar result at the Garden Creek Mound No. 2, in Haywood County,

N.C. He noticed that some of the excavated postholes contained a sandy fill near the bottom, and by plotting these in plan with a different key from other postholes he was able to define a house (Figure 36: 37).

Stratified structures represented by postholes at different elevations can be separated on the basis of the top of the postholes, a classic means of temporal separation of components (Figure 36: 38). Excavated postholes can also be classified on the basis of the angle of the postmold or posthole (Figure 36: 39), such as the leaner wall posts forming the outer ring of an earth lodge (Stephensen 1971: 29). From the angle of the leaner postmold in relation to the position of the main wall postholes, the height of the main wall can also be determined. Posthole and postmold shape can be used to classify posthole features, with the straight cut farmer's post contrasting markedly with the more tapered Indian postmold impressions in profile. Also, a hole dug with a posthole digger is recognized in some cases by its higher center (Figure 36:43).

After considering these 40 observable feature attributes, plus any others known to the archeologist, he can then turn his attention to classification of features distinguished on the basis of artifact association with features (Figure 36: 40–42). Unfortunately the tendency has been, and still remains in many instances, to view features primarily as

The formation processes of the archeological record are revealed in the profile of the 1670 fortification ditch at Charles Towne, S.C.

recipients of artifacts from which data can be recovered. As the chart in Figure 36 indicates, there is a multitude of attributes constituting data that must be recorded *before* the cultural items are recovered and analyzed. Postholes, pits, burials, ditches, trenches, and construction ditches for foundation walls are all valuable recipients of cultural items from which analyses and interpretations are made. A series of postholes can be classified into different cultural components on the basis of the artifacts recovered from them. The basic principle of *terminus post quem* is used to determine temporal periods represented by the artifacts recovered from these features (Figure 36: 40). Sometimes the presence or absence of particular items can be used as a classificatory device, such as the use of bone or stone wedges in postholes. A series of postholes with bone wedges might well form an architectural pattern allowing for the isolation of a house, or temporal, or cultural interpretations might be demonstrated (Figure 36: 41).

Cross mending of artifacts is an important means of associating features at one moment in time, such as the recovery of fragments of a white salt-glazed stoneware teapot from a number of features. The gluing of these fragments together joins the features as well, an observation adding valuable information for the interpretation of the features. The same applies to cross mending of fragments from various stratigraphic layers which bonds the stratigraphy into a single temporal unit (Figure 36: 42).

The classification of features on the basis of functional interpretation and designation by nomenclature oriented to cultural function is based on a group of attributes characteristic of particular features. Earth ovens, smudge pits, burials, cooking pits, storage pits, rock hearths, house floors, living floors, and use areas are observable data assigned cultural designations for analysis and interpretation (Figure 36: 44). Binford at the Hatchery West Site conducted an analysis of rock hearths, earth ovens, pits, houses, and burials through cluster and attribute analysis in order to define the cultural components represented by these features (Binford and others 1970). This type of multiattribute feature analysis combining a galaxy of attributes—width, depth, shape, texture, color, associated artifacts, orientation, ethnobotanical objects, and use area debris—results in a most sophisticated componential and cultural analysis.

The purpose of this study has been to point out some of the observations of feature attributes made by the archeologist who allows for making distinctions between features for componential and cultural analysis. To some archeologists this presentation has only stated the obvious, a standard archeological procedure used for decades. However, archeological reports still appear with the classic "pits, postholes, foundations, and profiles" level of observation and recording, suggesting a definite need for more rigorous observation and recording of data. For instance there are many historical archeology reports revealing structural foundations, and large expanses of supposedly observed and recorded excavated areas adjacent, but no sign of a posthole is seen. Scaffolding holes, postholes, and other subsoil disturbances almost always accompany historic structures; consequently, a drawing showing only architectural foundations is a highly selective type of data recording.

Other indications that a more rigorous observation and recording of feature data is needed are seen in the following:

1. postholes recorded as stylized symbols instead of as they actually are observed in the field;
2. straight interpolated lines for fortification ditch edges instead of actually plotted edges as observed in the ground, making for a neat but hardly accurate drawing;
3. failure to record trees and bush features;
4. failure to record the postmold as well as the posthole, the hole being a general representation of the position of the structure, but the postmold representing an exact position;
5. inconsistent recording of posthole and feature data, postholes being recorded only as incidental to some other problem of interest, or as they fortuitously are seen on wet days, with little effort being made to systematically record every posthole on the site;
6. palisades shown as stylized, schematic representations with no details and specific post positions shown;
7. entire site reports presented primarily through profiles, with little recording of plan data;
8. disregard of stratified data in features;
9. emphasis primarily on the artifacts recovered from features, missing in the process data of possible value in seasonal activity or temporal-functional relationships *within* the feature;
10. entire site reports presented on the basis of a series of 5-foot squares, with emphasis on stratigraphic data at the expense of features in plan, resulting in a lacunae in our knowledge of structures and settlement patterns.

Problems such as these can be overcome through more careful observation and recording of features and other data on a broader base, emphasizing a multiattribute approach in drawing distinctions between archeological features.

Besides emphasizing the need for more rigorous field observation the purpose of this study has been to emphasize the function of observation in the archeological process. The primary, basic, and central function of observation is illustrated in the paradigm in the chart in Figure 36.

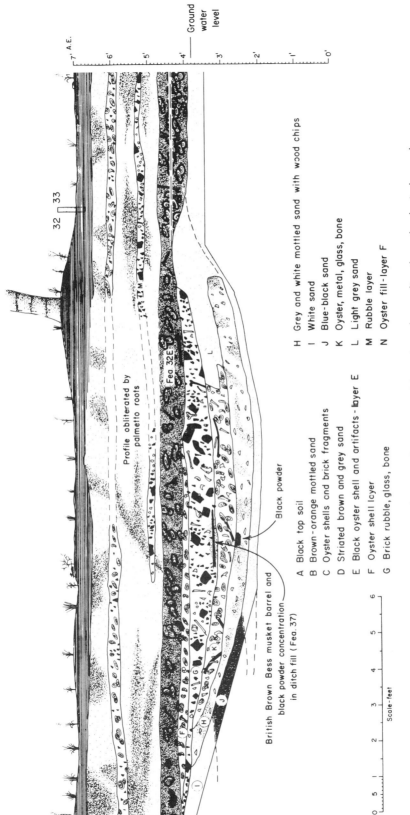

Ground water level

7' A.E.

British Brown Bess musket barrel and black powder concentration in ditch fill (Fea. 37)

Profile obliterated by palmetto roots

Black powder

Fea. 32E

Scale-feet

A Black top soil
B Brown-orange mottled sand
C Oyster shells and brick fragments
D Striated brown and grey sand
E Black oyster shell and artifacts-layer E
F Oyster shell layer
G Brick rubble, glass, bone
H Grey and white mottled sand with wood chips
I White sand
J Blue-black sand
K Oyster, metal, glass, bone
L Light grey sand
M Rubble layer
N Oyster fill-layer F

North Profile-Trench 32-33: Profile data recording an essential step in understanding the archeological record.

Theory with hypotheses makes fertile the observation of the data. When the archeological process of observation, analysis, and pattern recognition is completed, an explanation is invented to account for the culture process responsible for the observed patterned phenomena. The explanation is a genetic offspring of the parent theory and hypothesis, but was gestated in the fertile environment of field observation. This descendent tests the parent concepts and is the source for new hypotheses and theory, leading to more refined field observation. This paradigm of the archeological process clearly reveals the central function of observation, and is followed by several corollaries.

Theory and hypothesis without observation do not produce explanation. Thorough observation allows for more sophisticated analysis and problem solving, resulting in new and refined theory. Inadequate, inconsistent, incomplete, and careless observation will not develop into a reliable interpretation or explanation regardless of the sophistication of the theory and hypothesis. Observation, regardless of how sophisticated, is sterile without the parent theory and will not produce explanation. Theory is born of observation, thus observation is basic in the archeological process.

An important by-product of this archeological process is the preservation and interpretive explanation of the archeological record through exhibits of ruins, fortification ditches, parapets, burial houses, reconstructed earth lodges, structures and palisades. It is emphasized, however, that this by-product is not the goal of the archeological process, merely a shell produced from the gestation of cultural-historical interpretation and processual explanation.

The archeologist should guard against allowing the problems dictated by sponsors interested in structural detail for purposes of reconstruction for public display to become his archeological goal at the expense of integrative analysis and cultural interpretation based on broad and in-depth observation. However, if the archeologist accepts the responsibility of executing the archeological process to achieve his own scientific goals, he also has a responsibility to produce a product of some real use to the sponsor. An archeological report strictly limited to explanation of the archeologist's goals might still leave the sponsor wondering what to do next toward development of the historic site. Therefore, the archeologist should provide some suggestions for a master plan for the preservation of the archeological document for the development of the site within the framework of the archeological data.

Without such help in the form of plan and profile drawings and suggestions in a report to the sponsor, the archeologist has no reason to complain when the explanatory exhibits in the form of exposed ruins, rebuilt parapets, and palisades do not conform to the archeological evidence. He does have a responsibility to insure that the explanatory exhibits do not violate the archeological record.

Historical archeology is particularly encumbered with problem-oriented studies of narrow scope, wherein the problem consists of locating the foundation of a structure or a fort site. Indian site archeologists also have their albatrosses in studies centered on a narrow focus: the skeletal material from a site, sometimes recovered at the neglect of other types of data; the number of structures to be found in a stratigraphic cut of a temple mound, with no data recovered as to what the floor plan looked like; or the temporal sequence represented by the ceramics from a site through 5-foot test squares, with no information as to structural form or village plan that could emerge if the design only called for the 100-yard square instead of the traditional 5-foot or 1-meter grid. Our problem in such cases has been not so much a lack of problem, but a focusing of observation on circumscribed problems rather than detailed observation of attributes relevant to questions of broader scope.

Another traditional approach to the archeological process has emphasized the responsibility of the archeologist to observe intensively and carefully as many attributes of the data as possible so that a broad base for interpretation can emerge from the observation and recording process. This basic attitude has come under criticism for its frequent lack of problem orientation, and its sometimes apparent concern with observation and recording of data as an end in itself, resulting in challenges arising as to the value of site reports (Zubrow 1971: 482). It is obvious that no archeologist can possibly observe and record all the data that might be needed to answer all problems, but it does not follow that problem oriented studies in the new idiom are the only kinds of problems justified. (As pointed out above, the difficulty has often been too refined and narrow a problem rather than a question of no problem at all.) There is a basic corpus of data that must be observed and recorded in addition to any unique data requirements for specific problem solving, and it appears patently obvious that what we need is not only more narrowly focused observation for specific problem solving, but research using a broader base of multiattribute data recording from which hypotheses relating to culture process can be formulated. It is also apparent that with a greater concentration on observation and data recording that the scientific archeologist has an obligation to abstract pattern and offer explanation in terms of hypothesis and theory in an evolutionary framework.

Our problem solving is limited by our observation, and our questions can be answered only when our field observation and data recovery methods are as sophisticated as our theory. The trend now is to construct specific problems and collect specific data to provide the solutions, a

A Teacup, Wine Bottles, Razors, and Dividers lying on the floor of a burned home in Brunswick Town, N.C. are examples of in situ—de facto refuse.

step we certainly must undertake, but in the process we should not neglect the broader focal angle implied in an anthropologically or an historically based discipline.

Scientific archeology demands rigorous, controlled, consistent observation, with a base relevant to specific research designs. Theoretically weighty research designs and microscopic observation of data at the expense of the broad archeological record are not compatible within the paradigm of scientific archeology. Competent data recovery through relevant observation is prelude to any theory and forms the body from which analysis proceeds and new hypotheses and theory are created.

CLASSIFICATION OF THE ARCHEOLOGICAL RECORD

The need for careful observation exists throughout the archeological process, not only in the recording of features and architectural relationships emphasized in the previous section, but also in the associations, relationships, and location of artifacts. Michael Schiffer (1972: 163) has indicated the need for more explicit demonstration of the regularities of refuse dumping behavior, and has distinguished between primary and secondary refuse, terms long used but previously not explicitly spelled out, and what he calls de facto refuse. Primary refuse he defines as that discarded at its place of use, secondary refuse as having been discarded at a place not the same as the location of use (Schiffer 1972: 161). De facto refuse is composed of those elements that reach the archeological context "without the performance of discard activities" (Schiffer 1972: 161). Refuse remaining on the floor of a structure after its abandonment would be considered as de facto refuse, as would remains of objects in situ in a structure when it burned, neither having been intentionally discarded. However, the behavior involved in abandoning a structure after having removed the most usable and desired objects while leaving some unwanted de facto objects to be found by the archeologist is quite a different behavior from having all one's possessions burn in place when a home is destroyed by fire. For this reason I am suggesting the addition of the term in situ-de facto refuse to refer to the objects demonstrated to have archeological context relationships directly reflecting locational relationships in the systemic context. Floor level data from burned historic structures revealing placement of furniture, storage items, windows, and architectural hardware are examples of in situ-de facto refuse. I emphasize, however, such data are extremely rare, but the distinction between this and other de facto refuse resulting from abandonment should definitely be made.

A distinction can also be made between de facto refuse resulting from abandonment and that resulting from accidental loss. For instance, in the case of sand floors where any object is easily lost underfoot, the presence of coins, whole pewter spoons, whole knives and forks, whole medicine bottles, and complete ceramic vessels beneath the surface of the sand layer cannot be seen simply as primary refuse in the same sense as broken ceramics, glass, and bone fragments which would more clearly be defined as primary refuse. Whole objects such as this, in such a context reflecting accidental loss behavior, might well be referred to as primary-de facto refuse items in that they are in their location of use, but reflect accidental abandonment as opposed to intentional abandonment. Pins and beads falling onto a sand floor, or through the cracks of a wooden floor would come under this primary-de facto context, whereas a midden deposit of bone and broken objects scattered over the floor, or swept into a corner of a room would be considered as primary refuse.

In view of these archeological formation processes, it is clear that exacting techniques are required to isolate and record these distinctions in the archeological context in order to arrive at interpretations reflecting distinctions in human behavior.

One major addition to Schiffer's classification of the archeological record is suggested, and that is displaced refuse. Often primary or secondary refuse is displaced by natural erosion forces (Schiffer and Rathje's n-transforms. 1973: 169), or by cultural activity (c-transforms), creating a deposit that is displaced from its original location. This situation often

Whole objects such as Buckles, Spoons, Case Knives, and Coins lost in a sand layer on the floor represent primary–de facto refuse.

results from site use, landscaping, erosion control, and filling of depressions such as old wells, privy holes, cellar holes, and construction trenches.

The displacement of refuse from a primary or secondary context sometimes results in inverse stratigraphy, as later primary or secondary deposits are buried beneath earlier displaced refuse used as fill. This phenomenon is frequently seen to occur in the depressions of cellar holes, where the displaced fill layers above the floor level data earlier than the primary or de facto materials on the floor. This results from the accumulation of secondary cultural materials around the structure during the entire occupation period eroding into, or being pushed into the depression, over the later objects on the cellar floor which represent a moment in time before destruction of the structure.

This displaced refuse resulting in inverse stratigraphy was observed by Lewis Binford in 1959, and I have also frequently seen this phenomenon (Binford 1959: personal communication). This formation process should be distinguished from that which occurs when a cellar hole is used as a place for depositing secondary refuse postdating the destruction of the structure, which results in normal temporal stratigraphy. It is apparent, from this and other examples, that a significant formation process of the archeological record is that of displaced refuse.

A pistol lying in the fallen plaster layer above the floor level reveals that at the time of the
fire which destroyed the house it was located in a room above that in which it was found.

This classification of the archeological record on the basis of the
association, location, and relationship of artifacts is by no means a definitive one. As archeologists become increasingly aware of the importance
of such relationships for interpreting past human behavior and culture
process, more such methodological tools will be developed.

METHODOLOGICAL PHASES IN THE ARCHEOLOGICAL PROCESS

The archeologist should by all means be aware of the archeological
strategies available to him for recovering data relevant to his research
design. In gathering data for detailed pattern recognition and distribution such as used at Brunswick Town and other sites from which the
Brunswick Pattern and Carolina Pattern were delineated, the use of a
grid system for data control is necessary. Such an approach may well not
serve when the research design calls for another more efficient strategy
relative to the questions being asked. This section will deal with eight
methodological phases of the archeological process, particularly the four
excavation phases.

The archeological process can be viewed as eight phases, four of which relate to the collection of data in the field, the excavation phases, and four phases concerned with explication:

Excavation phases
1. Site survey
2. Exploratory excavation
3. Detailed excavation
4. Excavation of the 100-yard square

Explication phases
5. Analysis
6. Synthesis and interpretation
7. Explanation of the culture process reflected by the data
8. Explanatory exhibits on the site

In this study we are concerned primarily with the excavation phases relevant to research designs focused on the location and examination of archeological sites.

Phase 1

The first phase in the examination of an archeological site is the location of sites through surface survey, study of maps and aerial photographs to locate potential sites, and historical documentation.

Peripheral secondary refuse from a potter's shop in an abandoned cellar hole at Bethabara, N.C.

Phase 2

The sites located in Phase 1 are examined by sinking exploratory cores, squares, and trenches to obtain a sample of data regarding stratigraphy and superposition and to locate areas of major concentration of cultural data, postholes, pits, and artifacts.

Phase 3

Once the concentration of cultural material is determined, the spot is chosen for opening a larger exploratory area for more concentrated excavation of a more detailed nature. This area is usually some 50-feet square, or a long trench 20 or 30 feet wide and perhaps 100 feet long. The approach to excavating this area in more detail is determined to a great extent by the data revealed in the second phase of the project.

The third phase is used particularly where an individual house, camp site, chipping station, mound or ruin requires a more detailed stratigraphic or tightly controlled horizontal recovery of data, such as scatter pattern data, or thin lenses representing occupation levels. The decision as to what type of data recovery method is used is made by the archeologist and is based on his evaluation of the data revealed in Phase 1 and

One of two men killed in a battle between Whigs and Tories in 1775 at Ninety Six, S.C.

Phase 2 of the project. This decision is a major role of the archeologist, the application of judgment in the choice of methods he uses to extract the most data from the site in the quickest amount of time at a resulting maximum data–minimum cost ratio. Thus Phase 1 and Phase 2 predicate the research design of Phase 3 and the phases to follow in keeping with the overall research design.

Phase 3 is applied where Phase 2 tests revealed stratigraphic zones of cultural material and/or humus zones representing old ground surfaces or stabilized zones and/or occupation zones. If these occupation zones are deep beneath an overlying mantle of soil, it is necessary to remove the overlying soil, sometimes by machine to make the best use of time and money in obtaining the data these deep deposits have to reveal. In so doing the data from the top occupation zone may be destroyed, but again the archeologist must evaluate the situation and make a judgment as to which data are most valuable. In any case the top cultural zones should never be destroyed by machine until adequate sampling of these zones is carried out under Phase 2 procedures.

Once the overlying mantle of soil is removed to within a few inches of the deeply lying cultural deposits, the machine should be removed from the area and the zone approached by use of careful hand labor. The depth of the machine cut should always be controlled by constant super-vision by the archeologist, using the deep trenches cut during Phase 2 as a guide.

If the site has several cultural components that are located in the upper soil zone of the site, and if this soil zone is a foot to several feet in depth, with no visible stratigraphy, then the dissection of the deposit by arbitrary levels may be called for until enough data is collected to determine the superposition that may be present. This is a primary pur-pose of Phase 2, and if answered by the data recovered in Phase 2, the approach to the site in Phase 3 may be entirely different. Phase 3 or Phase 4 should not begin until the data revealed in Phase 2 are analyzed and evaluated.

If the topsoil zone contains virtually a single component, then it hardly makes for the best utilization of resources, human, temporal, financial, and logistic, to utilize a technique designed to reveal stratigraphic separation through superposition analysis. Such an unnecessarily precise and time consuming process sacrifices data such as features in quantity, house patterns, village patterns and relationships obtaining between them that can be obtained by using the procedures outlined in Phase 4. Phase 3 can well be carried out on a site at the same time that Phase 4 techniques are being applied nearby. Phase 3 is the traditional, detailed excavation approach to layers, levels, and features, and is always used once the features are located through Phase 4 methods of stripping of 100-yard squares to reveal the features.

Phase 4

If the site is a single component site as revealed by the cultural material recovered in Phase 1 and Phase 2, and this component is located primarily in the plowed soil zone with features extending into the subsoil zone below, then an ideal situation exists for application of Phase 4. A front loader or belly-loading traxcavator can be brought to the site to strip the overlying mantle of soil from the level at which the archeologist wishes to obtain a broad look at all features.

The machine should be carefully supervised by the archeologist, with an effort being made to leave a slight layer of buffer soil above the level of the subsoil surface. The surface of the subsoil or level to be examined is then schnitted (shovel cut) using a gang-schnitt technique in which the entire crew is lined up in formation and carefully supervised throughout the slicing process to insure a uniform cut of the soil level being examined. The features so revealed by this slicing method are then plotted with transit or alidade, followed by Phase 3 detailed excavation of the features themselves. To insure the most consistent reading of the soil document the archeologist should keep the schnitted surface damp by means of mist spray.

Features revealed by this method can be excavated and their contents analyzed, producing more data than would be possible in the same amount of time if the topsoil zone were removed and sifted by hand. Artifacts from features have a much greater time capsule and cultural context character and are conducive to a far higher temporal data-producing analysis than potsherds collected from the plowed soil zone, regardless of how meticulously that plowed soil zone is excavated—unless, of course, the plowed soil zone is characterized by a single component. If questions of distribution are being asked of the plowed soil zone, then no machine should be used. Generally, however, the plowed soil zone has been subjected to the mixing machine process of the plow for 100 or 200 years on many Southeastern sites. This will not eliminate the usefulness of the data there but certainly contributes to a characteristically small artifact size and often spans a long temporal range.

Needless to say, the approach of Phase 4 would not be used on sites where no plowing has been carried out, and the objects lying in the topsoil zone are virtually in situ as left by the occupants of the site. Most Southeastern bottomlands have been subjected to extensive plowing, and are therefore, characterized by the "plowed soil zone," a situation not so often seen in the Southwest.

If a research design is outlined wherein horizontal distribution of plowed soil zone materials is desired to produce data for comparison with underlying features, then of course no machine stripping such as outlined in Phase 4 should be undertaken. An important point emphasized here is the fact that the nature of the site should be considered along with the questions being asked in the basic research design to determine the method the archeologist will use in examining his site.

If settlement patterns are of vital concern to the archeologist and constitute a major element in his research design, then excavation of a limited number of 5-foot squares and trenches such as outlined in Phase 2 and Phase 3 will not reveal these data. If more data as to an Indian village are desired than the "possible" edge of a house and a few associated pits in a 20-by-100-foot trench excavated in the manner characterized by Phase 3, then archeologists must begin to carry their excavations beyond the first three phases of the archeological process outlined here.

We are now asking broad questions of our archeological data, and these cannot be answered if we do not improve and expand our methods, adapting our approach to our research designs predicated by the questions we are asking. We are no longer justified in excavating two seasons on an exploratory effort using Phase 3 procedures designed strictly around chronology when the data revealed in Phase 2 have already shown that the major soil zone is characterized by the presence

Gang-Schnitting in a Phase 4 operation to reveal the 1670 fortification ditch at Charles Towne, S.C.

of a single component! Such an excavation may well emerge at the end of a second or third season and not yet have the first indication of an architectural feature, or relationships that obtain beyond the microscopic area examined in the Phase 3 project. Under such a research design, even the perimeter of the occupation area is often a mystery after excavation is complete. If we insist on stopping at Phase 3, we should not ask questions that can best be answered through the application of extensive controlled sampling strategies, or through Phase 4 methods.

When Phase 2 has sampled adequately the various areas of the site and determined the relationships that obtain between the various levels and preceramic components, as well as the relative concentration of cultural material in various areas of the site, the archeologist must ask himself whether a repetition of this data collection through a Phase 3 project from the surface down is more valuable, or whether gathering data from a broad area of the site at a particular level would be the most productive of data recovery, through Phase 4 methods.

After adequate controlled sampling of Phase 2 has been carried out the archeologist may well make the decision to remove the upper, later components in order to reveal what is, in his judgment, a more important body of data in the deeper strata of the site. It is emphasized that this move *must* be predicated on the completion of Phase 2 with its recovery of control data on the upper occupation zones before machine removal of these zones to get at the lower zones is undertaken. If, however, the upper zones contain relevant information in themselves, Phase 3 methods should be used throughout the depth of the stratigraphic cut, regardless of the time required to acquire such data. Destroying valuable data for deeper levels is not justified, and it is only when more information of value will be gained than lost that upper levels can be judged as "expendable." If the most data can be obtained by spending three seasons on a single house site, then this Phase 3 type procedure should be executed, by all means. The archeologist must participate in this decision-making process if he is to recover the most data. The point here is that too often we find a slavish allegiance to methods long outmoded for answering the questions we are asking. It is hoped that we can begin to design our methods to fit our questions.

The following is a statement made some years ago that contrasts the archeological project that utilizes only Phase 2 and Phase 3, with one that launches into the methods of Phase 4, which:

> method provides for maximum speed, efficiency, and flexibility . . . to recover data from sites such as towns, cities, and forts whose features sprawl over many acres through woods and fields, valleys and hills. It is time to look beyond the womb-like comfort of the involvement with

dissecting burials, cellar holes and five foot squares if we are to meet the interpretive challenge presented by villages, ceremonial centers, towns, cities and fortified areas.

Too long have we practiced the ritual of the cult of the square, impotently arriving at feeble interpretations of complex cultures in extensive settlements from the meager evidence presented by a few postholes and a stratigraphic sample from a five foot square. We have often failed to adapt out tools to the scope of the project. We have used a spoon on villages and towns as well as burials. We have looked at cultures through keyholes when we should have been opening doors. This does not suggest the abandonment of the five-foot square, but it does emphasize that there are times when it is a totally inadequate tool, like excavating a village with a spoon. Through exploratory trenching to determine the nature and scope of the features, then totally removing large blankets of topsoil from extensive areas of the site, stripping football field size "squares" instead of minuscule five foot areas, we can begin to open a few doors. Once the archeologist is rewarded by the view of the culture revealed through such doors he is thereafter highly unsatisfied by peeping through keyholes (South 1971: 48).

Summary

The archeologist should go into the field with a theoretically based research design related to questions he is asking about past cultures, the remains of which he expects to examine. However, he should be prepared to fit his research design to the dictates of the site as the data the site produces are revealed through archeology. The phases outlined here are the means of achieving this accommodation of a theory oriented research design to the archeological realities of the site.

Excavation Phases

Phase 1 The sites cannot be studied until they are located. This is achieved through systematic sampling strategies, the goal of Phase 1, site survey.

Phase 2 The nature of the sites as to their underlying potential, stratigraphically and horizontally, cannot be known until exploratory sub-surface sampling is undertaken in Phase 2, Exploratory excavation.

Phase 3 Detailed dissection of important areas of the site for stratigraphic control and horizontal patterning cannot be accomplished without the microscopic approach of Phase 3, Detailed Excavation.

Phase 4 Questions as to settlement patterns, relationships between structures, types of structures, use areas of sites such as ball grounds, burial areas, dwelling areas, ceremonial areas, relationships between classes of features, etc., can best be answered by the methods outlined as Phase 4. If we know that a village site was spread out along a bottomland for a mile, would not the 100-yard square approach of Phase 4 be a better sampling method for studying the village than the microscopic view afforded by Phases 2 and 3, the traditional approach to the problem?

Phases 5 through 8 are not discussed in this chapter, constituting as they do the laboratory analysis, synthesis, writing of the report, and the explanatory exhibits developed on some sites. These four phases are as follows:

Explication Phases

5. Analysis of the archeological data
6. Synthesis and interpretation of the data
7. Explanation of the cultural process reflected by the data
8. Development of explanatory exhibits on the archeological site

The extent to which the archeological analysis can reveal the patterns of culture represented by the archeological data, the extent to which the analysis results in cultural synthesis and interpretation, and the extent to which explanation of cultural process represented by the data can be undertaken all depend on the approach of the archeologist in the field.

An excavated and stabilized fortification ditch and parapet on the left, with an unexcavated section of the ditch on the right.

If he stops his examination at the end of Phase 1, the amount of data is limited to surface finds and his conclusions must be speculative. If he stops his excavation at the end of Phase 2, his results can provide statements as to chronology and aerial distribution but he can say little beyond that. If he stops his examination at the level of Phase 3 he may be able to make a tentative statement about one house or structure, or part of a house or structure, usually relating to chronology and stratigraphy. Such excavations do not usually provide broad, horizontally distributed data allowing interpretation of settlement patterns, groups of structures, or village plans. It is for answering questions directed along these broader lines that Phase 4 is most effective and productive. There are sites that cannot benefit from the use of Phase 4 methods, such as relatively undisturbed sites, and masonry sites where machines would do severe damage to the archeological ruins. Again, the judgment of the archeologist must be used to keep machines away from such sites.

The analysis, synthesis, interpretation, and explanation of data of phases 5 through 7 have been dealt with in previous Chapters. Phase 8 brings a whole new concept into the discussion, with the use of explanatory exhibits on the site, such as palisades placed in the original ditches discovered by the archeologist, stabilization of ruins so that they can be exhibited and yet can withstand the rigors of being exposed to the elements, rebuilding parapets of earth beside fortification ditches. Sites such as Ocmulgee National Monument in Georgia, Town Creek Indian Mound and the Brunswick Town State Historic site in North Carolina, Jamestown in Virginia, and Charles Towne in South Carolina are examples of on-site explanatory exhibits of archeologically related features, but this phase of the archeological process is not discussed in detail in this study.

This study has concentrated on the first four phases in the archeological process, with emphasis on Phase 4, excavation of the 100-yard square. It has urged archeologists to add to the traditional three phases this most important fourth phase, with the hope that it can be employed more frequently in the recovery of archeological data, bringing our methods in closer harmony with the questions we are asking in our research designs.

EVALUATION OF OBSERVATIONAL SITUATIONS RELATIVE TO THE ARCHEOLOGICAL DATA BANK

In this section the concern is with the evaluation of observational or analytical situations in time. Any analysis of archeological materials must be oriented to a clear definition of provenience. Analysis of data from the plowed soil zone representing perhaps hundreds of years of occupation has a different analytical weight than data from a pit representing one moment of time if temporal questions are of primary concern. If questions of distribution of artifacts are being asked, then analytical weight would vary accordingly.

If we have an archeological site known from documents to have been occupied from 1720 to 1730, then our chronological period is established by documentation until archeology is able to confirm, deny, or elaborate on this document. When we excavate the site and find that none of the artifact classes about which we have chronological information indicate that the site was occupied at a time other than the decade indicated by the documents, then we have confirmed the historical documentation. The entire group of associated artifacts then have a feedback value into our data bank of knowledge. Thus we use our knowledge of certain classes of artifacts, such as ceramics, pipestems, and wine bottles as a check against the known temporal period and, if this is found to agree, then we have reason to assign the same temporal bracket to the entire group of artifact classes recovered from this provenience.

The same situation prevails when we have the same documentary control data, but upon excavation we find from the artifact analysis that there is obviously an occupation at a later time than indicated by the documents. Since we have tight stratigraphic and/or feature provenience control we are able to separate an earlier component from a later component, and we find that the earlier archeologically separated component has no class of artifacts dating later than our documented period of occupation. We then have reason to relate this group of archeologically associated artifact classes with our documented time bracket. The other, later artifact classes are then assigned a later chronological position both by virtue of their higher stratigraphic or provenience separation and by what knowledge we have in our data bank regarding the temporal position of these artifacts.

If, however, our excavation reveals a mixed deposit with no significant separation of materials by provenience, and artifacts are present from a period later than the documented time period, then we are forced by the archeological data to deal, in our analysis, with the entire temporal range represented by the artifact classes.

This basic methodological premise can be illustrated in a "Data Flow Diagram for Evaluation of Analysis Situations Relative to the Data Bank of Archeological Knowledge" (Figure 37). The short time span represented by data from a narrow documented occupation period and/or tightly provenienced archeological data results in a flow of associated data as a contextual unit toward the data bank of archeological knowledge. This data bank can be seen as a piggy bank into which information coins are placed, such as: (1) the chronological association of artifact classes as a time capsule; (2) the associative-functional, artifact feature relationships;

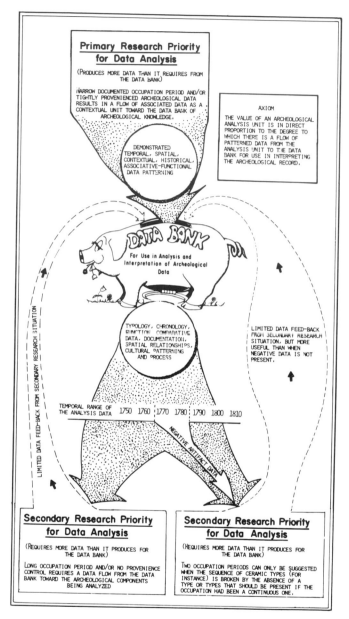

Figure 37. Data flow diagram for evaluation of analysis situations relative to the data bank of archeological knowledge (Pig chart).

(3) the spatial associations; (4) meaningfully provenienced horizontal and stratigraphic data in association with site features and architecture; (5) historical documentation; and (6) the associated data reflecting cultural

patterning and process as a contextual unit. Such analysis situations produce more data than required from the data bank, and therefore have primary research priority.

When the analysis unit represents a long occupation period and/or no provenience control, the result is that there is a data flow of information coins from the data bank toward the archeological components being analyzed. Since there is a long occupation period involved and no provenience control, virtually all information such as function, comparative data, chronology, spatial relationships, associations, documentation, typology, and cultural patterning and process must come from our data bank of knowledge toward the analysis and interpretation of the analysis unit. Because of this requirement for more data than it produces for the data bank, this analysis situation has a secondary research priority.

It is possible that two occupations can be suggested for an analysis situation representing a long period of time. This is when the sequence of artifact types is broken by the absence of a type or types that should be present had the occupation been continuous. Such a situation still requires more data than it produces for the data bank, and is still a secondary research priority situation, but it does have a limited feedback value into the data bank somewhat higher than when negative data is not present.

An example of the time when we can validly split a long time span ceramic collection is when white salt-glazed stoneware and other mid-eighteenth-century ceramic types are present, as well as pearlware of the 1780s and 1790s, but creamware characteristic of the 1770s is virtually absent. In the face of such negative data, and in the absence of other data to the contrary, we might suggest two occupation periods represented by the ceramic collection, separated by a period of nonoccupation in the 1770s. This does *not* allow us, however, to suggest that the bone or any other classes of artifacts can be similarly divided into groups reflective of two occupation periods.

It appears axiomatic that the value of an archeological observational unit is in direct proportion to the degree to which there is a data flow from the observational unit is in direct proportion to the degree to which there is a data flow from the observational unit to the data bank for use in interpreting the archeological record. A corollary to this is that in a primary or a secondary research situation the value of the data to future research is in direct relation to the competence of the archeologist in obtaining significant provenience analysis, interpretation, and explanation of the data in relation to the hypotheses dictated by the research design.

In view of the above remarks it becomes apparent for the purpose of defining the occupation period represented by the artifact classes in an analysis unit that we cannot validly select the artifact types belonging to the documented time period as indicated by the records and ignore or separate those that date later. In such an instance, the archeological record has demonstrated the incompleteness of the written record, and we should then deal with that occupation record. If we concern ourselves with listing artifacts used at particular time periods and divide our collection on this basis, we need not have done archeology to carry out what is primarily an exercise in the temporal arrangement of artifact types!

The archeologist faced with the analysis of a poorly provenienced and/or long time span group of artifact classes is sometimes seen to resort to what he may term "functional analysis" to avoid the mere exercise of temporal arrangement of artifact types. Limited information can be extracted from such analyses, such as the conclusion that plates were used to eat from, mugs to drink from, jars to store liquids, nails to hold wooden members together, shovels to dig with, lamps to provide light, drawer-pulls to open drawers in furniture, and other equally interesting conclusions. There is certainly nothing wrong with functional analysis, but again it is evident that the most data will emerge from our analysis situations when there is a narrow documented occupation period and/or tightly provenienced archeological data. In such primary research priority analysis situations there is more data flow toward the data bank than from it, for functional or other kinds of analysis.

If the archeologist finds himself involved with a secondary priority analysis situation where his level of operation is on that of the collector of relics or an antique dealer, then he may well ask whether his time might not be better spent in other pursuits. If in arriving at functional, socioeconomic, status, and other cultural interpretations from archeo- logical data the archeologist finds himself leaning on the documents as a crutch, and using archeological data primarily as padding to the his- torical record, then he is bastardizing the archeological profession. He should use documentary data, but the foundation of his interpretation should be archeological when his historical-temporal, historical social, historical-status, historical-function explications emerge from the archeological process. There should be a direct and positive nexus between the archeology and the documents in interpreting the cultural process represented by the patterning seen in the archeological record. If there is not this connection, then we are frosting history or writing fic- tion as a veneer over the data with which we began.

The archeological process requires a systematic, scientific carefully cited presentation where any conclusion follows from documented, demonstrated patterning of data. An alternative approach is characterized by terms such as "we might expect," or "it can be assumed," or "it stands to reason" that many wine bottles equal a tavern; porcelain equals a rich man; coarse earthenware equals a poor man; and from this "data" we leap to describing the life style of the colonial period in our "cultural explanation." Such an approach does not produce coins of information for depositing in our data bank of knowledge for use in the analysis and interpretation of archeological data.

Our comments here have been designed to emphasize the importance of data flow from archeological sites to the data bank of our knowledge. If our research designs are such that the questions we are asking can be answered primarily through a data flow from our existing knowledge to the sites we are excavating, then perhaps we should re-examine our questions and our research designs. If we find that having excavated site after site, and our reports are merely presenting a descriptive statement of architecture, the profiles, the features, and the artifacts as interpreted through existing data bank knowledge, then perhaps we should begin to turn our attention to those research situations having primary research priority. Such sites are kiln sites, stratified sites, short time span sites, and special use sites such as those used by silversmiths, blacksmiths, goldsmiths, and other craftsmen. Such locations are all potentially productive of data reflecting past lifeways. But equally important, and more so for processual studies, are those difficult to define, everyday, average, domestic, dwelling sites about which we know far too little. It is these sites around which we have concentrated our efforts in this book.

Archeological research designed to seek purely scientific goals is easier said than done, since archeological financing is most often not based on such research considerations. However, by constructing research designs and methods with an emphasis on data flow from research situations to data bank, we can increase the amount of usable and relevant archeological data emerging from excavations, regardless of the financial source of the research base. Scientific goals and mission oriented goals can be achieved in the process of cultural resource management, a point emphasized in the chapter to follow.

REFERENCES

Binford, Lewis R., Sally R. Binford, Robert Whallon, and Margaret Ann Hardin
    1970   Archeology at Hatchery West. *American Antiquity* **35** (No. 4); Memoir No. 24.
Dickens, Roy Selman Jr.
    1970   The Pisgah Culture and Its Place in the Prehistory of the Southern Appalachians; Ph.D. dissertation; Department of Anthropology, the University of North Carolina, Chapel Hill.

Keel, Bennie Carlton
 1972 Woodland Phases of the Appalachian Summit Area, Ph.D. dissertation, Department of Anthropology, Washington State University, Pullman.
Lehmer, Donald J.
 1954 Archeological Investigations in the Oahe Dame Area, South Dakota, 1950–51. *River Basin Surveys Papers.* No. 7, Bulletin 158. Washington, D.C.: Bureau of American Ethnology.
Schiffer, Michael B.
 1972 Archaeological Context and Systemic Context. *American Antiquity* **37**:156–165.
Schiffer, Michael B., and William L. Rathje
 1973 Efficient exploitation of the archaeological record: Penetrating problems. In *Research and theory in current archeology,* edited by Redman, Charles L. New York: John Wiley.
South, Stanley
 1955 Evolutionary Theory in Archeology. *Southern Indian Studies* **7**. University of North Carolina, Chapel Hill.
 1971 Exploratory Archeology at Holmes' Fort, The Blockhouse, and Jail Redoubt at Ninety Six. *The Conference on Historic Site Archeology Papers 1970* **5**, Part 1, August. Institute of Archeology and Anthropology, University of South Carolina, Columbia.
 1972 Archeological Excavation at the Site of Williamson's Fort of 1775, Holmes' Fort of 1780, and the Town of Cambridge of 1783–1850s. *Research Manuscript Series,* No. 24. Institute of Archeology and Anthropology, University of South Carolina.
 1974 The Function of Observation in the Archeological Process. *The Conference on Historic Site Archaeology Papers 1972* **7**:123–137. The Institute of Archeology and Anthropology, University of South Carolina, Columbia.
Stephenson, Robert L.
 1971 The Potts Village Site (39C019), Oahe Reservoir, North Central South Dakota. *The Missouri Archaeologist* **33**.
Stephenson, Robert L. and Alice L. L. Ferguson
 1963 The Accokeek Creek Site, A Middle Atlantic Seaboard Culture Sequence. *Anthropological Papers,* No. 20. University of Michigan, Museum of Anthropology, Ann Arbor.
Van der Merwe, Nikolaas J.
 1972 Soil Chemistry of Postmolds and Rodent Burrows: Identification Without Excavation. *American Antiquity* **37**, p. 245–254.
Zubrow, Ezra
 1971 Review of Big Juniper House by Jervis D. Swannack, Jr. *American Antiquity* **36**, p. 482.

Surviving structures such as this half-timbered wall aid the archeologist in interpreting archeological remains.

The Archeologist's Responsibility in Cultural Resource Management Studies

CONCLUSION

We have emphasized methods and accompanying theory used by the archeologist to explore the archeological record for patterning reflecting past human behavior variations and the processes responsible for it. In carrying out this process, the archeologist frequently finds what may at first appear to be a conflict of goals between his responsibility as an archeologist and that due his sponsor, who is financing his cultural resource management study. The view we emphasize here is that the archeologist can answer his responsibility in both areas. He must resign himself to 12-hour days to do so, but it can be done. The archeologist determined to abstract from his projects more than the minimum required by his mission oriented agency or his contract will find the time and the resources to conduct archeological science. Science is an attitude, a way of thinking, a process, a belief, a religion. Science is sciencing (White 1938).

The report emerging from any archeological excavation will reflect the theoretical base of the archeologist's research design. Archeology is increasingly being called on by mission oriented agencies to provide basic data for the interpretation and development of sites considered important enough by the agency planners to warrant scientific investigation. The sponsors of such projects have a right to expect that results of archeological work will have at least some relation to the questions for which they need some answers. Thus archeologists have two masters, the sponsor of their research, and their scientific responsibility. The fact that the sponsor may require architectural data for the purpose of reconstruction goals for public interpretation, or that his primary

317

concern is with the temporal period represented by an archeological site for purposes of authentication, need not bind the archeologist, preventing him from formulating a valid set of relevant problem oriented research goals of his own. He has an obligation to achieve his own scientific goals as well as his sponsor's developmental ones, and, it is hoped, to produce a report that will be of use to archeologists as well as to his sponsor.

Archeologists should clearly tell their sponsors what types of information might be expected to emerge from an excavation of an archeological site. Frequently sponsors are expecting from archeology answers that are not going to result from excavation, and it is the archeologist's responsibility to say where archeology can contribute to knowledge of the site and to delineate those areas where it is likely to produce few answers. Often the sponsor is looking for some direct parallel between the historical documentation and the archeological record, but often such an expectation is highly unrealistic.

Because the archeologist must satisfy the demands of his sponsor and his professional responsibility, he should not neglect either in his report. The report should clearly and fully outline the research goals of both the sponsor and the archeologist. This step should be followed by a statement of the theoretical base from which the search for these goals will be launched. It should then proceed to explain how these goals were sought through the archeological process, presenting a synthesis of the nature of the observations made. The data recovered should be presented in the form of a synthesis of the various analyses that were conducted on features, distributions, relationships, and artifacts. The cultural, historical integration and interpretation emerging from the synthesis should follow, with any resulting processual explanation relative to hypotheses and theory explained in a lucid form. Specific suggestions for further work should be made, as well as recommendations for historic site development if such is planned. In other words, basic scientific procedure should be followed in report writing, goal and hypothesis formation, observation and data collection, analysis, interpretation, synthesis, and explanation of the results, with suggestions for new hypotheses, future research needs, and recommendations for the stabilization and interpretation of the archeological remains. With this format the goals of the sponsor and those demanded of the archeologist in his role as a scientist can be met. This basic outline is summarized again for emphasis (South 1974):

1. outline of research goals and hypotheses
2. theoretical base from which the archeologist is proceeding
3. outline of the archeological process used to attempt to achieve these goals

The ditch outline for one of the bastions of the 1756 fort around the town of Bethabara, N.C.

The Palisade Ditch of the Bethabara Fort during excavation.

Placing palisade posts in the original Bethabara Fort Ditch.

4. analysis of the data
5. synthesis of the analyses conducted on the various classes and groups of data
6. cultural-historical integration of the data
7. processual explanation in terms of hypothesis and theory
8. suggestions for further archeological research
9. recommendations for stabilization and interpretative development of the archeological remains.

When a sponsor of a project wishes to evaluate an archeological report, he can refer to this basic outline and see whether or not the report he has in hand meets these basic minimum requirements. If what he has been presented is primarily a description of postholes, pits, and potsherds, then he has good reason to complain of its lack of significance.

The comments to follow are an appeal to archeologists excavating historic sites to orient their efforts toward the scientific, synthesizing format reflected in the above outline.

> The historical archeologist has an increasingly expanding responsibility to inquire beyond the mere validation of an historic site through correlation with documentary evidence; beyond merely listing the presence or absence of artifact types for establishing the temporal position of the site; beyond the revealing of architectural features for the purpose of reconstruction and restoration; beyond exposing ruins for the entertainment of the visiting public to historic sites; and beyond the process of recovery and preservation of relics from the past to be hoarded in repositories and museums! His view must be as broad as the questions being asked by archeologists, sociologists, anthropologists, ecologists, biologists, archaeo-parasitologists and other scientists who are increasingly turning to historical archeology to reflect some light on their special problems and spheres of interest. However, although archeology is broadening its scope, the primary emphasis will continue to be in the area of material culture where so much must still be explored . . . (South 1968: 54).

The demonstration of patterning of the material remains from archeological sites and the integrative synthesis of these data in terms of the explanation of progenital cultural patterns, are the direction historical archeology must take in order to emerge from the sterility of purely descriptive reporting and take its place among the behavioral disciplines. In historical archeology there is a present emphasis on goals aimed at greater accuracy, authenticity, validity, correlation, personalization, and public interpretation of "historical reality." This emphasis places the focus on history, with archeology acting as a handmaiden to the written record. This situation stems from the fact that historical archeology is stimulated and supported by a florescing historic site preservation-restoration-reconstruction-nostalgia phenomenon. Archeology does make a contribution toward goals dictated by heritage concerns, but these goals are secondary by-products of its primary function, the integrative explication of patterned material remains of culture stemming from human occupation.

The usual emphasis of historical archeology site reports is the following:

1. Archeology is used to "fill in" *historical* documentation.
2. Archeology is used to locate *architectural* features.
3. Archeology is used to recover *artifacts* which are then described in great detail, often to no apparent end (pseudoanalysis)
4. Archeology is "correlated" with historical documentation.

Pressure-treated posts are necessary when palisades are placed in original, archeologically revealed ditches.

Many site reports seldom rise above these levels of presentation, and the reason may lie in the willingness of archeologists to accept the sponsor's goals as the only ones of concern in a research project. With scientific goals, however, the emphasis must be on synthesis based on detailed analysis. Site reports must be firmly anchored in archeological data, with emphasis on integrative synthesis rather than on the analytical description of data, unless such analysis makes a useful contribution to our knowledge!

Therefore, to conduct an analysis of six gunflints or six projectile points from an archeological site, or an analysis of anything, requires a research hypothesis under which certain attributes are called for. The recording of no more involved an attribute than "feather-edging" on

A view of the stabilized ruins and palisaded fort during the process of historic site development at Bethabara, N.C.

creamware is on the same level as the multiattribute recording of a complex set of variables for the purpose of determining pattern through sophisticated statistical analysis, provided both statements are made within the framework of the postulates and hypotheses of a research design. The meticulous recording of attributes as an exercise contributes nothing new to our knowledge without the explanation for such data recording within the research design. Thus the illustration of artifacts simply as a matter of record is a useless procedure if better illustrations of the objects have been published elsewhere.

In 1955, J. C. Harrington recognized that historic site archeologists had a compulsion to illustrate every object recovered from a site and unfortunately such is still often the case:

> Unfamiliar as he is with the cultural material encountered, the reporter on historic site excavations feels that he must describe and illustrate every object. This procedure was often necessary with his Indian materials, for he had not been privileged to work with ceramic types which could be neatly characterized by such simple phrases as, for example "Wedgwood creamware" or "Lambeth delftware." He is inclined, therefore, to devote unnecessary space in his report to lengthy objective descriptions when a single word or phrase would suffice. In some cases, however, careful descriptions are needed, as of, for

example, the products of local craftsmen. Here, as in field methods, the necessary judgment and selectivity can be acquired only from training and experience (p. 1127).

Harrington's statement about "training and experience" might lead one to infer that only through experience could you acquire a sufficient grasp of the historic site materials to successfully avoid the description and illustration of masses of artifact data, but this is just not so for for an archeologist with a scientific frame of reference who can through a careful study of attributes write a cogent synthesis of data at least as good as the usual descriptive product, and considerably more relevant to questions asked.

Ivor Noël Hume has recently emphasized the need for archeologists to rid their reports of unnecessary descriptive weight:

> The illustration of a few rim sherds of common 18th-century ceramic forms that are already on record as having been found from southern Australia to northern Canada, contributes virtually nothing—unless they happen to be incorrectly described, and so warn the reader to beware of the whole report. I am not saying that this material should not be recorded or that any detail should be omitted from the final manuscript. But I am saying that a small number of copies of that report, cheaply

Parapets, palisades, and stabilized ruins, combined with interpretive signs provide the visitor with a bridge for understanding past lifeways.

duplicated, and housed in safe, known repositories, is all that is needed. Much more valuable to fellow archeologists, curators, and social historians, are research studies on specific topics, stemming from excavations and which have something new and useful to say. When money and publishing outlets are scarce, it is these studies that will be of the greatest practical value. (1973: 7)

The phrase "research studies . . . which have something new and useful to say" is critical for reflecting the attitude that can be used as a yardstick for evaluating the contribution made by an archeological report. This is another way of saying the report should be relevant to the questions asked.

In 1955, the field of historical archeology was not ready for Har-

After archeological excavation of fortification ditches is completed the same quantity of soil as that taken from the ditch can be replaced beside the ditch to form a parapet.

rington's advice. Only Harrington and a handful of colleagues were around to listen, and fewer still have heeded his remarks, as emphasized by Noël Hume's recent reiteration of the same point. However, within a few decades, historical archeology will be flooded with young minds bringing to the field the best of theory, statistics, and a scientific base of operation. Their reports will not be merely descriptions of what they found but will be defined by research designs anchored in a firm theoretical base, with scientific analysis and synthesis standard procedure toward testing laws relating to culture process.

As archeologists we must depend on our archeological tools for interpretive statements of archeological data, and not resort to the easy expedient of superimposing the historical preconceptions onto the archeological record. We do, of course, use both the archeological and historical data, but we should not use history as an interpretive crutch to prop up statements purporting to be archeological in nature. If we develop such habits, and then find ourselves in a situation where there is no documentation to lean on, we may well find that our archeological tool kit is empty, or that we do not have the skills to use the tools we have available. Such a leaning-on-the-arms-of-history approach is rendering a disservice to archeology by not utilizing to the fullest the information manifested in the surviving patterned material remains of culture from both history and archeology.

There is apparently an assumption in historic site archeology that archeological data must have a direct historical counterpart. There is, of course, nothing wrong with archeological-historical connections, but this is not the primary archeological goal for the archeologist. As archeologists we are dealing primarily with patterned material remains of past behavior, with the processes responsible for that behavior not necessarily recognized by the people or the society in the system from which the pattern emerged. Therefore, archeologists should focus their efforts toward the discovery and explication of patterns of material culture (Harris 1968: 359). The pattern he discovers may well have absolutely no historical counterpart; indeed, mutually exclusive data sets from the historical and archeological records almost appear to be the rule rather than the exception.

We urge archeologists excavating historic sites to become more selective in presentation of data. This admonition is aimed at the goal of making archeological research more usable by sponsors as well as archeologists. The examination of data is always a selective process. We cannot possibly list all the attributes conceivably of use of someone someday, and attempts at this often lead to absurdities such as measuring in millimeters the size and thickness of broken sherds of English ceramics (Krause 1972: 82). This apparent nonsense can be demonstrated to be relevant only if there is a research design calling for such measurement.

While interpreting patterns of culture we should not engage in pseudoscience misdirected toward meaninglessly translating a potsherd into a series of mathematically expressed numbers; or pseudohistory attempting to discover archeological equivalents to historical events; or pseudoarcheology involving endless descriptions of artifacts and features to no apparent end. Rather, we should selectively direct our efforts toward synthesizing patterns of material culture. In doing so, we reveal the patterns resulting from human activity. Such patterning may then allow us to gain insight into the behavior patterns of the people responsible for the archeological record for the purpose of formulating behavioral laws and through these gain an understanding of the processes at work within, and between, cultural systems. As we delineate change and dynamics between systems, we can begin to understand something about cultural evolution.

In this book, we have addressed our efforts toward this goal. In this chapter, we have tried to place this goal in perspective by pointing out the archeologist's responsibility to sponsors of cultural resource management studies as well as those obligations he has to the development of archeological science. This consideration is an ever-increasing one

Sodding of the 1670 Fort Ditch and repositioned parapet embankment stabilizes the archeologically revealed feature allowing the visitor to visualize the architectural feature seen by the archeologist as a soil discoloration.

constantly faced by archeologists undertaking cultural resource management studies (Lipe 1974). This point was emphasized by a series of
seminars held at Airlie House, a conference center in Virginia, under the
sponsorship of Charles R. McGimsey III, as president of The Society for
American Archaeology. The goal of the seminar on report writing was to
prepare guidelines for the preparation and evaluation of cultural
resource management studies which would be of use both to sponsors
of archeological projects and to archeologists.

This seminar, composed of Keith Anderson, Hester Davis, Rob
Edwards, Michael Schiffer, Stanley South, and Gwinn Vivian, addressed
itself to the construction of guidelines for the preparation and evaluation
of reports resulting from expended federal, state, and private funding of
archeological research. The primary objective was to define the content
of cultural resource management studies. It was also the seminar's objective to make it clear that in order to further the aims of the discipline of
archaeology investigators should not only address themselves to the
questions of project sponsor needs, but to those relating to current
archeological research needs as well. In order to achieve these objec-
tives, it was necessary to consider archeological reporting within the
framework of general scientific standards of reporting and professional
expectations. Cultural resource management studies are one variety of
empirical research in archeology. The seminar outlined general content
guidelines for reports of empirical research more precisely than had
theretofore been done. This basic scientific format was then used to
draft guidelines for the preparation and evaluation of cultural resource
management studies.

It is expected that the guidelines developed by the seminar will
become a basic document for guiding both sponsors and archeologists
involved in cultural resource management studies. The basic outline of
the guidelines developed by the seminar can be seen in the heuristic
device in Figure 38. In this figure the relationship between sponsor planning and archeological research goals, the archeological process, the
general scientific guidelines for report preparation, and the various
classes of reports dealing with cultural resource management, are
illustrated.

All the research represented in this book was conducted under the
sponsorship of agencies concerned with cultural resource management
studies toward developing historic sites for the education and entertain-
ment of the visiting public. None of this research was carried out under a
research design specifically aimed at simply recovering information
through "pure" archeologically relevant research.

The archeologist hoping to contribute to a science of archeology who
waits for the "right" scientifically motivated project to come along on
which he can demonstrate his archeological prowess will find himself

Figure 38. Milking the archeological cow (Cow chart).

without a sponsor, a shovel, or a trowel. A science of archeology will not be developed by those who wait, but by those who carry with them to each research challenge the scientific attitude toward inquiry. Such archeologists are responding to the broad cultural juggernaut of the twentieth century, irresistibly moving human inquiry toward explicit scientific thought and method in the research community.

REFERENCES

Binford, Sally R. and Lewis R. Binford
   1968 *New perspectives in archeology.* Chicago: Aldine.
Harrington, Jean C.
   1955 Archeology as Auxiliary to American History. *American Anthropologist* 55 (No. 6, Part 1).
Harris, Marvin
   1968 Comments by Marvin Harris. In *New perspectives in archeology,* edited by Binford; Sally R. and Binford; Lewis R. Chicago: Aldine. Company.
Krause, Richard
   1972 The Leavenworth Site: Archaeology of an Historic Arikara Community. *University of Kansas Publications in Anthropology,* No. 3.
Lipe, William D.
   1974 A Conservation Model for American Archaeology. *The Kiva* 39 Nos. 3–3: 213–245.
Noël Hume, Ivor
   1973 Historical Archaeology: Who Needs It? *Historical Archaeology 1973* 7. The Society for Historical Archaeology, Lansing, Michigan.
South, Stanley
   1968 What Archeology Can Do to Expand Historical Research. *The Conference on Historic Site Archaeology Papers 1968* 3. Institute of Archeology and Anthropology, University of South Carolina, Columbia.
   1974 Historical Archeology Reports: A Plea for a New Direction. *The Conference on Historic Site Archeology Papers, 1972* 7:151–158. Institute of Archeology and Anthropology, University of South Carolina, Columbia.
White, Leslie A.
   1938 Science is Sciencing. *Philosophy of Science* 5:369–389.

Index

P

Paca House, Maryland, 48
  ceramic analysis, 215
  ceramic formula applied, 224, 229, 258
Paca, William, 224
Padlocks, 99
Palisades replaced, 319, 322–324
Paradigm
  archeological, 5, 8
  humanistic, 6–7
  nomothetic, 4, 6, 8, 14–15, 20, 34–39
  particularistic, 20, 22, 31
  scientific, 8
Parapets stabilized, 307–308, 325, 327
Parker, Arthur C., 13
Particularistic
  archeology, 5–6, 8, 15
  barrier, 124
  paradigm, 20, 22, 31
Pattern, see Carolina Pattern; Frontier
     Pattern; Inventory Pattern; Kitchen
     Pattern; Mean Ceramic Date Formula
  adjusted majolica, 240
  empirical ranges, 120
  majolica, 238
  regularity, 87, 110, 122
Pattern recognition, 15, 25, 31, 35, 38–39, 43,
     84
  Carolina, 106–112
  Frontier, 125, 141–164
  Inventory, 190–198
  Kitchen, 167–171
Pawnee ceramics, 237
Pearlware, annular, 60, 65
Pennsylvania
  German-American pattern, 234
  German colonial artifact pattern, 186
  Pattern, 124, 186, 234
Peripheral secondary refuse, 47–48, 61, 179–
     182
  at Bethabara, 300
Personal Group artifacts, 95
Pewter, 193
  trenchers, 203
Pharmaceutical bottle, 171
Phases in the archeological process, 300–308
Phillips, Philip, 3, 232–233
Pig chart, 310
"Pin cluster," 70–71, 77
Pine Tuft, Florida, majolica formula applied,
     266

Pins and beads, Public House-Tailor Shop,
     68–71
Pistol, 299
Plog, Fred, T., 2, 14
Plow scars, 289
Polearm of archeology, 5–7, 14
  chart, 6
Polhemus, Richard, 222
Porcelain
  bowls, 86
  cups, 86
  embargo, 231
  repair, 86
  types, 210
Postholes, 278
  attribute recording, 279–280
Postulates, Carolina Artifact Pattern, 86
Power structure, 41–42, 125
Prediction, 77, 84
  group ranges, 118–119
  median occupation, 236
  pattern ranges, 147
Preservation, 281, 294, 321
Primary de facto refuse, 50–51, 68, 297–298
Primary research priority, 310
Probate inventory pattern, 190–198
  cluster analysis, 192
Problem
  defined in ceramic study, 203
  oriented research, 4, 295
  recognition, 15
Process, formation, 88, see Cultural process
Processing archeological materials, 97
Processual explanation, 318
Production systems, 235
Professional standards, 24
Profile data recording, 293
Progenital cultural patterns, 321
Provenience
  Carolina Pattern sites, 92
  control, 219, 309, 312
Pseudoanalysis, 321
Pseudoarcheology, 327
Pseudofunctional analysis, 312
Pseudohistory, 327
Pseudoscience, 327
Puaray, New Mexico, 245
  majolica formula applied, 271
Public House-Tailor Shop ruin
  activity variability, 111
  Bone, 71, 76–77
  burned floor, 66, 68